CW00687808

JUST A MAN

A NOTE TO THE READER

We completed this biography of Michael in the early summer of 2000. In September, as the world now knows, just as the book was about to print Paula Yates died tragically. As with so many things you will read in this story, we heard the news through journalists.

Of course, we were shocked. The last three years have been difficult ones for anyone who knew Michael. We thought immediately of Paula's children, and most of all for our niece and granddaughter, Tiger Lily. We just wished we could be there to hold her.

This book has always been a book about Michael, our brother and son, but Paula plays a role in any account of his life. However, even before recent events unfolded we had no desire to provoke new confrontations with Paula, and with her death we have no desire to be disrespectful to her memory.

So this is our story of Michael Hutchence. It is a story that for the sake of his memory – and for Tiger Lily – should still be heard.

Tina Hutchence and Patricia Glassop

TINA HUTCHENCE AND PATRICIA GLASSOP

JUST A MAN

THE REAL
MICHAEL HUTCHENCE

SIDGWICK & JACKSON

First published 2000 by Sidgwick & Jackson
an imprint of Macmillan Publishers Ltd
25 Eccleston Place, London SW1W 9NF
Oxford and Basingstoke
Associated companies throughout the world
www.macmillan.com

ISBN 0 283 06356 4

1 3 5 7 9 8 6 4 2

A CIP catalogue record for this book is available from
The British Library.

Typeset by SX Composing DTP, Rayleigh, Essex
Printed and bound in Great Britain by
Mackays of Chatham PLC, Chatham, Kent

To Michael, a beautiful, gentle soul;
and to all the children in the family

Acknowledgements

We would like to thank all those friends and family who allowed us to reach deep into their memories, pore through their journals, sift through old faxes and letters, and especially those who stood by us in the darkest days and who continue to send us love and support. We would especially like to thank Ross, Michele, Jonnie, 'Blair', Chris, Nick, Wendy and Sherine. And a special thanks to Gordon Scott Wise for his encouragement and patience.

Contents

PROLOGUE

Bitter Tears

There was nothing special about the first part of Friday, 21 November 1997. Two hours in meetings at my office, a dental appointment and back to the office where my nineteen-year-old daughter Erin cut a birthday cake she had baked herself. It would be my birthday on Sunday.

My husband Ken was there, along with Erin's boyfriend Joshua and my colleagues. They sang 'Happy Birthday' and I blew out the candles. After some joking around I called my mother and my stepfather Ross. When Ross came on the line he reminded me that it was just four weeks and three days until we were to go and spend Christmas with them on Australia's Gold Coast, where they lived.

I met Ken for an early dinner. When I got home I found an urgent message from my younger brother Rhett. He sounded almost hysterical. My immediate thought was that something had happened to our father. Rhett answered my return call, told me to sit down and asked if Ken was with me. I could hear Mother moaning in the background. 'What? What is it?' I asked. It must be something to do with Ross. I looked around for somewhere to sit. There was nowhere in my clean, hard, clinical kitchen. 'Please, tell me what it is.'

He was sobbing by now. 'Oh darling, it's Michael. He's dead.' For a moment I was suspended in time. Then I found myself sinking to the cold floor. 'No, no, no.' I was screaming now. 'It's true, darling.' I was adamant: 'That's impossible.' But I could still hear my mother in the background. 'It's true, Tina. Oh, Tina, it's true.'

'Impossible! How, how? Where?' I screamed; but nothing was coming out. Ken was staring at me, wordlessly.

'We don't know yet,' cried Rhett.

'Where is he? Who told you? It can't be true, it's those stupid, irresponsible journalists. They'll say anything. Who have you spoken with?' I was going to fix everything. My brother Michael Hutchence fronted the rock band INXS. In recent years he'd tended to be the family fixer but it was me who had taught him how to tie his shoelaces. I'd fix this. 'I'll call Martha,' I said – Martha Troup, Michael's manager. I'd restore the sanity, calm everyone down, repair this. In the family this had always been my job. But Rhett was sobbing again. 'Darling, we don't know anything yet, just that it's true and it happened at the Ritz Carlton. Mum's place is surrounded by television crews. Call Martha. Get a flight. Come home.'

There was a short, incoherent attempt at speaking to Mother before I handed the phone to Ken. I hadn't been able to ask about Paula Yates and her and Michael's daughter, Tiger Lily. I wandered around the house, screaming inside: It's impossible, impossible. It must be another lie. Ken turned on CNN. They were already reporting it. And then I remembered my children and went into my 'take charge' mode. I did not want Brent, who was twenty-five then, or Erin, to hear about their uncle on television – especially as I didn't even believe it. I paged Erin and without giving her time to return the call, I dialled Joshua's house where I hoped she would be. I spoke with Joshua's dad, briefly explaining what was happening. He told me that she had left for her apartment and Joshua had followed. I was worried sick that she would hear the news on her car radio.

Brent attends the University of Southern California, in Monterey Bay. I left an urgent message for him to call me too, hung up and dialled his pager. Meanwhile a call was coming through on my call waiting: it was Erin. She was laughing as I answered and made some crack about me checking up on her. She had not heard yet, but I didn't have much time before her phone would begin screeching with calls from her friends. She had just arrived home and was expecting Joshua any minute. I hesitated to tell her the news, hoping Joshua would arrive and be there for her. My voice dropped as I asked if she had her television on and she reminded me that she couldn't get any channels, and so only watched videos. For once I was glad that Erin had neglected to pay her cable bill.

'Mom. Mom? You're frightening me, what's happened?' As calmly as possible, I told her what I had heard and she broke down. Through her tears she cried, 'But Mom, are you sure, you know what those journalists are like.' I assured her that as far as we knew it was true and told her to have Joshua drive them both over to the house as soon as he reached her.

Brent finally called, in shock. 'How, when? Mom, it's on TV. Can they say that?' When did we all become so sceptical of the press? Brent sobbed and said he wanted to go to Australia. I told him to sit tight and I would get some details. My call waiting interrupted us. It was a friend calling from Sydney. She said radio stations were reporting that Michael had hanged himself. Impossible. No, they are wrong. They sensationalize everything he does. I don't believe it. I wouldn't believe that for a minute. I still did not know what had happened. The phone would not stop ringing, but with every call hope still jumped in my heart and I picked up, expecting to hear that it was all a mistake.

Still screaming inside, I walked over to look at the pictures in my living room. There were images of so many happy times with Michael. So many beautiful family memories, pictures taken in France, Australia, Hong Kong and London. There was Mother and Michael with Johnny Depp in Los Angeles last July, another framed photograph of me and Lenny Kravitz in the villa in the South of France. I stopped at a photograph of Michael and me taken right on the same spot where I was standing – Thanksgiving, 1996, almost one year ago to the day. I glanced down and saw that I was even wearing the same outfit. I felt like I was going out of my mind. Ken tried to comfort me, but I wouldn't stand still and snapped at him. He said that it was being reported over every television station, I must believe it. But I refused to watch or listen.

At last I got through to Martha. She was crying. Her phones won't stop ringing. Yes, it is true; but she does not want to believe it either. She tells me that she spoke to Michael earlier in the day New York time, when he had been with friends in his hotel room. Later, he had left two messages for her, one at the office and another on her home machine. His last message was painful, he just said, 'Marth . . . I can't take it any more.'

When I ask her if she has spoken with Paula Yates, her voice changes, lowers. 'No, I . . . well, anyway, I didn't want to deal with it. I couldn't. I sent someone over to her house.' She sobbed into the phone, flogging herself, because she was not there for Michael. I tell her she was the one person who was always there for him. For some reason, I do not even ask her about the circumstances surrounding Michael's death. Somehow I can't phrase the words, I am afraid to ask: if I do not actually hear the answer, maybe it has not happened after all. I tell Martha I am on standby for a 1.30 p.m. flight on Saturday. She is trying to get out on an early morning flight from New York, to connect with mine. We hang up together when we find that we are both sobbing so uncontrollably that we cannot speak any longer.

Various friends call, many of whom have been at my house on special occasions when Michael has been in town. The last time was just four months ago, in honour of Erin and Tiger Lily whose birthdays are only four days apart. Devastated, everybody is calling but nobody knows what to say. They mean well, I know, but who can make this nightmare go away? My friends all ask what they can do, try to convey their love and warmth, but nothing helps. This pain is here to stay.

Erin finally arrives. I had begun to pack in a helpless, floundering way, but she takes over so that my bag at least contains routine essentials and between us we deal with the constantly ringing phone. I walk around the house in an aimless daze. A cup of tea? How can I get anything past the lump in my throat?

I awake after a fitful sleep and the horrible truth slams across my brain, crushing that tiny moment of hope, of normality. There's my suitcase: it was not a nightmare. It is 5 a.m., Saturday, in California, 8 a.m. in New York and I call to see if Martha has made the New York to Los Angeles flight. Her husband Bill tells me she is going for the one thirty out of Los Angeles. This is real, not a movie reel although feeling seemingly surreal. As I go about my morning routine, I keep thinking of the old Skeeter Davis song, 'The End Of The World' . . . why does the sun go on shining . . . I stand under my shower, and I hear a woman scream. It is me.

The kids have slept over since we were all up most of the night anyway. Erin carefully places the last of my toiletries into my bag and agonizes about whether she should join me. I tell her she can take the day to make her decision or join Brent on his flight. Both Erin and Brent are just two weeks away from their first semester finals and thus already under considerable pressure. I suspect that Erin's primary concern is whether she can bear the pain of seeing her mother and grandmother in such agony. Erin and Brent have always referred to my mother by her first name, Patricia. These days however, Zoe, Rhett's little girl, calls her Grandma and I imagine Tiger will too. Oh my gosh – Tiger!

I thought back to when Michael was trying to come up with a name for his little Tiger Lily. His favourite was Hiraani, after a family friend. That was the name he chose. When Paula appeared lukewarm over the idea, he called me and asked if I could think of a suitable Asian or Pacific Islander name that started with an 'H'. I'm not sure if this was because he liked the idea of alliteration. Anyway, I faxed him with a long list of names. Of course the name 'Helena' was hard to resist (such a lovely name, even if its island origins are actually Greek), but felt this was unlikely to be the popular choice at the London home given Michael's previous association with Helena Christensen. No name seemed more beautiful or euphonious than Hiraani.

But what about the sweet little girl with the 'Michael' face now, how could she grow up not knowing her father?

Looking at the first pictures of 'Heavenly Hiraani Tiger Lily' which Michael had proudly showed me at Thanksgiving in 1996 was like looking at pictures of Michael when he was a baby. He was so proud when I told him this, and he beamed whenever someone commented on the startling resemblance. Before Tiger he had always been so proud when people commented on the family resemblance between himself and Erin. He would say, 'How did that happen?' I would tell him, 'Well, we do have the same mother, even if we don't look alike. I guess you take after her Kennedy side.' Somehow, that gorgeous full mouth passed me by, and landed directly on to my daughter's sweet face. And even now, the older she gets, the more she looks like him.

Neither Patricia nor I have ever sought to make a martyr of Michael. He wasn't a saint. He was powerfully attractive to women and he knew it, somehow managing to emerge emotionally unscathed from a series of complex relationships. As an artist he took creative risks sometimes and he had the sort of speedy energy that drew him towards any risky situation if the alternative was a dull and dreary one. All the people who truly knew and loved him understood this. He had a great, broad heart and would never have wanted to damage the faith and trust of those of us who loved and depended on him in any way. He may have been, as has been said, 'a wild boy' and humanly flawed for that. But essentially, he was just a man . . .

Ken drove to the airport where I presented myself at the Qantas desk in a daze, placed my passport and American Express card down and told the man that I had to get on flight 8 to Sydney as there had been a death in the family. He glanced at my passport and left to see a supervisor. When he returned, he said that I was wait-listed along with Martha Troup in business class but they would make sure I was on the flight. So what does wait-listed mean? Someone else said my daughter had called and I was taken to a back office where Erin was waiting on another line. As we weaved our way through the office, I could feel every pair of eyes upon me. I was only mildly hysterical but still screaming inside. Fortunately the Valiums my mother-in-law, Alice, had given me were preventing me from screaming on the outside too.

Erin said she and Brent would leave on the 10 p.m. Sunday flight and arrive in Sydney on Tuesday morning, local time. I sat there with a ticketing agent, my mind racing, and made the booking for a special rate they call Compassionate fare. Compassionate. I thought of Michael. He was compassionate, kind and good-natured. People loved him, so why would he not want to stay around for more of that love? Was that not enough? Most people would imagine that he had everything, but apparently he did not agree. Even though he had spoken animatedly of the future during our last conversation, six days before, I could tell that he was putting up a front. And, after all, he had been on Prozac for at least two years. No happy man has such a dependency.

I am directed to the business lounge, relieved that Ken cannot come with me. My husband is very uncomfortable in situations which he cannot control. I am feeling so vulnerable and numb, yet touchy. By now, he is feeling helpless in a different, nervous way and has been making inappropriate comments which only make me harder to reach. I don't want anyone's words of comfort, however well intentioned. Nothing they say will stop this bad dream and bring Michael back. He kisses me goodbye, wishes me a safe trip and I feel his eyes watch me disappear.

During that eternity in the departure lounge I send a fax to Mother and Ross as it's too early on the east coast of Australia to call.

I let them know I am arriving in Sydney on Sunday evening with Martha. I am feeling such rage and frustration about not knowing anything about the circumstances of Michael's death, I can't imagine how my poor mother's heart must be breaking. But I want to be there for her as soon as possible.

A Mother's Story

22 November had started out as a fun shopping day. My younger son Rhett, his partner Mandy and daughter Zoe Angel had arrived the evening before. Rhett was a bit disappointed because he had been in Sydney and prior to leaving he was to have met up with Michael for the first time in ages. But Michael overslept and missed him. Rhett and Michael had not had any contact at all in eleven months, mostly due to Michael's touring schedule, so Christmas 1997 was going to be wonderful. Michael was in Australia, on his final tour with INXS after twenty years together. He wanted to concentrate now on a career in films and had just completed a cameo role in a movie in Canada. He had several offers from producers and couldn't wait to finish the tour so that he could develop all this. Tina would be arriving on the Gold Coast in four weeks and this would be the first time in four years we would all be in Australia together for Christmas.

Ross and I had decided to spoil Rhett that year and surprise him with a new car. We had asked the salesman to deliver it to our house on Christmas Eve, filled with balloons and tied with a huge red ribbon with HAPPY XMAS RHETT printed on it. We had already derived so much pleasure from this and couldn't wait to see his face. Rhett had had a serious drug problem and had been in and out of rehabilitation for the past couple of years. I was so proud of him as he was committed to this effort, although it seems to me as though an addictive personality is something that Rhett must deal with for the rest of his life. What is wonderful is that he seems to be winning at the moment.

It was a sunny Saturday morning and while Ross went off to the golf club Rhett, Mandy, Zoe and I headed to the Pacific Mall to finish our Christmas shopping. We decided to go our separate ways and meet up in one hour in the coffee shop. I found some lovely dresses for Mandy and Zoe, did some shopping at the Lancôme counter, then collected the gold bracelets Ross and I had ordered for the two youngest granddaughters, Zoe and Tiger Lily. After this we decided we had done enough and headed home.

As we walked back past the beauty counter, I noticed the sales girls were staring at us oddly. It occurred to me that this must be because Mandy, who was walking a few paces ahead of me, was breastfeeding Zoe, as young women often do these days. Then again I figured it could just be Rhett and Mandy, as they do attract attention. Both are very tall and Rhett had dreadlocks at the time.

When we returned home there were numerous calls on my answering machine, mainly from journalists. One, whom I knew, said it was extremely urgent and would I please, please call her. Before I could answer her call, the buzzer on my entryphone started going crazy. When I pushed the button to see the screen I could see Channels Seven and Nine cameras in the background and hear voices yelling into the intercom that they wanted to speak to me. I sensed then that something was wrong and began to feel bewildered and scared. I decided to phone the journalist I knew, as I did not want to hear any news – good or bad – from a stranger. Before I could call her, she called back extremely distressed. I demanded to know what was going on. She told me the news that no mother ever wants to hear.

Disbelieving, I told Rhett to phone the Ritz Carlton in Sydney and ask for room 524, and demand to speak to Michael. He was told there was no answer in that room. Maybe he had changed his alias from 'Murray River' or changed rooms – he sometimes did this if unwelcome people had tracked him down. I then asked Rhett to get me the manager of the hotel, who eventually told Rhett that we should ring the Rose Bay Police Station. My heart started pounding. This was a nightmare. I had to speak to Tina. Rhett was able to speak to someone at the police station and they informed him of the situation, yet nobody called *me.* Not Michael's father, nor the detectives who were handling the case. Rhett phoned Tina in Los Angeles but only got her voice mail.

I looked down and noticed a fax Tina had sent me just a few days earlier with details of her Christmas plans. She'd added, 'I spoke to Michael about an hour ago. He sounded very content, said that overall the whole tour went well. I am very happy for him. He is very excited about the movie gig. He says he is booked to return to LA on the fifth – same day as me.'

Then she called. Rhett told her the terrible news. She was devastated and uncomprehending. Rhett handed me the phone and we just cried.

It was impossible to speak . . . there were no words to take away the stabbing pain in my heart, which was pounding as though it were going to burst through my body. The buzzer was still making such a noise, the voices still screaming into the intercom. All I could think was: Please make them go away.

Ross arrived home, briefly oblivious to the crisis. He immediately took control and made flight arrangements to go straight to Sydney. He is my rock and has continued to be, throughout it all. The rest of the day was a blur. I wanted to block it out of my mind . . . to sleep and wake up to a happy shopping spree, to listen to my messages on my answering machine and hear Michael's voice . . . 'Hi Mum. How are you? Where are you? Has Rhett arrived? How is Ross, is he at golf?' and to hear him say 'I love you Mum' as he always did before hanging up. He had called me just two days ago; he had sounded tired but happy to be in Sydney.

I did a lot of screaming the rest of the day. I could hear myself repeating the words to Rhett *'No! No! Why? How? It can't be true.'* I wandered around the house picking up photographs, putting them down. I walked out on the balcony and looked over at the beach, and the sunny Queensland sky. I thought of the day Ross had taken Michael out for a spin in a Tiger Moth. They had circled over our apartment building so I could take a photograph of Michael in it.

Rhett was sobbing uncontrollably. 'Why Michael? Why not me, Mum?' I imagined that he was possibly referring to his self-destructive tendencies. Rhett had done some serious and heavy playing at times – yet always seemed able to pick himself up from the floor of the pit.

I would run to the bathroom, dry retching, then come back to the living room to sit in stunned silence, trying to comprehend this madness, this intrusion into our lives. Rhett was speaking to Tina again. He was still crying. I suddenly felt a warm hand on my arm. It was little Zoe Angel. I looked into her beautiful blue eyes as she said, 'Grandma cry, Zoe cry, Daddy cry, Zoe cry.' We had all but forgotten this dear little child standing there with a slight frown on her face and struggling to understand what it was that had broken the happy spell of our morning.

I asked Ross to book us into the Ritz Carlton in Sydney. By morning I had changed my mind and we all stayed at the nearby Sir Stamford Hotel. I did not sleep well and kept waking with panic attacks. Like a zombie I got up and showered, threw a few clothes into a bag, dressed and made some tea. I waited for the rest of the family to wake, then for the car to arrive to take us to the airport to start the journey to hell. We learned of Michael's death through the media and I am still appalled about this. It would have been so easy for the authorities to contact me. I had found that over the years when Michael was in the spotlight, journalists never had any difficulty in finding me, so why couldn't the people in charge of this miserable situation? Michael's father Kell was also notified by the press. So often I hear in news reports that 'the name is being withheld pending notification of family'. It would seem that Michael's family should have been given the same respect. But this was only the beginning and a fragment of our nightmare.

We arrived in Sydney, Michael's birthplace. As we drove through those familiar streets I was reminded of my sweet son on every block. Huge posters of the upcoming INXS concerts were plastered on walls everywhere, newspaper shops with their placards outside on the footpath with Michael's photographs and bold announcements of his death. I closed my eyes and allowed my mind to fill with loving thoughts of him.

I was still in denial. It must be a mistake, someone else maybe, some other pitiable mother's son . . . not my Michael. My Michael loved life, he was an adventurer, he loved his daughter, his whole family. Then I remembered that when he called me five months ago from Vienna I had sensed sadness in his voice when I asked how things were going. He said, 'I can't take it any more, I don't want to finish this tour.' I told him it would not be a good idea to pull out now, to hang in there and very soon he would be free to accept film offers and finish the solo album which meant so much to him. He cheered up a little, but his mood was so low, I could still 'feel' it in his voice. So I changed the subject to that of his beautiful daughter Tiger. In normal circumstances this would lift his mood, but not today. Again he said, 'I can't take it any more, I've had enough.' He elaborated about the fighting between his partner Paula Yates and her ex-husband Bob Geldof, how much it was costing him in the courts, and his concern about his own investments. He had a feeling that something was not right. He had tried to keep track of everything, as he had already lost a lot of money through having acted on advice that had backfired, and did not want this to happen again. I had never heard Michael as depressed as this.

At the end of that conversation he asked us to meet him in Los Angeles, his next stop. When we arrived there he was waiting for us in the lobby of the Mondrian Hotel and his mood was clearly brighter. He was happy to see us and I was relieved.

On our arrival at the Sir Stamford we were *told* we would be using the name 'Edwards' while staying there. This was presumably to protect our privacy. We decided to worry about this later, but knew it was going to make things difficult for family and friends to contact us. My sister Maureen had phoned Kell to get my unlisted room number, and Sue, his wife, said she would not disturb him as he was too upset. My sister had only just heard about Michael's death an hour after having her bag, which contained her address book, snatched. She was kept on the line for at least fifteen minutes before she was able to talk to someone. Fortunately I phoned her and told her our new 'name'.

I phoned Kell and he suggested we come to his apartment as soon as possible to talk and make the necessary arrangements. Almost immediately a driver called to suggest that we be down in the lobby in about fifteen minutes. I phoned Rhett's room to let him know we were going over to Kell's but he was not there. When Ross and I went down to the lobby to meet the driver we were met by the minders and led towards the garage. Then, when we got out of the lift, we saw a police car and were told it was to take us to the morgue.

This shocked me. It was so final and we still knew so little about what had happened. I was unprepared and did not want to get into the car. It was such a sudden, cruel way to see off my darling son Michael. Why hadn't Kell primed me for this, given me some details? Most of all, I needed a hug, a kind word from the father of my child. I needed some comfort, anything to help take away the pain and help me begin to come to terms with the fact that we had lost the son we both loved.

We were driven to the morgue in the police car and a few seconds after we pulled up Kell and Sue and his sister arrived in a car driven by Tony Woodall, a bodyguard employed by Michael's financial adviser, Colin Diamond. Rhett and Mandy arrived with Zoe immediately after us.

It was time for me to view Michael and I took my pounding heart and shaking body into the room. Ross was trembling, too, as he took my arm. It was his nightmare as well. I did not know what to expect and I was feeling ill and dizzy. I finally focused my eyes on my son, then touched his forehead to brush the hair away from his eyes. He looked so beautiful, but felt so cold . . . it was as though he had fallen asleep in the snow. Touching his thick, dark hair brought to mind the time I had cut a tiny curl from his head when he was a little boy . . . a lock of shiny chestnut brown hair streaked with blond from the sun. Ross walked outside after a while to give me some private moments with Michael. Then Kell came in and we stood there together, neither of us able to speak, emotion enveloping us as we gazed at our beloved son. I wanted to shake him, wake him and ask him '*Why, Michael, why?*' I talked to him, I prayed for him, kissed his lovely face and hands and walked away.

We were driven from the morgue to Kell's apartment where we had to make some decisions about the funeral service. Zoe Angel played on the floor as Rhett, Mandy, Kell, Sue, Ross and myself tried to be focused. Tony the bodyguard hovered. Sue made some tea as Kell suggested the funeral directors and I suggested the flowers. Iris, I thought, the beautiful blue flower, which was in abundant bloom in the garden of Michael's villa in Roquefort les Pins, in the South of France. This was his favourite flower, as well as mine. After this was agreed Tony interrupted and went with Kell into another room for a short, private discussion. We had only briefly touched on burial versus cremation and no decision was made. Then Kell suggested he should be cremated and a big memorial stone be erected. I did not want this, as I remembered reading what had happened to Jim Morrison's grave site in Paris. Even now his followers still sit on his monument and party, and the French authorities have now requested that it be removed. I remember Rhett saying, 'What does it matter? Michael was an atheist.'

We discussed the press. They were on a vigil outside Kell's place, as well as our apartment on the Gold Coast, and now they were lining up across the street from the Sir Stamford, lenses trained at our windows. It would only get worse in the days to come. I clearly remember Kell saying, 'What we need is a Harry M. Miller type.' Harry Miller is Australia's best-known public relations person. He handles all of our big celebrities and has a lot of clout, rather like Max Clifford in Britain – and sometimes as controversial. As it happened, I had met Harry three weeks before at a book launch in Sydney and we had talked about Michael. Harry had expressed his desire to involve him in a project. I told him that Michael would be back in Australia in a couple of weeks, gave him Martha's contact numbers and passed Harry's numbers on to her. Kell asked me to call him and discuss the media problem. Even amidst my grief and confusion I did not know how Harry could control the press totally, especially with Paula arriving in the morning. I advised Kell to sleep on it as I did not want to ring Harry without any firm plan. I had no idea what was involved, or what it could cost us.

We talked on about the torture Michael must have endured during the past three years. This period was the only time in his career that I could recall him getting a persistently negative press. It was always hurtful to read, and it worried Michael, I knew.

Tina was due. We were driven back to the Sir Stamford.

My flight was finally called. The attendant assured me that Martha was waiting at the gate and said there was no need for me to hurry as the staff had been advised to seat all passengers before we boarded. She offered to take me down some back stairs, so I didn't have to face anyone with my swollen eyes. She also told me she had arranged for my children to be escorted to the business lounge the following evening, and handed me two mini-bottles of wine in a bag, I rarely drink, but I recognized this as a kind gesture. The attendant was obviously feeling helpless. I had gone through most of her Kleenex whilst she tried to steady me outside the lounge.

Martha, looking so tiny and sad in the deserted waiting area. Martha may be short in stature but she's as sharp and astute as New York businesswomen come. I dare say she could get away with calling anybody who is anybody in the music industry, at any time of the day or night. Michael relied on her judgement heavily. They spent many hours travelling together, going to business meetings, planning the future. She used to say that she wanted her tombstone to be engraved with 'Here lies the only woman Michael Hutchence did not go to bed with.' We embraced and just shook our heads helplessly before being taken on to the plane.

Throughout the thirteen-hour flight, the whole crew was very gentle with us. Many of the flight attendants came by and expressed their sympathies. We settled in and went over the turn of events in so far as we were able at this stage. I had seen and spoken with Michael frequently over 1997 as he had been on tour in the United States but Martha filled me in on some things I had missed in my brother's life in the last three months, and some of the facts about his death as she understood them. She explained that she had called the London home on Friday, only to catch Paula in a foul mood, furious with her ex-husband, Bob Geldof, who had been knighted by the Queen in 1987 following his inspirational work for famine relief in Africa.

Paula had hoped to take the two younger Geldof girls, Peaches and Pixie, to Sydney. INXS were there on the Australian leg of the

'Don't Lose Your Head' tour. Michael had given me the impression in our last conversation that the children would be arriving closer to Christmas – he wasn't keen to have children around on a tour and besides, he understood that this year marked Bob's turn to have his children for the holidays. It sounded as though Bob wasn't keen for them to go this early *and* not have them for Christmas. However, there was nothing to prevent Paula from going to Australia with Michael's daughter, Tiger Lily. Michael could enjoy the time between tour dates with his little girl and have his family get reacquainted with her. The Geldof girls could join them later, as in Christmases past. But I thought that just days away from the first night of his last tour with INXS, the last thing he would have needed was the extra stress of family difficulties. However, as I know myself, things aren't always easy where children are involved after a divorce.

When we last spoke he told me that he had run into his former girlfriend of four years, the supermodel Helena Christensen, and he'd been reminded of many old insecurities deriving from that relationship. I had commiserated with him about the upcoming tour, which he was dreading – the fact that it would mark the end of INXS made it especially emotional for him. I reminded him there were not many tour dates and besides it would be Christmas in five weeks when he could have a break before returning to Los Angeles to complete this watershed in his career.

I had spent some time in LA with the girl whom Michael had been seeing for the better part of the last four months. She is an intensely private person, and I will simply call her Blair. He had given her airline tickets to most of the tour dates, and had appeared to be very relaxed and happy with her. It was no secret to Paula, the band, his close friends and family members that Michael still found other women interesting. Paula might be the mother of his child, but he had denied all reports that he had any intention of marrying her. He lavished all his pure love on his little daughter: it was clear to me that his devotion to Tiger was quite a separate issue.

Martha also stated that she had spoken to the person who had packed Michael's luggage for Sydney. I did not see the significance of this as anyone close to Michael knew that he often had whoever was to hand pack his bags. He was usually running late and in all those years of travelling, he never did learn the fine art of packing lightly. On reflection I supposed that she was assuring me that he had not left the United States with any illegal substances. I had not given this any thought, as although I was dimly aware of my brother's drug indulgences, I was also under the impression that for the most part, he was in control of them. It sounded as though Michael had been considerably more depressed than he had let on to me, which was so typical of him. He could be angry that people automatically expected him to be content with his life and always had reasons why it was not so hot to be Michael Hutchence, rock star. Then again, many times, if you were to display signs of concern, he would brush it off, and reel off a string of stories of recent good times and expectations of more in the future.

She told me that upon hearing the tragic news she had instructed the tour manager to take care of Michael's hotel bill so that he could collect the phone log and check who Michael may have spoken to that night. She added that it revealed that Michael had called Bob Geldof. It seemed to me that this would be a job for the investigators. What would it matter who he had called in his final hours – they had obviously been unable to help him.

We discussed the possibility of foul play, agreeing that Michael was not into pain of any kind. In my experience, Michael had an extremely low tolerance for physical suffering. An accidental overdose would make more sense. What we had heard of his death seemed to me such a brutal way to commit suicide. However, it was later explained to me that when a person takes his life by hanging, there is no pain, he simply loses consciousness. Somehow the certainty that Michael's death was a suicide had already begun to take hold. That is not to say that this explanation didn't hold its own awful bafflements – it just seemed to be the only explanation.

During the flight to Sydney, I noticed that the news was not on the monitor, and we did not get a newspaper. Later Martha said that a flight attendant had told her that they made the decision not to play CNN or hand out newspapers out of respect for us. I tried to sleep. I was worn out, but even the Valium did not help: I only saw my beautiful brother's face every time I closed my eyes. There were so many unanswered questions. I tried to remind myself of the good times, instead of asking myself 'why?'

Just prior to landing, the purser came over and assured me that we could disembark before the other passengers. Outside the customs area the band's minders were waiting with welcoming, yet grim faces. We all hugged and made our way to the car, with Martha throwing out questions immediately.

On the ride to the hotel, Martha was enquiring about the state of the five remaining INXS members. They went through a roll call. Where is Andrew Farriss, how is he doing? What about Kirk Pengilly, Tim Farriss, Garry Gary Beers and Jon Farriss? It sounded as if all five of them were in total shock, and definitely in need of her. The question was, I thought, who was going to comfort Martha? We were told that Australia's Prime Minister, John Howard, had made a very respectful statement about Michael and that on the whole, everything had been positive. They meant in the press of course, but I kept thinking of the more obvious: my brother died alone, he took his own life – what is positive about that? The autopsy would be in the morning, Monday. Martha said she wanted to see him and asked me if I did too. Of course I wanted to see him, I needed to. I looked out of the window and everything reminded me of Michael. Over the years I had driven down those same streets so many times with him, or on my way to see him. Then something caught my eye, a newspaper stand. I can't explain what it felt like to see a large picture of your brother, and across the top of the page the headline, 'MICHAEL HUTCHENCE DEAD AT 37'. I was still screaming inside, 'You're wrong, it's a mistake.'

CHAPTER ONE

The Loved One

In the days and months following Michael's death it seemed the words most often posed to me, and the ones I heard myself repeating over and over, were 'Why? How could this happen?' and 'Did you know something was wrong?' No doubt anyone who has lost a loved one to suicide, especially when there is no apparent, glaring reason, will ask these questions. We have also had the added pressure of media speculations. On the surface Michael would seem to have had it all. You would think that it would be enough to be talented and wildly successful in your chosen career, especially when this success transferred into fame and all the enjoyable excesses that go with it. And to have the sort of exotic good looks that attracted women effortlessly. Michael was also one of those special individuals who inspire friendship from both men and women. He had good friends, and the most loving and supportive of families.

Perhaps to get some measure of Michael's inner feelings, you need to appreciate the dynamics within the family and climate in which he was raised. Crucially, I can tell you that Michael was a most loved child, happy, well-adjusted and affectionate.

As a member of the immediate family, it seemed to me that it was almost impossible to imagine Michael failing no matter what he chose to do with his life. He had tremendous encouragement from our parents, and I always recognized that Michael was the favoured child. This had less to do with any deficiencies on our parents' part – I knew myself to be deeply loved too. It was more to do with Michael's endearing nature. I now know that birth order and gender play a major part in how a parent relates to a child, thus influencing personality, and therefore outlook on life. In many families there has always been a special place for the first-born son – it's as simple as that. Or as complicated if you happened to be a younger son, like Rhett.

Another issue is that of an 'overlapping' family. Mother and I had been a family with an absent father when we were joined by Kell, who became my father. We have never gone in for designations like step-parent or half-sibling. After our parents' divorce, Kell married Sue and later Mother married Ross. Although Rhett was fifteen at the time, Michael seventeen, and I was involved with my own young family by then, this made everyone's role more salient. That is, each of us adopted a more pronounced role, separate and unto ourselves. This differs from a conventional family where everybody knows what role they are to play within the family. We were no longer accountable, each having learned to become responsible for their own lifestyle, with no one to answer to, or feel responsible for – except by loving choice.

It helps to look carefully at Michael's background. Not through the stories written in the tabloids by those who interviewed him throughout his career, because during those times, he recognized that he was selling albums with his 'wild boy' persona, a character he referred to as 'the other Michael Hutchence' – the performer, the character people saw on stage. I was about nine when I learned how valuable good press and public relations could be. Mother's friend, who represented the advertising agency handling the public relations for the Rin Tin Tin television series, had me write a fan letter to Australia's very own Rin Tin Tin (a dog who appeared in the Australian commercials), rather than the more distinguished American canine who performed heroic rescue acts week after week in a kids' TV adventure series. The Australian dog, a German shepherd named Lofty, actually belonged to my mother's friend. The letter was written by a copywriter. I just had to copy it in my own childish handwriting, then it was reprinted in the newspapers to launch an advertising campaign. I remember that the original copy arrived late, sent to the airline terminal right before I was to catch a flight back to Melbourne. In my haste there, I made all kinds of mistakes, but they liked it because it made it more authentic. When my grandmother cut it out of the newspaper I had no interest in it at all, because it wasn't really mine. This taught me a valuable lesson; don't believe everything you read in the newspapers.

You cannot even always rely on the 'serious' news sources, as Michael, and eventually the rest of the family, found out. When people outside the immediate family refer to our 'family thing', as if there were a deep-rooted secret upon which others might speculate, I must admit I do not know what they are talking about. More than half the population comes from what is referred to as a broken home. Besides, Michael was only six months away from leaving home to begin his journey with INXS when our parents were divorced. I would say that he had a better, more stable start in life than most – and that includes Rhett and myself. However, Michael's death has had an astounding impact on us all, not just because we loved him so, but as you will see, he had become the symbolic patriarch.

I began to write about Michael immediately after his funeral. I have always resorted to pen and paper when I have felt passionate about something – particularly when there didn't seem to be a way to articulate things and at times when I feel that there has been some great injustice. I'm not one for verbal combat – never have been. Michael was the same – I guess he was able to express his passions in his songs. Neither of us could face friction in any of our relationships and tended to retreat into silences rather than have confrontational, angry scenes. With Rhett it's a different matter. I don't know why, but sometimes he almost seems to thrive on argument.

With Michael's passing I was faced with the greatest unresolved conflict of my life, a divided family and a rage against the press who were getting everything so wrong. I was angered by Michael's needless death and outraged by the behaviour of many of those whom he had trusted and in some cases paid handsomely to oversee his affairs and generally take care of him. It was torment to see some of those people – possibly for money – talking freely about family matters about which they knew next to nothing. People who barely knew him claimed close friendship. I suppose some of this was inevitable but it made me burn with a desire to set the record straight. Michael had homes in Australia, London and France and he was a generous host whenever his schedule permitted. But he was basically on tour or in the studio for ten months of the year, living out of suitcases in hotel rooms. The other guys in INXS were effectively his brothers, but basically he hadn't had time to develop as many deep friendships of the type that so many others now claimed.

I wearied of reading newspaper reports riddled with mistakes or lies about Michael's unhappy childhood and his estrangement from his family. I particularly hated to read this sort of nonsense because it basically defamed the character of the loving brother I knew and who could not now correct things. There were stories about the family feuding over his estate and others about his plans to marry Paula – all, again, untrue. In his life Michael had abominated the intrusions of the media and had sought to protect what little privacy he had. He would have been appalled by the terrible untruths about him now being unleashed. I began to feel it was almost a duty to speak for him.

One leading Australian newspaper wanted Mother and me to cooperate in a special tribute edition to Michael about three months after he died. We declined. When the 'tribute' was published, written by someone claiming to be a close source, we were horrified to read that Michael supposedly hadn't been close to either of us, and that you could count the times he had seen me on the fingers of one hand. His relationship with Mother was similarly dismissed and distorted. Some would argue that Mother and I should display a lofty indifference to all these lies and basically treat them with contempt and disdain. Who are these cowardly, nameless troublemakers, anyway? What do they matter? But in our raw and grieving state only months after Michael's death I felt that something had to be done.

At first even the minor inaccuracies rankled. But I was not going to explain that Michael had his life and I had mine, that I had no need to follow him around from gig to gig like a groupie as was suggested. Why would I when we cherished extended periods of precious and private time as a family in France and the Gold Coast? When there was a special reason and if I could easily get to a gig, sure I went, particularly in the early stages of his career. Why not? But as the nature and complexities of the lies intensified it became imperative to write the truth, most especially for the sake of Tiger Lily and his niece Zoe Angel in the future. I owe it to them to write an honest record of what happened and to sketch a truthful portrait of their loving father and uncle. I began to reconstruct every conversation I'd had with Michael over the past two or three years, dig out every note or fax from him and to confront the fact that, yes, he had been pretty unhappy although he seldom showed or admitted it. I made calls to people who I hoped could supply fragments of answers to the mystery of his death – Bob Geldof, his old friend Andrew Farriss and his long-time love and forever friend Michele Bennett. And I set about writing of the Michael Hutchence I knew as a child, a teenager, a glorious young adult and finally the troubled man he became.

It has been very hard over the last couple of years to keep my dignity intact, while trying to ignore some of the stories which have been written about my family by various so-called friends, who decline to give their name. Sadly, these stories are repeated over and over in the tabloids. You choose not to protest publicly to accusations made by people who should know better; this in turn leads to strangers sending you hate mail. I wonder how any of these people can sleep at night.

I have kept a diary for as long as I can remember so it wasn't so odd, after I discovered that Tina, too, had been keeping notes, that we decided to work together on a book about Michael. It was my idea and Tina was reluctant at first but soon we found that there was some small therapeutic benefit in the work. I needed all the therapy I could get. I even found I was becoming ill so Ross took me to stay with Tina in LA for two months. So patient and understanding when I collapsed into tears yet again, Ross loved Michael too. So that's how this book began. In California we found we had a little peace and privacy. The media did not hound us so relentlessly – at least not at first.

I had thought that nothing could hurt me after the shock of Michael's death. But we were not being allowed to grieve and start the healing process in the natural way, so things just kept getting worse and worse. Like my daughter I felt helplessly wounded by all the lies about Michael, particularly when they were perpetuated by people who claimed to be his friends or who had benefited from his kindness and loyalty when he was alive. Tina and I began a back and forth process of faxing and exchanging drafts, correcting and integrating our memories. Sometimes as we worked together and spoke on the phone we were even able to laugh.

Maybe that gave us enough strength to begin litigation against the executors of Michael's estate in April 1998. Our reasons will become clear. We were relieved to be able to resolve that litigation in May 2000.

In the early fifties, our mother Patricia Kennedy had owned her own modelling school in Melbourne. It was a wonderful playground for a curious little girl. Often when a child was needed for a show, or a shoot, I would fill in. Or if my mother could not find a babysitter, I would accompany her and just observe all the activity in the dressing room. I was always fascinated by her chameleon qualities when she herself modelled. In those days, it was rare to find make-up artists and hair stylists at a shoot or backstage; the model was on her own. A professional model would carry an enormous bag filled with her own props – gloves, scarves, shoes, jewellery, hairpieces, and of course make-up. Mother was very clever about changing her appearance for every photographic set-up. If it was a catwalk show, she would carefully lay out her accessories ahead of time. With the help of a dresser, she would perform the most amazing transformations at lightning speed and appear beautifully poised in a fresh outfit and ready to sweep down the runway. Superwoman could not have made a faster change. Later on, when Mother was learning the art of make-up, her close work with cameramen, and years of experience in front of the camera, for magazines and television commercials, was invaluable. I have only the utmost respect for the beautiful, dedicated models of that era: they truly were the supermodels.

Mother had been very much in demand both for print and the catwalk and was based in Sydney, where she eventually became a make-up artist. Days are long for a make-up artist – on set before the sun comes up with an average day of twelve hours, which leaves little time for taking care of a child. I remained in Melbourne with my grandparents and great-grandfather, but from a very early age I flew alone to be with her, and I enjoyed it.

Michael always kept a very special framed photograph beside his bed at his house in the South of France. Visitors to the sixteenth-century villa would find most of the displayed photographs on the first level, depicting happy group shots of the immediate family – Mother, Kell, Rhett, Michael and myself in Hong Kong. But the photograph with the place of honour on his night stand was not that of a current girlfriend but a very glamorous picture of Mother, taken in the 1953 'Gown of the Year' awards and wearing a spectacular creation.

I married Tina's father when I was seventeen. He was a lot older. My mother and grandmother had also been child brides. I realized very early in our marriage I had made a mistake, the marriage didn't last, but it gave me the beautiful daughter who is also my wonderful and true friend, always there for me in a crisis – as I hope I am for her.

After divorcing Tina's father I had a child to rear alone. I was teaching deportment and modelling in Melbourne, which eventually led to opening my own school. I modelled as well as taught but became more interested in the other side of the camera. Television work was the next step, and it was when I was booked for commercials that I found out exactly what I wanted to do.

I flew to Sydney for my first television commercial and was sent to make-up. This was a first for me, as we always had to apply our own make-up when doing a fashion show or photographic shoot, except for the big shows or special sessions. My first experience in the make-up chair was frightening. Few were experienced in TV make-up and I thought I looked as though I had hepatitis, left with a white neck and hands to display the products. But I was booked regularly and spent a lot of time flying back and forth between Sydney and Melbourne for commercials – and also a lot of time in the ladies' room trying to tone down my garish face.

I moved to Sydney when I was offered the position of manageress of a new modelling school. I took it on the condition I could still do commercials when they were offered. I needed the money as I was saving to bring Tina to Sydney. It was becoming increasingly important that she should be with me, much as she loved her grandmother.

Then I met a make-up artist who knew exactly what she was doing, so I hired her to teach TV make-up at my school and sat in on every class. Her name was Joan Von Adlerstein. We became very good friends and Joan would always ask me to help her when she was busy. I was an avid student as I knew this was going to be my own career. Once when Joan went on a skiing trip she asked me to take over her bookings at the studio and her night classes at the school. she had a bad accident on the slopes and ended up in hospital for months, so I continued standing in for her. I had done OK up until now, but I had not had anything too difficult to do, but she had given me confidence. I studied from a book and practised on anyone who would allow me to. Joan's fracture was a bad one and by the time she was able to return to the studio there was still ample work for both of us. I continued.

Years earlier my younger brother John had been shot dead in a stupid and terrible accident. He was with a group of friends celebrating a birthday. One of the boys had returned with a borrowed rifle from a hunting trip, and hadn't checked to see if there were any bullets left in the barrel. My brother's friend picked up the gun and accidentally pressed the trigger. The one bullet left pierced my brother's heart and he died instantly.

I mention this here because my mother never recovered from the tragedy and spent years grieving, as if unaware that she had three other children. Then she focused all her attention on Tina, becoming obsessive and even telling people that Tina was her child. It seemed to help her get over the grieving at last and I knew it gave her pleasure, but her possessiveness worried me rather. As time went on she began hiding my letters to Tina, making excuses why Tina could not fly to Sydney for weekends. So even recent family history wasn't all idyllically sunny. Maybe I felt I had something to repair with my children.

Kelland Frank Hutchence was the first in his family to be born in Australia. His parents came from the United Kingdom. Kell's mother Mabel, affectionately called Mabs, was widowed in her fifties when his father Frank, a sea captain, died. His sister Croy was also widowed and lived in Port Moresby, Papua New Guinea. When Kell met Mother he was a very popular bachelor about Sydney. Considered a 'good catch', he was much in demand at dinner parties and so forth. He was well educated and travelled internationally on business for the firm of importers he worked for. Always a well of amusing stories, Kell was very engaging to be around. Sometimes, though, I heard him saying things I thought were critical of people he'd been nice to. He was also physically attractive, and fancied himself a David Niven lookalike.

He was thirty-seven when he met Mother but still lived at home with his own mother, who spoiled him devotedly. Today most women would consider such an arrangement rather off-putting, but in those days, long before the sexual revolution had turned, few 'nice' women were willing to go home to a man's place after a date anyway. Kell may well have had fun with willing partners on his travels but in Sydney he observed polite convention. He was known to date beautiful women, too, and models in particular. At a time when Australian men were being accused of rampant chauvinism, he was the epitome of the cultured gentleman. Where most Aussie males would not dream of even ordering flowers for a woman, Kell could be seen walking down the street with red roses and a bottle of fine wine. He created an image of himself as the true romantic, wining, dining, and dancing at the most exclusive restaurants and clubs.

My first meeting with Kelland Hutchence was in December 1958. I was with my friend Leah McCartney who had just returned from overseas as the reigning Miss Australia. She was meeting her boyfriend and insisted I join them for a Christmas drink. When we were introduced Kell said to me, 'One of these days I'm going to marry you!' I didn't take this seriously, but after that first meeting he was most persistent, with a daily bombardment of proposals, phone calls and roses. Even my students, who saw some of this, added to my sense of pressure with their questions. Amid fears, soul-searching and against my instincts, I accepted his proposal. On the 'big day', I got cold feet. My sister Maureen was my bridesmaid and I told her of my doubts and that I couldn't go through with it. Naturally, she wasn't happy. She was all dressed up and there was a church full of guests waiting.

So Kell and I were married in January 1959. I had accepted his proposal on condition that he adopt Tina, and he promised he would. Three months later I became pregnant with Michael. We were happy then, and excited about a new addition to the family. Kell and Tina had a nice relationship and Tina was happy to hear she would be getting a baby brother or sister. Tina stayed on with my mother for the first few months of our marriage as Kell and I were living with his mother, and I was still trying to 'get Tina back' from my mother as gently as possible – altogether a rather complicated situation. Kell gave Tina a locket with Hutchence engraved on it, but as time went on he seemed to avoid any conversation about her adoption. This was a constant worry to me and it caused strain in our relationship. I did not take marriage vows lightly, nor any other kind of promise.

Michael was born at the Mater Misericordiae Hospital in Sydney – an easy birth, as Tina's had been. He was such a placid baby, always smiling, loved his food, loved his bath, loved being on this earth and a joy to be around. Kell was a very proud father and adored his son but it soon became apparent that he did not have the time it takes for family life. He continued to travel frequently on business, sometimes being away for months on end. Tina was attending school and would rush home to her baby brother: she did a lot of babysitting in those days, but she seemed to love it.

An incident that burns in my brain, which neither Mother nor Kell remembers, took place the evening that I finally arrived in Sydney to live with them. When they picked me up at the airport I was startled to see my mother in a maternity outfit; she had always been so svelte. I had not seen her in eight months and now she was four months pregnant. This was curious: only other kids' mums looked like this. When we stopped for dinner on the way to their apartment Kell drank several cocktails and a bottle of wine. Mother was taking care of herself and was not drinking. They had a disagreement over Kell's drinking. Mother took off her heavy gold bracelet, one of many that Kell was to give her over the years, and threw it on the floor. From my point of view, as an eleven-year-old starting a new life in a new city, this did not look promising. Fortunately they patched things up that night, but we always had a well-stocked bar in our home, and my parents continued to disagree about Kell's liquor consumption.

Looking back on it now I understand how difficult it must have been for them both. Mother was a little edgy: it can't have been easy being pregnant after eleven years and to be fair all this was new for Kell in his late thirties, until recently a bachelor who had shared a well-run house with his mother. In just three and a half years, my parents ended up with a teenager (me), a two-year-old (Michael), and a newborn baby (Rhett). Kell's domestic life had been so well ordered before, so maybe it's not so strange that he wanted to escape on his travels rather a lot.

Soon after my arrival in Sydney, Kell presented me with that heart-shaped locket. It had a hand-painted rose on the front and was backed in gold. He said it was a special day and asked me to turn the locket over. It was actually engraved with 'Christina Elaine Hutchence'. I had a new name. Overnight, I was Tina Hutchence. He explained that he had gone to a lawyer and adopted me. Wow! Now he wanted to know what I was going to call him. I had avoided calling him anything and it had been uncomfortable. He asked me if I could call him 'Dad' or 'Daddio' or 'Pops' or something like that. I chose Dad. This was going to be a new beginning. I would also soon have a little sibling and we would be a regular family. This meant so much to me as I had always felt that my own father did not want me. Kell and I became good friends after this and I trusted him with my secrets. Before now, I had found it difficult to explain my family situation to the nuns at my convent school or my friends there. I did not know any other children who lived with their grandparents and great-grandparents. Actually, now I think I was fortunate to spend so much time with them, but in the fifties, I was a novelty to other children.

Kell fussed over Mother so much while she was pregnant with Michael, so concerned about getting her through doorways or in and out of the car, you would have thought she was about to give birth to triplets. I would be less than honest if I said I was not jealous of Michael before and immediately after his birth. It seemed as though he was the only show in town even then. And it was obvious that both Kell and my mother looked forward to this birth with heightened emotions. It was a new beginning for them both after all. This was also Kell's first child, and although my mother's second, she had been a teenager when I was born. This time she was mature, relaxed, and confident. We all worked on the nursery, painting it a bright lemon – a sensible colour, as we could not predict the sex of the child. This was before anyone knew about the effect of colour on moods and ultimately one's behaviour; now they say that bright yellow can make a child excited to the point of practically bouncing off the walls!

Mother was booked to do some maternity fashion shows and her friends held a mammoth baby shower. Bob Rogers, a popular disc jockey at the time and a family friend, gave Mother an André Kostelanetz album titled 'Music for Pregnant Women' which she played during her afternoon rests. The music had a big orchestra sound, a choir, horns and violins. It was very beautiful and soothing.

On 22 January 1960, while we were living in Lane Cove, New South Wales, Michael Kelland John Hutchence was born. He was named John for my uncle, John Kennedy, Mother's younger brother. It has been reported in various newspapers and even in biographies that Michael's second middle name was Frank. I have a copy of his birth certificate and the only Frank there is his father, Kelland Frank. My parents were extremely proud of the 'little prince', as I secretly called him, and why not? Michael was an adorable baby, although his arrival certainly turned the household upside down.

Having this brother was like having my own little living baby doll. Although at twelve I'd not had any experience with babies, I began babysitting duties about one week after he came home from the hospital. I found that I was pretty good at it. We started off with two hours and progressed to a full day. Most of the time, I did not mind babysitting as we moved houses so often and it was somehow something stable. We moved three times in the first year alone. Kell switched companies and they would relocate him to different cities or states. I was shy and introverted which made it hard for me to make friends, and although he was too tiny to understand what I was rambling on about, Michael became my confidant. I felt most comfortable being a little mother and I felt responsible. When I babysat I could have Michael all to myself, without anybody being nervous that I might drop him. I bathed him, fed him and lulled him off to sleep when he was restless. I rubbed cream on his gums when he was teething. He would chew on my long hair and get it caught in his tiny fingers and the more I shrieked, the louder he would gurgle.

The first time Mother and Kell went out for the evening, they hired a nurse. I was mortified. How embarrassing, how come it was all right for me to take care of him during the day? What was the difference? Besides, I had just begun high school and was perfectly capable of taking care of myself. It felt quite unnecessary to have a nurse in the house – I had been so careful with Michael. Never once did I prick him with a pin when I changed his old-fashioned cotton diaper; I was careful with his delicate skull; I took him on walks. As the months went on and he began to recognize us, I was eager to be the first one into the nursery in the morning to come to his 'rescue'. He would be so grateful for a friendly face to pick him up. He would stop crying and give me a big smile. As time passed he was able to pull himself up, holding on to the side of the crib, bounce up and down and holler only to grin as soon as he saw a loving and familiar face. From very early on it was obvious that he instinctively knew that if you smile, someone will smile back.

I failed to realize it at the time but due to Kell's career changes, this was only the beginning of a nomadic life for us all. I attended approximately six schools in three different states between the ages of eleven and fifteen. I rarely had the same uniform as everybody else. Once, I even took correspondence schooling for two months while

Kell was out of the country on business and Mother and Michael and I spent a brief period in Melbourne.

And then there were five. On 21 August 1962, Rhett Bradley Hutchence was born in Brisbane, Queensland. By then I was fourteen and we had been in the same suburb, even the same house, for all of a year so I was beginning to have a social life. Babysitting was no longer all that appealing, especially with two of them. I sometimes asked a friend in to help. I was only allowed one friend at a time, because it was thought I might not keep my mind on my job otherwise. I began calling both boys 'Babe'. I do this with my own children now and I called Michael 'Babe' until the day he died.

From the start, it was obvious that Rhett was going to be a handful. He was so different from Michael. He was not a happy baby and he let us all know about it. It is possible that his irritable disposition was due to allergies – he was allergic to cows' milk for a start. His paediatrician had my mother mix up a formula using goats' milk. Every morning she would line up the bottles and bring the milk to a slow simmer. It had the foulest smell and even though Michael was only two, he would walk into the kitchen in the mornings holding his nose. Rhett was even more fractious when it was time to change his diaper. When he could speak, his favourite word was 'No'. He shook his little head before the words would form and when he could finally speak, he had the deepest voice for a child. 'Nnnnno.' And to this day he is still contrary. For instance, if you were to point out the beautiful white snow he would likely say 'Well, it's actually grey.' I felt protective of Rhett because I really did not feel that he was getting the kind of attention that Michael commanded when he was a baby.

Rhett was tiny and helpless as a newborn, with huge, dark, tear-filled eyes. He only slept in short snatches. Sometimes, Mother and I took turns getting up at night for him as she became so worn out from her long days with the two of them. With the lack of sleep, Rhett was cranky much of the time, and so too were Mother and I. Kell was not affected as we were: he continued to take overseas business trips and barely had time between them to notice the disruption in the household.

Rhett seemed to have arrived into this world an unhappy baby. There are studies to suggest that whilst most babies are categorized as 'easy', others are harder to warm towards. There is the smaller percentage, the babies who are 'difficult'. These babies have intense reaction to change, find it more difficult to adjust, and more importantly they are difficult to soothe. This sounds just like Rhett. When Rhett cried and Mother attempted to cradle him his body would stiffen and he would become rigid. There was just no telling how he would react to a new person, sound, or even a toy. Of course, as this was more than thirty years ago, studies to help understanding were not available, and my parents were not equipped to handle Rhett's special needs. They reacted as most would, with a certain amount of exasperation.

Michael, in the meantime, became an adorable little toddler, up to all kinds of cute antics. He was not angelic all of the time – he had his own fractious moments and could be stubborn, but in general he was easy to be around. He had even learned the words of a song – actually 'his' words to a song. From the time he rose in the morning until he closed his eyes at night he sang over and over, 'Up the magic dragon lived by the sea' (instead of 'Puff the magic dragon'). To stop him, I taught him another song, I chose Mary Wells' 'My Guy'. He skipped around the house singing 'no handsome face could ever take the place of my guy', which I'm sure sounded peculiar coming from a little boy, but it was the only song I knew all the words to, at the time. When he had been singing this for about two months, we progressed to another.

Even though I was only a teenager, I believed that Rhett was being deprived of a major influence for his ultimate self-esteem – his father's love and attention. It seemed to me that Kell did not even try to pretend that he was interested in this little boy. It was truly sad to see what I observed as the detachment Kell exhibited towards Rhett compared to the enthusiasm he displayed for anything that Michael was involved in. Rhett craved his share of attention, and when he could not get it, he automatically did something to seek it, agreeable or not. As time passed I came to think that Rhett had realized that in order to get attention he had to raise some disturbance. Eventually his allergies subsided, so he was not as cranky and he slept longer hours. He still had some medical problems but after a hernia operation he became physically very strong. But I wondered whether the greater, deeper, damage was done.

*

I loved my boys – all my children – equally, but Rhett was quite a handful. He became distinctly fussy about his solid food. I will admit that I found it tiresome, especially if I suspected that he was simply seeking attention. He hated vegetables, peas in particular, and if a single pea had touched anything else on his plate he would refuse to eat anything at all. He wanted to live on chocolate, which may have been an early signal of an addictive personality. As a toddler he would kick and bite if he did not get his way. He could be extremely bad tempered and really needed a man around to control him. With Kell away so much, I hated having to be the disciplinarian and 'enforcer' all the time. But Rhett also had his endearing side and as he got older he could charm his way out of any trouble. He was smart and funny, but he didn't like to be cuddled as Michael did. After having had two children who were quiet, cheerful and easy to raise, I suddenly found my life revolving around a hyperactive child.

Even then, back in the early sixties, studies had been made of such children and their special needs but when I tried to discuss this with Kell he dismissed all that as mumbo-jumbo. However, Kell wasn't there most of the time when Rhett was throwing tantrums.

We eventually moved back to Sydney in 1963. This was our first home in French's Forest, a relatively new neighbourhood then and even thirty years later it has not changed much. Driving down the main highway leading there, the trees are so thick, you cannot detect the little pathways leading off the road to the houses thirty yards back. If you have never been there before you would think you were going to come face to face with a kangaroo. In fact they do have 'koala crossing' signs along the road. Nowhere could have seemed more safe and wholesome a place to raise children and we were surrounded by other young families. By now I had left school, having found it difficult to keep up with the curriculum after so many moves. I was envious of the boys, as they had not begun their schooling or serious friendships and seemed unaffected by the nomadic life we had led.

In the early hours of 23 November 1963, I awoke to a quiet house. It was my sixteenth birthday. Suddenly, there was a commotion and my mother, in tears, burst into my room to tell me that John F. Kennedy had been assassinated in Dallas, Texas. On that terrible day, it was very hard to get out from under the cloud of the huge tragedy of that loss. The sadness and bewilderment was of course felt all around the world, most people who were old enough to comprehend the story can remember where they were when this happened. I remember the impact on the average Australian was enormous. I am sure that hearing the newscast over and over must have had some effect on my mother who could not help but think of the loss of her own brother every time she heard the name John Kennedy. We sat at the breakfast table unable to speak of anything else. Michael, who was not quite four, did not know who President Kennedy was and I remember he was very confused with the adult talk and the gloom surrounding the day.

Kell spent most of the following year overseas on business. Mother occasionally worked on commercials but spent most of her time caring for the boys who were a handful. The garden, both front and back, was full of eucalyptus trees, 'gum trees' as we refer to them in Australia, and for a child this was like having your own forest. Michael was as curious as a child could be and Rhett, of course, wanted to follow his older brother everywhere. Although the yard appeared to be a wonderful playground, with all the deadly insects, snakes and spiders making their home in the Australian countryside, Mother was pretty nervous.

Kell returned from another business trip in November of 1964, and announced that he had accepted a job as Managing Director of an import/export company, importing Haig Scotch Whisky, and Moët et Chandon champagne for restaurants and hotels in Hong Kong. He was to depart immediately, while Mother, Michael, Rhett and I would join him in January. For once we were all glad to be moving, despite our pleasant neighbourhood. After all, we had been up and down the east coast of Australia; it would be exciting to move to a foreign country.

Shortly before we left Australia, I was visiting friends in Melbourne and my mother arranged for me to meet my biological father. She had contacted him to let him know I was there and he asked to see me before I went to live on another continent. I had deliberately put him out of my mind as it was less painful that way. In any case, he had not attempted to contact me and, after all, I had a new father now. My mother's friend took me to a coffee shop and left me to wait for a man I only knew from old photographs. Then a man with sad, puppy-dog eyes – my eyes – came over to me. He was much shorter than I had remembered, but then I had been so short the last time I set eyes on him as a four-year-old. With what might be considered a lack of tact and sensitivity, he had brought his children from his second marriage with him and they kept staring at me. Finally, the little boy said, 'We have a photograph of you on our mantelpiece, but you look a lot different now.' The photograph he was referring to was apparently taken when I was three. The memory of this excruciating meeting remains very painful, not least because I felt so sorry for this man. Where do we learn to become a parent? We just do the best we can. Obviously, it was not the greatest idea for me to meet him after so many years without contact. We have never spoken since.

When I arrived back in Sydney, in early December, we barely had time for Christmas. But of course we had to make some effort for Michael's and Rhett's sakes. Mother and I shopped and wrapped gifts, but we decorated the French's Forest house sparingly, for we were surrounded by packing crates. The house was being rented out while we were in Hong Kong. Since Kell's contract was for only three years, we might as well keep it on just in case it didn't work out. We all four went to the local physician for our inoculations: cholera, typhoid and smallpox. Mother and I took turns taking care of the boys, the shots made us so ill, and it was a miserable Christmas and New Year's Eve.

Then it was time for our passports. We went down to the government office in Sydney to deal with the required paperwork. Mother and I learned that we actually had to go to Melbourne for our birth certificates – in those days such documents were not trusted to the post. We returned to Sydney, had our photos taken and went to sort things out. Then there was a problem. My birth certificate did not match my name. Where were the adoption papers? There must be a paper trail. But there were no adoption papers, as Kell had not actually adopted me after all. He later explained that when he went to the lawyer, he was told it would be easier and less expensive simply to change my name. What difference would it make? I guess it wouldn't have made any difference if I was never going to get married on foreign soil, apply for a passport, a green card, citizenship in another country, or an assortment of other significant matters that can come up in a lifetime. The authorities finally relented and granted me a passport in the name of Christina Elaine Hutchence after my mother had explained the situation and pleaded with the agency to make an exception. But I never got over the feeling of betrayal when I realized Kell had brushed my adoption aside as too much effort. It meant that the last five years had been a lie, as he did not care to officially make me his daughter, or, most importantly in his eyes, a Hutchence.

In 1985, by when I was living in the United States, I went into the Australian Consulate to renew my passport and was informed that I could not have a new one under the name I had used for twenty-six years. I sat in the office of the Consulate General and cried my eyes out. I had never been known as anything else. My professional name was Hutchence, even through two marriages, I had kept my name. The consul could not help me, those were the rules. I would have to get a formal name change, which could only be done in the country of origin. Fortunately I worked for Continental Airlines at the time, so I was issued a temporary passport, flew to Sydney, changed my name legally to Hutchence, and was back in LA within the week.

Mother also had a problem as she could not obtain a birth certificate, and the authorities insisted her father was 'unknown'. She was frantic. She had always known her father was Stephen Patrick Kennedy. She was Patricia Kennedy. Her father was killed when she was twelve years old – while attempting to cross the street, he was run over by an ambulance. Fortunately in the mid-sixties, for both Mother and myself, it was still possible to talk your way into something like a passport under the name you were generally known under, if you looked decent enough. They gave her a certificate of citizenship and she was finally given her documents. But the whole incident evidently offended Kell's superior sensibilities. At the time, Kell maintained that we were the only five people in Australia with the name of 'Hutchence', and very few outside Australia. Ironic now to remember that when I was caught skipping school, he said, 'You must remember, you're a "Hutchence", think of the name.' I remember that Kell took the news of the birth certificate very hard. He even told Mother that he had married a 'bastard', although her parents certainly had been married. Although the marriage survived another twelve years, they were rocky. It seems to me that he has always felt a false sense of greatness due to his surname.

*

I had never been out of Australia before, and needed a copy of my birth certificate – which I had never had – to obtain a passport. I decided to go to Melbourne, the city of my birth, to obtain this, and also take the children down to see my family as I had no idea how long we would be living in Hong Kong. I went into the office of Registrar of Births in the city and made an application for my certificate. To my surprise I was told there was no record of my birth. I insisted there must be some mistake and asked them to search further. Once again, no record. I went home and told my mother what had happened and she was adamant I should go back and ask again. I went the following day and returned home tearful and empty handed. I asked my mother if she had something to tell me about the circumstances of my birth.

Meanwhile Kell was calling, wondering why I was spending so much time in Melbourne. I tried to explain my problem as delicately as I could, but when he spoke to my mother and she told him there wasn't a problem, he preferred to believe her. I returned to Sydney with the children. Eventually I received a letter two weeks later informing me that my mother (using her maiden name) had given birth to a female child – but declared the name of father unknown. My mother never spoke of this again. The man I had always known as my father had been killed when on crutches crossing Melbourne's busy Collins Street – ironically right outside the offices of the Registrar of Births and Deaths.

I had brought Tina into this marriage on the understanding that Kell would adopt her legally. I especially wanted this when I became pregnant with Michael. I had waited a long time to be able to have Tina living with me permanently and I wanted her to feel part of the new family. When he failed to follow through with this, even though he told her he had done so, it was only a matter of time before he would be caught in the lie. Tina was very hurt by this and at seventeen years old, it damaged her self-esteem, and did little to deepen her trust in men.

In Vince Lovegrove's book about Michael, on which Kell collaborated but later regretted, the author says that Kell thought seriously about taking the little boys to Hong Kong and leaving me behind. Kell is quoted as saying, 'I thought with the help of amahs [servants], that I could survive in Hong Kong with the boys because I knew the city well. But somebody told me I couldn't get them out of the country without their mother's permission. Then I realized it would not look good with the company if I rolled up with two children, telling them I had split with my wife. So I told Pat about the job, and she was on the next plane out of

Melbourne, headed for Sydney.' According to Lovegrove, he also recalls that even though his company provided a flat, a car, and hefty expense account, he was not settled when we arrived two months later. This caused the company to spend much more on our move as we had to take up residence in the Hong Kong Hilton.

I was astounded to discover, according to Vince Lovegrove, that Kell had possibly intended to leave me behind. We had discussed this potential job change and move together, and when he was offered the job, we agreed he would accept – although I believe he had already made up his own mind. As he had to return immediately, we agreed I would follow on within two months with Tina, Rhett and Michael. If Lovegrove is right, Kell would have taken his children at two and four years old away from their mother. There are many other stories in that account of Michael's life, particularly in dealing with his childhood, where if Kell is being quoted accurately he has selective memory. If so, I can only assume this is because he was rarely around during Michael's childhood, since he had to travel so much on business.

It's also worth noting that while Mr. Lovegrove's book claims to reflect 'unprecedented access to all [Michael's] blood relatives' and even thanks Tina and me for our 'special inspiration', I can state publicly that neither one of us contributed a word to his book. If I had, he would know for a start that I have not been married five times. He also acknowledges for her help Michael's grandmother, Mabs, who had been dead for almost fifteen years at time of writing!

CHAPTER TWO

The Golden Playpen

The nine-hour flight to Hong Kong in January 1965 was, with a five-year-old and a two-year-old, exhausting. Our first taste of the climate we were about to experience came when we stopped over in Manila. It was around four in the morning and we were escorted across steaming hot tarmac. I had never known such humidity. We were already feeling like wrung-out dishrags and now here we were with two tired, whining little boys.

We finally touched down in Hong Kong. It is the most amazing landing, frightening if you are not expecting it. The sun was just up and first we seemed to be landing in the ocean and then flying low enough to peer through apartment block windows before hitting the runway just before the ocean beckoned again. Kell was waiting. We had not seen him in two months. He had a car ready and we crossed over to Victoria Island by ferry, as there was no tunnel in those days. Our lives would never be the same after this move. Rhett, Michael and I forever became gypsies.

Life in Hong Kong was a series of fascinating adventures. We started out at the Hong Kong Hilton where we had a suite with large bedrooms either side, one for Mother and Kell, the other for the boys and me. Hong Kong is very cosmopolitan, but even in those days the ratio of Asian to Caucasian was about 90 to 1. Michael and Rhett had Beatle haircuts and their hair was blond, which I guess is hard to imagine as they both grew up to be so luxuriantly dark. Rhett especially was very fair then. When I took them downstairs in the elevator, local people would touch their hair. This did not bother Michael too much, but Rhett would get agitated and brush the strangers' hands away, complaining loudly. I would try to pacify him, explain that it was a compliment, but he was much too young to understand. That was just the way he was, very easily provoked whilst Michael would just frown and put up with it. Sometimes he liked the attention and by being agreeable, he commanded plenty.

In the very first week, there was a cocktail party in our honour. Mother took me out to buy a suitable cocktail dress, then she sent me to have my hair professionally styled. I felt so sophisticated, but of course I was far from it. At the party I met a photographer who suggested to Mother that she bring me around to his studio for some test shots. A photograph of Kell was published in the Hong Kong *China Mail* the next day with an announcement that he was taking over as Managing Director at Guthrie and Co. I still have that clipping and many more press stories on all of us from our years there. I did do the test shots and my modelling career started slowly to take off. I was not print material, but I was a skinny five-foot-six and could do a mean catwalk down the runway. I didn't have many other career options because I did not speak Cantonese. One of the shots from that first photo-shoot was used in the morning English language newspaper, in an article written by Terry Burke, an Australian journalist and scriptwriter, who quickly became very influential in my mother's career as well as my own.

Terry would call and say, 'OK, meet me at 3 p.m. outside of the Star Ferry. I will have a script, and a cab waiting. You can learn your lines in the cab. We're going to the studio to do a live promo for the Sunday *China Mail*.' Upon stepping into the cab, I would be handed a script based on my real life. I still have an original one, which reads:

Tina: I really have to get up early to get the *China Mail* at my house.
Alana: Why is that?
Tina: Because once my two little brothers get a hold of it, you never know – aeroplanes, paper dolls . . .

I couldn't always be sure if the other person was even going to be speaking English, sometimes the crew would have to give me hand signals to indicate my cue when she had completed her line.

It was so much fun living in the Hilton. We did not have the means to prepare meals so Mother and I were off the hook. Room service was fun at first, then we tried all of the restaurants in the hotel. Eventually, we knew everything on the menus. Of course the boys thought that the whole twenty-six-storey complex was our home. I had to be a light sleeper, because often when I opened my eyes in the morning, the door to our side of the suite could be wide open to the hallway, and I might hear Michael and Rhett running up and down as if it were merely an extension to our house. I was a teenager of the sixties, I wore curlers and baby-doll pyjamas to bed and did not relish going into a hotel hallway to retrieve my two little brothers. They also found the elevators fascinating. Mother and I would find ourselves frantically pushing buttons, trying all floors to catch the two little mischief-makers after they had got loose. Eventually we moved into our own apartment.

Sometimes I've wondered if those days gave Michael such a taste for the luxurious yet impersonal room-serviced existence of life in expensive hotels that he was driven to replicate them as a touring rock and roll superstar. But really I had no idea then just how those years in Hong Kong would impact all of our lives. Initially Mother and I were less than thrilled about moving to the Far East, after all, the place to be in the sixties was London. Who ever heard of anyone moving to Hong Kong? It became obvious to me later that this move from Australia, the land that was still being referred to as 'white Australia', to these multicultural surroundings compounded a nomadic existence that we have all experienced in one way or another. Due to the nature of Kell's business, my parents entertained constantly, and I found myself conversing with adults most of the time. Instead of jeans, I wore couture. Rather than beach dances with Billy Thorpe and the Aztecs, I attended cocktail parties with Sergio Mendez and Brazil '66. Dinner parties resembled the United Nations, every guest was from a different country.

This new lifestyle and the glimpses of other worlds it presented would forever set us apart from our peers in Australia. And just as I could never be the same teenager, this would also be a very different childhood for Michael and Rhett. Michael attended a kindergarten where he was in a minority; he learned his nursery rhymes in Cantonese as well as English. He began to speak a variation of English accented by Cantonese phrases and mimed when he could not get his point across to the servants verbally. Some of these skills may have contributed to his later powers as a lyricist and stage performer. Rhett was just a toddler and spent many hours playing with the cook's little boy who was about his age. They did not start out speaking the same language, but within a few months they were each proficient at the other's. Michael and Rhett seemed to accept their new environment more readily than the adults in the family.

Kell was very busy with his new responsibilities. Mother had become bored with the lunches and teas and had gone back to modelling and make-up. Michael and Rhett were being kept busy with pre-school and kindergarten. Rhett was now learning his nursery rhymes in Cantonese and becoming very fluent. He was a very bright three-year-old, copying everything his older brother did, and yet he was physically superior. He demonstrated this one day, while the two were lying on the floor quietly watching *Romper Room* on television as they always did. The programme always ended with the hostess on the show picking up a mirror, and signing off with a catchphrase that each week used a different selection of popular names – for instance, 'I see Tommy, and I see Lisa, and I see Adam and I see you.' Obviously, the names were chosen to take in as much of the audience as possible. Very often, she said the name Michael. On this day, Rhett jumped up and, without provocation, slugged Michael, who began to cry. When asked why he did this, he screamed through tears of frustration, 'Because she always looks in her mirror and sees Michael, and never sees me.' How do you explain this to a three-year-old?

Many years later Michael said he wished our parents had named him Rhett, as it was such a great name, so different, a perfect stage name. Rhett was tough in every sense of the word and he was a natural leader, strong willed, determined, highly intelligent and with a remarkable memory. Throughout his childhood, Rhett remained this way. He breezed through his classes. The only problems he had in school were when he corrected his teachers. By contrast, Michael did not excel in school, and he had a slight lisp, which I suspect held him back from speaking up in class. He could charm himself out of many situations, but he always had to work harder to pass his grades. His report cards inevitably read, 'Michael is a dreamer, he needs to get serious about his education.' As Rhett progressed from one grade to another, Michael envied his younger brother's gift for reading an assignment once and understanding it. In adulthood, he would make up for it by being a ferocious reader. He read constantly on planes and while he was touring. It became important to him to be thought of as an intellectual and he looked for the same in his partners and he hated to imagine that people might dismiss him as just another rock-'n'-roller with a supermodel girlfriend. As he went through life meeting new people, he would grill them on every detail of their job, their hobbies, their lifestyle. When doing so, Michael's eye contact with them did not flicker and he had the gift of making the other person feel that they really were interesting. Now maybe part of this came from sheer, effortless charm, which isn't always too profound. Nonetheless, it made people feel good. At other times I guess he was making up for his lapses at school. When describing a new love interest, he would always begin by briefing us on the girl's intellect. By the time he was in his early thirties he seemed to have some knowledge of just about any subject that you could bring up. He was obviously well travelled, but he made sure that he was also well versed in the history and culture of most every country he visited, be it for business, pleasure, or an INXS tour.

Life in Hong Kong was very good for all of us, especially the children. We all made many friends, some of whom we keep in touch with today. Kell was not travelling quite as much as before, which gave us a more stable home and at last I felt that we finally had the potential to become a family.

It was easy to fit into the lifestyle there, as there was so much to do. When the boys were settled in their schools, they were kept extremely busy. Most of all, they loved to go to the Ladies Recreation Club swimming pool. There was an instructor there who was wonderful with the children, but would not accept them for lessons until they were five years old. I booked Michael in for classes but this of course bothered Rhett who had to wait another two years. Michael took to the water immediately and would enter every race. I bought a swimming aid for Rhett to strap to his back so he could at least enjoy himself in the water. He began to see how long he could hold his breath, face down in the water. For this reason, when he began his first lesson he would only swim underwater and had to be taught to swim on the surface. They both became excellent swimmers and divers.

We were always anxious about Michael's asthma, fearing it might be a family blight as his aunt suffered from it. But actually Michael was a very healthy child, easily dealing with routine childhood illnesses, infections and the occasional bout of bronchitis. Certainly nothing affected his swimming or other sporting activities. It was only as he approached adulthood that the asthma sometimes troubled him – but never to the point of serious debilitation.

Kell changed positions a number of times. He started off in the liquor business and then took a job with Mandarin Textiles, who made up couture for Lanvin and also had their own label, Dynasty, which was sold in their boutiques at the Hilton, Mandarin, and Peninsula Hotels. The line was very popular with tourists. As a result I had the most incredible wardrobe, as I was lucky enough to be the sample size. We had to entertain a lot at home, which I loved, and our social life was really exciting. Music seemed to fill our house from morning to night. I loved soul singers like Aretha Franklin and Dakota Staton, Ray Charles, and I didn't mind the Beatles and Tom Jones. But I adored Sinatra. Michael said in an interview that his love of music came from me.

I read that an American film crew had arrived in Hong Kong to search for locations for a movie called *Strange Portrait*, starring Jeffrey Hunter and Mai Tai Sing, directed by Jeffrey Stone. I figured work would be better than gossip and giggle, as I'd become bored with that and did not care for bridge, so I approached the production office to see if a make-up artist was required. I was hired on to the crew. The first assistant director was an Englishman by the name of Peter MacGregor Scott who, years later, produced the Batman movies. In 1995 he asked Michael to record 'The Passenger' for the *Batman Forever* soundtrack.

When we finished filming, the producer asked me to stay on for another movie, so after only one week's break we started on the next production, which was titled *Sumuru*. It was to star Shirley Eaton (the Golden Girl in *Goldfinger*), Wilfrid Hyde-White, Frankie Avalon, George Nader and Klaus Kinski and it featured a separate cast of dozens of girls from the American beach party movies. I asked Tina to join me as my assistant as she had been around me long enough on various productions; it was easy to teach her.

Klaus Kinski, the father of Nastassja, had brought his wife and daughter with him to Hong Kong and they were staying at the Hilton. When visiting the set, Michael and Rhett attempted to talk to the sweet young Nastassja, but she was very shy, and they had to coax her to play. During filming, Michael had his sixth birthday and I invited Nastassja, who was also six, to his party. Many years later I read an article written by a friend of Paula's in an English magazine where it said, 'Michael's mother entertained often and amongst those who partied hard with her was Nastassja Kinski and Michael Caine.' Now, I have never met, let alone worked with, Mr Caine and quite how hard he would have wanted to party with a six-year-old remains a mystery. My Michael may have been the instigator on both of these stories which have been repeated down the line in many interviews, including some with Paula. He learned the art of a good yarn from Kell, and he learned it well.

Michael and Rhett enjoyed coming to the set and knew the rules. Any noise and you're out and you don't get another chance. They also liked to play with my special effects kit and many a time I found to my horror they had used my 'blood' to give authenticity to the wounds suffered in battle by their GI Joes! Apart from this they had what seemed to be a hundred little plastic soldiers. They were the most popular kids in the neighbourhood, because they would siphon 'movie blood' out of my make-up kit and use it on their little warriors. Rhett would have made an excellent make-up artist. His simulated bruises, burns and cuts on his friends sent many a parent into shock. I continued working on film, as whenever there was a production crew in Hong Kong, I would be contacted. The opportunities were too good to pass up, especially when one is getting paid to travel; besides the boys were very busy with their school work, sport, and music lessons.

Michael's interest in girls began early, when he met a very pretty English girl in his swimming class and was quite besotted by her. He was about eight. One day he and a few friends were playing with a ball at a nearby park, and this same pretty little girl came by with her friends and joined the game. Michael suddenly decided to kiss her, then stepped back very embarrassed and tripped over a rockery landing on his arm which had twisted behind his back. He was taken to the Queen Elizabeth Hospital, a public one where the majority of patients were Cantonese. He had broken his arm, and they kept him there for three days and fed him Chinese food for breakfast, lunch and dinner, which he loved. He was pretty adept at the chopsticks by then. His arm had to be reset as it was slightly crooked. From then on he had problems swimming competitively so he had to give it up, although he continued to enjoy swimming and water-skiing for his own pleasure.

Eventually both boys joined cub scouts, learned judo, kick boxing, chess, archery, and studied music. Michael studied violin, even though he was threatened daily by Rhett to stop the terrible noise or he would cut the strings. I had hoped that Rhett's many outside interests would tire him out and make him calmer, but his hyperactive tendencies did not abate. Michael would spend hours on a model plane, only to have Rhett smash his little masterpiece in a tantrum. There was a daily barrage of irate mothers at my door, standing there, with a crying child. I was forever apologizing for black eyes and bruises and hurt feelings. There was a stream of letters from Rhett's teachers, not about his grades, for he was an excellent scholar, but because they simply could not control his naughty behaviour. Amidst great disapproval from Kell, I took Rhett to one doctor after another while we lived in Hong Kong, as I had read of findings in the States that might have helped him, but not one of them could make any difference. I wonder now if Rhett resented all these consultations and examinations.

In our apartment on Old Peak Road we had two amahs. Servants are customary in Hong Kong. Whatever their name is, you put 'Ah' before it. This is the polite way to address a servant. They would in turn address all males (Kell, Michael and Rhett) as 'Master' and Mother and I were called 'Missy', as in Master Michael and Missy Tina. We had a 'baby' amah, for Rhett and Michael; and a 'cook-general' amah to take care of the cleaning and meals. Kell took it upon himself to interview prospectives, so we went through quite a few in the beginning. He once employed a very pretty, young girl for the care of the boys, she said her name was Huh so naturally we referred to her as Ah Huh. She didn't last long, she kept going missing, until we found her downstairs with the chauffeurs wearing one of Mother's favourite outfits. Mother did the hiring from then on.

We went through quite a few general amahs before settling on Ah Chang, who had left her family in Shanghai to find prosperity and freedom in Hong Kong. She wore her hair in a long braid down her back, secured with a black ribbon. Her uniform consisted of black pants and a traditional, crisp, white 'mao' jacket. You could always hear her coming, as she had a habit of shuffling, instead of picking her feet up. Her manner appeared to be stern but she had a heart of gold, and I loved to hear her laugh. She had to struggle to maintain a certain control as she was constantly being outwitted by Michael and Rhett.

Kell made a habit of calling at the last minute when he planned to bring people home for dinner. Mother would go to the kitchen and tell Ah Chang how many extra guests we would be entertaining that evening. Mother would say, 'One Missy and two Masters come home with Master; six o'clock, dinner. We have curry, OK?' Ah Chang almost always questioned Mother's orders: she wanted 'Master' to tell her what he wanted her to serve. Mother got so cross about this, she once dialled Kell's office, and had him tell Ah Chang himself. I always thought that Kell secretly enjoyed this inequality of the sexes. Before Hong Kong, he had spent a major portion of his adult life in the Far East, and it was obvious that he felt comfortable with local customs, his favourites being that men are more important than women, and that boy children were more valuable than girls.

Ah Chang was with our family for eight years. On his way home from school one day Michael found a scraggly little tortoiseshell cat he named Tinkerbell. He entered her in a competition and she miraculously won first prize. The morning edition of the *China Mail* featured a photograph of Michael hugging the scrawny feline. Tinkerbell was thereafter spoilt by the family. She slept in Michael's bed and Ah Chang made sure that she was fed fresh fish only, from the local markets. On a trip to Sydney, I picked up some new kind of dry cat food and asked Ah Chang to give it to Tinkerbell. Of course Tinkerbell had been living the luxury life and turned her nose up at the dry food. Ah Chang maintained that it was because she was a Chinese cat; Australian cats must be different, she insisted.

Tinkerbell had a female kitten at around the time *Bewitched* was a popular television show, so Michael named her Tabitha. She was just as feisty as her mother, and together they terrorized Ah Chang. The word for cat in Cantonese is 'mao'. A day never went by without Ah Chang screeching about the 'maos'. They made her life a misery; as she turned to admonish one cat, the other would leap up on the kitchen counter and make off with a portion of the family dinner. Tabitha hadn't been with us very long, when Rhett was given a pair of strawberry finches, exquisite tiny birds. Ah Chang hung their cage high so that the cats would be deterred from seeking out any snacks. It worked for a short time, until one night there was a gruesome commotion. By the time we had gathered on the porch, all that was left was an empty cage, save for some beautiful red feathers and of course Ah Chang wielding a broom, as she chased a defiant Tabitha into a corner. Michael ran to defend her and as Tabitha cowered, red feathers hanging out of her mouth, Ah Chang screamed what we understood to be Cantonese obscenities.

My social life was really looking up. It was a very carefree time in my life. There was no need to babysit the boys any more, as we had a baby amah for that. My brothers loved to play pranks especially when I had friends over to the house. My friends thought they were cute, but I was constantly embarrassed. They delighted in saying anything in front of anybody and all the while I was trying so hard to be sophisticated. One new craze was go-go dancing – in cute miniskirts, *Shindig*-style, nothing sexy. I had three girlfriends and one of them had an uncle who was a disc jockey. He hired us to 'go-go' at one dance, calling us the Telstar Dancers, after one of the first American spacecraft. The *China Mail* put us on the front cover of the paper and offers began to come in. We landed a contract on a television show, which was the Chinese version of *Shindig*, so it was imperative that we come up with an endless variation on routines. Fortunately we had a large living room at my parents' house in which to choreograph and practise our dance routines at full volume. Michael was in charge of playing the same song, over and over, until we could get the routines down – he was very precise about it, too.

Michael and Rhett would position themselves on the floor and watch us go through our routines, sometimes mimicking the moves. I thought Michael was going to be a drummer, the way he beat time with his chopsticks, moving his shoulders up and down, his head cocked to one side and mouthing the words to the songs. He was so serious, watching to see who was out of sync. Rhett made funny faces at us and complained that we were playing the same song, over and over, and why couldn't we do it this way or that? During his career, Michael of course gave many interviews, drawing upon experiences in his lifetime, some real, some imagined, and some realities with a lot of imagination thrown in. On more than one occasion, he told an interviewer that while in Hong Kong, his sister had been a go-go dancer – in a cage! I am happy to report that this story was imagined.

There was some wonderful music being generated by a number of British bands; the Rolling Stones, the Beatles, Cream. One of the girls in our group arrived back from a vacation with a Rolling Stones single which took our breath away. It doesn't seem so shocking now, but 'Satisfaction' was the most irreverent piece of music I had ever heard – and I took great delight in playing it over and over, until Michael and Rhett knew the words by heart. My friends thought it was just the most fun, to ask them to do a duet on this one. Rhett couldn't always remember all the words, so to make up for it, he would scream out louder when Michael got to the 'satisfaction' part.

Our parents exposed us to Frank Sinatra, Tony Bennett, Count Basie and Ella Fitzgerald so we all grew up with an appreciation of good music. I think Kell looked upon my move to this 'new' music as rebellion. The conflict in Vietnam actually allowed for some very interesting and enduring music to filter into the tiny, British Crown Colony of Hong Kong. Droves of American servicemen were coming to Hong Kong for rest and recreation and bringing with them some popular, new American music. I wore out at least five recordings of Buffalo Springfield's 'For What It's Worth' during 1967, by playing it over and over until Kell threatened to smash the stereo if I didn't return to 'Satisfaction'.

Living on a relatively small peninsula did not preclude us from moving house. We went from the Hilton in the Central District of Victoria Island to an apartment halfway up the Peak; to a house in Stanley, which stood on a cliff and overlooked its own private beach and pool, and back to two different homes on Old Peak Road before heading to Kowloon on the mainland. All this in six years, and not counting three months spent back in Australia! Nomadic as we had become this didn't seem particularly disruptive at the time but perhaps it continued to encourage a sort of rootlessness in us all. Certainly I've never been frightened to move on or move away if I wasn't happy somewhere.

Whereas life in Hong Kong was carefree for the rest of the family, it was a stressful time for Kell. Business is fast-paced and someone is always waiting to step into your job. Kell's tolerance for prescription drugs escalated. On top of this, most business was conducted along with a social affair and drinking, all more acceptable in the sixties. It was normal to have cocktails and follow up with wine. Sometimes it was impolite to refuse.

By the time I was eighteen I was also working with my mother. I had never been all that interested in make-up before this. When I realized that it was fun, that I could meet some really cool people and was being paid very well I decided that this was the career for me. I learned by fire. Mother handed me a make-up sponge and Panstick, and told me to match the actor's colour. I know I must have made mistakes in the beginning, but the actors were very patient. I did a lot of hair too, not that I was qualified, but it was the sixties with the hairpieces and such; if you knew your way around a teasing comb and kept a can of hairspray handy, how could you go wrong?

I liked the American actors. They would say things like 'Hey, it ain't brain surgery, let's have some fun and get it in the can.' They were disciplined and mindful of time-wasting tricks. The first thing you learn on a US production is that time is money – lots of money. English crews were very different from the American ones. Very civilized, but slow. They took tea breaks. The American actors would then say, 'We're not filming an epic here, let's shoot this thing. If we wait any longer she won't need the old-age make-up.'

Altogether I was having a wonderful time on the sets. I sometimes joined the actors for dinner and drinks in a nightclub called the Den, which was in the basement of the Hilton. Since the whole cast and crew was staying at the Hilton, it was always crowded. One night we were sitting there when my parents came in with a large group of business associates. I'm not sure what was being said at their table, Kell was looking pleased with himself, but my mother was visibly miserable. I watched this for half an hour before seeing my mother rise from her seat, stop the waitress who was about to place drinks on another table and speak briefly with her. Then she took a drink from her tray and without saying a word she stood over Kell and poured it over his head. She turned on her heel and calmly walked out of the nightclub. I do not know what she was upset about, but I later asked her what she had said to the waitress. She replied that she was asking what the different drinks were; after all she wanted something sticky, and creamy. She said if you are going to do something like that, you may as well make it worth the trouble.

On a couple of nights when typhoon warnings prevented me from making it home, I shared a room with an actress named Patty. She was so bouncy and sweet, a typical blonde, tanned California girl. She missed her boyfriend back in Malibu. She said he was an actor too. He was on a television show called *The Big Valley*, with Barbara Stanwyck and Linda Evans. Patty was so much in love. She said he would be a big name some day and talked endlessly about their home in Malibu and their hobbies. He called often, usually in the middle of the night as he could not get used to the time difference. I assumed they were getting married. Patty must have ended up with a broken heart, because after I moved to the US I heard that he had married Farrah Fawcett – the actor was Lee Majors.

Marvin Westmore made quite an impact on my life. He is third generation in the Westmore make-up dynasty; his father, Monty Westmore Sr, designed the make-up for *Gone With The Wind*. His brother Michael is in charge of the *Star Trek/Deep Space Nine* make-up at Paramount. Marvin grew up on movie sets in Hollywood and is completely unaffected by this legacy. He was in Hong Kong on a movie starring Burgess Meredith and Jeff Bridges. Mother was helping him with the make-up as it required prosthetic pieces and extra hands. Although I was busy on another movie at the time, I stole away and managed to spend as many hours as possible on their set, hoping his talent would rub off on me. Mother became Marvin's guide to Chinese culture and he showed us some of the magic behind the Westmore make-up techniques. Marvin is also an excellent chef, and demonstrated his talent in our kitchen on weekends. Spending time with people like him made me want to live in the United States. I really enjoyed the casual, friendly attitude of the Americans and I began to save and make plans to move to California.

If Mother was working and I was free, it was my responsibility to collect Michael and Rhett from school. Kell needed the chauffeur, so I would get a taxi to the school and back again. One day I was getting out of the cab, paying the fare and trying to hold on to both Rhett and Michael, when Rhett suddenly broke free from my hold and took off across the road, towards the house. I could see another cab coming from the opposite direction. Michael and I froze with terror, and watched helplessly as Rhett ran smack into the side door of the moving cab and bounced off into the middle of the road. The cab he had collided with came to a screeching halt. Fortunately there had been no other traffic on the road. I grabbed Michael's hand and ran to Rhett who was lying flat on his back. He was dazed, and the cab driver got out and began yelling at me in Cantonese. Michael screamed something back at him, also in Cantonese, defending his big sister. It cannot have been very flattering, because the man only became more enraged. I scooped Rhett up and carried him inside the house, with Michael running behind. We had Rhett checked out. Fortunately, he only had a slight concussion, which didn't surprise me a bit, hard headed as he is. Boy, was I in trouble that night when Mother and Kell came home. Rhett really milked it for about a month.

We were all used to Kell's business trips, to Australia for the beef he was now importing or to Europe for the liquor. Occasionally he would depart late at night and only be away two days and those times upon his return we would hear nothing of his whereabouts. These trips always seemed a little mysterious and when I enquired about them at the breakfast table he always changed the subject. It wasn't until much later, after leaving Hong Kong, that Michael told me what Kell had been doing on these short disappearances. Apparently he got word that the American officers in Vietnam were interested in purchasing meat that still resembled something you might barbecue. They were willing to pay very well for it in fact. As a man always looking for 'the big one', he saw this as his opportunity. He arranged flights to Saigon, where, late at night, he switched to a barge with frozen beef, left over from supplying the hotel trade, and he would head up the Delta to a prearranged drop-off destination. I was intrigued, after all it was all very cloak-and-dagger. One night his barge had a close call. It was caught in crossfire and went down, which left him to swim to shore. He never went back again!

Then again, while I am quite sure that the basics of this wonderful story are true, Kell has always had a charming way with a yarn. It is never complete fairy-tale, but the truth is always embroidered. Kell could mesmerize us with his stories, telling them in such a way that even if you know he is embellishing, it would be difficult to put a stop to it. By the time Michael hit his mid-teens, he too was known for his storytelling. It was not unusual for him to tell one story on the same evening to two different groups of people in two entirely different ways. Sometimes he would hear a good story from someone else, and make it his own. I have heard my own real life stories back, only more colourful when relayed with Michael at the centre of them. This trait would cause much heartache in the aftermath of his death.

Some time in 1967, the Chinese Revolution was beginning to have repercussions in Hong Kong. The mainland shut off our supply of water, so the government decided to split the city into four sections, and ration the supply. We were allotted four hours of water every fourth day. Think about it: just four hours of running water every four days! We stored the water in huge tubs and used it sparingly. The trick was to get a friend in each section and do the rounds all week to be sure to get a bath each day. Rhett and Michael were intrigued with this set-up, it meant that bath time became a big production for their amah and they would get to stay up later to watch television. We also had curfew, as the revolutionaries were getting very aggressive, even leaving packages containing bombs all over the city. Between 7 p.m. and 7 a.m. if you were found on the street, you could be arrested. So in order to continue a social life, we had to be sure to reach our destination by 7 p.m., and then all-night parties would begin. For a teenager it was a glorious, legitimate excuse for not coming home till morning.

Kell thought that it was getting dangerous just to be in the city. He stayed on, but sent us to Australia by sea. I left kicking and screaming, as I knew I would be miserable in Sydney after living in Hong Kong all that time. We had finally been in a city long enough for me to record telephone numbers in ink. I had made many friends and had initially refused to go, as I finally felt as if I belonged somewhere. We returned to our house in French's Forest and Michael and Rhett were enrolled in a local school. Mother returned to the film industry and reluctantly, I took a job as a junior buyer in Sportsgirl, a women's clothing store. I moved out into my own apartment, and an English nanny, fresh from a vacation in Katmandu, was hired for the day-to-day care of Michael and Rhett. But a few months later Mother returned to Hong Kong, with the boys.

My parents had decided that I would remain in Australia, partly to shield me from tensions at home and partly mindful of the expense of my travel. This decision made a tremendous impact on my life, and not, might I say, for the better. Although Australia is a beautiful country, with wonderful qualities, I felt like a stranger in my homeland. The lifestyle was so alien to what I had become accustomed to and I no longer had friends there. For eighteen months I lived in Sydney while my parents and brothers continued to live in Hong Kong. It is interesting to me now that Hong Kong, by now one of the great transit ports of the world, held a sense of belonging for me. Almost twenty and feeling like an alien who had been dropped on another planet, I tried to make friends, but most people I met were experimenting with hard drugs. Although I drank alcohol, I had not been exposed to drugs and it scared me to be out of control. I finally actually refused to make friends, deciding that I would be leaving Australia soon anyway. I lived to work and while most people around me loved Fridays, I dreaded going back to my apartment knowing that I would have to find some way to kill the pain until Monday morning. Scotch was my friend until I found that with my weight (less than eight stone on a five-and-a-half-foot frame), adding a sleeping pill could put me out for twenty hours. Eventually I found a doctor who prescribed Valium. I had found the drug of my choice. Fortunately for me, I do not have an addictive personality, and I never became a Valium junkie.

I had letters from Michael and Rhett and my mother, but I cannot find a single one from Kell during this period. When I finally made my way back to Hong Kong I realized why my parents had been so distant: they had not told me that they were separated. I don't think the boys fully understood the situation, because while they continued to live at the family house in Kowloon, Mother spending her days taking them to their swimming practice and other activities, joining them for dinner as a family, and even attending business functions with Kell, she returned to another apartment on Victoria Island at night when the boys had gone to bed. Kell had refused to move out of the house, so this was the only way she could handle the situation with minimum disruption to the boys' lives. Mother eventually moved back into the Kowloon home when she and Kell decided to try once more to keep the marriage together for the sake of the boys.

Obviously I can't help wondering how all this impacted on an eight-year-old boy. His mother was there for him, yet not there all the time. His grown-up sister was all but out of his life and the amahs were his only female constants. Maybe his pattern in later life – that of invariably getting involved with someone new without making a clean break from his existing relationship – stemmed from a fear of abandonment and a need to keep something or someone in reserve in case the new love let him down.

When he was eleven years old, Michael made his first recording. A director of one of Hong Kong's big advertising firms, Ling, McCann, Erickson, asked me if Michael could sing, as he was looking for an English boy to sing Christmas songs for a record. I took Michael to the studio, and a Chinese gentleman handed him a list of songs – 'Silent Night', 'Jingle Bells', etc. Michael sang loud and clear and with a bit of prompting with the words, he got the job. He was paid HK$300 (US$50). We eagerly awaited his big début, having been told that it would be sold in Dodwell's department store. The big day arrived and we hurried to the store. We searched everywhere, asked every sales person and at last we were told it was not in the music department but in the toy-shop. It had been made into a scratchy little orange disc, about four inches wide, which could only be played when pushed into a slit in the stomach of a twelve-inch-high, extra rotund, plastic Santa! But this was an exciting day for Michael, scratchy sound or not. Was this Michael's first significant career move? I have since lost my Santa and disc. But if there is a toy collector out there with a fat plastic Santa, a slit in its belly and a tiny orange disc with a scratchy sound, I would love it.

When he was twelve Michael went on to King George V School in Hong Kong. He enjoyed drama, music, folk singing, choir, archery, and loved arts and crafts. As I write this, I am looking through my photo albums and magazine clippings, where I have come across an article written by Gerry Agar, a woman once hired by Paula Yates to 'boost her image'. Ms Agar claims that at the age of eleven Michael was wandering the Bronx in New York, alone and lonely, while I was going through many affairs and husbands. A shame the magazine neglected to check the facts.

Tina saved and planned for a trip to California. She had been there four months when she called one day and announced she was getting married. Although we had not met Tina's fiancé in person, we had had many phone conversations with him and felt comfortable with her choice – and after all, she was an adult. If she had the courage to relocate to another continent on her own, we had to have faith in her decision.

At the time, Kell was the Managing Director for the Dynasty fashion house in Hong Kong. He commissioned his Spanish designer Miguel, to create something breathtaking for Tina. When I flew into California just two days before the wedding, Tina had not even seen, much less tried on her gown, head-dress, or shoes – they arrived with me. But everything fitted perfectly and she looked beautiful. It was a pity that she did not have the rest of her family with her, but over the years we have learned to accept this as part of our restless lifestyle. Twelve months later she gave birth to her fine son, Brent.

CHAPTER THREE

Sydney, Los Angeles, Sydney

When we returned to Australia in late 1972, Kell and I continued to stay together for the sake of our sons, who we settled into school in Sydney. On his second day of school, Michael found a friend in Andrew Farriss, who came to his aid in the school yard. This friendship would last twenty-five years.

For a large, young country with a comparatively small population, made up of many immigrants, many Australians can be intolerant of accents and teenagers can be brutal. We all came away from our stay in Hong Kong with a slight accent. It remains a city composed of the relocated – relocated from every city in the world. You live there constantly hearing these foreign brogues and it becomes impossible to escape the temptation to imitate. Michael became a master mimic, and by the time he returned to Sydney he had been going to a predominantly British school. Now, Australians like to make fun of the upper-crust British accent more than any other because to them it tends to sound snobbish and stuck up, while Australians traditionally pride themselves on being unpretentious.

So here was twelve-year-old Australian Michael, second day at an Australian school where he may not have been throwing out friendly vibes. Even before the kids attempted to get to know him they had a routine with all new students. Partly based on a new student's appearance and accent, they would tease and harass them, throwing tennis balls and heckling the unfortunate newcomer. If you stood up to them, you could win their respect but that was easier said than done, especially for the kids with an accent to mock. The culture shock was almost unbearable, especially for a shy boy who had left his friends in another country and who was on the verge of becoming a teenager. In an interview with *Spin* magazine many years later, Michael said, 'I'm Australian for sure, but I lived in Hong Kong until I was about twelve or thirteen. I had a problem with Australia. In the first place, I hated it. I had all the same prejudices in my head that the English have about it, hats with corks dangling to keep the flies away, and kangaroos. Once I got there I realized it was different, but I couldn't believe the people where I went to school. I just hated the place.'

Fortunately for Michael, Andrew Farriss had been a new student not long before, and he had made friends with another student who intimidated the others with his height. This guy Paul was already close to six foot, and when he and Andrew saw a group of boys hassling newcomer Michael, they stepped in. Andrew and Michael did not become instant buddies, but gradually developed a respect for one another that grew into their lifelong friendship.

Kell had decided to open a factory in Maitland, a small town outside Sydney, which is where he would stay Monday through Friday, returning for weekends. Rhett was still behaving in a disruptive and destructive manner, and may have been having trouble dealing with the fragile state of our marriage. He had been caught taking shots at cars with a BB gun, he was also found drinking alcohol, and there seemed no limit to what he would try. We decided to buy him a motocross bike and encouraged him to take up the sport with Michael. He loved this and they would head off for the day together, returning home exhausted and covered in mud from head to toe. If Kell could not get home on a weekend, I would have Michael and Rhett hitch the trailer to the back of my car, load the dirt bikes, and drive to a country town for the weekend. I loathed the drive but I was determined to try and keep some semblance of family life. Besides, they loved those bikes and the trails, which were few and far between in Sydney.

One Sunday Kell hitched the trailer to the car and apparently did not push the bolts down hard enough. We were descending a hill on the way to the mini-bike trail and I overheard Rhett jokingly say to Michael: 'I say Mike, that looks like our trailer.' Michael yelled out, 'It *is* our trailer.' Just then I could see the small vehicle, containing the boys' bikes, pass us by and careen across the road into the corner wall of a chemist shop, smashing the corner bricks. It narrowly missed the front window. It was a good thing it was only 7 a.m. in a sleepy little country town, it could have been disastrous with pedestrians present. As it was, the bikes were safe and it only cost us the repairs to some brickwork.

I had gone back to my career as a make-up artist. Kell had mortgaged our house to start up the factory. It was at this stage that I decided that I did not want to keep up this façade any longer, I wanted a divorce. Each time I tried to discuss a divorce or separation, Kell would object vehemently and tell me I could leave but the boys would not be going with me. He threatened he would come and take them back. I decided I had to take them away as far as possible, as I did not want my children involved in a tug of war. I felt then that Kell had been all but invisible throughout this marriage. It was hard being both mother and father, more difficult I believe when parents are still living together – yet apart. Due to his work commitments Kell spent so much time overseas that he was never in tune with our day-to-day lives. We had been on the move constantly, with his ever-changing career. I just felt that there was nothing left in the relationship, least of all trust.

The divorce laws in Australia at the time were such that there were only two legitimate grounds, adultery or a two-year separation. Kell has a lot of pride, and he could never believe that failure in our marriage would be due to anything on his part. After all, he was never there! I felt totally trapped as we had worked all those years, but our house was mortgaged to capacity and there was nothing to divide anyway. At this stage Rhett was thirteen years old and Michael fifteen. I knew I couldn't leave them both behind and could not afford to take care of them both. Rhett was impossible for me to control, Michael had even come down on him for his behaviour towards me. I talked to Michael, told him of my dream, my plan, my secret – and this became our secret.

One day I just snapped. I had been offered work in Los Angeles, with Marvin and Michael Westmore. They had asked me to study corrective make-up with them, which would lead to working with cosmetic surgeons to help their patients camouflage facial disfigurements. This was a new area and the more I thought about it the more I wanted to have the opportunity to practise this form of make-up. And I would be nearer to Tina as well, of course. My plan was to stay away for two years of separation, then return to Australia and divorce Kell. If it all went well and I could afford it, I could have Rhett join us, although I had no illusions that

Kell would help us out. For the next three months I saved so as to have as much cash as I could. Michael kept asking: 'When are we going, Mum?'

As our departure day approached worry was making me fear for my sanity. The practical chore of packing – often a nightmare aspect of moving – was light relief. I was dreading saying goodbye to Rhett and trying to explain. I still remember the day I told him as one of the worst of my life. I was torn up about being parted from him and driven with guilt about my decision. There was so much uncertainty ahead for Michael and me in California and I truly believed that, for the time being, Rhett would have a better life, secure with his father. I felt inadequate to deal with complaints of his smoking and drinking, his bullying of other boys at school and his general aggressiveness. I was convinced that he needed the influence of a strong man in his life and, although I hated separating the boys, I believed that Rhett was the lucky one. I write this with deep pain, even today.

The day finally arrived and when Rhett came home from school I sat him down and told him that Michael and I were leaving for America. He wanted to go with us and I told him that it may be another three months before I could do that as I would first have to find somewhere to live, settle Michael into school and settle down to work. I promised I would send for him as soon as I could. He wanted to come to the airport with us. Friends arrived to drive us and it was a sombre ride. Naturally Rhett was upset and he started to cry and said, 'I promise I will be good if you take me.' I told him to be good for his Dad and hopefully it would only be a couple of months before I could send for him. As we stood at the gate, the last passengers to board, I looked at Rhett's face and wanted to turn back. But it was too late. My heart was breaking, realizing what I had done. Michael was so quiet and so was I. But Michael was the only one not crying. I gave Rhett one last hug, Michael said his goodbyes and walking to the gateway, said, 'Come on Mum, if we're going, let's go.' There was no turning back now. I said goodbye to my friends who took Rhett back home to Kell. He would be back at the house by now, as it was a Friday evening and he was going to be home that weekend.

The trip to Los Angeles was painful, neither of us saying too much, except for me trying to reassure Michael that things would work out as planned. It must have been painful for Michael also, although he didn't show it much, probably because of his love for me and possibly because he was curious to find out what lay ahead for him in America.

*

In 1975, while living in San Jose, I awoke to an emotional call from a sobbing Kell. 'She's left me and taken my Michael. Is he there?' Why would Mother and Michael be with me? Mother had spared me details of her plans. This could not have come at a worse time as my own marriage was falling apart. I tried to calm Kell down so he could explain what had happened, but he was incoherent through most of the conversation. I reminded him that he had another son and asked if Rhett was all right. He explained that while he was in Maitland, Mother and Michael had packed up and left. I told him if I heard anything, I would get back to him, and asked him to do the same. I never forgot his words, not just 'Michael', but, 'my Michael'.

It had been twelve months since I last saw my family, in August 1974. I had taken my son Brent to stay at the family home in Belrose, New South Wales, to introduce him to his Australian family. Brent was fascinated with Rhett, whose twelfth birthday we celebrated, and Michael who was fourteen at the time. He followed them around the house each afternoon as they came home from school. The boys found that it was a full-time job keeping an enthusiastic two-year-old out of their stuff. Michael spent ages in the garage, absorbed in his dirt bike. Photographs from that visit show a mesmerized toddler covered in grease sitting next to the young mechanic, Michael. The age difference between Brent and Michael was twelve years, the same as between Michael and myself. It was reassuring and rather touching to watch him care for Brent with patience and enthusiasm as I had done with him.

On our first day at the Sydney house, Michael made quite an entrance, as he crashed through the front door with tremendous force, scattering school books everywhere. He had sprouted upwards since I last saw him. Skinny, with hair almost to his shoulders, he was at the age where his voice was breaking, and as he talked animatedly, I could detect that a soft lisp was still there. He had arrived with his 'best mate', Andrew Farriss. Andrew was shy, serious, and quietly spoken. His family was from Perth and he was the middle one of three brothers and also had a sister. He and Michael talked about poetry and music but Andrew seemed to clam up whenever I jumped into the conversation.

The boys were wearing their Davidson High school uniforms. I still have Michael's hard-cover *Concise Oxford Dictionary*, which he used during those years at school. He has scrawled his name and classes on the inside of the cover. I forget how it came to me but it remains my favourite dictionary. One time when I offered it back, he told me to keep it for Erin and Brent, which I did, and I now safeguard it as a keepsake for Tiger Lily.

Now, within a few hours of Kell's call I heard from Mother, who had landed in Los Angeles. She and Michael were on their way to San Jose and they flew to San Francisco about two hours later. Michael was now fifteen. He had not changed very much in one year, although his teenage skin was bothering him. I don't think Mother really thought about the logistics of her plan, she just knew she had to get out of the marriage. I guess she wanted to keep things 'clean' by not involving me.

The first thing we did was to get Mother and Michael an apartment nearby, and enrol Michael into high school. Almost immediately after they arrived, Mother bought Michael a yellow dirt bike. He spent many hours maintaining it and eventually entered into a competition where he came second. He was pretty happy. But just as things were settling down, I had a frantic call from Michael in the middle of the night. Mother was having what we would now recognize as a panic attack, brought on by all the complexities and stresses of her flight. I drove over right away and by the time I arrived she had calmed a little. Michael was pale and was relieved to see me. Mother was breathing into a paper bag to prevent hyperventilation, as my doctor had advised. It was really only then that I began to learn what had been going on for the past three months, all the planning and pain. I was relieved that Mother had a job lined up to take her mind off things. Mother, Michael, Brent and I soon came to share a house in Studio City. My three-year-old Brent was at nursery school and Michael enrolled at North Hollywood High, so Mother and I could both work.

Kell's business ventures weren't going so well in Sydney, and he went to Manila to pursue new prospects. Rhett went with him. During this period in Rhett's life his relationship with Kell understandably improved. The economy in the Philippines enabled them to have people to cook and clean and keep house for them, and the departure from subversive peer influence in Sydney and Kell's strong discipline combined to give Rhett a good life and calm his aggressive tendencies. Also, he would have had all his father's attention to himself. I reminded myself that I could not expect the same quality of life for two growing sons and myself in California if I took them both.

The legal implications of my move had not even crossed my mind. It was actually against the law to take the fifteen-year-old Michael away from his father without consent. But Rhett's hurt was profound and left deep wounds. No one can be surprised about that. Kell would not allow Rhett to join us, even for a holiday.

In a different world – today's – I might have handled things in another way. Back then I felt that I had such limited choices and all of them terrible. Thank God the law is kinder and more just towards women in my situation now. As you might imagine, I have given a great deal of thought to this over the years. I know that I would not have done what I did if I hadn't felt myself approach the verge of breakdown, feeling under such pressure.

Working as a corrective make-up artist was very rewarding but sometimes very stressful. It can be very draining emotionally to work continually with the medically referred client. The work involves helping people, who have congenital disfigurement or problems caused by illness or by accident, through the use of make-up techniques. It was difficult for me to settle, though it helped when Tina arrived with Brent. Michael and Rhett wrote to each other during their first year apart and Kell wrote to Michael too. I was more than happy about that. When within weeks of my move, I had word that Rhett and Kell had moved to the Philippines and Rhett had settled into the International School in Manila, Rhett and I started corresponding too. I still have many of those letters and from my reading of them now it is evident that he was being well cared for, and that his relationship with Kell had improved enormously. His first letter to me started off by saying, 'It's so hot here the wax in my ears is melting.' He told me about a German teenager who had stayed the night and left with Kell's briefcase containing a few thousand dollars in cash. He went to the boy's home the following morning and recovered the case with most of the money intact. Kell gave him a reward. He said he liked it over there and wished we were there with him or better still, wished he were in America with us. He did not sound at all angry or upset, he said to give his love to Michael and everyone and he loved me very much. I still have that letter and showed it to Rhett recently. He read it and said, 'And I still do love you, Mum.'

Much later, when Michael returned to Australia, Kell tried to convince him that he had been deprived by the move to California. But Michael's memories of life there, of North Hollywood High, of his drama classes, the freedom he enjoyed, the friends he made and the music scene were all happy ones – as he confirmed to me when we spoke of the whole wrenching episode. He felt his teenage years in California steered him towards work in the entertainment industry and the life he had loved so much. In later years his long-time friend Richard Lowenstein said Michael spoke of this period in his life as something special. He spoke fondly and proudly of times spent on film sets with me. It seemed to steer him towards the possibility of working in film. I will never know if my sons would have turned out differently if they hadn't been separated and maybe it's pointless to speculate as they already had such distinct and different personalities.

I was working as a receptionist at the Nieman Marcus beauty salon. I would run around the house in the morning desperately trying to get Michael and Brent ready for school. Michael seemed to like all the differences between North Hollywood High and Davidson High, from the basic curriculum to the atmosphere, which encouraged a free expression of ideas and originality of ambition. The dress code was so casual he could wear jeans. Every day upon arriving home, he had something to show us. He loved how the African American kids danced, and he practised their moves, with Brent as his audience. He used a ten-speed bike to get around, and sometimes, if I was going to be late from work, he would swing by and collect Brent from pre-school. By now, Michael was spending most of his free time listening to music, mostly Elton John, and writing poetry.

The only thing that seemed to bother him was his skin condition. Mother knew he was fretting over severe acne, so she took him in to see the best dermatologist she could find, always driving him over to Beverly Hills for his appointments. With time Michael gradually saw improvement but it was a slow process and well into adulthood Michael sought treatment, latterly to deal with the residual scarring. However, as a make-up artist who has worked with medically referred clients, I am aware that teenage acne can leave deep psychological scarring no matter how well the complexion clears. I once heard that later on when INXS was up for an award against another popular Australian band, some fans of their rivals held up a sign which called

Michael 'crater face'. INXS took home the award but this display of mean spirit surely must have cut deeply.

Most of the time Michael was very cheerful and occasionally mischievous. Once I left the keys in the car while I ran in to a shopping mall for a quick pick-up. When I came out to the parking lot, my car had vanished. I panicked. I had left Michael in the car with Brent in his car seat. Out of the corner of my eye I saw a police car and as I approached I noticed that the person they were detaining was Michael. He had driven my car into another parking space for a laugh. The patrolmen had seen him and pulled him over to check his licence, which did not exist. I had to do some fast talking and of course left myself open for a lecture about leaving minors alone in a vehicle with keys.

Mother loved being around film people. One young actor she worked with had several offers on a script he had written but refused to sell it unless he was cast as the lead. Eventually he raised the production money himself – and the Rocky phenomenon was born. Shame she didn't keep in touch with Sylvester Stallone: she could have done great work for some of those fight scenes . . . Still, her career was blooming. She went on location to Little Rock, Arkansas, on a Roger Corman production called *Fighting Mad*. The lead actor was Peter Fonda. Thirteen years later, Michael would also be working on a Corman movie, *Frankenstein Unbound*, filmed at Lake Como, Italy. Along with Michael it starred John Hurt, Jason Patric and Peter Fonda's daughter Bridget.

I tried to find activities both boys would be interested in. Once, I planned a camping trip in the mountains without checking the weather report. Of course it snowed and we ended up sitting in a cabin for the whole weekend. I thought the trip was a let-down, but to my surprise Michael and Brent thought this was cool, as if we were stranded or something. I had brought along enough food for about three weeks. At home, mostly we went to movies or had friends over to swim in the pool. Michael's bedroom had French doors, which led directly out to the pool, and he took every opportunity to enjoy it with his friends. He was always very patient with Brent and babysat him for me at times. Around this time, I also began to ease back into the film industry, taking over some of Mother's work as she was still laid-up from a major fall. Thus I met Erin's father, Jeff, who was a film editor.

Once, when Mother was on location, we had a note from Michael's school, which said they wanted a parent/teacher conference. I went in my mother's place. His teachers were just concerned about Michael's grades. Nothing new about this – teachers were always worried about his grades, and he had not changed his study habits since his days in Hong Kong when his teachers called him a dreamer. He was not particularly interested in maths, science, biology or chemistry. He was keener on music, drama, art and English. The problem was he was required to get passing grades in the other classes in order to graduate high school. As it is with many young adults who tend not to be academically inclined, he would complain and argue that with his goals, maths and science would be pointless. Having gone to many schools myself I sympathized with him in having to change over to a completely different curriculum. He did make some effort, but not enough to stop us fretting over his poorer grades.

I would have liked some of the teachers who had complained about his performance, to have held a conversation with him by the time he was in his late twenties. By then he had proved himself to be a dynamo. His vocabulary was fantastic, he was very eloquent, and it seemed that he could hold his own on any subject – pretty much self-taught. I have read many erroneous stories about this period in Michael's life, giving the impression that Michael was depressed due to Mother bringing him to the United States for eighteen months. This is ridiculous, although, perhaps I can't blame the writers, for even Michael had several versions of his life story, depending on who his audience was. All I can say is, I was there, and we had a lot of fun times, and many quiet heart-to-hearts. He was interested in politics and had specific views on how a country should be run and what was right and what was wrong about anything you could mention. He was too shy to show me his poetry. He spoke of the acting profession and lamented that Australia was not the place to launch an acting career. If he was missing Rhett, he never said so. Occasionally we would go somewhere and he would say 'Wow, imagine what Rhett would say if he saw this!' But, I don't ever remember him actually complaining that he missed him. Of course, he may have kept it to himself, but he never indicated that he was suffering in any way. He knew he was the favoured child and that Mother would have sent him back, with sorrow but without question, if that had been what he wanted.

After Michael's death, it didn't help things that Kell was reported as saying that Michael's age for his California period was twelve. If he did, he must have had a lapse in memory. Saying he was only twelve makes a big difference. It would have meant that he was too young to say he had no desire to move to the United States. Michael came here of his own free will. He kept the pending move a secret even from his brother, and he was very excited about it. Kell was also reported as having stated that Michael returned to live with him in Sydney when he was given sole custody of the boys. Michael was actually nearly seventeen when he returned to Australia. Where he was concerned, there was no question of child custody in the divorce.

About six months before Michael and I were due to return to Australia I had a bad fall on a movie set and was unable to walk. I was confined to bed for approximately one month and afterwards the doctors told me I needed at least six months' physical therapy as I limped around on crutches. I had been receiving many letters and phone calls from Kell who was now back in Australia and, having accepted that we would divorce, asked me to sign some papers so he could sell our house. He argued that if we did this, we could each buy a small house or flat. I resisted, as I did not want to sell our home; however, I did not know what would happen in the future as at that point it was impossible for me to stand, let alone work. I decided to send Michael back, hoping to follow very soon, but it was at least six months before I could travel. Tina was a wonderful and constant nurse, cook and carer, totally dependable and never complaining. This is in her nature – I observed those characteristics in her dealings with Michael, Rhett, her own children and her friends. Nonetheless it was a worrying time for me with an impending divorce, separation from both my boys now and my inability to work.

I eventually arrived back in Australia and went to Kell's rented house in Belrose. Kell had indeed sold our home. He had a live-in housekeeper for the boys and he was off back to Manila on business. According to Vince Lovegrove, I didn't want to keep the house, so he'd sold it and paid off his debts. So much for there being enough money for each of us to buy separate homes! When Kell left for Manila, Rhett, Michael and I stayed on in the rented house, and after almost nine months of constant physiotherapy, I was able to walk and think about working again. I resumed working for the Grundy organization, on a TV 'soapie' called

The Young Doctors. This ran for eight years in Australia. This was perfect for me as it was steady, I knew my hours, had a regular wage coming in, could plan my time and usually be home in the evenings to prepare dinner for Michael and Rhett, unlike location work and the crazy hours I was more used to. By the time I arrived in Sydney, I could see that Rhett and Michael were happy to be with each other again, although as before, they had separate friends. Michael had renewed his friendship with Andrew Farriss, and became serious about his music.

By the time Michael returned from California Andrew had already pulled together a band which he called Doctor Dolphin. The other three members were Davidson High classmates Kent Kerny and Neil Sanders, and a bass player from Forest High, Gary Beers. Gary had been recruited mainly because he already had a car – a rarity among Australian teenagers back then. Andrew had been providing the vocals, but Michael eagerly joined Doctor Dolphin as lead singer, as shaking a tambourine did not qualify as contributing instrumentally. His voice was tentative at first, but although Doctor Dolphin never did venture beyond the rehearsal stage it proved to be just what he needed to test his range.

While Doctor Dolphin experimented in the Farrisses' garage, Andrew's almost twenty-year-old brother Tim was already booking his band, Guinness, for local weddings and parties. Tim and his friend Kirk Pengilly had been playing together for about six years and were eager to progress. Tim and Kirk – who both played guitar – used various line-ups throughout high school, even auditioning Tim's younger brother Jon on drums. As Jon was only nine years old it did not work out. Kirk had been the creative force in Guinness, writing the material and singing. But it was Tim who was to become the driving force that would bring the original line-up of INXS together. He had observed Doctor Dolphin and was impressed with three elements: his brother's keyboard prowess, Gary's talent on bass guitar and some special qualities in Michael's voice. Michael was relaxed in rehearsals and showing signs of becoming an impressive frontman. Tim asked them to join him and Kirk, and they rounded it out by giving Jon another chance. At sixteen, Jon was finally old enough to join his brothers in the band.

After a short rehearsal period, the band débuted as the Farriss

Brothers. Their first public appearance took place on Tim's twentieth birthday, 16 August 1977. After this, Tim and Kirk set about in earnest to make it a success.

The band practised all hours, sometimes in the Farrisses' garage and sometimes in ours. They also used rehearsal halls in the beach suburbs of Mona Vale and Avalon. Michael was truly driven and focused and I was very happy for him. Kell was completely opposed, however, and said that I should not encourage it. He thought Michael should get a 'real' job, that it was unrealistic and that he would never make any money out of the music business. Kell thought he should be looking for a white-collar job and that I should not be encouraging him to get into 'my' business of performing and entertaining. I thought that he should follow his dream.

Michael was also getting involved in his first serious romance, with a very sweet girl called Michelle Nagy he'd met at the school bus stop. They would talk on the phone for hours, travel on the school bus together and see each other on Sunday afternoons at her house or ours. When he was practising with the band, she would go and watch.

Then Jill and Dennis Farriss decided to move their family back to Perth, about three thousand miles from Sydney. Jon Farriss was still in school so there was no question of him staying in Sydney for the sake of the band. Instead the others set about following the Farriss boys to the west coast. Michael took a job at the Wentworth Hotel as a waiter after school to save money for the trip. The job only lasted a short time, as it was tiring getting there after school and not arriving back home until after midnight.

Rhett became increasingly aggressive as Michael's departure loomed because he wanted to go with him. There was no possibility of this as he was barely fifteen and still at school. He objected to every argument I put up and would not see that, quite apart from his age, Michael had to find his own way and could not be responsible for him. One day he became so angry at the thought of Michael's departure that he lashed out and hit me as Michael walked into the kitchen. Michael was so outraged that he took hold of Rhett and held him down and gave him a lecture on how women were to be treated. He said, 'If I ever hear of you treating a woman, especially our mother, this way ever again, you will certainly know about it!' I understood Rhett's anger, as he felt that he was being abandoned once again, but there was no solution.

His aggressions simmered after Michael's departure. It took a long time for Rhett's temper to subside and I'm afraid I was never able to help him much, no matter how hard I tried. I loved Rhett and I know now that he loves me, but it has taken many, many long years and many buckets of tears to get where we are today.

The day finally arrived and Michael called Michelle to say goodbye. Though he missed her a lot, time and distance proved to be too much for such young ones to sustain their relationship. Kirk came to collect Michael and I handed him a food-care package for the long drive over. With mixed emotions we said our goodbyes; sadly, but with great hopes. When the car was out of sight, I walked back to the house and into the kitchen to find an envelope on which Michael had written, 'Dear Mum, Take care of yourself and get yourself something nice with this. Sorry it can't be more – don't worry about me. Love, Michael xxx.' The envelope contained a $20 bill, and I have it to this day.

The drive across the Nullarbor Plain, the longest, loneliest stretch of road between the coasts, took approximately three days. The distance approximates that between Los Angeles and Miami, or from London to Marseilles and back. Michael used to tell the story of how they spent the trip smoking dope and stopping to cook out of Kirk's wok in the middle of nowhere. Later on he described the scene to me as if it were out of a Fellini movie. 'We stopped late at night in the middle of the desert and Kirk pulled out his wok and Tupperware containing diced vegetables. Before we even had the chance to start a fire for the food, we looked up to see little eyes bouncing everywhere. It was the kangaroos leaping all around us. Kirk was completely unfazed and went about cooking up this Chinese meal. We found ourselves sitting there in the empty outback, sharing a Chinese meal, kangaroos staring at us.' When Michael first recounted this story to us, he didn't mention the part about the grass. Later on we heard him tell it in a television interview, adding the dope bit. But by then it was ten years after the event.

I worried a lot about Michael while he was in Perth, even though he had 'family' there in Andrew's parents, Jill and Dennis Farriss. He would write telling me of how it was a learning experience for all of them. They did learn to look after each other. Early in 1978 I received a letter from Michael. He wrote about having a massive headache for over four days, but having to keep up singing anyway as they couldn't afford to turn down jobs (they were averaging $100 a week). Apparently the doctor couldn't find anything wrong, but Michael was in excruciating pain when he belted out some of the songs. He enquired after Rhett, asking if he was still being aggressive, and told a story about the band's new jeans being stolen off the clothes line. He told me that he watched *The Young Doctors* whenever he could just to see my name on the credits, and thanked me for all my support – 'You are a wonderful person and take care of yourself. I love you.'

I also have a card from Michael, postmarked Perth, Australia, 27 July 1978. He details the band's exploits in mining towns and such in Western Australia. He writes that the band is attempting to write their own songs. Not understanding the inner workings of the music business at the time, I thought they were making it hard on themselves. Who would go to see an unknown band playing unfamiliar music, I wondered.

I was pregnant with Erin and she was two weeks past her due date. California is approximately sixteen hours behind Perth, and so it appears that by chance he mailed the card around the same time I was entering Cedars Sinai to give birth to Erin, who was born on the 26th – which happens to be Mick Jagger's birthday. Interestingly, in the card, he wishes me a 'happy birthing day'. Even though it wouldn't have taken an Einstein to know that his card could well coincide with my daughter's birth, he always loved that story. It gave us a sort of spiritual connection.

As soon as the six band members reconvened in Perth, Tim and Kirk set about getting them work. Andrew, Tim, Garry Gary (as Gary was to start styling his name), Kirk and Michael were renting a house not far from the Farriss family home, where Jon was still living while he completed his last year of high school. The house where the band lived was just as you may imagine. The five eldest members were taking full advantage of the local female talent, free beer at the local gigs, cheap marijuana, and plenty of spare time. Mother worried more than I did about this lifestyle but we both knew there was nothing we could do about it except hope he'd behave responsibly. Michael was especially taken with a girl called Ananda who he claimed had been presented to him on a leash at a party. I never really believed the story, but it got a lot of mileage and the girl was for real. She was a throwback to the sixties, poetry readings and such, and this appealed to the hippy dreamer in Michael. Neither my mother nor I were privy to all the fun goings-on in that house, but they were five young men out on their own for the first time, they survived and came through it just a little more grown up. I don't think I would want to know all the details.

Tim Farriss was the undisputed leader. He was the eldest and at that time the most ambitious. At twenty, he had no doubts as to what he wanted and he wanted this band, the Farriss Brothers. He saw their stay in Perth as a rehearsal and prelude to serious success. He and Kirk took care of the business side of things as the other four concentrated on sharpening their musical talents. They took charge of collecting the money after the gigs, paying the bills and dividing what was left for each of the members to live on, which was little more than pocket money during that first year. Tim was always thinking up ways to promote the band, which was not easy in sleepy, remote Perth. It may be the capital city of Western Australia – which is Australia's largest state, claiming approximately one third of the total land mass – yet it is the most sparsely populated one, with only 800,000 residents in 1978. On the south-western coast of Australia, Perth is a beautiful green city with great beaches on the Indian Ocean. But to its east and north there is desert.

Perth was out of touch with the music scene then, and there was very little live entertainment going on in the pubs. The band was forced to organize their tour to mining towns and fishing communities, where men are men at the very least. It was particularly hard on Michael because he was a sensitive, eccentric young performer and a nonconformist, and there was no room for that sort of thing on the pub circuit in Australia, let alone in tough mining towns. Many of these audiences assumed that Michael was homosexual and there was very little tolerance for that in Australia in the seventies. Michael used to tell us that all the escaped convicts must have ended up in those towns! About Port Hedland he once said, 'They have this central area with six pods coming off and there's red dust everywhere. They have dust locks; it's like nowhere else. You have to walk into a room and whoosh! All the dust gets blown off you, and you go to a dust-free area. And they have wet canteens and dry ones. The first, to get pissed in, and the other to eat in. These last were seldom crowded. The people there are all desperadoes. We played there New Year's Eve one year. It was one of the most horrifying experiences of my life.'

After ten months in Western Australia, Jon was old enough to leave home and the band made their way back to Sydney where they set up house at Newport Beach, a northern coastal suburb. Once there, Tim began his promotional assault in the parking lots of all the pubs on the north shore of the harbour. One day, while he was sticking Farriss Brothers flyers under windshield wipers he was approached by Gary Morris, the manager of the immensely popular band Midnight Oil. He asked Tim about his band and on the spot offered them a support gig. This led to Gary Morris becoming their first manager. It was an incredible break for the Farriss Brothers, and they never forgot it. Morris was not happy with the name of the band and for a short time they became the Vegetables. Soon after this, at the suggestion of Midnight Oil roadie, Colin Lee Hong, the Farriss Brothers was changed to INXS. I later learned it was a name that definitely suited them at the time, as they had become known for their excessive behaviour both on and off stage. The parties at their house at Newport Beach were legendary, while Michael's antics on stage, flinging himself around and up and down, and dancing like nobody else, gave the audience the impression that the band was still partying as they worked. What's more, to get audience attention while they were on stage, they wore anything you would not find on anyone else. Sometimes their outfits were downright geeky, but at least no one else was wearing them.

They first appeared as INXS at a pub date, on 1 September 1979. Two years after getting together as the Farriss Brothers, they had the same line-up, one that would remain the same for another eighteen years. Experimenting with images and sounds, INXS continued to support Midnight Oil and other local bands, gathering an enthusiastic following. They had begun to write their own material in Perth where nobody was interested in anything other than top forty hits. Now they were free to express themselves in their own powerful way.

The first time I saw Michael performing was soon after the band returned to Sydney, and played at the Dee Why Hotel, a very popular venue at the time, renowned for its dedication to the Aussie bands. Playing pubs was a good starting point in more ways than one; character building to say the least.

It was a Sunday afternoon, and my sister Maureen and I decided to go along and support the boys. There must have been approximately thirty-five people in the bar, about twelve of whom were bikers, including two 'biker chicks'. All the same we sat up front and were very impressed with Michael's singing. It reminded me of that of the young Frank Sinatra. There was a certain tone to his voice – at times tender, yet with a dangerous edge to it, which could develop unexpectedly into some great raw roar or slide into the moodiest of blues. He moved very sensually as well, lithe and graceful sometimes, unashamedly raunchy at others. I could see how he took on a different persona on stage and that one day the camera would love him. Of course all his brothers in the band were brilliant too, but at that gig, seeing Michael the musician for the first time, my eyes were drawn to him. Naturally I was the proud mum.

We applauded enthusiastically after each song. Meanwhile, the two 'biker chicks' were giving us strange looks and loudly criticizing us for even being there. They probably thought we should be taking high tea at a ladies' club.

After the first set, Michael walked over towards us, the others following to thank us for being there. We both stood up to give him a hug, and almost fell flat on our faces. The floor was so thick with spilled beer from the previous night, our heels had stuck! Meanwhile the girls were staring at us as no doubt they couldn't believe that the band would even know the likes of us. From then on, the atmosphere was decidedly more friendly, and we stayed for the second set. The next time we went to see them perform at the Dee Why Hotel they were in a larger room, and the queue to get in was three blocks long.

CHAPTER FOUR

In Excess, like I-N-X-S

Up to now Michael had sent us tapes of the Farriss Brothers performing covers. The one I remember most clearly is their version of the Rolling Stones' 'Brown Sugar', and another, 'I Shot the Sheriff'. Once in a letter with the tapes, Michael wrote that, unlike most frontmen of Australian bands, he felt that he sounded 'American'. When I listened recently to some of those early recordings I can't agree with him. I took a call from Michael around this time and he said 'Yeah, we're really excited. This guy wants to be our manager, and he's changed our name to In Excess, like I-N-X-S, and he wants to buy us special outfits for the stage.'

'That's great, Babe. He must really believe in you if he's willing to spend money up front,' I replied.

'Well, um, yeah I guess. But he wants us to appear behind bars.'

'You mean like a jail?'

'Kind of. They would be made out of lights.'

He was losing me. 'So how's the audience going to see the band if they have lights shining in their eyes?'

'We haven't worked that out. We'll have to think about it. The thing is he wants us to be mysterious and inaccessible for a year or two and build up the momentum.'

INXS was not as excited about this idea – 'inaccessibility' was even to extend to being effectively incognito and not giving interviews – and when I called him back a month later, he said they had a new manager. Gary Morris did not have the time needed to promote the young band now known as INXS, but decided to help out a friend as well as the band, by putting the two together.

Wendy Murphy Moss is the former wife of Chris Murphy, the

manager who took INXS to its greatest triumphs. Wendy and I have remained friends since early 1980 when I began taking my family to Australia on a regular basis. Wendy describes her first encounter with INXS this way: 'It was late 1979 but I can remember it like it was yesterday. Chris had a call from Gary Morris, the manager for Midnight Oil, who were doing extremely well at the time. He said there was this young band who needed a manager . . . They were playing at the Penrith Leagues Club. Chris was looking for a band to represent, and we went along that night. I was eight months pregnant with Stevey [their first little girl], but insisted on going. We were immediately impressed, Michael was shy, but he still had stage presence; the other five band members were excellent musicians.' Soon after becoming their booking agent, Chris signed the band to a management contract.

Although Wendy is not mentioned with Chris when journalists describe the beginnings of the phenomenally successful band, I can tell you that she had a lot of influence. When he initially signed INXS, Chris and Wendy were living in Windsor, approximately two hours by car from Sydney. In the first year Chris worked twelve-hour days. Maintaining their home was not easy for Wendy with a new little baby, fourteen horses, and an absent husband. But she persevered until Chris had an accident when he fell asleep at the wheel on his way home from a concert one night, after which they moved to Mosman, in the city. By now Chris had INXS touring every little town in Australia and the band members found it pointless to keep up the rent on a house they were not occupying. In the first year at the Mosman home, Michael stayed in their spare bedroom whenever the band was in town and became part of the family. Later on when Stevey was christened, Michael became her godfather.

For the next three years, MMA, standing for Mark Murphy Associates, was run from the Mosman home. Mark Murphy, Chris's father, had died at the age of thirty-four following a heart attack and his mother took over running the company for a while. Chris met Wendy when she started work there. Chris eventually took over and was in the process of bringing the little company into the twentieth century.

This was a very good time for young bands in Australia as far as live music went. But while there was a healthy business in pubs and clubs, making money as a recording artist in Australia has always been tough. Overseas artists like ABBA were more valued, and anyway Australia just does not have the manpower to support a large, indigenous music industry. The population for the whole of Australia in the early eighties was under fourteen million, roughly the same as that of Los Angeles. And it was cut off from the rest of the world by sheer distance, making it hard to break out beyond Australia's shores. But Chris and the band shared an invincible ambition to succeed internationally, and Chris made a plan.

From 1980 to 1983 Chris spent nine out of twelve months either touring with or negotiating for the band. I thought he exuded the perfect combination for a successful manager: he had a healthy ego, he was tenacious, determined, ambitious and aggressive. There was no way he was going to take 'no' for an answer. Even better, believing that musicians should be free to create while a manager took care of the business, Chris stayed out of the studio, unless invited to be there. In early 1980 Chris played a demo tape for former AC/DC manager, Michael Browning, who owned the independent label, Deluxe Records. It was a rough demo recorded when they were still the Farriss Brothers. Recognizing the power of their stage performance, Chris then dragged him down to see INXS live at a small theatre in a southern beach town. Browning was impressed with them, he felt there was something special. He was especially taken with Michael and they negotiated a five-album deal.

When Chris told the band this they were ecstatic. It was what the constant rehearsals had been for, the freebie gigs in tiny overcrowded pubs. The band and Chris shared a vision which went far beyond Australia, and they now knew they were on their way.

In June 1980, Michael sent us copies of 'Simple Simon' and 'We Are the Vegetables', the first single the band recorded with Deluxe. I was really surprised, and impressed and proud. I played both sides for anyone who would listen, telling them the songs featured my little brother. Michael also sent us press clippings, tapes, flyers, anything. I think he assumed that because I lived in California, there was a good possibility that I could get them a deal in the United States. But I was far removed from the music industry, and even as a motion picture sound editor, my husband Jeff was rarely involved with the music decisions.

Soon after 'Simple Simon' was recorded, the band began work on their first album. After playing live each night, they went into the studio and worked until the sun came up. This went on five or six nights a week. They released their début album titled *INXS* in October of the same year, and it included a hit single 'Just Keep Walking'. The group kept on touring, consistently the hardest-working band in Australia, even rehearsing when they had a night off. Jeff and I witnessed this when we took Erin and Brent to Sydney that year. We virtually had to follow the band around to gigs just to see Michael. The first time I actually saw Michael perform with INXS was at the St George Leagues Club in the heart of Sydney, and I believe we paid $5 at the door. Jeff and I followed Chris Murphy backstage before the show and when he opened the door to their dressing room, the aroma of pot wafted out into the hall. Chris walked in ahead of us and admonished the band for partaking before a show. He made a big deal out of it. I don't know if it was for our benefit, but I was impressed.

By now Michael was living with Vicky Kerridge – tall, attractive and blonde, with a well-bred air and terrifically supportive of the band. She had met Michael at her local milk bar where she was buying some cigarettes and he was buying some rolling papers. As we stood in the crowd with Vicky, waiting for the band to walk on stage, I was nervous for Michael and excited at the same time. The place was not packed to capacity, but it was certainly not embarrassingly empty. They finally walked on, and when they started up, and Michael threw himself into character, I was mesmerized. I had not expected such full on, in your face presence. The drunks down in front were showing their appreciation by shaking up their beer bottles and letting Michael have it when he came close to the edge of the stage, he in turn shaking up his own cans and spraying it over the crowd. One big guy sprayed him every time he moved to his side of the stage. Eventually Michael yelled, 'If you don't stop doing that, I'm going to get to like it!'

I could not believe how Michael was whipping the crowd up and controlling all of the space on the stage. It was such a metamorphosis. There was my sensitive, soft spoken brother, strutting up and down the stage, looking menacingly at the crowd – which I knew he couldn't actually see due to his poor eyesight – all along blasting into the microphone. Occasionally he would sprinkle his act with a four letter word, as in 'How y'all fucking doing tonight?' I loved it, it was insane and fun. But he was so good at being this stage character that

I also found it slightly disturbing. It occurred to me then what an excellent actor he was. I understood what he was creating and I thought I would burst with pride. Vicky yelled something in my ear, which I never forgot. She shouted, 'Aren't they great? They're the loudest band in Australia!' Her conviction was so strong, she totally believed in Michael's ability to make the magic happen.

We went backstage afterwards to congratulate them. There was a warm, friendly feeling there and the band members were genuinely grateful for our support. Lots of down-to-earth, Aussie joking around, honest enthusiasm and hugs. They didn't have much in the way of a road crew then and mostly carried their own equipment: it would be a while before there were entourages, limos and fancy hotels. Who cared if I was mildly deaf for two days, I thought; they were fantastic. As an encouraging gesture, I went around to Vicky's apartment the next morning and handed Michael an envelope containing $150 in US currency, and told him to purchase the boots he had been telling me about – an item of stage gear he really coveted.

In 1981 INXS actually played almost 300 shows, criss-crossing Australia on three separate tours. Chris Murphy spaced the tours out so that he could give them special names and thus keep up the interest even though the band was playing the same place every two months. There was the Stay Young Tour, the Tour With No Name, and the Fear And Loathing Tour. Life on the road was not at all glamorous. There were plenty of girls and parties, and a certain amount of available drugs, but accommodation usually meant the cheapest hotel, with three people to a room. They used two vans for two crew members, six band members and the equipment. The usual routine was to take turns sleeping on the way to the next town so that no money would have to be wasted on a hotel. They sometimes managed to sneak all eight into one modest hotel room. They survived on lots of fish and chips and soggy hamburgers, and a combined determination to conquer the world.

In March they released their cover of a sixties hit called 'The Loved One', which had originally been recorded by another Australian band called the Loved Ones. The single, which was well received, had been produced by Richard Clapton; himself a fine singer and songwriter. Chris Murphy had managed him previously and approached him to produce INXS's follow-up album. Australian record producers were in short supply in those days. The second album, *Underneath the Colours*, was released in October, and went to number 15 in the Australian charts. Clapton also produced the album's breakout single, 'Stay Young', for which INXS also made a video. It had a home-made look, just friends and their children dancing around the band who were playing on the beach. They enlisted everybody's help of course. Mother did the make-up and held reflectors when the sun began to go down. It was shot in Clontarf, on the beach in front of a house belonging to our parents' friends, Elizabeth and Oliver Campbell, who had a daughter with the beautiful name of Hiraani. As a teenager, I had babysat all of the kids at the Campbells' home during summer vacations. We all hold fond memories of those summers and that house, and Hiraani and her family still live there today.

Working in the studio helped define the inner dynamics of the band. Each member had excellent, creative musical qualities. Andrew, however, was proving to be a standout from the rest. He took the helm and became very specific about the musical arrangements. Michael's poetry was emerging into comments on society and relationships. His lyrics would later take on sensual love themes.

Michael sent me some newspaper clippings, which have long since yellowed. In an interview Jenny Hunter Brown makes this observation of Michael: 'He stares quite fearlessly, slightly surlily, out at the milling pub crowd. And for a moment Michael Hutchence echoes the late Jim Morrison. He clamps both palms just beneath the microphone and clenches them. He's twenty, fit, a fine dancer. He swings side to side with the mike stand as access in a mutant, Austral skank.' She continues, 'A great mat of damp curls flopping over one angry eye, he shoots out each rounded word like a rocket off a pad. Michael has reason to look fearless, he is fronting one of the brightest new bands on the horizon.' To another writer Michael said, 'I like to build a show rather than start at a high level. It should be like sex, y'know? It should slowly build and build, then you have your climax . . . then encores if you're lucky.' So there he was, fresh off the launching pad and eager to build his 'sex god' image.

This was enough for me. There had been a lot of excitement over Danny Sugarman's biography of Jim Morrison, *No One Here Gets Out Alive*, and there was talk that it was to become a movie. I was a fan of Morrison's and in January 1981 sent a letter to Mr Sugarman care of his publisher, in a naïve effort to convince him that Michael could play the lead role. After the polite preliminaries, I said that I'd heard about a possible film and waded on, 'With all modesty I must tell you that my brother Michael Hutchence is the only person to play the lead! Here for your review are some press cuttings on him and his group "INXS" (in excess). Very truly, Tina Hutchence.' I don't know what I thought would happen when Mr Sugarman received this, but I was hoping that he would insist that the production company take a chance on my brother. An unknown, twenty-one-year-old, lanky kid from Australia. We can dream can't we? I never heard back.

In 1981 Michael called me to ask if Chris Murphy could stay with us while in Los Angeles to try to get them an American recording deal. The band only had the budget for one night at a hotel. Success did not, of course, occur overnight in the United States, and Chris was our guest more than once. As it happened on that initial visit, we were due at the Golden Reel Awards dinner on his first evening. Jeff and his partners were nominated for several awards that year. That afternoon when I collected Chris at the very rock-'n'-roll Sunset Marquis hotel just off the Sunset Strip, he confessed that he had a huge hangover and was feeling nauseous. I was driving Jeff's Jaguar, and Chris was concerned that he would ruin the interior, so I took it easy and drove close to the kerb in case he had to vomit. Jeff came up with some magic potion in the bar and we got him steady enough to attend the awards dinner. We had asked my girlfriend Lindsay Bloom along to partner Chris. Lindsay was co-starring on a television series called *Mickey Spillane's Mike Hammer* with Stacey Keach, and her actor husband was away on location. Chris was not prepared for the event and we had to borrow some clothes from Lindsay's husband's wardrobe on the way. After we sat down at our table at the Beverly Wilshire Hotel, someone approached Lindsay to ask if she would be a presenter, as another actress had called and made her apologies. Lindsay agreed. I thought Chris was going to explode: this was his first time in the United States and on his first night out he was squiring a famous actress! His eyes were popping as he scanned the room for more famous faces. Slightly overwhelmed, he was drinking everything in sight. It didn't take him long to catch on though, and his confidence improved with each visit.

Once I picked him up in my new car, with INXS number plates. He was 'INXStatic'. He brought INXS T-shirts with him and I wore mine constantly; he pulled out crumpled INXS posters from his luggage and I immediately had them framed. He always tried to keep me up on my brother's progress in those early days. We all wanted success for the boys, there was a real feeling of teamwork. During one visit he handed me a glamorous press shot of Michael, which I thanked him for, but placed aside. He was disappointed as he said that women really loved Michael, he was surprised that I did not make much of a fuss over the eight-by-ten glossy. I reminded him that Michael was my brother and it would be strange to display this kind of photograph of him in my home, along with family snaps. Besides, I could not understand the fuss that was being made over his sexual aura.

Chris replied that Michael had a certain magnetism, one that he had not yet learned to project fully on stage. That would take time. He confided that he was having a problem getting Michael to loosen up on stage, to speak to the audience and take control. For all of his talent, Michael still seemed to have low self-esteem. This seems unbelievable now, when I look back on the dynamic, unconstrained, performances Michael is remembered for, but Michael was a shy, very private person. However, Chris had no need to worry, for by the time INXS began their first shows in the United States, he had come up with a plan which involved Michael appearing on stage wearing layers of clothing, above the waist, which he could gradually peel off. It gave him something to do between songs. Removing layers of clothing as he weaved his magic on stage became a fixture of his act; and I always thought that it meant he was removing layers of himself for the audience to see.

Judging by the female response, it worked very well. However, Michael always called upon his alter ego, the other 'Michael Hutchence', to face the large crowds. This together with the fact that he was practically blind without his glasses helped tremendously because he could only see as far as the first three rows, therefore he could only gauge how many people were in the audience by the applause. I once asked Michael how he managed to walk out and perform in front of huge crowds – he told me he never got nervous. He said he used visualization techniques. 'The night before or the afternoon of a performance, I close my eyes and play it in my head – just as I want the performance to go. I see the crowd, which of course I can't, and build them to a crescendo.' As far as I know he used this technique for many years, visualizing and then walking on stage as that alter ego. In the latter years as his pressures increased, he came to depend on other, dangerous, crutches.

Kell sent Rhett from Manila to spend two weeks' vacation with us in California. Rhett was seventeen by this time and he arrived without any pocket money, very little luggage, and a message from Kell to make sure to get him a haircut and, by the way, he needed some new clothes. I picked him up from Los Angeles international airport, brought him back to the house in Burbank and within an hour detected the aroma of marijuana. I followed the smell into the living room where I found Rhett reclining on a couch. I couldn't believe it, he had been in the country less than two hours and he had found an illegal substance – had he brought it with him? I asked him how he had managed to slip it through customs. He replied that this was not necessary. After going through customs in Honolulu, he walked out into the terminal and someone was dealing right there. I learned that in those days if drugs were around, Rhett would find them a temptation. Fortunately, Erin was a baby, but Brent was old enough to notice, and I was so angry that I was shaking when I asked him not to do this around my children – his nephew and niece. Episodes such as this were to become a regular occurrence, and would only escalate over the next seventeen years. I'm not unrealistic about drugs and know that many people experiment with them, especially in their teens. I don't believe that every one of them will progress – or descend – into hard drug usage, or that all illegal drugs are equally dangerous. But I didn't want drugs of any kind being used around my children.

Two nights later Rhett wanted to go to the Hollywood Palladium to see the Ramones. Fortunately we also had my New Zealand girlfriend Annie staying with us and she offered to go with him. When I drove them to the venue, he was wearing combat trousers, with pockets all down the front. As they attempted to pass security, Rhett was patted down. All hell broke loose. Fortunately he was not carrying pot and they apparently missed the flask of scotch he had in one pocket, due to the Swiss Army knife he had in another, which was classified as a weapon. It was confiscated and he was told that he would not see it again. The guards weren't to know what we in the family had realized for years: never, ever arbitrarily use or even ask to borrow something belonging to Rhett without being prepared to put up with some major opposition. He has always had this strange outlook on material possessions, what is his is his and if you are a relative, what is yours is also his – end of discussion. For instance, Rhett has an eye for antiques and collectibles. I also have a collection of interesting antiques. He once took a liking to a commemorative 1893 Chicago World's Fair Columbian stamp keeper I had. Once when he visited me, it walked out with him. I called him and he owned up but said I would have to 'steal' it back. I did. Then he did. Then I again retrieved it and locked it away.

He made such a disturbance upon hearing the news that he would not get his knife back, that they asked him to leave. Annie panicked, stepped in, and reasoned with the men. She suggested that she be responsible for the knife, and hold it in her purse. This request must have presented these toughies with a dilemma: here she was, a courteous, well-dressed woman in her mid-thirties, politely begging that they waive the rules, in order for her to enter into a pit of raucous teenagers. She promised not to brandish the knife during the concert – they finally yielded, and she and Rhett walked through the door. I think Annie earned Rhett's lifelong respect that evening.

Michael was always popular with girls and when he moved on to a new interest, he usually salvaged the friendship. I believe this was due to his own fear of rejection and dislike of confrontation. Unfortunately for him some girls are not so easily dismissed. One day I answered my door and standing there was this waify, cute, hippie, Mia Farrow type. She was not unlike another girl to feature in his life, Kylie Minogue, but this was Ananda, the girl from Perth. I expect my son had reckoned that since she lived approximately 3,000 miles from Sydney, it was doubtful that she would be paying any calls. But here she was standing there with a big smile. I phoned Michael and we arranged for him to come over for lunch. Ananda and I waited and waited. Finally I ducked into my bedroom and made another call to Michael: no answer and he was now two hours late. I was panicking, I had 'hippie girl' in my living room. I had run out of conversation after about an hour and she would not start lunch without Michael.

He finally phoned and told me he was at Vicky's apartment, which was around the corner from mine. I informed him that Ananda refused to eat until he arrived. His answer was, 'Mum, go tell her that I am not coming unless I know she will not growl at me!' She really had him quite concerned, and I was the mediator. I finally talked him into coming over and we sat down to a strange but reasonably pleasant lunch. I never saw Ananda again, and this non-confrontational habit of moving on became a pattern for Michael.

Not long after this incident I was to meet the girl who was to become the love of his life. Michael had called me and asked if I would do the make-up on his next video for the new single 'The One Thing'. He also asked if I could organize a couple of the actresses on *The Young Doctors* to appear in the video. As it was being filmed on the weekend the girls were happy to do so. Michael had become friends with the assistant director Soren Jenson so he asked him if he would like to direct. Michael arrived that day with Michele Bennett. This was to be my first introduction to her as she lived in Melbourne. They became inseparable and were obviously very much in love. Soon they were living together in Sydney, sharing a house with their friends Jenny Morris and Nick Conroy. We saw a lot of them – weekend barbecues, dinners – and met Michelle's parents which seemed to give a stamp of permanency to this relationship. Michael bought a small cottage in the Paddington district of Sydney and he and Michele moved in. He started to collect some possessions – furniture, paintings – and continued to do so on his travels around the world.

INXS was tearing up the stage in a tiny club in Melbourne one night when Michael noticed a strikingly beautiful girl. She had long dark curly hair, full lips, dark piercing eyes and was poured into a body-hugging black dress. He was struck with a bolt of lightning. He played it cool but enchanting: this was his ultimate weapon – the charming yet somehow detached character. After the set, he joined her with some friends and found out she was in her last year of high school and one of her subjects was Cantonese. As he had spent most of his childhood in Hong Kong and was still vaguely familiar with the language and intrigued by the culture, he felt this meeting was meant to be. There was electricity between them. Twenty-year-old Michael, who believed strongly in a deeper connection than mere sexual attraction, and seventeen-year-old Michele, who was drawn to Michael's gentle inner side, felt an instant connection. He felt that he had found his soulmate. Michele Bennett would be his live-in love for seven years and, beyond this, his good friend for life. She is the only woman Michael actually told me he had considered marrying.

Michael had only recently moved in with Vicky, so the relationship did not take off immediately. Michele, who lived with her family outside Melbourne, was a girl with principles. There was no question of her going back somewhere with him after the show. Their next encounter was some months later when Michele went to see another band, the Models, at another club and halfway through, felt eyes boring into her back. She turned around to see Michael standing about twelve feet in the crowd. She shyly acknowledged him and once again they spent the evening deep in conversation. Once again she went home with her friends.

Michael and Michele saw each other only when INXS happened to be playing a Melbourne date until she graduated from high school and took a job in a beauty salon in Toorak. One day while she was crossing the street, she ran into Michael. He invited her to the concert that night and from then on they began a phone courtship. He would call often and at odd hours. Through their conversation Michele sensed a kindness and caring about Michael. She realized that on the one hand he was extremely vulnerable and easily injured, to the point that if he felt that he had inadvertently hurt someone he cared for, he would be upset and mentally flog himself over the incident. At the same time, she could see that he could be quite steely and determined towards something that he felt passionate about. He expected a lot from people, especially himself.

Michele's parents were charmed by Michael and eventually allowed her to move to Sydney with him. She packed up her car with all of her clothes and one lamp as her contribution to their flat. They were obviously mad about each other. We all loved Michele and from the very start considered her to be part of the family. At the time it never occurred to me that he would ever be with anyone else. At first they settled into an apartment in north Sydney with singer Jenny Morris and another lifelong friend, Nick Conroy. It was an idyllic, carefree time for all members of the household, each with his or her own goals and dreams. It was a most exciting time for Michael, with INXS beginning to capture the small success waves, and anticipating and longing for the big ones.

In these lighthearted, heady days on the brink of huge success, with Michael's manic touring schedule, the foursome still found time for vacations, usually long weekends. Michael was working very hard and now bringing home the most money he had ever seen. One weekend they hired a houseboat on the Hawkesbury River. With so much planning and excitement, you would think that they had taken a private yacht on the French Riviera. On the first day, Michael climbed up to sun himself on the top deck, and removed his shorts to lie down in his swimsuit. As he lay there, a breeze came up and carried his shorts overboard. In the pocket was his week's wages, a whopping AUS$200, an enormous amount of cash for him then. He alerted the others that he was diving in after it. Michele objected strenuously as the boat was surrounded by poisonous jellyfish. All the same, both he and Nick tried in vain to rescue Michael's hard-earned money.

He decided to give Michele a ring for her birthday. He saved for months and took Jenny with him to choose a diamond. He finally found one he could afford. You would need a magnifying glass to see the stone, but to this day it is treasured by Michele. With Michael's encouragement Michele took up modelling. She remembers that he instilled confidence in her. He constantly told her to stand up straight and to remember that she was special. He convinced her that she was capable of achieving anything in life, and consistently reminded her to keep a positive outlook, to smile even when she was afraid and above all to believe in herself. She has told me many times that she is grateful to Michael for this. Michele's modelling career took off and Michael was very proud of her and often boasted to others that she was actually doing better than she was. I don't think this is a bad thing as we all tend to exaggerate a little about the people we love because we want others to care about them too or at least to rate them. But Michele is a very reserved person, not in the least bit conceited, I doubt she has ever known how beautiful she really is. So she would always correct him, pointing out that she had only had two photo-layouts in *Vogue* and not the front cover as he had stated. Despite their youth, Michael's frequent absences, and the pressures of the music business, the relationship blossomed. Michele discovered that Michael was absolutely committed to her. He proved to be an impetuous, enthusiastic partner and a true romantic. Much about his love for her was expressed in his lyrics at that time.

By now Michael was making enough money to purchase an old car, although automobiles would curse him all his life. He went through many used European cars during this time when he rarely had a valid driver's licence. It was important to him to have the luxury and freedom of owning his own car, which is funny because I remember the standing joke at Chris Murphy's office was always that they had to send a ride for Michael if they wanted to be sure he would be at the studio or gig on time. One car he purchased early on literally had all of its wires crossed. When he threw the light switch, the left indicator would go on; if he touched the choke, the windshield wipers would start up. Soon after he bought this automobile, and while he was away on a tour, he instructed Michele to have all the wiring repaired. She did so right before he was due home. When she went to collect it, she was so happy with the great job the mechanic had done. Driving it home she was excited, thinking that she could hardly wait for him to take it for a drive himself, finally a reliable car which did not break down. Suddenly, as she was crossing the Sydney Harbour Bridge, there was a shuddering from the hood and to Michele's alarm it ripped off and blew over the top of the car and on to the roadway behind her. Miraculously it missed hitting any other cars. She continued home with the hood on the back seat. Proof of Michael's car curse yet again . . .

Various other cars belonging to Michael broke down at the most inconvenient times, often on the way home from performances. Usually he would simply jump out and grab a cab or hitch a ride home. The roadies got so used to finding Michael's cars scattered around Sydney, they would either start them up and deliver them to his house, or simply unload his belongings and take these over. While Michael was on the road, Nick would watch out for Michele and they would use Michael's vehicles. One day they used one to go to the beach and parked it at the top of the driveway upon returning. About an hour later they heard a commotion out front of the house and ran out to investigate. Michael's car, which he had not even had a chance to drive before going on tour, had simply rolled out of the driveway and smashed into another vehicle. Nick must not have engaged the parking brake. Fortunately, Michael was developing a sense of humour about his cars by then and took the news in his stride.

Michael was spending more time on the road than at home. He set up a lock-up in Sydney and eventually another in Hong Kong. Quite often Murphy's office would send someone over to throw everything of his into boxes. Clothes, personal letters, special keepsakes that he would accumulate while on the road. After a time he would forget about them and the boxes would be sent off to the lock-up.

Michael's love for motor bikes never left him. The first 'toy' he purchased when he had enough money, was a second-hand motor bike. He left this parked at my apartment block when he began his road tours, and it sat there for weeks at a time and began to rust as I lived close to the beach. The bike could be seen from the road. One day my doorbell rang and I opened it to face a large leather-clad and, to me, threatening figure. The intruder said, 'I believe the owner of that bike downstairs lives here.' My heart jumped, I wondered if the bike had been stolen and sold to Michael illegally. He continued, 'Bring him out here.'

I did not know whether to slam the door and call the police or just scream for help. I finally stood my ground and told him my son was the owner and he was working. I decided not to tell him that he was not actually living there. To my great relief my visitor said that he wanted to buy the bike! We exchanged phone numbers and I promised to get back to him. When I contacted Michael he said that he would give it some thought. My leather-clad friend called back a day or two later and made an offer which Michael accepted. When the man came around to give me a cheque, I told him to make it out to 'Michael Hutchence'. He said, 'You mean the one who sings with INXS?' I assured him it was and he offered me $100 more if I could get him an autographed photograph! We made the deal. As he was leaving, he asked me if he could have some water for his dog, which was sitting patiently in his car. I filled a small plastic container with fresh water and watched him take it to his car. I assumed he would have a bull terrier or something; they say that dogs resemble their owners. To my surprise, he opened the car door and lifted out a tiny poodle. You just can't read people by their appearance.

Michael's love of bikes continued: the next one he bought was a red Harley Davidson – which again he left in my garage while he toured. Before leaving he attached a note to the bike which said:

* NEVER REV ENGINE – HARLEYS CAN'T TAKE IT!
* WARM FOR 2 MINS BEFORE RIDING
* DON'T RIDE IT – IT WILL KILL YOU OR I WILL IF IT DOESN'T – NOT INSURED!!

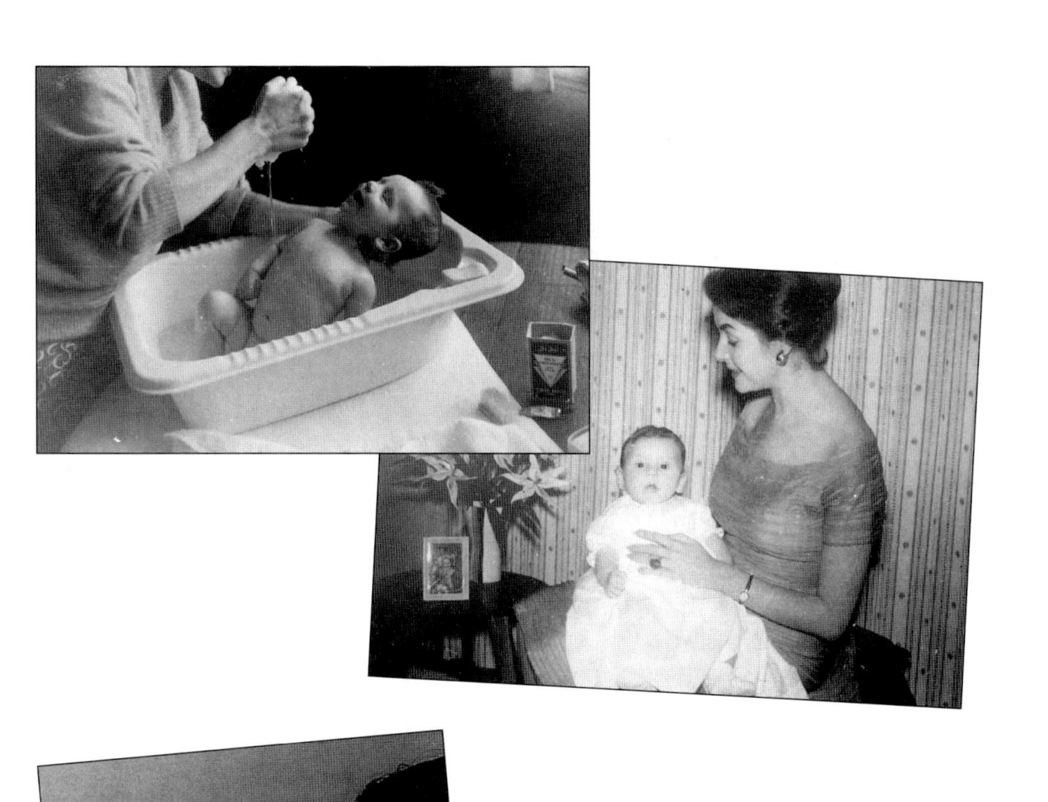

Top left: Bathtime for Michael at four months. He always loved water. **Above:** Michael, aged three months, in Patricia's arms on his christening day, Lane Cove, Sydney, 1960. **Left:** Michael, sixteen months, with Tina, thirteen, right after his first haircut, 1961. **Below:** Michael the folk singer with friends, Hong Kong, 1971.

Clockwise, top left: Patricia with Peter Fonda. Filming in Little Rock, Arkansas, 1976. **Top right:** On the day of Patricia's wedding to Kell with friends Leah McCartney (Miss Australia) (right) and Monique Rosenblum (left), January 1959. **Right:** Patricia at the Gown of the Year Parade in Melbourne – the picture Michael loved. **Below right:** A photo of Patricia's mother aged nine, a gift from Michael in 1993. **Below:** Patricia, Klaus Kinski and Tina (who was an extra in the movie in which he was starring) in Hong Kong, 1968.

Clockwise, top left: Michael and Rhett visit Father Christmas, 1963. **Top right:** Rhett (clowning) and Michael with our beloved Ah Chen, who wore a thick plait all the way down her back. Michael's cat Tinkerbell would chase the end of it as she bent over to clean or pick something up. **Right:** Rhett and Michael in Hong Kong watching *Romper Room*, in their usual positions – on the floor, 1965. **Below right:** The family in Hong Kong: Patricia, Michael, Tina, Rhett and Kell, 1969. **Below:** Michael, the serious young model for Jardine, Matheson, Hong Kong, 1972.

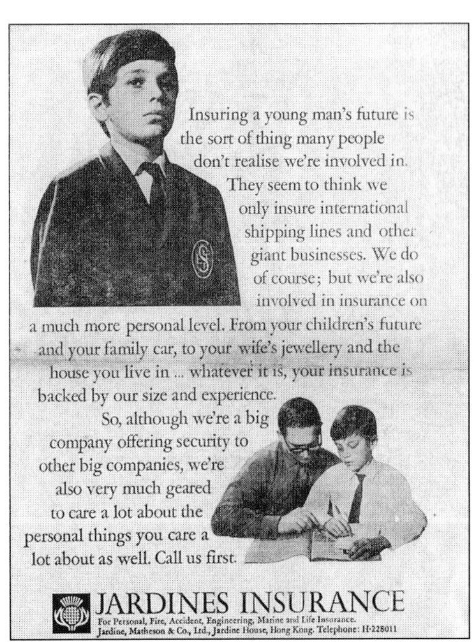

Top left: Michael (aged eleven) and Rhett (aged nine) at Coolangatta Airport before returning to Hong Kong, 1971. **Top right:** Michael the boy scout in Hong Kong. **Below:** Back in Australia. Michael (left) and Rhett are ready for a day of motorcycling after hooking the bike trailer up to Kell's car for the trip to Maitland, 1973.

Left: INXS's first visit to LA in 1982, where they stayed with Tina. Kirk, Michael and Andrew with Tina's good friend actress Lindsay Bloom, who not long after this became a brunette to play Velda the secretary on *Mickey Spillane's Mike Hammer.*

Clockwise, top right: 'X' tour in 1990. The songwriters, Michael and Andrew, taking a break.
Right: An early pub gig in 1979. Andrew Fariss (left), Michael and Gary Beers before he became Garry Gary.
Below: The making of the video, 'The One Thing'. This went into high rotation on MTV in the US. Michael is wearing Patricia's Spanish hat and in the foreground is the table set for the famous 'food orgy' scenes. Patricia did the make-up for this video.

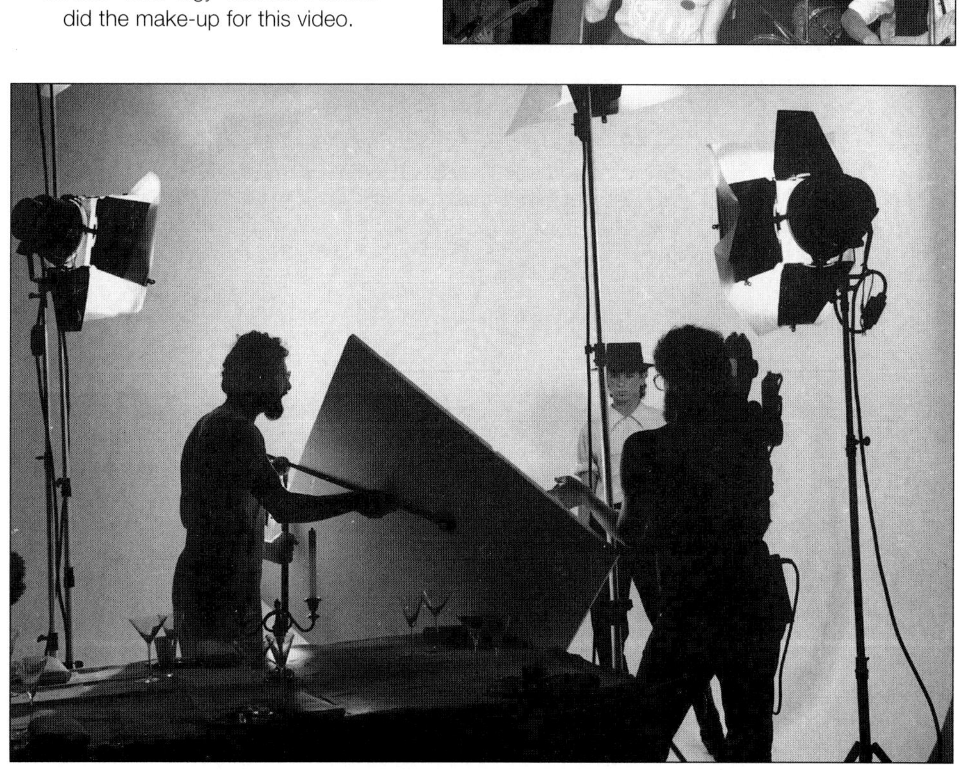

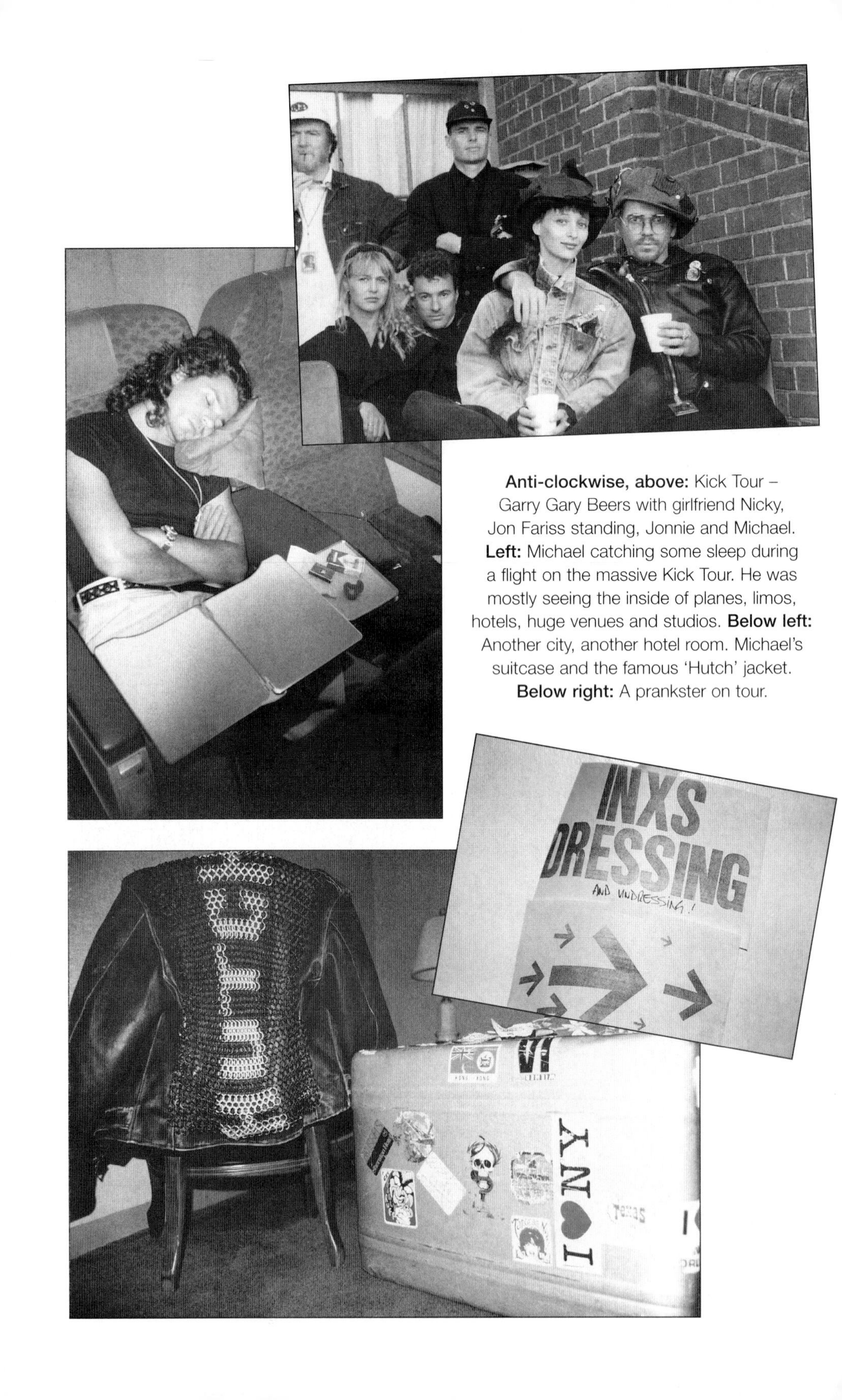

Anti-clockwise, above: Kick Tour – Garry Gary Beers with girlfriend Nicky, Jon Fariss standing, Jonnie and Michael. **Left:** Michael catching some sleep during a flight on the massive Kick Tour. He was mostly seeing the inside of planes, limos, hotels, huge venues and studios. **Below left:** Another city, another hotel room. Michael's suitcase and the famous 'Hutch' jacket. **Below right:** A prankster on tour.

Left: Johnny Depp, Patricia and Michael at the Greek Theatre, July 1997. **Below:** Sherine Abyratne, singer for Big Pig, Michael and Jonnie on the night Paula Yates began her pursuit.

Above: Kate Moss, Naomi Campbell and Michael in Monaco, 1996. **Right:** Michael, model Gail Elliot and Richard Gere, 1993. **Below:** Ray Charles and Michael Hutchence, November 1993. (East West).

INXS play Sydney University. (Ross Glassop)

INXS's first overseas tour was in New Zealand in January 1982 and I can remember how excited Michael was. They toured as support to Australia's number one band at the time, Cold Chisel, whose members were notorious for their unrestrained drinking, wild backstage punch-ups and overall unruly behaviour. But this tour came at the end of a five-year, multi-platinum career and by then Cold Chisel was famously completely out of control. There was far too much drinking before going on, and since they were on the verge of breaking up, the band members were at each others' throats. It was an education for INXS – in what not to do.

Chris Murphy and Deluxe had been trying hard to break the band into the United States, without any luck. Chris felt that they needed a major label behind them. The band felt so strongly about the potential for Michael and Andrew's song 'The One Thing' that they spent their own money to record it using Mark Opitz as producer. He had a respected track record and had also produced several albums for Cold Chisel. Chris took 'The One Thing' to a meeting with WEA Records and they offered him a deal. However, it was not the deal he wanted. With heart-stopping determination he held out until eventually Warner's A&R (Artist and Repertoire) manager, Gibson Kemp, worked something out which he could consider. Chris wanted a commitment from WEA Australia, that they would support and promote the band internationally. This was not the standard deal in those days. Yet eventually Gibson came back with an offer to sign the band for Australia, New Zealand, Japan and South-East Asia. Chris accepted.

When Chris was attempting to get INXS a record deal in the United States he worked harder than anybody I have ever known. He often spent a week in our home going from one meeting to the next, making calls all over the globe at all hours. He never seemed to sleep. On one visit I answered a call for him and the man on the other end of the line said he was Molly Meldrum. Peculiar name for a man, I thought. Having lived in California since 1971, I had no way of knowing that Ian 'Molly' Meldrum was a pivotal influence in Australian rock music. I handed the phone over to Chris who turned pale. He cupped the receiver and rolled his eyes before greeting him as if he were royalty. When Chris left town I sometimes collected the videos he had left with prospective recording executives – the ones who were not remotely interested in the band. I spent many days driving Chris to meetings, listening to his frustrations, sometimes joining him with record company personnel for shmooze dinners. Chris's managerial instincts were extraordinary. He had more conviction than anybody I had ever met. We would check out other bands and he would walk out announcing that INXS could blow them away.

On our visits to Sydney in the early eighties, Wendy and I were kept busy with the children in the home, while Jeff often tagged along with Chris on band business. But don't imagine that because Wendy organized the home-front, she had nothing to do with INXS's ultimate success. To the outside world, Wendy may have looked like the typical homemaker, but I saw something entirely different. As the office was in their house, she would take and make business calls, do the grocery shopping, iron clothes, arrange loans and overdrafts for MMA, do the laundry, find investment properties, cook a meal and so on, and on . . . She also has a talent for spotting good investments and she put this to work for the band when they began to see royalty cheques. Very early on, she arranged to purchase three properties for the band. She chose two luxury units in the heart of Sydney overlooking the harbour, and a block of apartments in Kirribilli just north of the city. Michael and Michele moved into the top floor of the Kirribilli apartments building and Jon Farriss took the apartment below. Wendy and Chris also invested in the properties, which actually made it more profitable all round, and they still own some of these properties today. Part of their aim was to prevent these young musicians from waking up in their mid thirties to find themselves with nothing to show for all their hard work – these were Chris's own words. I was so grateful that my brother was blessed to be in such good, sound hands.

Not long after the deal was signed with WEA, INXS released 'The One Thing' to an enthusiastic radio audience. Gibson then worked out a deal with Polygram in Europe and the United Kingdom. The final frontier would be the United States and Canada.

In 1982, prior to settling down to work on what would prove to be their first international album, Chris steered the main writers in the group to make a trip to Los Angeles, New York and London. Their first stop was with us in Burbank, and Chris had warned them to watch out for Jeff's potent margaritas. This, of course, was the first thing that they asked for. Along with Michael came Andrew Farriss and Kirk Pengilly. Michael and Andrew stayed at our house, Kirk with a nearby friend who had two very attractive teenage daughters who often babysat for me. At the time I thought this would be the safest way to go considering Michael's already growing reputation with girls. I found out much later that I was wrong: sending Kirk to my neighbour's house was like placing a coyote in amongst the chickens. After this visit, I found the girls far too busy to babysit when any of the INXS boys were in town, as they all started dating each other, and remain friends to this day.

Chris had come through Los Angeles beforehand and he left me with some specific instructions on where he wanted the happy threesome to sightsee. He had planned for them to take in some live entertainment at the Roxy, the Rainbow Room and the Whiskey-A-Go-Go. I asked a girlfriend to help out since I was busy with my children and too tired to go out at night. Besides, I was chauffeuring them around enough and assumed that Michael would be less than thrilled to hang out with his sister for his entire visit. Debra, the friend I asked to help, was a very pretty twenty-six-year-old aspiring actress. She had an agent and was doing well modelling and picking up small acting roles. As I remember, it was not an easy sell as she was already being squired by some of the most eligible bachelors in Hollywood. Eventually I promised that I would do any favour she wanted if she would just take Michael and the other two on a night out. Just one night.

'Wellllll, I don't know. How old is he?' said Debra.

'Twenty-two, but he's well travelled, and he's cute, really. They all are. Pleeeeease?' I begged. 'You'll be doing me a huge favour.'

Debra broke a date, called two of her friends and arrived at my house to collect Michael, Andrew and Kirk for the evening. I led the girls back to the den where Michael had been assigned the job of reading a bedtime story to three-year-old Erin from a Dr Seuss book. Only, he was not following the story, instead making up his own. She was so familiar with Dr Seuss's words, that she was correcting him. He was taking no notice of her and this was revving her up to shrieks of laughter. Debra looked charmed.

Much to their embarrassment I played some of the band's music before sending them off, hoping they would all have a halfway decent time. This was their first taste of Sunset Strip. They went to the Roxy and took in an act simulating the Doors. Around 3 a.m. Andrew arrived home in Debra's car to raid our bar and pick up some grass. I remember being concerned that he wouldn't find his way back to Debra's apartment and Jeff drew a map. I imagined that Michael and Kirk had sent the most sober of the three musketeers to do the job, even though he had only been in the United States four days. Four days, slightly intoxicated and he's driving a strange automobile on the other side of the road! I flashed to the last instructions Chris Murphy had given me. Make sure they have fun and see the shows, but watch the margaritas and stuff, Michael, Andrew and Kirk were adults and I was aware that they had been enjoying 'stuff' for a long time. I didn't partake in 'stuff' but it really was not up to me to lay down any rules under these circumstances: it wasn't as if the children were around. I decided that I had done my job if the evening was going well. The girls drove Andrew and Kirk home in time for breakfast, but we did not see Michael for another twenty-four hours. When he walked in he slept for fifteen hours straight.

It was soon obvious that Michael and Debra were attracted to each other. They had the same sense of humour and laughed a lot. It was an intense, mostly physical connection. Debra was charmed. She had recently disentangled herself from an abusive relationship and Michael was a refreshing relief. She remembers him as being sweet, young, and shy, gentle and vulnerable and very family oriented. He evidently spoke to her of his loving feelings towards his family, and was unlike any of the self-assured Hollywood types she had met, and they found it hard to keep their hands off each other. She took him to see a movie at the famous Mann's Chinese Theatre and he insisted on sitting in the balcony – to make out. All of a sudden I was seeing a lot more of Debra as they were going everywhere together. Horse riding, walks, sightseeing – and a lot of time spent at her tiny apartment. I kept hearing, 'Where's Michael? Have you heard from Michael?' from Kirk and Andrew. Even though he had not hidden from Debra his deep feelings for Michele, Debra found Michael to be a tender and sensitive lover – something which many women would find intensely appealing about him.

The boys weren't too grown-up for some more innocent pleasures and I arranged for us to visit Disneyland. When we were standing in line at the Jungle ride – Michael, Debra, Andrew, Kirk, Erin and me – a security guard approached us and took Kirk aside. It seems they had spotted him rolling tobacco in papers and assumed the worst. Roll-your-own cigarettes were almost unheard of in California at that time, they were certain that it was a joint. Fortunately it did not take them long to deduce that Kirk was using regular old tobacco. These days, of course, that too is seen by many as something akin to a crime! But even though he was playing hard during this visit, Michael was already preaching the philosophy of healthy mind healthy body. While preparing breakfast each morning, I could watch him through my kitchen window going through the movements of Tai Chi. Over the years he would take on yoga, weightlifting, and kick boxing. But it never occurred to him to give up illegal substances, I'm afraid.

Although Jeff and I were planning to take the children for a vacation in Sydney in a little over a month, when it came time for Andrew, Kirk and Michael to leave for New York it was a tearful scene. Debra and I drove them to the airport, waved them goodbye and as soon as they were out of sight she announced that she was going to Sydney too. It was the first time I realized that Michael could be devastating for women. Six weeks later when we touched down in Sydney with Debra, Michael was waiting outside of customs looking very nervous, because Michele knew that Debra was aboard, was not exactly thrilled about it, and was staying clear of Sydney. I handed Debra over to him and wished him luck. He had not asked me to discourage Debra from going: on the contrary, he had made his first call to her from New York, just six hours after departing Los Angeles. I decided to stay out of it: Michael was old enough to run his own life.

Just before our visit the band had completed the video for 'The One Thing', for which Jeff had given them the creative concept. Chris had called and asked Jeff for some ideas and they went for one which involved a banquet scene. I walked into the den one day and he was on the phone to Australia, saying, 'A food orgy, yeah, listen to me. Just have masses of food on this long table, and they should be devouring it, Henry VIII style, ripping legs off of turkeys, taking a bite and throwing them down. Decorate with some great-looking girls to hand feed them, and the guys should be looking good too, spend some money on wardrobe. Interchange it with a stark stage with the band playing. Use a hand held camera and get plenty of close-ups. If I can't be there to direct, I want to cut it.'

The video had a big-budget look about it because most of the technicians who worked on it were professionals, but their talents came free to INXS. For instance, Michael had met the young director Soren Jensen on Mother's soap, *The Young Doctors*. Since it was being shot on a weekend, he agreed to do it. Not only did Mother take on make-up artist and wardrobe duties, she even talked two beautiful actresses from her show, Suzy Stenmark and Karen Pini, into appearing for free. Karen, an accomplished seamstress, also designed and sewed some of Michael's stage wardrobe by this time. However, in this video, Michael wore store-bought clothes topped off with a Spanish hat belonging to Mother. He liked the hat so much that he continued to borrow it until she finally gave it to him. Michele was also featured in the video – in fact, it was her first introduction to the family.

Shortly after we arrived in Sydney, Jeff reviewed the footage and suggested some cuts. Chris Murphy had complete faith in Jeff's artistic decisions as he was an award-winning editor. Within hours, he was in an editing room cleaning up the flow of the video, which would be INXS's début on American television screens. Jeff recognized that the key was Michael's interaction with the camera. He was a natural, completely comfortable with it, having a sultry, sensuous way of moving every muscle in his body, as he gazed into the lens. No matter what the rest of the band was doing around him, he was completely focused, continuing to look to the camera as if it were a woman he was flirting with. Music Television Video (MTV) Channel placed it on heavy rotation in early 1983 shortly after they were signed by Atco Records for North America.

Michael was often in the studio with the band during this trip, recording their third album, *Shabooh Shoobah*, so Debra would come sightseeing with us. I noticed a gradual change in her style. I said nothing until she showed up one day in a short skirt, bobby sox, and heels. The Hollywood in her was slowly disappearing and the Ohio she came from had vanished from sight. She proudly said Michael was now choosing her wardrobe! I wasn't sure what to make of this apparently passive behaviour on the part of my friend coupled with what seemed like an odd desire to control on my brother's side.

During the following four years, though Michele and Michael stayed strong in their love for each other, Debra would float in and out of Michael's life. Some time later, on the day before the band arrived in California to play some college shows, I had a call from Chris Murphy to tell me where they would be staying, and he specifically asked that I should not tell Debra that Michael was in town. His concern was that Michael keep his mind on business and he did not want to rock the boat with Michele as she was a calming force in Michael's life. Chris had booked the band into a small, inexpensive motel on the Strip area of Sunset Boulevard. Sunset runs from downtown Los Angeles, through Los Feliz, Hollywood, West Hollywood, Beverly Hills, and all the way out to Santa Monica on the coast – about twenty miles. Debra had a part-time job at the Old World, a popular restaurant on Sunset, just across from Tower Records and Spago. When I looked up the address of the motel, my belief in fate was confirmed. The motel was directly across the road from the Old World restaurant! I gave the news to Chris, who did not believe me at first and then muttered some exasperated obscenities into the phone as it was too late to change accommodation for the band.

Michael, of course, was sitting at a table with the rest of the band when Debra arrived for work two days later.

Debra and Michael were not in love, although she says she always had a special place in her heart for him. She always described him as a spiritual, intuitive being, somehow always seeking the deeper connection when they talked. The two spoke for many hours, with Michael occasionally exposing his darker side. He made a disturbing statement to her on at least one visit; he told her that he did not expect to live to the age of forty. He did not elaborate and, being an actress and knowing all about performers' angst, she took the remark in her stride. The last time she saw him was in the spring of 1986 when she was seven months pregnant with someone else's child and surprised Michael by appearing backstage. He thought she looked radiant and was quite keen on the idea of a quick fling for old times' sake as he liked the idea of making love to a pregnant woman. Debra declined – but it was a happy reunion none the less.

On his visits to New York throughout 1982, Chris had been talking with Atco Records, a subsidiary of Atlantic. He had shown them videos of the band in action, but their look and sound was so different from everything that was on the market at that time and the label was not convinced. Chris knew if he could get them to see the band live, he would have a deal. He invited Atco Managing Director Reen Nalli out to Australia. It proved to be one of the best moves he would ever make. The band was in great form and the fans responded as usual. Not only did she sign them on the spot, but they sat up till dawn mapping out a plan to break them into North America.

Following their signing with Atlantic Records in the United States, Chris made sure that INXS were setting up their business affairs properly by introducing them to a Sydney attorney called John Gray. In 1983 junior lawyer Joanne Kelly was just starting a promising career in the same firm. Although her expertise was in litigation and her dealings were not with Mr Gray but with his partner, Joanne often noticed a flurry in the office when Andrew, Tim, Jon, Garry, Kirk and the leather-clad Michael strolled through the doors. Joanne was one of the few young women who was not moved to stare at the young men – her musical tastes leaned towards opera. Fifteen years later as a successful partner with another law firm, she would find herself deeply enmeshed in a puzzle, fighting for justice for Michael Hutchence, a man she never knew.

In January 1983, one week after Michael's twenty-third birthday, INXS appeared with Men at Work, Cold Chisel and The Angels in front of 45,000 people in a musical event billed as 'Narara Music Festival' in Narara, New South Wales. INXS put on a show-stopping performance and a fan presented Michael with a baby lamb, which made for great press.

When INXS came over to play their first US shows supporting Adam Ant soon after this, I was worried that people would not know of them and therefore not support them. I bought a load of tickets and handed them out to the girls at the local Burbank high school. I did not know there was such a thing as 'will-call' where friends of the band picked up complimentary passes the band left for them. I spoke to my babysitters, asking them to spread the word and I handed out INXS T-shirts with instructions to wear them 'all of the time'. It was at a time when girls were slashing their T-shirts with a razor blade. The craze had not reached Australia, so when Michael saw this he asked one of the neighbouring teenagers to cut his up. I was very popular with the local teenage girls, never at a loss for a babysitter.

When Wendy arrived shortly before the first show and found out I had actually bought tickets, she laughed uncontrollably and told me I was never to do that again. Wendy had me buy *Billboard* and all of the other music trade magazines, and she showed me what to look for in the weekly numbers to chart INXS's rise. I was talking with her one day, and said how great it would be now that they would not have to worry so much about money. She explained the logistics of taking a six-piece band on the road in a country the size and density of the United States. She told me that this little tour was costing them $100,000. How naïve can you get? I was stunned, having imagined that a tour was for making money. Apparently, the idea is that a band goes on tour to promote their music, hoping that they will sell a lot of compact discs in the stores, and thereby recouping their investment and driving up sales. It's like advertising.

Wendy, Chris, Jeff and I drove down to a little dive in San Diego to watch the band do a warm-up before hitting the larger stages in the US. I could tell Michael was nervous before the show. Wendy and I were in the tiny dressing room with Chris and the band, because this was a rough bar and we were not going to stand out there by ourselves. Wendy is a smoker and I am not, but when she turned around to help Tim who had a problem with the zipper on his pants, she handed me her cigarette. I was holding it awkwardly, when Michael squeezed by, noticing the cigarette in my hand. As he snatched it from between my fingers he was angrily concerned for me, saying, 'Tina, that's disgusting, don't start now!' Moments later, Wendy turned back around and said, 'What did you do with my cigarette?' I pointed to Michael as he stood in front of us stubbing out the cigarette – he was in his own world, oblivious. I can't remember Michael having a girlfriend who smoked cigarettes or any who were too keen on alcohol, but he had a very different attitude towards other drugs. I have often thought about this, given his own subsequent dependencies.

When INXS started up that night the audience was mostly noisy and uninterested and it didn't get any better. In fact they just got louder so that they could be heard over the music. This was very different from some pubs in Australia where I had watched the patrons just get up in Michael's face and yell at him, spray beer on him and then get into it. This crowd was just ignoring them. Wendy and I jumped around and showed our appreciation, hoping that it would be infectious, but it did not help. I was so disappointed, I wanted everyone in the bar to put down their drinks, stop talking and take notice. What did these people know? My brother and his friends would be headlining the Ritz in New York just two months later. I found out very quickly at the first show with Adam Ant, that a support band does not actually get much support from the audience who are impatient for the performance of the main attraction. Very often in those first US shows, INXS would be knocking themselves out on stage to a very small, unenthusiastic crowd. This could be hard on a band who were successful in their own pond.

The Adam Ant entourage had a routine. After the show, two roadies would come out to the backstage door and choose 'lucky' fans, girls of course, who would be taken to the inner sanctum. Wendy and I watched as these men would go, 'You, you, you, no, not you. Yes, you with the green top, no your friend can't come.' Etc, etc. They had a strict backstage policy not allowing support bands to stay backstage after their set, and they would not allow them to have guests backstage. For a friendly group such as INXS, this was a very alien policy, but it taught them another valuable lesson, and you will never hear an unkind word from any bands who have supported INXS over the years.

By now INXS had three gold albums in their homeland and their Australian mentality saw them through. Australians don't take themselves seriously. Having faith in their talents and eager to succeed, the band members were good-natured about the whole thing. I chauffeured the local high-school girls in their INXS T-shirts to every show between Los Angeles and San Diego, east to Palm Desert and north to Santa Barbara. It was not necessary for me to encourage them to rush the stage or scream, enticed by the cute Aussie boys, they did it on their own and, gradually, INXS found a following.

Following their tour with Adam Ant, the band played a small theatre in Hollywood. When I attempted to go backstage I was stopped and told, 'You can't go back there yet, the Go Go's are meeting with the band.' The Go Go's were very hot at that time and I wasn't offended, on the contrary, I was thrilled for the attention INXS were attracting. Shortly after, Michael appeared and excitedly told me they were going on the road with the all-girl group. It is rumoured that this was a wild tour, with band members from each group sleeping with each other. I can only say that Michael was very difficult to contact during this tour, rarely in his hotel room. Their tour manager said that if he were missing anybody he would just call up the tour manager from the Go Go's and make sure the errant member was at least on the Go Go's bus. They also opened for the Stray Cats and the Kinks.

*

1983. A letter to our mother from the Daytonian Hilton, Dayton, Ohio, said that things were going well with the tour and the album – 'on a super bullet at 64. Probably keep going too.' All the critics seemed to like them. Again he lamented that he missed Michele and Rhett and me, but concluded that all the hard work and time away from home would pay off, especially for the next album.

After the release of *Shabooh Shoobah* in the United States, and especially with 'The One Thing' playing repeatedly on MTV, it was not necessary for me to drag my friends to the live shows: they were calling for tickets. The band was now signed to a major US recording company and I no longer met them at the airport, as the record company was sending vans or limos for them. Once, early in his career, Michael called to let me know the band had arrived at the hotel and incredulously described how the driver had 'gifted' them a huge amount of pot. His words were, 'Wait till you see it. I mean it's like a tree branch!' I had trouble faking enthusiasm about this. After all, I would have thought that the idea was to make sure these young men enjoyed a lengthy career.

On one of the hottest May weekends in 1983, INXS played the massive US Festival, on a ranch in the San Bernardino Mountains south-east of Los Angeles. They performed in front of 150,000 people. Others appearing that weekend included the Pretenders, Stevie Nicks, U2, the Clash, Van Halen, A Flock of Seagulls, David Bowie, Judas Priest, Mötley Crue and AC/DC, to name a few. Jeff and I arrived without backstage passes. Not realizing the enormity of the open venue, we were herded on to a ranch where they seemed only to be serving beer. Without water, or even a soft drink, I became dehydrated within the first two hours and we were coming up against a brick wall at the backstage gate. We finally spotted Gary Grant as he came out to watch INXS in the sound tower. The young Australian band was in the early line-up of the first day, an unenviable slot. Most of the crowd is restless and waiting for the more well-known bands to come on. The stage was already set up with the equipment for upcoming performers so INXS had a much smaller stage area from which to work the crowd. As we stood next to the sound tower watching the performance, I was very nervous for Michael. But INXS put across a tremendous performance and even earned an unexpected encore. The audience, all MTV babies, went wild for 'The One Thing' and 'Don't Change' – both on high video rotation. These two songs would become staples on set lists for US tours for the next fourteen years for INXS.

Although I was feeling light-headed due to the heat and lack of water, I refused to miss a second of this momentous performance. It was very exciting for them, and the crowd had gone nuts. After INXS left the stage, Gary told us he would be waiting at the gate with the passes. He hurried off ahead of us and as we approached the back-stage, I felt myself sink to the ground. Jeff did not notice and just kept walking as I rolled into the only shade I could find, the underside of a parked truck. When I came to, I was being carried by a very large Texan, wearing a stetson. Once again, I was in front of the backstage gate, and this time asking for a medic. Security ushered the cowboy in, and he deposited me in a room under the stage. This was the makeshift first aid station. I was administered an ice pack and periodically checked. My name was taken, and I passed out again. When I came to, I heard a doctor say that he thought I should be sent to the local hospital. I remember trying to speak, to tell them that I needed to let someone know where I was, but I could not get the words out, and before long I was in an ambulance.

At the hospital, which had a huge area set up and ready for casualties from the two-day concert, I was finally able to recover, and was discharged to a waiting ambulance who returned me to the backstage area. After roaming around for a bit, dodging television cameras, which were recording impromptu interviews, a number of bands who were waiting to go on, and many party revellers, I found Andrew Farriss and a very worried Jeff. They were waiting for me because everybody else was on the bus and ready to go back to Burbank. The plan had been to celebrate the successful day with dinner at our house. As I attempted to leave the backstage area, I was once again informed that I was not wearing the correct security pass. I was standing between Andrew and Jeff. Andrew just said, 'This is bullshit, we're leaving, and she's leaving with us', and they each took an arm and we charged through with Michael following.

I was in no shape to cook so we sent out for pizzas and Jeff made batches and batches of his famous margaritas. When the late news came on, the only band they featured from the US Festival was the new, young Australian band. There were Michael, Kirk, Andrew, Jon, Tim and Garry all strutting their stuff on national television. Sure they were used to being seen on Australian television with a possible

15 million viewers, but this was the United States, a country with three hundred million people. We sat around the television in silence and wonderment before switching channels to see how many other networks were carrying the same footage.

During this first tour of the United States in 1983 the band met the legendary record producer Nile Rogers. He was impressed with their sound and energy and shortly afterwards, they went into the Powerhouse Studios in New York with him and laid down 'Original Sin' in two takes. Backing vocals from Darryl Hall were added later.

Michael had written the lyrics to a song called 'Brand New Day' while the band was touring the southern states. He was inspired as he watched children happily interacting in a front yard, oblivious to their colour, and its potential to divide them as they reached adulthood. The title was changed to 'Original Sin' and when it hit the airwaves it caused a furore. Michael's lyrics 'black boy, white girl, black girl, white boy' caused bomb threats to radio stations who dared to play the song. Astonishingly, years after all that the civil rights movement had achieved, it was banned on many stations in the United States. In an interview with Australia's *Penthouse* magazine Michael said, 'I thought, every day those kids wake up, the possibility is they'll be a little more prejudiced than the day before.' He added, 'I don't think one thin page of words can change the world, but it can push things around. It made all the right people angry.'

Following their international success, certain basic security measures were put into place. One of the most dramatic changes was the implementation of pseudonyms. It was one thing to have the itinerary with hotel phone numbers, but the trick was to know the correct name each band member might be registered under. The switchboard wanted the name of the guest. Imagine asking for your own brother under the name of Mr Fabian Sparkle, Mr Dick Strangelove or Mr Fred Flintstone – just some of Michael's pseudonyms. Many times Michael would call, give me his room number and forget to give me his alias. Thank goodness the road managers kept their given names. I was forever calling Gary Grant, calling Sydney from my home in Burbank, to get my brother's pseudonym while he was sitting in a hotel ten miles away in West Hollywood. Band members would then get bored and make up new names between cities. Some of the other names Michael used over the years were Mr Kafka,

Monsieur Venus, Mr Pussycat, Mr Harley Davidson, Admiral Nelson – and, of course, Mr Christensen. Sometimes we were given pseudonyms when we stayed at the same hotel. On one visit to South Australia our mother travelled as Wilma Flintstone!

Michael and Michele were still together though at times it was not smooth sailing, especially when Michele had to put up with rumours of Michael's infidelities. One time they were sharing a house in Sydney with Chris Murphy's assistant, Gary Grant, who was tactless enough to gleefully read out stories on Michael's love life from magazines. This sort of thing might well have enhanced Michael's appeal to a female audience but Michele was less than amused. It threatened her self-esteem and ultimately the relationship itself.

Michael would often call her from the road, he hated being alone and had trouble sleeping after a big concert. He would socialize with other band members after a show but he would be lonely after everyone else retired and that's when he would call Michele. It relaxed him to speak with her. Most times, he was soothed just listening to her voice and they spoke almost every night. When he found himself repeating his frustrations about life on the road and their forced separations, she turned her thoughts around by reading to him, often simply passages from whatever book she had to hand. Early on she realized that it calmed him almost immediately, taking his mind off his fears and insecurities, lulling him into a deep sleep. One night he called her apartment in Sydney from his hotel in Tokyo. He was desperately tired, and so wired from the show, just like a little child after a birthday party, he could not sleep. They spoke for some time then she began reading to him, until she heard snoring. She made noises into the phone and even hung up but of course it did not close the call out and she realized that he would be getting a huge phone bill from the hotel the following day. With the yen ticking away, she finally had to run over to her neighbour's house to call the hotel reception desk to have them close Michael's line.

Michael continued to make these calls to Michele throughout his life. She was always there for him and assumed that the other women in Michael's life accepted this as part of their friendship.

CHAPTER FIVE

Rocking the Royals and *Dogs in Space*

After completing their fourth album, *The Swing*, and with the controversial single, 'Original Sin', at number one in Australia, INXS embarked on their first world tour in early 1984 with an extensive, sold-out set of dates in their homeland.

At the same time Jeff and I were involved in divorce proceedings. We had different ideas about family life. I wanted someone who could be at home for dinner occasionally, and Jeff's sound studio was so busy that it kept him away from home twelve to fourteen hours a day. His day began at 11 a.m. and continued until the early hours of the morning. If he wasn't in the studio during the weekend, he would be sleeping. He is a perfectionist and when he painstakingly took his time on an MTV project for INXS, I felt the pressure every time Chris Murphy called to ask when it would be ready. Hearing the angst in my voice he would jokingly say, 'OK, how about I fly some girls in to get him coffee? Margaritas? Anything?' He would tell me how much money it was costing the band even though Jeff was not charging for his services. He and Jeff would have disagreements over what footage should be in the piece. Jeff has a good eye for direction and he puts so much into a project, he can forget who it belongs to. I was wishing that he had not got involved with any of the band's projects. To Chris's credit he never divulged to the band that the project was running over budget because of Jeff's determination to do it his way. He protected Michael from the heat.

When Jeff and I separated, he agreed to allow me to take Erin to Sydney for six months. The plan was for us to take over Mother's apartment while she moved into a friend's place just three blocks away. Mother had just opened the Advanced Makeup Academy, a school teaching make-up artistry for the motion picture industry. I was to give classes while Erin attended Neutral Bay Primary. Mother arranged a small homecoming dinner for me on my first evening in town, as it was Michael's only free night from the tour.

Rhett called in the early afternoon to say that he was out in the country, but was heading back into town and would see me for dinner at Mother's. We have always been so used to catching one week here and ten days there, usually on family vacations, that we try to get in every minute when we are in the same city. I told him to slow down, I would be in town for six months this time. Around 6 p.m. as Erin and I were heading out the door, the phone rang. It was the Bankstown Hospital. Rhett had been involved in an accident. Apparently, Rhett had been hurtling down a hill on his motorcycle behind a small car, and when it had suddenly stopped to make a turn, he had been unable to avoid ramming into the rear of the car. His motorcycle was totalled, but fortunately he was thrown clear, landing on his backpack. He was not wearing a helmet so it was amazing that his injuries were confined to two broken wrists and a slight concussion. The nursing sister said it would be futile to come to the hospital that evening.

I ran over to Mother's with the news. She was frantic and Michael, Michele and I had to restrain her from rushing to the hospital. Michael admonished himself, saying he should not have given Rhett the motorcycle in the first place. Beside himself, he also wanted to go directly to Bankstown Hospital but I reiterated what the sister had said. Michael agreed that they probably would need the time to clean Rhett up and give him painkillers and, after all, we had been assured that he had only minor injuries. We had an early night and arranged to meet early the next day.

The following morning, Mother, Erin and I collected Michael from the apartment he shared with Michele and drove to the hospital. We were all shocked when we saw Rhett. He had not been cleaned up, and blood was caked everywhere. His wrists and hands were taped all the way to his fingertips and he was moaning in pain. My mother became faint. Michael stayed in the room with him while I took Mother into the hall and summoned the head sister who explained that when Rhett arrived at the hospital, he was so high they could not risk administering any medication. In fact they were waiting until the afternoon to do any surgery.

As I walked back into Rhett's room I noticed a backpack under his bed. Michael was looking pale and worried. He was stroking Rhett's hair as they had a whispered conversation. I pulled the backpack up and placed it on the end of the bed and Rhett said, 'That's it.' The aroma of grass overtook the stench of the hospital as I loosened the drawstring. Michael told me to hold on to it and we would take it back with us. Rhett had explained to him that the bag had gone in the back of the ambulance with Rhett before the police found it. Apparently the grass had just been harvested.

On the way home, Mother sat in the back seat and Michael drove, as I wondered if he currently had a driver's licence. He spent so much time touring out of the country little day-to-day annoyances often eluded him, and he had a habit of misplacing travel documents and important things like that. His life had got so fast and busy that he could not keep track of routine things that other people just tick over with. Approximately thirty minutes out of town, Mother opened the backpack. Touching it, smelling it, she asked, 'What is this?'

Michael and I looked at each other sideways. I felt just as guilty as if I was the one who had been transporting an illegal substance. I was thirty-six going on fifteen again. Michael finally said, 'It's OK Mum, I'll take care of it', just as Mother was asking, 'Is this marijuana? Oh no, what if we are pulled over, just what we need . . .' I didn't blame her for being upset. We had Erin in the car as well, but thankfully she was doing her usual 'little Erin thing', reading intently and taking no notice of the adult talk. At least that is what I thought at the time: subsequently she told me she was always listening. As I remember, the main concern was Michael's career and his reputation. The newspapers could have a field day with the headlines should we be pulled over. We dropped Michael at his apartment and he disappeared with the backpack.

Michael continued with his concerts, and for the next three days we made the trip out to Bankstown to visit Rhett. He was not at all happy to have missed INXS's big show in Sydney, especially when Erin excitedly relayed the whole evening to him. She was six years old and this was the first live INXS concert she had seen. Even though the band had stayed in our home and she had watched recording sessions, most of their concerts had been in venues where alcohol was served.

Around this time I noticed a difference in security surrounding Michael. The men employed to protect the band were no longer courteous towards family, partners or other backstage visitors. In one incident, while manoeuvring Michael and Michele to their car, two of the security personnel demonstrated such zeal in their protection for Michael that they forgot that he was holding Michele's hand. She was wrenched back by some fans, and knocked to the ground and trampled before anyone noticed that she was not in the car. After that Michele refused to go backstage, preferring to meet Michael at a designated location after the show.

When Rhett was released from hospital, it was decided that he would come home with me. Life with a wounded Rhett and a six-year-old in a one-bedroom apartment was interesting to say the least. Rhett would want to sleep in but I was on a schedule. Erin was in school and I was working part time at the Academy for Mother. She and I would take turns taking care of Rhett. His casts began just below the elbows and extended all the way down to his fingertips, which made it difficult for him to do anything for himself. He would sit in a bubble bath while I washed his hair. When he emerged from the tub, I wanted to comb the tangles out of his hair, but he refused – I was making him look too square. He figured out a system of laying the towel across the bed, which would allow him to rub his head over the towel until the hair was sufficiently dry. Within a week he had dreadlocks. He loved it. Eating was another adventure. He was unable to even hold his knife and fork and as he sat at the dinner table, Erin would kneel up on the chair next to him and see how close she could get the food to his mouth. When he was in the mood for a walk, I sent Erin with him. I could look down from my sixth-floor balcony and watch the two misfits. Six-foot-tall Rhett in a poncho to cover his casts and little Erin walking beside him holding on to the two longest fingers he had dangling out of the end of one cast.

One day I left him in the tub while I went on an errand. When I returned, he was still sitting there, with one arm submerged in the water. He had been insisting that the original doctors had done a bad job setting his wrists, and he was about to prove it. As the softened cast came away from the arm, it was obvious that he was right. His lower right arm appeared to be deformed. I made an appointment with the doctor to have the other cast removed and make arrangements for him to go into the Royal North Shore Hospital to correct the problem. Within days he was admitted into the RNS where surgery was successfully completed and pins inserted.

Rhett took full advantage of his hospital stay this time. Rhett spent a major part of the time playing tricks on the other patients as most of them were not ambulatory. He was sending out for pizza at all hours, and calling me before visiting hours, requesting hamburgers from a favourite grill. Michael was busy with the tour; however, he arranged for various beautiful girls to deliver à la carte meals to the hospital.

Soon after he left hospital for the second time, Rhett and I went to see INXS together, and before the last encore, he took off towards the side of the stage, his poncho covering his casts. Fearing that he would not be given an escort backstage, since again we had not been left the correct passes, I ran behind him, but we were separated. By the time I found him, he was involved in an altercation with one of the security people who obviously did not recognize him, or believe that he was Michael's brother. Rhett was not going to take this man's obstruction and he attempted to push past. The man grabbed one of Rhett's wrists which, due to the poncho, he had not noticed was in a cast and pushed it up behind his back. Rhett screamed in agony. By the time we straightened that one out, and arrived backstage, I think Rhett was darn sure he was going to make everyone feel guilty over the incident. He had every right to be angry with the management people whose inefficiency had caused the confusion over backstage access, and of course had suffered horrible pain, but this was no reason to be angry with Michael. Michael's first reaction to Rhett's outburst was that of astonishment and hurt. He then calmed Rhett down and changed his focus to the party at hand. Placing his arm around Rhett's shoulders, he cajoled him into telling everybody about his accident. There's no doubt that my brothers loved each other deeply but however hard Michael tried to protect Rhett from himself the more inflammable the atmosphere became. As Michael's renown grew Rhett drew attention to himself in other ways. Nothing much had changed since they were children.

Upon my return to California I had to find a job which would not keep me away from Erin for crazy hours. This meant the movie industry was out. I also wanted work which would allow me to spend vacations with my family in Australia. I eventually went back to college, gained a travel agent certificate and joined Continental

Airlines as a reservations agent on their international desk. I think the only reason they chose me to go on their exclusive international roster in Los Angeles was that I had the right Aussie accent. Michael was very proud of me for going back to school – you would think I was studying brain surgery to hear him talk of it. I also took full advantage of the staff travel opportunities by flying all over to take in INXS concerts and visit Michael on the road. Sometimes I travelled on the tour bus to the next venue.

After one fantastic performance in Omaha the band returned to the dressing room exhausted. Before they could cool down, the promoter stopped by to insist that they make an appearance backstage for the local critics and such. It was a gruelling, fast-paced tour and when they were taking the bus on to the next city directly after the show, exhausted, they would flip coins to see who would make the next appearance. The loser this time, Michael, put on his 'I'm so excited that you enjoyed the show and love the album' face, and ventured out to meet and greet. After a short time he came back and told me about a girl he had just been introduced to who had been running a conversation with him while fingering a hole in the crotch of her jeans. Her whole conversation had centred around the sensations she was experiencing while looking into his eyes and masturbating, in the middle of a room full of partygoers! Michael was pretty blasé about it, but if he enjoyed the experience I think it was because it made a good story to recount later. I was oddly fascinated: what a strange business he was in.

These were some of my favourite times with Michael. In the early days I simply shared his hotel room and later on he would organize a room next door. We stayed up most of the night talking; sometimes I ironed his clothes and sewed buttons back on while we caught up with each other's lives. We went to movies and shopped for clothes – he was always searching for the unusual as he was very mindful of 'not looking like some guy in the front row'. I have never been a very demonstrative person and always felt uncomfortable backstage despite the fact that I often wanted to be there to offer solidarity. It always seemed so pretentious, with everybody trying to make like they are great friends with the band members and that they are somehow there, because INXS especially invited them. *Not* because they happened to know someone, who knew someone, who could get a 'will-call' ticket and backstage pass. That is why there are often two backstages – the ordinary one and the inner sanctum. Most of the hangers-on in the former hardly crack a smile at anyone else in the room, as they are too busy trying to appear 'cool'. I guess it's the same in any business – you have to do a certain amount of public relations schmoozing and every time a musician has a new album out they have to go through the whole process again. Some might enjoy this aspect of the work, but Michael wasn't one of them.

Much as he liked women, Michael didn't particularly welcome the attentions of groupies. The girls would try to get into the band limo, to party on, when this was not what most of the members of INXS were about. When these girls were backstage they often tended to look at me as if to say, 'Aren't you a bit out of place? Give it up!' until I was introduced as Michael's sister. It is amazing how pleasant people could be when they heard those words. I just resented it. Why couldn't people be friendly without the knowledge that you were related to someone in the band?

I cut back on attending INXS concerts altogether after an incident in the mid-eighties. I was standing on the balcony of the Hollywood Palladium with my 'All Access' pass clipped to my dress, when Chris Murphy came up to tell me he had left his pass backstage and could he borrow mine? I didn't think anything of it, assuming that I could talk my way back after the concert. I was wrong, the security people, not INXS's usual crew, refused to let me through. Even at the time this seemed to me to be somehow emblematic of something I had sensed before – that the people surrounding Michael weren't as decent and reliable as they had been in the past. There was some irony in the fact that the more successful INXS became the less control they had over the machine that ran them and Michael, cushioned as he was in some ways, wasn't even always aware of this. One of the penalties of success, I suppose, is that a person can lose touch with reality without realizing that, far from being out of control of their destiny as they were before, they are 'managed' to the point of being in an almost childlike personal oblivion.

Anyway, that evening I spent an exhausting and frustratingly long time dealing with increasingly rude refusals to let me go backstage when I'd decided that I wanted to, surrounded by sneering groupies who looked at my tailored silk dress (I'd come straight from the office) with an offensive mocking pity. I won't go into all the tiresome details but it was only because Michael happened to spot me in the unseemly crush, and enveloped me in his arms, that the barriers came down for me. The reluctant heavies let me through, to the evident astonishment of the ladies in waiting. After that incident I felt much as Michele back in Australia did and preferred to meet Michael somewhere else after the show.

1985 was a huge year for INXS. The band performed for close to 50,000 fans in three shows in Australia. Immediately afterwards they began recording *Listen Like Thieves*, their first collaboration with Chris Thomas. In May, while recording continued, they appeared at the Countdown Awards, Australia's equivalent to the Grammies, and walked away with six major awards: Best Album (*The Swing*), Most Popular Group, Most Popular Male Performer, Best Songwriters (Michael and Andrew Farriss), Most Outstanding Achievement, and Best Group Performance in a Video. Little did they know this was just the beginning. For INXS would continue to dominate the Australian music award shows for the next five years. This was a huge unprecedented accomplishment. In July they played a Live Aid performance with the beautiful backdrop of Sydney Harbour, which was beamed around the world. *Listen Like Thieves* had its final mix in London in August and they began a world tour in Australia the same month. They toured South America in October, while the first single was released to glowing enthusiasm in the United States. They then returned to Australia to perform in a charity concert in Melbourne, before heading back to the West Coast of the United States to headline a few sold-out shows, ending up in New York for more sell-out performances.

INXS was invited to perform at a charity concert in Melbourne's magnificent Victorian State Arts Centre in November 1985. The event was billed as 'Rocking with the Royals', because special guests included Prince Charles and Princess Diana. The concert coincided with Victoria's 150th anniversary and the International Year of Youth. All parents of the band were invited. It was one of the most memorable concerts in INXS's career. Melbourne was all lit up and our car just crawled along St Kilda Road, which was wall to wall with people standing in line to catch a glimpse of the popular royals and their favourite rock groups. The show, hosted by Molly Meldrum, included performances by Kids in the Kitchen, the Models and I'm Talking. They had erected three giant video screens outside the Arts Centre so that 40,000 excited, dancing fans could also enjoy the night.

I was seated just a few seats behind the royal couple and could clearly see Prince Charles attempting to snap his fingers in time to the music while Princess Diana was unabashedly rocking around in her seat. After the performance, the artists were presented to the royals, which was a great thrill to them as well as to us parents. Michael and Diana remained 'friendly acquaintances' until her death just three months prior to Michael's.

If 1985 was a grand year for the band, it was a tough one personally for Michael and Michele. She was now travelling more for her modelling agency. Sometimes this worked out well and she and Michael could meet up in places around the world. Other times it was disastrous. She was in Ibiza during the Live Aid performance and had to travel from hotel to hotel to find one that was screening the event. She missed the special royal performance in November, due to work in London. But she did manage to fly from a fashion shoot in Milan to New York, to meet up with Michael for her twenty-third birthday in early December. Christmas holidays were especially difficult considering the many months the band spent on the road. Between them Michele and Michael had parents in Melbourne, Sydney and Hong Kong; and it was rare to get more than a week to enjoy these special occasions – there were five other members and their families to consider as well. The band was usually playing New Year's Eve and it was especially hard on Tim's wife Buffy, as they had children.

One insane Christmas, Michael and Michele left Sydney on 23 December to drive fourteen hours to be with her parents and their friends in Melbourne. They stayed over two nights and left 26 December, to drive back to Sydney for rehearsals the following day. When they arrived back they were told that rehearsals had been cancelled due to the Farriss brothers taking a fishing trip. Nobody had thought to call Michael to let him know. Michael would become furious when these goof-ups happened but rarely would he fully display it to his band mates. Perhaps this tendency to avoid displaying appropriate anger – rather connected to his non-confrontational attitude to women – contributed to a build-up of unresolved inner tensions.

Michael's 1986 diary gives a glimpse into the pace the band was keeping. His first entry is dated Tuesday, 31 December 1985. He writes about the beautiful fireworks on Sydney Harbour, which he had gone to see with Michele. The pyrotechnicians shoot them off the bridge on New Year's Eve, and it's a spectacular sight, especially if you are lucky enough to be on a boat. That particular year, they synchronized the display to INXS music, which was thrilling for Michael. His next entry is Friday, 3 January 1986, 'The end of my holidays – had a good time but not long enough of it. This is so hard for Michele and I.'

He also lamented the fact that although he'd enjoyed his holidays, they were a meagre six days, and he'd wanted to spend more time with Michele. But INXS were off to Coober Pedy, in the middle of Australia, for a gruelling three-day shoot for the 'Kiss the Dirt' video. It's one of the hottest, dustiest, most miserable places on earth in summer. They had a scare on the return flight when a wheel on their small chartered aircraft exploded on landing.

He also talks about how much he misses Michele, even expressing hope that they'll have a child together in the future. He describes her as 'brave and beautiful' – and although he's excited about the tour, starting on 8 January, he's not so willing to leave Michele.

Nonetheless, INXS's first world tour kicked off in New Zealand with their first show in two weeks. They picked up a Double Platinum award in Auckland. He notes that on his flight to London (in first class!) he read 'Simone De Bouviere's' *An Easy Death*. When they arrived at Heathrow on 14 January, he found his bags had gone missing, containing all his clothes – and even his traveller's cheques. His first interview was the following morning. At the end of the week, they travelled to Newcastle to tape the music show *The Tube*, hosted by Jools Holland and Paula Yates (although he mentions neither of their names).

He obviously found himself too busy, because the next entry is in August, regarding a property for sale in Australia, and then the final November entry. 'Songs written: 1. Mystify 2. Monkey On My Back 3. Tiny Daggers.'

In June 1986 I flew to London for ten days. INXS were on their third world tour in two years, and would be playing London's Royal Albert

Hall. Until INXS arrived in London, I stayed with my friends Tina and Gibson Kemp who were also close to the band, Gibson having been instrumental on their early negotiations with Warner Electra Asylum in Australia. As soon as I arrived Michael called and suggested that I tag along with the band on a 'photo op' which was to take place in Hyde Park. We found dozens of photographers waiting in the park. I tried to stay out of the way and just observed. Michael was asked personal details about Michele and he told them that she was no longer modelling, that she had recently embarked on a career as a television journalist. This was news to me and I was surprised that he made such a statement to a member of the press. That evening we dined at one of his favourite curry houses and I asked him about Michele's new career. He said that she was thinking about it, and he liked the idea, as the rock 'n' roller with a model girlfriend was so clichéd. But he did not tell me that he and Michele were actually having difficulty coming to an agreement about her career. She wanted to pursue other avenues and although he wanted her to have a career, he also wanted her to be available to go on the road with him. This is what would eventually split them up romantically, although they would always retain a deep friendship.

On the afternoon of the show he was concerned to find that he did not have his asthma ventilator. Michael always tried to travel with an extra inhaler because although they can be bought across the counter in some countries, as we found out that afternoon, in the United Kingdom, you require a doctor's prescription for the kind he needed. As he went off to sound check, I desperately tried to talk several pharmacists into selling me one. Finally I contacted Michael at the venue to let him know that I had had no luck. No problem, he replied, a doctor had given him a supply. This sort of panic situation would happen often throughout Michael's career. I would be frantic, unable to find something he would tell me he desperately needed and he would forget to tell me when a publicist, an assistant, a roadie had taken care of the problem. I didn't spend much time with Michael when he was surrounded by these people and it rarely occurred to me that he had a crew who were getting paid to take care of him.

Although the fact that one of these 'fixers' had found a doctor willing to supply Michael with an inhaler was a relief to me, it brought a serious point home. Asthma is a serious, chronic illness and the drugs prescribed to control it are complex ones – which is why in Britain supply is generally monitored. The condition is more than just a tiresome inconvenience, although like many asthmatics Michael made light of it and refused to allow it to restrict his life. I always wished he'd be more watchful about conditions that could lead to an asthma attack, even though fortunately his were few and far between. Today I was put in mind of the 'Dr Robert' of the old Beatles song – an expensive private doctor in London who supplied all manner of drugs to the rock élite of the day and I only hoped that the good doctor that the fixer had found had at least some knowledge of Michael's particular requirements. I can only wonder and worry about how the strong drugs usually prescribed for asthmatics might have interacted with the recreational ones which Michael was increasingly resorting to.

After the show Tina Kemp and I went on a bus with the rest of the band and friends to a charming little bar. Michael was paying a lot of attention to a particular girl and seemed uncomfortable when I noticed. Obviously it was like cheating in front of Michele's friend and he looked torn. I whispered to him that it was his life and that I was not there to judge him. He still looked embarrassed, especially when the girl continued to come on to him. When we decided to leave Michael walked us out to a taxi. This would not be the first time such a scenario would take place – he was definitely not faithful on the road. I never knew if I should be flattered because he thought so highly of me that he wanted to avoid showing his flaws, or insulted because he thought I could be censorious.

Soon after this visit to London I planned a return to Sydney. Brent wanted to complete his schooling in California and was very involved in baseball. Although I would miss him, I found his logic completely sound. Anyway, as I was working for an airline company I could arrange flights for him at any time for almost nothing. I sent Erin ahead and I left three weeks later with my furniture for a new start. When I arrived in Sydney, Erin was already making friends in her new school. I quickly found an apartment and another job with Continental Airlines. I was on the reservations desk, which meant that I was attached to a headpiece and a computer – along with approximately twenty-five other people. The computer detects which station is available, and selects that reservations clerk to take the call. The call 'pops' into your headpiece and away you go. A month after starting this job, INXS was due to fly into Sydney from the United States and I knew they were not travelling Continental Airlines. A call popped into my line and I answered 'Good afternoon, Continental Airlines. This is Tina, how can I be of service?' A male caller identified himself as 'Rick Hutchence', Michael Hutchence's brother! Really? I was both amused and astonished as he spelled my surname for me. He went on to tell me that his brother was arriving back into the country on tour, and he had forgotten the flight number and time of arrival, so could I please tell him.

Well now, this was interesting. I looked up and saw that my supervisor was away from his desk. What is the most fun I could have on a boring Friday afternoon, I wondered. I went through the procedure of informing the man that I could not possibly give out that information; it would be a breach of security. It had nothing to do with the fact that INXS would be travelling as VIPs – by law this information can only be given in an emergency. I told him that he would have to call the proper authorities, in this case the police, and they would then contact us. He became very irate and enlightened me on the fact that he could have me fired for insolence. Now it was time to 'enlighten' him about the fact that I was Michael's sister and that we did not have a brother called Rick. He became even more agitated and roared into the phone, 'What would you know, we don't even have a sister.' He then demanded to speak with a supervisor!

I obliged and turned the call over to a reservations agent sitting next to me. She had listened intently to my conversation and had made it obvious that she was longing to take over. She identified herself as the supervisor and listened very patiently to the man thundering through her earpiece. When he had finished, she very calmly told him it was his unlucky day because Michael's sister did indeed work for Continental Airlines and he had just been speaking with her. She said that he could not possibly be Michael's brother because she had met Rhett Hutchence. 'Rick Hutchence' slammed the receiver down. Giggling uncontrollably, we could hardly wait to share this story with the rest of the reservations desk. Just then, another call popped into my line. It was the supervisor and he too had been listening to the second part of the conversation. We never were reprimanded, I think he enjoyed the call as well. When I told Michael about this, he made two tickets and backstage passes available to the Sydney Entertainment Centre show for Continental

Airlines to offer to their reservations staff with the most call volume in one day.

After the concert we were invited to a small reception where the band was presented with platinum records for *Listen Like Thieves*. The next day Erin wrote a sweet little story on the events of the evening, and gave it to Michael who said he would cherish it. He and Michele treated her to lunch that day and she took along her favourite book, Sam Shepherd's *Fool For Love and Other Plays*. This was a very sophisticated book for a little girl barely eight years old to be reading, I admit, but then Erin was always a ferocious reader and Jeff and I had allowed her to be exposed to a wide range of writing. Michael was always impressed with Erin's choice of book and he loved this particular collection of plays. When Christmas came that year and we could not find another copy of the book, she gift-wrapped her dog-eared copy for him. He was so touched. Over the years at the end of faxes, he often made a point of mentioning some particular novel that Erin might like.

By the mid 1980s Michael was spending very little time in Australia. He was touring and recording all over the world and found a permanent address unnecessary. To alleviate the tax burden, he had taken up residence abroad, though this was mostly on paper only. In fact he still owned the cute little house in Sydney's Paddington, where he and Michele lived when he was in town. Eventually it had to be rented out. As I understood it, he could not live in Australia, especially in a place which he owned, without being taxed heavily. It was Kell who had first recommended that he take up residency in Hong Kong, although he was advised not to make it public.

By the end of 1986, the single and video for 'What You Need' was an international hit and had catapulted INXS into a perfect place for stardom in the USA. At the same time Richard Lowenstein, who had directed the video, was waiting for Michael to make some time to star in his movie *Dogs in Space*. Michael and Richard had formed a friendship based on mutual respect during the filming of the 'Burn For You' video in 1984. Richard had hoped to star Michael on his *Dogs in Space* ever since.

INXS's success came at a price. Michael's free time was badly restricted and there never seemed to be enough of it to recover from being energetic on stage, working on a new album and being unfailingly witty, polite and intelligent when confronting journalists. I was sure that he was experimenting a lot more with drugs, not that I ever witnessed the evidence of this. But I had heard enough rumours, and I was worried by his frequent trips to the restroom, wherever we were. I was sure he was taking cocaine but this didn't scare me as much as it might have done since I'd known a lot of occasional users in LA. Of course dependency is a terrible thing and can lead to people's business and private lives collapsing. But where Michael was concerned I hoped and assumed he did it sometimes, just to keep up the pace of recording, performing and touring – and for relaxation.

Two days before Christmas 1986, we sat around the tree at a friend's house in Sydney, as Kell played Santa Claus. These days Mother and Kell held separate Christmas celebrations. There was Michael, Michele, Rhett, Erin, Kell's new wife, Sue, a long-time family friend, Croy, some friends of Kell's and myself. Brent was with *his* father, in the States. Kell handed Michael a beautifully wrapped book about the pursuit of excellence and the people who have attained great success. His inscription suggested that Michael was well on his way to being a contributor to a future edition of the book. He turned around and picked up an oddly shaped gift and tossed it at Rhett. It was a leg of ham. To this day I cannot understand what motivated such a peculiar choice of present. The only thing that comes to mind is that Kell, who had no tolerance for street drugs, had read somewhere that it was pointless to hand over money or anything which could be exchanged for money to a person with a drug habit. There was horrified silence and it was obvious that Rhett was holding back understandable tears of hurt, jealousy and frustration. The pained look on Michael's face showed that he suffered with his brother.

Four of us adjourned to the kitchen where Michael lit up a joint and handed it to Rhett. Michele and I did not indulge but we listened as the brothers consoled each other. We heard footsteps and I approached the doorway to head off the newcomer, thinking that the brothers could fly out the back door. As I stood there, hands clasped behind my back, talking to Kell who was oblivious to the pain he had just caused both brothers, someone crept up behind me and pushed the joint through my fingers. Kell did not even notice the strange aroma as I stood three feet from him. I was petrified that Kell would notice and think I was joining in. I glanced around to see Michael with a huge, mischievous grin, and Rhett and Michele peeking around the kitchen door. Michael and Rhett thought it hilarious to put me in a position of possibly being caught with something so alien to my lifestyle. It made me feel and act guilty even though I hadn't done anything wrong, but still Kell did not notice anything unusual about my stammering and fidgeting about the room. Michael and Rhett were at their best when they were in on something together. They were very competitive about pranks and witty conversation. Rhett could usually outdo his brother when it came to pranks.

This appeared to me to have been a very confusing, painful time for Rhett, who was at this stage fighting his battle with illegal drugs while watching his brother seemingly effortlessly climb to the top of life's pile. I must admit that at that time I was unaware of the full extent of Rhett's addiction. I do not know if he was very good at hiding this from me or if I was so naïve. When I finally confronted him about his excesses midway through 1987, not really being aware of what substances he had been indulging in, he casually told me it was heroin. I felt heartsick and scared. I only knew it from the outside, of course, but from what little I had read or heard I believed it to be a drug that killed. Rhett airily brushed away my concern and said he had it under control, he knew what he was doing. Then he informed me that Michael had been the first to try it and told him it was not that big a deal. Rhett's point was, why not go after Michael? He gets away with everything. It was a familiar chorus, Michael manages to taste everything and when he does, he is cool and he gets away with it. Why not come down on him? I didn't believe Rhett, but cautiously confronted Michael who admitted that he had tried heroin once or twice, but that it made him feel ill.

He said that he felt it was necessary to get into the role of Sam for *Dogs in Space* – a heroin-addicted singer in a punk band. Michael had spent two months filming *Dogs* in Melbourne in March and April 1987. It had been a long haul to get to the actual filming since the project's inception three years earlier at the Cannes Film Festival. Richard Lowenstein had only known Michael for a few months when they met up in the South of France and spent an interesting all-nighter, topping it off with a breakfast meeting with an Australian film producer. Richard was pitching an idea to her while Michael was at the table, more or less asleep in his croissant. The woman was unimpressed with Richard's ideas until he told her of a story he had, which centred on a punk band living in a house in Melbourne in the late seventies. It was based on a real-life character, a singer by the name of Sam Sejavka who had struggled with heroin addiction. Richard told the producer that Michael had already agreed to be in the film, when in fact he had not even written the script. The producer showed immediate interest, which propelled Richard to actually put the script and funding together.

Michael kept his close friendship with Richard and they plotted and planned to get the project in front of the cameras. He had huge respect for Richard's work and longed to associate himself with his style of creative-cool. One night Richard arrived backstage with Nick Cave, the lead singer of Birthday Party, who was the epitome of hip-nonconformity. Michael had been a fan of Cave's for a long time and although he was too shy to push headlong into a conversation that night, they presently became friends, and that friendship became stronger when they both came to live in Britain in the mid-nineties.

Richard got lots of encouragement for the *Dogs in Space* project, especially as Michael's involvement was known, but unfortunately each time the money required to back the film was in place, things were held up by Michael's INXS commitments. Michael became quite anxious about this, worried that he would lose the role to someone else. He desperately wanted the chance to play this character and when he did get to the set he was absolutely wholehearted about his work there. But when he insisted that he had only tried heroin to help him get into the 'Sam' role, I did not let him off the hook. I told him it hardly seemed necessary to actually try heroin. That is why dramatic reconstruction is called 'acting'. He reiterated that it had made him feel ill, and that he had only tried it twice. As usual when Michael could not win an argument he threw on the charm. He laughed at me, and gave me the familiar chant about me being so square – can't believe you were a teenager of the sixties, loosen up, enjoy life, you take it all too seriously and so on. By the time he was through with me, I decided that I must not be much fun to be around. I also fretted that by challenging him in this way I'd given him every reason to hide his excesses from me in the future.

The family continued to vacillate between refusing to indulge

Rhett if he showed signs of drug use and coddling him when he appeared to be straight. It is shocking to say now, in the light of what I now know about prescription and illegal drugs, but I think we were in constant hope that it was just a phase and he would find a career and the drug dependency would go. He did not see the family very often. When he did he could be sweet and thoughtful and appeared to have his problem under control, and when you only catch small glimpses of someone it is hard to get a fix on their psyche. The problem was that when he was having these problems we – Mother, Kell and I – were not equipped to distinguish when he was fabricating a story to get funds for his habit, and when he truly was in need of food or rent money. At that point, he refused to go to a professional for help.

CHAPTER SIX

The Rise and Rise of INXS

Australian Made was a phenomenal Australian tour conceived by Chris Murphy who put together nine Australian bands, the cream of the crop, including the Models, the Divinyls, Mental As Anything, I'm Talking, the Saints, the Triffids, and former Cold Chisel front-man, Jimmy Barnes. Seemingly on the brink of international star-dom, INXS would headline. What made this venture so extraordinary and ground-breaking was the logistics. As well as all the planning and organization for the travel, accommodation and security for nine very popular bands, there was the road crew and travel companions of each of the band members to consider, all moving around a vast, sparsely populated country. It would take a mastermind to syn-chronize this into a money-making venture, and Chris Murphy proved he was up to it.

Months before, in an early promotional gambit, INXS and Jimmy Barnes had recorded a screaming, rocking version of an Easybeats classic, 'Good Times'. Of course any song Jimmy attacked was screaming and rocking and Michael was up for the challenge. They recorded it at the Rhinoceros Studios with Mark Opitz at the helm. I joined Michael for dinner one night and he took me back to the studio to observe the fun. Jimmy, known as the working class man's rocker, was one of Michael's favourite people. That night I sat in the control room as Michael and Jimmy laughed and sang and held everyone in the studio mesmerized.

One week before the start of the tour Michael met Chris Bailey, the lead singer and songwriter for the Saints, and that summer the two would forge a lasting friendship. Chris was never the typical rock and roller. Though he sounds as if he was educated in private schools and walked the halls of Oxford, he had left school very young and was, like Michael, largely self-educated. Chris says that he had never been seriously impressed with INXS and assumed that Michael would be just another womanizing, hard drinking singer with nothing more to talk about than his guitar strings. Well, if Michael was the charismatic man of rock and roll, Chris Bailey is its poet. In fact they would eventually and rather immodestly refer to each other as Byron and Shelley in a private joke.

Chris and his wife Pearl, and Michael and Michele became inseparable. Chris called him Mick and found him to be very happy with fame and his position as the international pop star but saw that this was by no means his only dimension. Michael had never before been on the road with someone he had so much in common with, they were both gregarious yet loved the classics. Fuelled by alcohol, the two men talked all night about the great philosophers. Michael was impressed by Chris's vocabulary and intellect and felt challenged to prove himself an equal. Chris Bailey truly wanted nothing more from Michael other than his friendship. The fact that they never discussed business, and very rarely did they even speak of music tells it all. Chris would become the friend he would seek when he wanted to step out of the fame bubble. Chris observed, 'Rock and roll is a mean business, and Mick was not a mean person.'

In 1987 INXS recorded *Kick*, which was to become their most successful album – indeed, one of the most successful albums of the decade. You wouldn't have guessed it at the outset of recording though, with band members musically unprepared which was unusual for INXS. They had been a tight band and were in the habit of working well together in the studio. Michael and Andrew had never made a habit of always sitting down to write together, but by the time they got to *Kick*, their personal lives diverged so much that they were now writing on separate continents and sending material to one another. Michael tended to write down ideas and phrases all of the time and only when it came to the crunch would he put it all together. He constantly wrote on scraps of paper and on the backs of envelopes. Sometimes Andrew presented Michael with twenty-five tapes to listen to. Michael would pull out his pieces of paper and start fitting the lyrics to the music. They began recording *Kick* at the Rhinoceros studios in Sydney with Chris Thomas at the helm and, almost immediately, he realized that they lacked enough material to complete a whole album. He sent Michael and Andrew away to write and one of the gems from this collaboration was 'Need You Tonight'. They put the finishing touches to the vocals in Paris and final mix in London with Bob Clearmountain. It was released in October and became an immediate success due in part to the band's constant touring and MTV following.

While Michael was in Europe completing *Kick* he called Michele asking her to drop everything and take a vacation in Greece. Michele, who was producing music videos by that time, could not break away. In fact they had already mutually split as a couple partly due to Michael's reservations about Michele's determination to carve out her own career. He simply would not take her desire to work seriously. During this call she told Michael that he should take the time to be alone, get into his own head. She suggested that he extend himself, to go somewhere alone, to a destination other than a resort so that he could do the thing he loved best: read and explore philosophy. She could not be talked around but he did go to a Greek island alone. It was disastrous: Michael was hopeless by himself, somehow he'd never acquired the resources to be contented alone. About a week later he angrily called Michele to tell her that he had taken her advice, and along the way had rented a bike and had an accident. And by the way, he was having a miserable time. This churlish, childish outburst was presumably aimed at making her feel guilty enough to come and rescue him, but she couldn't or wouldn't. This all sounds petulant and selfish, but to be fair Michael was twenty-seven years old and he had been surrounded by five constant companions (the band members), management, roadies, and fans for most of his adult life. He wanted time off, but after travelling with others for so long, he had trouble being by himself. He was looking for someone who would just be with him on a constant basis for a while.

When in Sydney Michael lived within walking distance of the make-up academy and often used to call in and take me around the corner to a little coffee shop. I recall the day he came to tell me that he and Michele had decided to split up. He just popped in and asked me to come for coffee. I was in the middle of a class and I had my assistant take over as he looked very upset. When we sat down he told me that it was mostly his fault as he had spent too much time away from Michele. His career was keeping him overseas more and more and Michele was just beginning her career in Australia. She had some strong views on making it on her own. He was on his way to the gym and asked me if I thought he looked very healthy, adding that he was taking good care of himself. I said he looked very healthy, but not very happy. He said he was concerned about the situation with Michele as he loved her very much. We finished our coffee and he walked me back to the Academy, we hugged and said goodbye again, as he was leaving for another tour. I watched him walk away looking so lonely and somehow had a feeling that he and Michele would never, ever break off their relationship. I was right, they never did. Until the day Michael died, he loved her.

I answered the phone at my house in Sydney. It was Michael calling from Hong Kong.

'Hey Big Sis, what's the story!'

'Hi Babe, good to hear your voice. When will you be here?'

'Well, I don't have a definite date yet, but I'll let you know. I'm not arriving much before December first. Tina, I have someone with me.'

'A woman?'

He laughed that laugh he had when he had been smoking and pushing his voice to the limit. 'Yes, someone special.'

I was disappointed, because I was still hoping that things could somehow mend between him and Michele. I had always loved Michele and assumed that she and Michael would eventually marry. However, by the time we finished the conversation I was pleased for him because he sounded so positive, which suggested that whoever this person was, she had the capacity to make him happy.

'What's her name? Tell me about her.'

'Ummm. Well, you'll like her.'

'Well, tell me more . . .'

'Ummm. Well, you know, first of all her name is Jonnie.'

'And Jonnie is short for?'

'It isn't short for anything. She's American and her real name is Tina. Her parents are amazing people, she spent most of her childhood on a commune. Her best friend is Rosanna Arquette whose family also lived on the commune, and they both changed their names to Rosanna. But I call her Jonnie.'

'Well that explains everything.'

'She has small, delicate features, with large, sad eyes. Actually I see her as a modern day Audrey Hepburn. She's a model. She doesn't seem to like modelling,' he continued, 'I've been trying to encourage her to take more work, she's up for a big contract right now, though, I think she prefers to use her brainpower.'

This was a bit ironic, given the reasons for his split with Michele, but I was keen to meet this Jonnie. 'You must bring her out for Christmas. Is she there, can I speak with her?'

A soft, nervous, voice came on the phone. 'Hello Tina? Michael has told me so much about you, I feel I know you.' She won me over right away. That conversation was the beginning of a friendship, which endures to this day. I invited Jonnie to come out to Australia with us for Christmas during that conversation and she did make it, the following year. Jonnie and I have been amused over the years when she has been described as two different women – Rosanna and Jonnie – but always as a tall, leggy, long-haired, blonde beauty. Though a beautiful Christie Turlington lookalike, in reality she is of average height and has always worn short to medium length hair, and is a brunette.

She had actually met Michael briefly while she was modelling in Japan with Michele. Michele told her about her boyfriend who was in a rock band and she played his music constantly. INXS came through Japan while the two young women were working together. Michele invited Jonnie to join them for a drink and to meet the band. It was a very casual meeting and there were no sparks between Michael and Jonnie – after all, he was with Michele. Michael did something, however, that impressed her enough to tell a friend. There was an Australian girl at the club, a fan who recognized Michael. She approached him and flirted overtly, in front of Michele. Michael was trying to be polite and friendly as always with fans but when the girl became insistent, Michael took her in his arms and dipped her – all the way to the floor – and dropped her. He walked away, leaving the girl on the carpet. This demonstrated to Jonnie that Michael respected Michele and their relationship.

A year or two later Jonnie was staying in Laguna Beach, California, when she had a dream. It was so strange and slightly disturbing that she noted it in her diary. In the dream she was in Paris, walking along a familiar street with some other people when they came across a man whose face she could not make out. Someone in her party said, 'I want you to meet Michael.' She awoke wondering who this 'Michael' was. That very day, she had a call from her friend Rosanna Arquette, who had been invited to the Cannes Film Festival and had the opportunity to take a guest. The two Rosannas were on a flight within the week.

That year, 1987, Wim Wenders' *Wings of Desire* was the hot property. The tiny, blasé town of Cannes is unrestrained during the annual May Film Festival. Hotel space is at a premium, and people walk the streets day and night, all hoping to be noticed. Michael was strolling down the main concourse with his friend, Michael Hamlyn, who would later produce *Priscilla, Queen of the Desert*. This was before Michael bought his own villa in the South of France and he was a guest of the Hamlyns. He was there for no other reason but to take in the ambience of the Film Festival. As he and his friend made their way through the streets, taking in the spectacle, they ran into the Rosannas. So the two Rosannas met up with the two Michaels. Jonnie enquired about Michele Bennett and Michael was quick to tell her that he was no longer seeing her, although the friendship was intact. That evening she dined at the Hamlyn place, and spent her first night with Michael. She recalls that the *Hotel California* album played over and over and Michael asked her to 'please stay', as if he did not want to be alone. She was not comfortable with him that night, recalling that, even though they had shared a thoroughly amusing evening, he retired sad and angry at nothing in particular. He just seemed to have this angry aura about him, 'a darkness', she said.

In speaking with other women my brother dated over the years, I was surprised to hear this same description of Michael, in particular when speaking of their first evening with him. I have given much thought to this and have come to the conclusion that Michael was showing signs of depression all along and hid it from his family. A mysterious, brooding persona can of course be irresistible to women, and they just accepted it as part of the artist within. The following day Jonnie returned to the hotel where she was sharing a room with Rosanna Arquette. After three days they returned to Paris where Rosanna A was meeting her boyfriend Peter Gabriel. Jonnie was disappointed that Michael had not called but she would soon find out that he had in fact tried many times to contact her during those last three days in Cannes. The hotel rooms in Cannes and Paris were under Rosanna Arquette's name and each time Michael called to leave a message for Rosanna, Rosanna Arquette did not respond, dismissing perhaps rather thoughtlessly this 'Michael' who was leaving odd telephone numbers for her to call back. But by chance Michael and Jonnie ran into each other in Paris where he was recording the vocals for the *Kick* album. He was staying at the St James and since the Rosannas were not thrilled with their accommodation, they moved over to that hotel as well.

After ten days in Paris, Michael was due in New York for a meeting with Nick Egan on the album cover design for *Kick*. Nick was a good friend of Michele and since she and Michael had not been apart for very long, he did not want her to hear he was already seeing Jonnie. Theirs had been such a long, close relationship, he did not want to hurt her and he thought that she might assume that he had been seeing Jonnie all along. To protect this new relationship, he introduced Rosanna as 'Jonnie', pulling the name out of the air. The cover-up did not last very long as someone recognized her from a Ford Model Agency card and the word did get back to Michele. The false name endured, however, and my family still refers to Rosanna as Jonnie.

She returned to Los Angeles and Michael flew back to Australia and kept calling during their separation. Jonnie still has tapes from this period: 'Michael here, where are you?'

Back in Australia on a tour of Queensland, Michael read that the Premier, Sir Joh Bjelke-Petersen, had ordered authorities to remove condom vending machines from universities. Sir Joh was also vehemently anti-abortion and had even suggested that bar owners refuse alcohol to homosexuals. Michael was incensed and decided to speak out against Sir Joh's offensive and antiquated ideas at his next concert. Not only did he speak his mind, he threw condoms out into the crowd. This in itself was not illegal but Michael used obscenities to describe his thoughts on Sir Joh. As a result, the next concert, in Darwin, was thick with police and charges were sought against Michael the following day. However, he had left the country by then on his way to a vacation spot before preparing the tour. By the time he returned to Queensland fifteen months later, his attorneys had resolved everything. One advantage at least, I suppose, of being a rock superstar . . .

Michael was only in Australia for a short time before leaving for

New York. Immediately after he left Sydney I had a call from Sam Evans, Chris Murphy's assistant at MMA. She wanted to know if she could give Michael's contact number to Australian actress, Virginia Hey. I was surprised that Sam was even asking me as Michael could certainly take care of himself when it came to beautiful women. I was familiar with Miss Hey's work, as she had been featured in the *Mad Max* movie for which Jeff had edited the sound. She had been a guest at a party Michael had hosted on his trip to Sydney. I remembered her as being an exceptionally tall, sophisticated beauty, with a wickedly intellectual but naughty way with words. I figured he could handle her phone call, so I told Sam to go ahead and give Virginia his contact numbers. According to Michael, this led to a brief, intense affair. Michael was actually besotted by Virginia. So enchanted was he that he spoke of fathering a child with her. He said he wanted to live with her and settle down. But although Virginia's qualities would have been more than enough for most men, Michael remained insecure and somehow needed to continue to give in to temptations elsewhere. On one level he was preparing to make a commitment to one woman but in fact he just wasn't ready.

He told a story of his last day with Virginia. He said that he had an interview with Paula Yates, whom he had met briefly on an English television show, *The Tube*, in 1984. Michael left Virginia in their New York hotel room while he met with Paula two floors below. When he returned much later, Virginia was sitting on the bed, sewing up his shirts. Well, that's one version. In her autobiography, Paula has another, in which she claims Virginia was sitting in the dark with a pair of scissors, and threatened to kill Michael, herself and Paula. Virginia says that when Michael returned to their hotel room two hours late, dishevelled and with lipstick on his clothing, she was just sitting on the bed watching TV. She said that he had been making excuses before she had even accused him of anything, and appeared as if he had been wrestling with a 'gorilla in lipstick'. I tend to believe Virginia's version.

When Paula's interview appeared in the London magazine *Time Out* some months later the highlights to our family were some entertaining lines from Michael:

> *I'd like a baby, but not just one woman. Maybe five women. I guess you'd have to have some kind of arrangement; I love girls in*

Chanel; I like Australians, they're straightforward, dry, laconic . . . we're so lucky to have a country at such a raw stage . . . my father is an importer and exporter, who lived in China. He's a firm believer in China, a capitalist pig. He went back to Oz and went bankrupt a couple of million times so the dynasty's had its ups and downs . . .

There were some provocative observations from Paula too. Noting that Michael resembled 'the logical conclusion of thirty years of pop star attitude', she describes him variously as dangerous, appealing, shy and sensitive. It is an altogether flattering piece, written with her usual wit. Michael told Paula in the interview that he would like to be in films, and that he was brought up on film sets and always wanted to be an actor. Paula said that when she returned home from this interview, she placed a photograph of Michael on her refrigerator surrounded, depending on which account you have heard, by either fairy lights or wishbones. Bob would occasionally pass by and scrawl something on the picture and she would replace it with a new one.

Virginia says that she expressed absolutely no rage. She is an intelligent, secure and articulate woman. She wrote Michael a letter in response to his betrayal and it hit him so deeply that he never discarded it. Virginia bravely said to Michael the things that most women would like to say to a man whom they had caught in a lie, accusing him of being a 'self-indulgent, irresponsible, careless, insincere, spoilt brat'. Bravo from women everywhere!

Michael did not like confrontation of any kind and faced with a stress-overload he reacted like a cornered child and fled back into the arms of Jonnie. By the time the short romance with Virginia was over, Jonnie was in Japan and without notice Michael appeared at her hotel. It was such a snap decision that he landed without a visa. The authorities gave him only three days in the country. Three days to convince Jonnie to move to Hong Kong with him. He did just that, and they spent the next two years together. Apart from Michele, Jonnie is the only woman who shared his life on a constant basis, including going on tour with him. They spent no more than two nights apart over two years.

I guess there must be some significance in the fact that I became friends with most of Michael's most important women, have been able to speak to many of them since his death and remain closest of all to Jonnie and Michele – the two who may have loved Michael best.

Jonnie was surprised to see his humble little sixth-floor walk-up flat in the middle of the noisy, overflowing city on Victoria Island. He shared the small apartment with Jon Farriss. She was impressed that he should live such a simple life away from the spotlight. Life in Hong Kong was an adventure every day. Michael was very proud of the city of his childhood. He delighted in guiding Jonnie towards appreciation for the Asian culture, the sounds, smells and sights. She accompanied him several times to an office in the Central District, occupied by his financial adviser, international tax consultant, Gordon Fisher. From this office, Fisher, a Scotsman, and his associates – another Scot called Andrew Paul and a Queensland barrister, Colin Diamond – had set up corporations which operated trust funds for a number of clients, including Michael and Jon Farriss.

From the beginning, Michael did not have the time, indeed did not want to take the time, for the business side of his work. Although he believed in investing for the future, he just wanted to concentrate on creating music. He also wanted to paint, to act.

After several months, Jon Farriss expressed his wish for a larger place and they all agreed to move to a rented house in the exclusive Stanley district. As a child, Michael had lived in Stanley, in that house which looked out over a cliff to the China Sea. The house that he moved to with Jonnie and Jon sat on a bluff, the porch covered in bougainvillaea and with a magnificent view of the tiny islands surrounding Stanley. Jonnie and Michael made this their home base. But they travelled often, soon going on the road for the *Kick* album. This world tour, billed as the 'Calling All Nations Tour', would take them through Europe, the United Kingdom, Canada, the United States, South America, Asia, Australia, and would last eighteen months. Jonnie gladly gave up her modelling career and rapidly learned to take care of Michael on tour. Her focus was always on his comfort, his health, his moods. She made herself unpopular at times, but it was all for Michael's well-being. She made a habit of standing at the back of a venue when the band did their sound check to make sure Michael's voice was being pumped up above the music. She would complain to the sound crew, who, at first exasperated, came around to seeing that she was simply trying to elevate the entire performance.

During this tour, Michael began distancing himself from the other band members, often travelling separately and only showing up for sound checks and shows. He rarely socialized with the rest of the band, preferring to be with Jonnie. Band meetings were kept to a minimum and Michael, always eager to please, often gave in to consensus, but came away frustrated and angry as he felt that he was carrying more of the load than the others. There was press in every city and it was natural for them to request an interview with flamboyant front-man Michael. It's hard to do the same thing night after night, month after month. He wanted to keep the shows fresh and he came up with ideas, but the rest of the band did not want to change anything.

1988 was another extraordinary year for INXS. After ten years of constant work they were harvesting their fruits. In March they played three sold-out nights at Radio City Music Hall in New York City. *Kick* hit gold and platinum in Australia along with *The Swing*; *Shabooh Shoobah* also went gold, *Listen Like Thieves* platinum. *Kick* passed the quadruple-platinum mark in the US and they had their first number one US single with 'Need You Tonight', helped greatly by Richard Lowenstein's video. By May 'Devil Inside' and 'New Sensation' also made it into the top five in the US charts. Accolades in the United States alone were impressive. In September they swept the MTV Music Video Awards with the clip 'Need You Tonight/Mediate'. It won in five categories: Best Video, Best Group Video, Best Editing, Breakthrough Video, and the one that really counts, Viewers' Choice.

If not handled correctly, a tour becomes one's whole focus. Every show is important but it is exhausting to be surrounded by people and activity all the time. The outside world seems not to exist because life is a collage of planes, hotel rooms, limousines, venues, restaurants and adoring fans. It is an unreal existence where you can become worn out yet are cut off from the family and friends who could help put things in perspective. The days leading up to and beyond *Kick* were especially frenzied, a time when Michael needed someone who could be constantly on his side. I will always be so grateful that he spent that time with a caring confidante like Jonnie. She never asked anything from Michael. Not recognition, nor help with her career. Raised in a culture which embraces harmony and tranquillity, she follows yoga and disciplined diet and tried her best to pass this on to Michael. I have never seen him so physically fit as he was in those two years, although they were actually the toughest touring years of his life.

While INXS were touring California with *Kick*, Brent and his friend Milan accompanied the band back to their hotel after the show and they partied on. Brent and Milan were still in high school and had classes the next day. They were having such a good time with Michael and Jon Farriss who had a skateboard and was riding up and down the corridors, that they forgot the time. By 6 a.m. they realized that they had a class at seven, so Jonnie and Michael packed them off to school with a care package from the party. When they arrived in front of the school, they found healthy sandwiches, fruit, chocolate milk and Corona beers in their bags.

When INXS was in concert there were many requests for 'will call' and backstage passes. Jonnie tried to weed out the friends and family from those who were not, calling to make sure the right people had tickets. Michael told her that in the past, people had their feelings hurt when this was not taken care of. She made up the lists and after the concert if anybody was missing backstage, she would go out to find them. She knew that the unhappy party would forever hold it against Michael, even though he had nothing to do with it. She was the only one of Michael's partners who was mindful of such things.

On one such occasion after a concert in Birmingham, England, she remembers the offended party was Paula Yates who arrived with friends and no backstage passes. Jonnie obligingly took them back when she complained to security. The Australian band Big Pig was supporting INXS on the European part of the tour and Michael's friend Sherine Abeyratne, the very curvy lead singer with Big Pig, who had also sung with him on 'Burn For You', was standing next to him, deep in conversation when Paula arrived backstage. Sherine says that most people were surprised when she walked in, because you would have expected her to be at the Wembley concert with Bob Geldof, not the Birmingham show with girlfriends. She remembers Paula walking directly up to Michael without even noticing that the two of them were speaking and that after he introduced them she may as well not have been there. In all her years touring with bands, Sherine had never before witnessed such aggressive 'come-on' lines from a woman to a man. She says that even the most zealous groupies don't usually attack their prey that hard and fast. After only a few minutes of this, Sherine remained next to Michael but shifted her attention to another conversation to her right, which included Jonnie. It was a noisy, crowded room so only she could catch both conversations. Every now and then she would look at Michael out of the corner of her eye. Finally Michael turned from Paula and grabbing Sherine's arm, he whispered in her ear, 'Get me out of here, this woman's a full-on predator.'

Bob Geldof's memoir *Is That It?*, published in 1987 and written during happier times where his relationship with Paula was concerned, recalled with affectionate humour her dogged pursuit of him when he was hugely successful as the singer with the Boomtown Rats. He referred to Paula as 'the limpet'. She was clearly not to be distracted from her goal then – or now.

Paula Yates actually loomed large even during the time that Michael was with Jonnie on the *Kick* tour. Jonnie can remember being in their hotel suite in Paris when a call came through. Dismissing Jonnie, who picked up, Paula insisted on speaking to Michael. Obviously Jonnie could only hear one side of the conversation. She heard Michael ask, 'Why would you do that? I'm with Jonnie, why would you bring Fifi?' Slamming the phone down hard enough for it to jump off the hook, Michael told Jonnie that Paula had told him she was leaving Bob. Certain that he would be pleased to see her, she planned to meet Michael in Paris. She said that she was packing a bag and bringing her daughter Fifi with her. He tried to humour her when she suggested that he tell Jonnie to leave. This was not the first of such calls. In the past, moreover, she had even arrived in the hotel lobby and using the house phone, called up and refused to leave until Michael came down to see her. While he dressed, he would curse and wonder out loud what could be wrong with this woman. He would tell Jonnie he was meeting Paula at the bar, and an hour later – sometimes two – he would return. He would tell Jonnie that they just talked about Paula's marriage. Jonnie recalls that the phone calls from London were regular: whether they were in some place in middle America or South America, Paula found them.

Midway through the *Kick* triumphs Michael found that he could get away with anything. He distanced himself from the other band members and often voiced resentment of Chris Murphy who was no longer a hands-on manager. Rather than truly looking out for him, the roadies and the rest of the crew let Michael think whatever he did or said was OK. After all, he kept that down-to-earth way about him even as he experienced the excesses. As long as he could fall back into that 'Australian slang speak' he did so well everybody believed that he still had two left feet on the ground. When, in fact, he was pushing all of his senses to the limit. It took all of Jonnie's strength and attention to keep him focused.

U2 had two of their videos nominated against INXS in the 1988 MTV awards – 'Where the Streets Have No Name' and 'I Still Haven't Found What I'm Looking For', and INXS won for 'Need You Tonight/ Mediate'. In the course of this, Michael and Bono became friends – they respected each other's talent and integrity – after being introduced by Michael Hamlyn, who was nominated for both U2 videos. But it was INXS who left the LA ceremony with seven major awards, prompting host Arsenio Hall to remark, 'Is that band fresh or what?'

The evening of the awards ceremony itself was not a happy one for Michael, however, despite INXS sweeping the board. It began on a low when the limousine arrived and Rhett announced he was not ready, and brought the mood down by fretting about his appearance and complaining to Michael about it. He was in a bad mood because he wanted to invite some friends but it was not like a concert where Michael could arrange for extra people to go along. You actually had to have a ticket. As with most major awards ceremonies, it was televised and nominees had to be in their seats by a certain time. Beforehand Michael was in a room full of people, including Richard Lowenstein who had come over from Australia – it was his creative and directorial work that had secured several of the award nominations. Rhett was delaying their departure. Things did not improve after the show. Despite discouragement Rhett had invited friends and Michael was placed in the position of having to explain why he was arriving at the 'after' parties with extra people. Michael and Jonnie had a disagreement when he insisted on staying out too long at the parties and looking for cocaine. At one stage she got out of the limousine and began walking back to the Four Seasons hotel. Michael attempted to walk with her, finally coaxing her back into the car. When they returned to the hotel and friends departed Michael became depressed. He could not give any specific reasons, just said that his life was not worth living. Jonnie had seen his mood go up and down all evening. She tried to reason with him and he seemed to calm down, but he was pacing the room when suddenly without warning he rushed for the French doors to the balcony and threw one leg over the railing. Jonnie was frantic as she ran after him, grabbing his other leg. He was in despair, sobbing by now, and it took all of her strength to speak rationally to him to restore some sanity. After they were both exhausted, she was able to coax him back into the suite.

Speaking with her today, she only remembers his moods that night and cannot recall anything specific that he was unhappy about. He simply seemed generally discontented with his whole life. Finally, by the time the sun was up, she had soothed him to sleep. Until now she has never discussed this incident with anyone. As before where Michael's indulgences and delicate state of mind were concerned, not only did it get brushed under the carpet but by the time he awoke in the afternoon he seemed restored to the happy, witty, charming Michael that he knew most people expected him to be.

But Michael was finding some time to enjoy the rewards of his labour and success. While in Los Angeles he purchased a picture by Alberto Vargas, famous for his super-fantasy-glamour 'Vargas Girl' pin-ups of the 1940s. He also paid a handsome sum for a handwritten poem by John Lennon. As with many of Michael's lovingly chosen keepsakes and pieces of art, he would never get to enjoy them. Without a permanent address, he had them both put into storage, this time in Los Angeles.

In October 1988, with his father in financial difficulty, Michael handed over a deposit for US$250,000 and signed a letter of credit with the Standard Chartered Bank of Hong Kong for facilities to house Kelman Industries Limited, Kell's office. That Christmas, 1988, INXS was coming off the road from the *Kick* tour, and looked forward to being with their families. Michael and Jonnie would be in Sydney. I was having a friend out from California, a record producer I had met on a trip back to Los Angeles. An attractive man, he had called me often since I arrived back in Sydney. I had no reason to believe he was interested in anything other than a closer relationship with me. He called me to say that INXS was playing San Diego before heading back to Sydney so I arranged for some tickets and backstage passes for him. He was apparently there in San Diego just as Michael made his stage entrance, and yelled out to him, 'Tina sends her love'. Michael turned back over the noise of the crowd, smiled, waved, and thanked him. This man called after the concert, thanking me for the tickets and mentioned he would be alone for the holidays so I invited him to Australia.

Christmas dinner was going to be at a little place Mother had found for Michael and Jonnie in Sydney. We arrived late with the Aussie baked vegetables Michael had requested, and so as it turned out actually missed all the excitement. As I pulled up I saw several firemen walking out the front door and getting into an enormous fire truck. Apparently the dishwasher in the rented townhouse had not been used at all in the week they had been there – they had eaten out most of the time. Tidying up before everyone arrived, Jonnie had filled it up and flipped the 'on' switch. Within minutes it had begun to smoke. She called the fire department when she actually spotted flames licking from inside the dishwasher! A team of big, capable Aussie firemen soon arrived at the front door and Jonnie waved them to follow her through into the kitchen. So taken were they by the sight of the fabulously toned and olive-skinned Jonnie in her tiny red mini dress bending over the dishwasher, that they almost missed the culprit: a wooden spoon lodged in the water-filling mechanism. They only spotted Michael, who had been looking on in amusement, as they were leaving.

It was a long day but another good Christmas. Although Kell was in Hong Kong with his new wife Sue, Mother was there, along with Rhett and several people from the Australian music industry. I thought it was my imagination when my new friend seemed more interested in Michael's plans for the future than in our dinner together, but I put it out of my mind. That Christmas I gave Michael a rhyming dictionary amongst other things, as I thought that it would be a tool for his trade. Michael and Jonnie gave me a wonderful picnic basket filled with fine china and silverware. Jonnie gave Michael an easel and art supplies after all his references to taking up painting. They gave Mother superb tickets for a Sinatra concert. Mother had a magnificent pin made for Michael. It was approximately four inches in length, and featured a beautifully carved Asian face, surrounded in gems. He wore this on several award shows, carefully placed there on his tie where Mother could see it on TV. Jonnie loved the pin so much that Michael left it with her when they parted. Three months after Michael's death, Jonnie gave it back to Mother in a typically unselfish gesture.

There was a party on New Year's Eve, at Michael and Jonnie's. The plan was to continue on to the Sydney Show Grounds where there was a huge party, featuring a live performance by Grace Jones. We took off in a caravan of cars, stopping in on a party at Jon Farriss's house on the way. We were a pretty happy group. Michael had about six VIP passes but there were possibly nine of us. It was a sell-out show. He tried to talk us all in but the gatekeepers were having none of it. There is no such thing as a star system in Australia, they don't care who you are – and actually, Michael liked that. My date took someone aside and whatever he said worked. Michael did see the humour in that, making a joke about the irrelevance of his fame and its potential to generate tax revenue for Australia, which of course he did, but not to the extent that they would like, since his home was out of the country.

We were directed to a VIP room, which looked down on the stage. Way past the time for the show to begin Michael was asked into the manager's private office. Later we heard that Ms Jones had refused to go on, unless she could have her money up front, in cash, and this wasn't available. At the request of the promoter, Michael went in and talked to Ms Jones, not without making some comment about not even being able to talk the ticket taker into letting him bring some friends in. Whatever Michael said, it worked and soon after, Ms Jones appeared on stage. Everybody was so wasted by this time, it could have been Mary Poppins up there. My friend the record producer was spending most of his time at the bar talking to some girls, while I was chatting with Chris and Pearl Bailey. Michele was there also – this was the first time she had met Michael and Jonnie as a couple. She was dignified and friendly and dateless. I was impressed, and so was Michael.

Next morning, I was awakened by the phone. It was a girl asking for the visitor – apparently he had written my number on her napkin. I threw the phone at him. Not thirty minutes later, there was another girl on my phone. He was in the shower so I asked her some questions. She said that he had told her that he was staying with the Hutchence family. I told her this was not the residence of the 'Hutchence family' and hung up. By the time he was out of the bathroom I had packed most of his belongings and ordered him a taxi for the airport. I really questioned myself after this incident and I closed the lock on relationships once again. Michael always asked why I stayed by myself, how I could survive without a mate as he had trouble being alone. For me it has been easier that way. Many times Rhett has said that it wasn't always easy being Michael's brother. For me this was the hard part of life: I always questioned myself and my friendships. I found it hard to trust.

A day or two after that incident, I went to my mailbox and found two soggy letters for the visitor. They were from two different girls. One of them was half opened, with polaroids of a girl in a negligee falling out. 'Hope you're having fun with the Hutchence family, I miss you' was the inscription. My mother had a brilliant idea. She suggested I send them back to the girls but first, I should exchange the envelopes. Los Angeles must have been unseasonably chilly for that man for a couple of months.

Michael used to say that Jonnie was amazing, that she could not be mean to anybody. While she was with him, she protected him from people who took advantage of his generosity. At restaurants, Michael would automatically pick up the bill; I saw Jonnie putting a stop to this many times. He was too soft-hearted to say anything when the bill was placed in front of him so Jonnie would simply pick it up, do a quick calculation and announce a figure for each person to throw down. Some people resented her for this, but she had his best interests at heart and he was actually grateful to her for taking the pressure off of him. During this time when it was no secret that he was making incredible royalty money, friends often asked for loans and it was hard for him to refuse. She took care of all the potential unpleasantness when this happened and took the brunt of criticism by being the one to say 'no' when the hangers-on and the sharks moved in.

The first time I saw Kylie Minogue in the same room as Michael was at a club where a party was being held after the last show of the *Kick* tour. I was surprised to see her there with Jason Donovan. Not that there were no other celebrities around but wholesome Jason and Kylie just looked so out of place amidst the heavy rock and rollers. At the time Erin was a diehard fan of *Neighbours* so I asked Michael to introduce me so that I wouldn't feel stupid about asking for an autograph for Erin. He replied that he did not really know them and that I should just introduce myself. Michael was completely out of touch with that aspect of who he was and who I wasn't. Some people treated me differently when he was not around and when he was not at my side many people did not recognize me even if I had met them a dozen times.

I had never asked for an autograph before but I would be a heroine with my daughter if I braved it to get this one. The music was deafening as I approached Kylie and Jason so it was not until I was right in their faces, that I realized they were having an argument. Too late, they were glaring at me. I charged ahead and introduced myself as Michael's sister and gabbled that my daughter was a fan and could I have their autographs? I figured they should be flattered, with all of the other noteworthy people in the room. Jason obliged first, snatching the paper and pen out of my hands, then handing it to Kylie. She scribbled something without looking at the paper and glared again as she shoved it back. I thanked them and walked away, wishing the floor would open up and swallow me. I vowed never to approach people without Michael again. But I was a special Mom the next morning when I produced the autographs for Erin.

That *Kick* party was actually a lot of fun. Jonnie came by and said they were congregating downstairs to go back to their suite at the Hyatt Regency. As we walked out past the dance floor, Kylie was dancing with Jon Farriss's girlfriend. Michael didn't seem to notice and shuffled me out into his limo. We were a small group in his hotel suite, and every time someone got up to leave, Michael would try to stop them. It was as if he did not want the tour to end. I can only imagine that at the end of sixteen hard months on the road he must have been feeling lost without an itinerary to tell him where he was headed the next day.

Unlike the rest of the band, Michael only took a short break before throwing himself into *Max Q*, a solo venture with Ollie Olsen. Actually, Michael never thought of it as a solo album, because it was a collaboration with Ollie and six underground musicians. They began recording at the Rhinoceros Studios in Sydney and when Michael was due in Los Angeles to present a Grammy Award to Tina Turner, he took Ollie with him. Ollie, Jonnie and Michael stopped off in Tahiti for a vacation on the way and true to form Michael arrived without a visa, but was able to talk his way through immigration. For the short break in California which followed, Michael and Jonnie rented a house in Malibu while he and Ollie continued work on the *Max Q* project. Jonnie had a friend, Richard, who was very knowledgeable about guitars. He had a knack for finding just the right instrument to suit the person and the purpose. Even though he didn't play all that well, Michael wanted to purchase a specific guitar and Richard came up with a beautiful cherry-red, thin-line, hollow-body Al Kiola which I am told is a beautiful piece of equipment and Michael finally learned to play the guitar better. During this collaboration, Michael referred to Ollie as 'a mad musical genius'. They were an odd couple and the ambience at the studio was always interesting: Michael with his friendly, engaging, extroverted manner and Ollie who was so caught up in his underground music, barely noticing if someone new walked in the door. They continued to work on rough demos for the album in Los Angeles and returned to complete the project in Australia. Michael felt such a sense of accomplishment while working on *Max Q* which, by the way, was named after Ollie's dog.

Later, in a *Spin* interview, Michael said of 'Ghost of the Year', a song written by Ollie:

> *I like the lyric, 'I'm counting on you to count my blessings/to count the fingers on my hand/That's the amount of time I've got/I'll always feel drowned.' Which is a very interesting way of putting it. You become this public property. Ollie's saying you're always counting on the public to deal the final blow. You know it's inevitable. And you have to love them for it in a way. You have to accept that that's the way it goes. Otherwise you'll spend the rest of your life talking about how you were an ex-pop star. Which I'm not interested in doing.*

Around this time Michael began complaining about Chris Murphy. He felt that he was holding him back from doing solo work. Getting free time to do the *Dogs in Space* project had been like negotiating with the United Nations. At first there would be a break in the tour and then Chris would negotiate more dates after committing to Richard Lowenstein. US *Rolling Stone* had wanted to feature Michael on the cover alone. Chris refused their request, saying that the other band members should have equal coverage. *Rolling Stone* chose to pass, which was disappointing for Michael. It seemed that Michael's status as a charismatic rock star was worrisome to management and his band mates. It is a narrow way of looking at things, because Michael's success could only strengthen INXS's popularity. Where would the Rolling Stones be without the tremendous following of Mick Jagger and Keith Richard? Often during this time, Michael would say that he was having his attorney go over his contract. Chris had set up offices in London and New York by the mid-eighties, and he hired Martha Troup to run the US office.

Martha eventually married Bill Leibowitz, the attorney who helped Chris negotiate the band's recording contracts. Michael felt that Chris was no longer working for the band and in particular in his best interest. Royalties had been split fairly evenly to avoid conflicts with other band members even though Michael privately felt that he was expected to work harder. He co-wrote the largest percentage of the material and thus received higher publishing royalties along with Andrew Farriss, but was expected to do most of the interviews while the other band members could take time out. Actually it was not all the fault of the other band members – most of the time the request was for Michael only. He had never before complained so bitterly as now.

Martha was introduced as Michael's personal manager. During those weeks in Sydney she was very nice to me, and she was falling over herself to take care of Michael. I think she genuinely cared about him. Shortly before *Max Q* was about to be released, I called Martha in New York and she expressed her frustration that Michael had not featured in the advance publicity. She thought it would have a much better chance if it stressed his involvement: after all it was coming on the heels of the highly successful *Kick* album, why not use his fame? I had to agree with her. I wondered if Michael might feel torn if such a situation arose; if he had success on his own it might discourage him from continuing with INXS. I thought this might be at the heart of the problem – certainly, Michael was discontented. I agreed to speak to him about it.

Of course I cared about the band and I had respect for Chris's major involvement, but Michael's welfare was my priority. Not long after this Chris cut ties with Martha, but the seed had been sown and Michael's friendship and respect for Martha deepened. I too felt that Martha had Michael's best interests at heart. Even though *Max Q* was not a commercial success and Ollie Olsen had written most of the music, Michael thought it was among his best achievements. He had displayed such joy and passion during the recording sessions, I think he felt it validated him as a musician. But I think not being in a position to publicize the album, capitalize on his name, feature on magazine covers and so on, really hurt Michael and the project. No amount of consoling and dissecting could cheer Michael up, and I shared his frustration. 'How are you supposed to sell albums if nobody knows who *Max Q* is?' I asked. Even the album cover was a put-off – a hodge-podge of different facial features belonging to everybody who had played on the album, made to look like one face. Even I knew that potential fans needed a strong image to identify with. But although Michael was disappointed that his fans did not embrace *Max Q*, he was encouraged when it did well critically, winning no fewer than three *Rolling Stone* Awards in 1989.

Rhett had become particularly unstable and drug dependent. He would call Michael for money and put a guilt trip on him. Michael had so much and he so little. Abusive calls would come from Rhett under the influence. Michael would literally throw the phone at Jonnie to handle the situation. This drove a wedge between Rhett and Jonnie, because she had to play the bad guy. She was a lover, personal assistant and peacemaker, given Michael's rather passive nature. He suggested that Jonnie arranged for Rhett to move to Los Angeles and stay with a friend of hers. Michael thought that Rhett just needed to be away from Sydney. He already knew some people in the independent production houses and with Jonnie's help Rhett began working on music videos and commercials in all facets of production. He was very good at it too – reliable and resourceful.

Whilst visiting Rhett in Los Angeles, Michael, who never learned his lesson with the automobile, again went looking again for the perfect car. He heard of a 1964 Aston Martin, which was being sold privately. He took Rhett to the showroom to try it out. Rhett was thrilled when Michael slid behind the wheel and took him for a spin. Arriving back at the showroom, Michael told the broker that he would take it. He and Jonnie returned shortly with US$150,000 cash. His friend Nick Egan came along and videoed the transaction for some reason. I guess it was a kind of ceremonial occasion which they wanted to record.

When Michael left Los Angeles from that trip he asked the dealer to have the car stored until he could decide where to have it shipped. It sat in storage for a long time before arriving in the South of France. Much later I spoke to the person who brokered this deal and he told me he was surprised when Michael paid in cash. It would seem that it was very trusting of Michael to hand that much cash to someone he did not know. It was not as though he could get much of a formal receipt for it, just the pink registration slip. In most instances a buyer would want more protection if ever there was a dispute over who legally owned the car.

Like many wealthy people, Michael was now making considerable efforts to lighten his tax burden. Houses, cars, properties, even businesses can be placed under trusts with company names. These companies are often set up in the British Virgin Islands, Cayman Islands or Liberia where the tax burden is low. Michael's name would still not be on them of course unless in a beneficiary capacity. Royalty cheques could also be paid into such a trust, by one means or another.

In the northern hemisphere spring of 1989, Jonnie accompanied Michael to Lake Como in Italy to film *Frankenstein Unbound* for Roger Corman. Michael had been thrilled about being offered the role of the poet Percy Bysshe Shelley, opposite Bridget Fonda's Mary Shelley. Jason Patric, John Hurt and Raul Julia were also cast. Michael and Jonnie made a friend in Jason Patric who would later use Michael's villa in the South of France to hide out with Julia Roberts when she broke her engagement to Keifer Sutherland. Michael and Jonnie spent an idyllic summer filming and exploring the countryside and Lake Como continued to be a favourite retreat for him. But despite everyone's hard work on the movie, it did not do well at the box office. Michael was disappointed but he learned that no matter how talented the actors, you couldn't be sure that a script would work once it got to the screen.

Filming completed, Michael took Jonnie on a Harley to the South of France and they visited Gordon Fisher across the border in Monaco. Jonnie remembers that Fisher worked such odd hours he sometimes nodded off during conversation. She was also aware that Michael was often worried about money, even during this time, with the obvious success of *Kick*.

CHAPTER SEVEN

Educating Kylie

Upon their return to New York from that meeting with Gordon Fisher, Michael, without warning, walked out of the hotel one day, leaving his clothing and his American Express card. Forty-eight hours later he called Jonnie to say he was in Hong Kong and he was not coming back. He had left the credit card to ease his conscience. Once again, avoiding confrontation at all costs, Michael had taken flight, literally. Already out of her mind with worry and now devastated, Jonnie called a friend to help her check out of the hotel. She stayed with a girlfriend for a short time trying to deal with a broken heart and hoping Michael would call. He didn't, so she used the Amex to buy a ticket to Los Angeles where she hoped to rebuild her life. Jonnie went through a lot of pain and anguish, but nobody ever stayed angry with Michael for long and within weeks they had sorted things out and remained friends until his death.

I never knew Michael to be without a special woman in his life. In the past when relationships were looking a bit out of kilter, I too begged him to take some time on his own but he could never do this. Like many other performers, he needed people around him all of the time. Michael especially craved the company of women. He was a true romantic and loved to play the role of man-in-love. It wasn't long before we knew of his new romantic solace.

INXS was due to be back in the Rhinoceros Studios to work on the *X* album in late 1989. I was hearing rumours that Michael was seeing Kylie Minogue but I dismissed them immediately. Kylie was a huge TV star both in Australia and the UK after the long success of the soap *Neighbours,* and was on the brink of a considerable recording career of her own. Nonetheless, her image was that of a pretty pixie who might not have the qualities of worldly and womanly sophistication that Michael had come to be attracted by. I thought wrong, for quite soon Michael called from Hong Kong and confirmed the story. But what had happened to Jonnie? He told me that he wanted her to 'fly, do her own thing'. He felt that she was always there for him but that she needed something of her own. He said that they were still friends, that he loved her, though he felt she needed some solitude. I thought, look who is talking! And I still couldn't quite believe it about Kylie: she was so uncool . . . My fickle daughter, who only a year ago had been thrilled with Miss Minogue's autograph, agreed when I told her the news. But Michael was smitten again.

'She's great, fantastic. She's so underrated. You'll love her.'

I thought, well, let's give her a chance, after all, this is Michael's choice and we need to get to know her. Arriving home three days later, on the afternoon of my birthday, there was a huge box of long-stemmed red roses at my door. The note inside was from Michael. It read, 'Happy, happy Birthday, may this be your brightest year. Love, Michael xxx'. When I checked my messages, Michael was on there, asking me to meet him for dinner and a movie. When he called back to make dinner plans he did not mention that Kylie would be with him but I had a feeling she would be. He liked approval. When I walked in I went over to the maître d' to ask about the table and before I could open my mouth, someone grabbed me around my waist from behind, then I was spun around and scooped up and spun around again. 'Hey Baby, lookin' good!' We kissed and hugged and over his shoulder I could see this little girl standing behind him and smiling. He put me down and introduced me. I did not mention that we had already briefly met. Kylie hugged me warmly and wished me happy birthday. This was unexpected and a nice start to the evening. I firmly decided to throw out all of my prejudices and opened my heart to her.

We went to the table, ordered and talked nonstop. I was careful not to bring up subjects that could make Kylie feel uncomfortable, but there were plenty of family things that had to be discussed. Michael spoke of Erin, he told Kylie proudly about her advanced taste in literature. Shortly after this dinner, Kylie appeared at the Sydney Hard Rock Café and was presented with one of their embroidered denim jackets. She gave it to Erin who, at age eleven, was not much smaller than Kylie at the time. Kylie has fantastically photogenic features, a 'child woman' face, certainly one of the most recognizable women in the world. When she excused herself to go to the bathroom during my birthday dinner a nearby table of Japanese businessmen stared after her and spoke animatedly. Michael said, 'Isn't she great? So down-to-earth, like the girl next door.' Well, yes, if the girl next door was used to being ogled all of the time. I genuinely liked Kylie but I still didn't get it. Michael was wearing a hat and shades, at least trying to be incognito. But here he was at a popular restaurant with a young woman who didn't even try to be anything other than 'Kylie'. It got worse at the theatre. We stood in line to buy the tickets and when Michael had to rush off to make a phone call, I was left standing with Kylie in the middle of a large lobby surrounded by about two hundred people, all staring in our direction.

Mostly thanks to attending Michael's gigs I've had shoes ripped off my feet, earrings torn from my lobes and hair pulled out of my scalp when running from backstage door to a waiting car. I am not fond of being in open areas with celebrities. I asked Kylie if we could find a quieter place to wait for him. Concerned that he would not find us, she did not want to budge. I finally coaxed her over to a corner and stood in front of her. This is not difficult. I'm slight, but Kylie really is petite. Finally, Michael returned and we went into the darkened theatre. We left just as the credits came up, and raced outside to the manager's office where we waited until all theatres were emptied and it was safe. We headed outside with Michael holding both our hands and laughing. As we stepped out of the main door and it slammed shut, a group of kids nearby recognized Kylie and then Michael. The chase was on. 'Run!' Michael yelled. And boy did we run. Up and down alleys and across streets looking for a cab. When we found one, and settled into the back seat laughing, I wondered aloud why I had been running, and we all laughed some more.

At the beginning of this romance, Michael and Kylie were careful not to be photographed as a couple. Apparently there was a big price tag for the first photograph of the two together. I will never understand the dichotomy. A person in their business begs to be noticed. When they begin to make waves they employ a publicist to keep their profile high. They willingly sign autographs at any time and are thrilled when someone acknowledges their work. When they make it big and don't have to pay to have their name in the press, they resent being recognized. I say make a deal with a photographer, pose for the pictures to get it out of the way, and split the reward. Surely with the mystique gone, harassment would end also? Even after the reported fifty-thousand-pound bounty was paid by a British newspaper for the first photograph of Michael with Kylie – a blurred thing captured through a telephoto lens – the press continued to hound them. People venturing into a fresh relationship can feel capricious, sceptical, and unsure, but add to this the pressure of being under a public microscope, comments made in the press and on the airwaves daily, and chances are that paranoia would be running high.

I had been working on writing a professional's make-up book and when I finished I went up to the Gold Coast in Queensland, where I had quite a few friends who had moved there for the beautiful weather. After a couple of weeks, I decided I liked it there and thought about opening another make-up academy. I talked this over with Tina and we decided this was a good plan. I returned to Sydney, packed up and moved to an apartment in Paradise Waters, and set about finding the right premises to occupy. This did not take too long and once again I was running another academy in Surfers Paradise, too.

One day I had a call from Michael asking if he could spend a few days with me. I was so happy as we did not get to see each other too often. This meant we could spend some quality time together and catch up on the past months. I had heard that he was seeing Kylie Minogue and like Tina originally I dismissed this as rumour until she called and said she had been out the night before with Kylie and Michael. I found it difficult to believe as it seemed an unlikely pairing. Young Australians have grown up with Kylie. She and Jason Donovan had been an item both on and off television, and in fact were recently married on their show. Michael and Kylie an item? I don't think so! Michael arrived at my home only long enough for us to exchange a few words when the phone rang, it was a girl for Michael. I handed him the phone and walked away to make lunch and give him some privacy. Half an hour later he came out to the patio and we sat there for some time discussing family, his life and then it came out that he was now seeing Kylie. He told me that he had met up with her in Hong Kong. I was surprised as she seemed so young and so unsophisticated and he was so worldly. We had only just finished our lunch when the phone rang again – it was Kylie again. Another long conversation. After that call we went for a drive and took a walk around Marina Mirage and then had some coffee at a café. Unfortunately it was school holiday time and Michael was besieged by young fans, so there wasn't much time for more family chat. He signed a few autographs and then said, 'I can't handle this.' We went for another drive before going back home and as we entered the door, the phone was ringing. Again, it was Kylie. She was certainly persistent, and I felt somewhat agitated at this interruption of my private time with Michael, but I did not say anything as I thought Kylie must be feeling somewhat unsure of herself in this relationship, as young girls do. Kylie was very much protected by her family and I think her only relationship up until then had been with Jason. Michael stayed a few more days and there were many more phone calls, but we did find time to talk and it was so good to see him. He told me that he had been spending quite a bit more time in France.

The press had suggested that Michael was corrupting Kylie; the truth is more that he was educating her. Kylie was smart and listened and learned. He gave her confidence which enabled her to take better control of her career. I did not have too much to do with her but from my observation the more control she had the nicer she grew. I know how frustrated Michael became as the years went on and he felt he was losing control over his career and finances. It is ironic to think that as he was instilling so much confidence in Kylie he was beginning to lose control over his own personal affairs. When Michael and Kylie split up, she was devastated. But they were able to maintain a lasting friendship. Kylie has indeed turned into a beautiful girl, the total professional, and a huge international star.

By Christmas 1989 the Kylie relationship was still thriving. We spent Christmas Day at an apartment they had taken at the Connaught in Sydney. Brent was spending Christmas in California. Mother, her sister Maureen, Erin and I arrived at noon with Christmas dinner, to find Michael was still drunk from the previous night. In fact, we had to wake him. Kylie had flown to see her family in Melbourne, Rhett had stayed the night at the Connaught and was still also sleeping it off. Along with some friends, the brothers had been thrown out of the pool area due to some rowdiness. Rhett had been playing with a new Swiss army knife, which Michael had given him. There was a bit of an accident, and someone in their party had sustained a minor injury to his hand. It would be kind to say that the place was a mess, the maid not working over the holidays, and the activities of the previous night were much in evidence. Empty bottles, dirty dishes and loads of leftover boxes from food deliveries were scattered everywhere, even surrounding the tiny, sparsely decorated Christmas tree. Kylie had managed to prettify this a little before her departure to give the apartment at least a bit of Christmas cheer. Rented movies like *Breakfast at Tiffany's, Citizen Kane* and *Casablanca* were stacked high. Michael said that he had been amazed to find out that Kylie had not seen some of these classics.

Rhett's former girlfriend Lisa and her husband Billy Zane arrived along with others from the music industry. Lisa and I talked about life in Los Angeles and I commiserated with her on green card problems. I was getting homesick by this time and was planning to return to the United States. This Christmas there was nothing memorable for some reason. It seemed that everybody was preoccupied with future plans and places. Rhett was returning to the United States, Mother was making a life for herself on the Gold Coast, Kell was still living in Hong Kong and had not made it back for the holiday, and Michael was concentrating hard on his new INXS album when he and Kylie weren't being hounded by the press. On New Year's Eve, we started out at the Connaught and moved on to the home of some friends. Kylie was sitting next to me drinking something that finally gave her loose lips. Casually, I said, 'So, you never told me how you got together with Michael.'

She talked of a friend who also knew him and said that this Nicole had arranged it all. As simple as that. Just goes to show that even the famous call on their friends to help in matters of the heart. Kylie revealed herself to be a sweet girl from a close-knit family who strove to protect her. She is also a very sharp entertainer who keeps her finger on the pulse of trends and Michael obviously had real affection for her. He was very protective which was fascinating to observe as up until now everybody had been taking care of him. He was very excited about the relationship and really tried to keep the press at a distance so that it could develop in privacy. But the public was fascinated with the whole 'innocent Kylie, bad boy rocker Michael' aspect, and I think they were doomed from the start. He had never experienced this kind of curiosity and intrusion on his personal life because he had never dated anybody this famous. Kylie was used to being followed by the press and she handled it much better. He told me once that he looked upon her as his 'work in progress'. This was not said in an unkind way. Kylie was eight years younger than he and part of his enjoyment of dating her was in sharing his knowledge of literature and the great movies. Also Michael was used to filling large venues and putting on live shows, whereas Kylie was just beginning to move into that side of her career.

I was thinking of retiring and taking a real holiday. When Michael returned to Hong Kong he sent me a card with a note saying he could not believe I had never been to Paris. He said that when I was ready to go on a visit, I should phone his Sydney accountant and he would arrange a first-class round-the-world ticket for me. He had bought a house in the South of France by then and had a young French couple installed there to take care of it. This was to be a get-away home, a holiday house for the whole family to enjoy. Shortly after this as fate and fortune would have it I met my future husband. Ross had been a widower for two years. He was an ex-Air Force pilot who had joined up young and had retired a highly decorated Group Captain. We had decided to go on a world trip together and married in Reno, Nevada. We then planned to go on to Los Angeles to see Tina and then to New York where Michael was touring with INXS. Our family lived in such a nomadic, disparate way that this was a way of trying to get together whenever and wherever we could.

Some time in early 1990 Michael told me about a villa he had bought in Roquefort les Pins. He suggested that I might want to move there and live in the front cottage. He thought I could help him by managing it for him, but due to the children's schooling I had to decline. His idea was to rent the main house and garden out for location shoots when it was not in family use. He said he had paid around 1.5 million dollars in cash. Later I learned from his housekeeper that he had bought the house from the manager of Duran Duran. Evidently Simon Le Bon called often during the summer to ask about its availability. As usual with Michael's purchases it was set up under a company name, and this one was Leagueworks Pty Ltd, with an address in Monaco.

A sign across the main gate reads 'Vieille Ferme Des Guerchs', which roughly translated means the 'old farmhouse belonging to the Guerchs', the family who originally owned it; but it looks like anything but an old farmhouse. It is a magnificent place, about 400 years old and stands on about three acres of lush gardens inland between Nice and Cannes, not far from Grasse where the most beautiful perfumes in the world are created. The main house is a two-storey farmhouse with relatively small rooms. It has five bedrooms each with an adjoining bathroom and from the two larger bedrooms on the second floor you can see the Riviera coast in the near distance. It also has a large kitchen, dining room, living room, playroom, music room and downstairs is a basement large enough for a two-bedroom apartment. Some wonderful family times were to be spent there and some bleaker days, too.

In early July Erin and I arrived back in Los Angeles. It was a joyful Fourth of July that year. We were glad to be back, staying with friends in the short term. From the moment I returned I was in touch with Jonnie daily. She had begun a new career as a photographer and was trying valiantly to pick up the pieces of her life. We needed to keep the connection and she was still nursing a broken heart. With her talent and courage she soon founded a successful casting agency which still flourishes today. I also spent time with Rhett who was still working in Los Angeles. Most of the time it was to help him with some day-to-day annoyances or we met for early dinners before he went on somewhere else. Neither of us felt comfortable socializing with the other's friends. I pushed at the subject of therapy and he vehemently rejected the idea. I felt that he was running away from the real problem, which was that he used drugs to kill the pain, could not stay away from them and yet he loathed himself for it, which ironically only encouraged his usage. The more I pressed, the less I saw of him. Eventually Michael sent him to New York as Rhett was convinced that it was too hard to stay away from temptation in Los Angeles. Both thought a new start in another city would help.

In late summer that same year Michael called from the Mondrian Hotel in Los Angeles and came over for lunch by the pool. I brought up the subject of Rhett and Michael said he was doing great. Not so great I told him, I had heard the previous day that he was seen in New York doing some really bad stuff. Michael said he was sending him money to keep off that and refused to believe it. I told him that he had to stop supporting Rhett because in doing so he was contributing to his problems and suggested that we get some people to help us get Rhett into the 'Tough Love' programme. This is where you get the person's friends and family together to confront him, with a counsellor from Tough Love rehabilitation centre present. The idea is to make it serious enough that he will leave with the counsellor that day and spend whatever time it takes at the rehab centre to force him into staying clean. Michael would not buy it; he had people watching Rhett, he said, and he was doing just fine, adding that Rhett was afraid to step out of line in case his living expenses would get cut off. I knew Michael meant well, but my information was very reliable. I felt helpless. I had counted on Michael eventually coming round to my point of view. This time it was almost a pride thing: he already saw himself as head of the family and therefore he knew better.

When I asked Mother not to send any money to Rhett, she said that she hadn't in ages and asked me to speak to Kell about it. He also said that he would refuse to send Rhett money. I was worried that his drug dependency would eventually kill him. He had been lucky so far. Michael, the protective big brother, had to come to terms with his decision when Rhett found himself in some serious trouble in New York some months after this. Michael of course, as usual, literally bought him out of it. I kept insisting, 'He's not learning this way.'

In the lyrics of Michael's song, 'I'm Just a Man', are the words, 'My brother's sane, his heart is so strong; he's killed some pain, and to himself nearly did the same; it washed away, into the cruel sea; like everything, that's built upon the sand; flesh and blood, flesh and blood.' This was close to the bone. The only thing he did not address is the cause of the pain and I believe it began in Rhett's infancy, the fact that he was a 'difficult' baby. I know that not all of these children lose themselves in drugs, but think about the way in which the world responds to a child with that hectic temperament, and you can understand how Rhett was not always getting the positive feedback that an easy child like Michael might inspire. Rhett began to lose himself in drugs relatively young which made it harder for people to warm to him. By the time he was struggling with serious drug abuse, Michael was being accepted and embraced by the world and maybe feeling unnecessarily guilty about the capriciously diverse way that fate had handed out the cards for Rhett and himself.

Chris and Pearl Bailey spent Christmas relaxing with Michael and

Kylie at the villa in 1990. Michael had a three-week break from the INXS '*X*' tour schedule after completing a gruelling two months in Europe, including four straight nights at Wembley Arena in London. Kylie had helped Michael choose appliances and furniture for the villa and it was all very comfortable now. She tried out some recipes and chatted with Pearl and the men did what they always did whenever they got together – drink a large amount of alcohol and stay up talking all night. Michael and Chris remained great friends, each respecting the other's talents. But Pearl recalls that while Kylie was trying hard to be the perfect hostess, things were not all smooth between her and Michael. There were tensions and they were not quite as loving as they had been.

Michael joined INXS in Mexico City on 11 January 1991, playing two sold-out shows to an audience of 100,000. Six days later they played the Rock in Rio Festival to another 100,000 fans, along with a line-up which included Ziggy Marley, George Michael, Robert Plant, Billy Idol, Donna Summer, Run DMC and Guns n' Roses. This marked the beginning of another seven months on the road, taking in South America, the United States, Canada, Australia and returning to complete Europe, where they played many festivals and benefits for huge audiences. Before reaching Mexico City he had already begun a phone romance with Helena Christensen.

INXS came through Los Angeles in late January 1991 and gave a warm-up performance, actually a hush-hush show, at the Whiskey-A-Go-Go. I took my friend Jill, as I knew Michael would be glad to see her. Jill, one of my teenage babysitters from 1983, had given so much support to the band and she and Michael had hit it off so well before. The show was special, intimate and like a private party. I looked up to see Belinda Carlisle, now forging her own solo career, draped around a banister on the balcony above. She was mouthing lyrics with Michael, as were most of the guests. I resisted the temptation to ask Michael if they had been an item, but throughout the performance she never took her eyes off him. Afterwards at a party at the Four Seasons it was nice to see the band greeting Jill but I was worried about Michael. I felt he was distant. We locked ourselves into a bathroom, the only place that was private, and we talked. I told him my fears, about some unflattering things I had heard that he had said about various members of the family. I only half believed what I'd heard but it bothered me if Michael could not talk to us if he was troubled. A mutual friend had told me that he had heard Michael at a party complaining about our complex family affairs and the fact that he no longer wanted to spend time with me because I never looked happy and didn't know how to enjoy myself. I felt he was pulling away from us. We were such a small clan and he had seemed to be the thread which held us together.

Michael cupped my face in his hands and said, 'Tina, don't listen to, or read, the garbage. People are always quoting things that I do not say. I love you. We will always be close.' It was really difficult to look into Michael's eyes and not believe him. We walked outside and he asked Jill for her new number. Two days later, he arranged for her to meet him on tour but he spoke of Kylie most of the time they spent together. This was not unusual, he and Jill had a long-standing, unusual friendship and he knew he could discuss anything with her. She said he referred to Kylie as his 'baby' and still seemed captivated with her then. Jill's perception of Michael's feelings for Kylie are interesting, given the apprehension he had instilled with Chris and Pearl Bailey just two months before.

New York looked wonderful when we arrived in February 1991, snowy and bright. When we entered our suite at the Plaza we found it fragrant with flowers, champagne was on ice and a fire glowed in the hearth. Michael had arranged all this. In his welcoming note he explained that a car would collect us and take us to the INXS concert at Meadowlands that evening and he would meet us there. More champagne and flowers greeted us in the limo. Michael and Ross had yet to meet and I thought all these wonderful romantic gestures boded well for their first encounter.

At Meadowlands we were met by Michael's friend and head of security, Jeff Pope, and whisked backstage to Michael's dressing room where a feast was laid out. Sushi, prawns, lobster, salmon, oysters, fruit and yet more champagne were all beautifully set out for after the show. The only other person in the room was a striking girl wearing a long white dress. She had long dark brown hair, dark tan skin and the most unusual green eyes. We just smiled at each other, then Michael appeared behind me and gave me a big hug. We laughed, so happy to see each other again. I introduced him to Ross and they seemed to take to each other. Now there was only one more family introduction to go for

Ross and that was Rhett. We'd not had much contact over the last two years as he'd been travelling and mostly living in the United States. I would not have to wait much longer as Michael told me that he too was in New York.

This was the first INXS concert Helena had seen. She had that in common with Ross. Her name was dimly familiar but now, of course, I could place the face from a hundred glossy magazine covers – Helena was one of the most successful models in the world. When the show was over Jeff and the security came to collect us to take us backstage again. We had some supper then happy and elated we went back to our hotel making plans to meet up for a family lunch the next day. Before retiring, I decided to pop a note under Michael's door to ask him to invite Helena too. Next day as we waited in the restaurant, in walked Rhett and his date, along with Michael and Kylie! Confused? So were we.

I had no idea what was going on and felt somewhat embarrassed in case she had seen my note to Michael inviting Helena. There were a couple of frosty moments but we had an enjoyable lunch. Kylie looked adorable. We talked about her family and she proudly told me that her grandmother had made the outfit she was wearing. It was quite an uncomfortable situation for all of us. Rhett is always quick to size things up and he started telling jokes which lightened the atmosphere somewhat but Michael was rather quiet until he got into conversation with Ross about his days as a fighter pilot. Over the years Michael loved to hear these stories and grilled Ross constantly for more. We stayed two more days in New York but did not see Kylie again. INXS continued their tour in the Lear jet that had 'INXS' painted on the side in large letters. I was very concerned about them travelling from city to city in that plane as the weather was extreme and snow had to be scraped off before each take-off.

We said our goodbyes, flying to London by Concorde and on to Paris, which was everything I had hoped it would be for Ross and me. We went on to Venice and then flew to Nice to be met by Michael's driver Claude and driven to his villa in Roquefort. This was to be my first visit to this lovely old house and we would come to spend many wonderful times there with family and friends. We had all heard so much about this house which Michael had bought as a getaway to relax and enjoy his solitude. He would write there, party there, and over the years enjoy cooking for friends and family.

The grounds have the most magnificent old trees, some of the ivy-clad trunks seem almost as wide as the house. Scattered throughout the garden are old lamps also covered in ivy and rows and rows of lavender bushes. There was a rose garden, a herb garden, a vegetable garden, lemons, grapefruit, orange, apple and even olive trees. Michael eventually had the olives pressed for oil and bottled it with his own label. He used some at the villa and gave the rest away to visitors. We were to walk around the garden many times with Michael over the years. After this initial visit we were to return to the villa annually and each time Michael would walk us around to see the improvements he had made, his chest puffing with pride. This garden was Michael's great joy and he spent a lot of time and money and care on it.

On that first visit we noticed that the house was sparsely furnished, but over the years Michael collected notable pieces of furniture and paintings, some of which he shipped from places all over the world. Most of his belongings had been stored in Hong Kong and Sydney but now he was sending for them to fill this retreat. Everything was in keeping with the casual style of the house. The oversized dining table, huge side buffet and squashy sofas all contributed to an appropriately light, airy and Mediterranean feel.

When Helena started going to the house it took on a more feminine and romantic look. There were lots of white bedspreads and tablecloths and there were always dozens of candles, which would be lit each night in every room. Candelabra would be taken on to the patio overlooking the pool where we would dine in the summertime. We ate outside on this patio often, and I can still smell the lavender and see the overhead blanket of wisteria. Michael often treated us to his own bouillabaisse, along with wine from his own cellar. I was so pleased that he had this heavenly oasis to escape to, 'to smell the roses' so to speak. He referred to it as the family home and encouraged us to invite friends to stay, even when he could not be there. When we had friends coming in, if at all possible, he would go to the airport and greet them himself, he was so proud to share the place.

One Friday in 1991, after Mother and Ross had left to meet Michael in New York, Jonnie called to say she was going to be away for the weekend. I happened to be in a blue mood and she suggested that she call her friend Richard to keep me company. She had dated him for seven years before going out with Michael, he remained a friend and she thought he would be the perfect person to cheer me up. When Richard called I realized that he was the same Richard who had found the Al Kiola guitar for Michael in 1989. He had a great voice and an attractive phone manner. After a long conversation we arranged to meet for dinner. Being cautious of anyone knowing where I lived, and not wanting to be stuck somewhere, I told him I would pick him up. Erin was so delighted: this was a Date. No, it was definitely not a Date I told her, but we did become engaged three years later.

Michael called and I mentioned that Jonnie had introduced me to someone special. Before I could get his name out, Michael said he knew because he had just spoken with Jonnie. With almost breathtaking insouciance he had called her in despair after Kylie walked out of the Plaza! Michael was inconsolable over the break-up with Kylie, even though it was he who had initiated it. His calls to her were less frequent and of course he blamed the pace of the tour, but rumours of Michael's philanderings were flying around everywhere. Kylie had confronted him in his room after she had flown in especially to see him and there was nothing to do but admit that he was seeing Helena. I have the impression that Kylie is a straightforward person who simply cannot tolerate infidelities. The fact that he was so upset over Kylie's heartbreak was so typical of Michael, who wanted everybody to be happy. He wanted to get away with murder via stealth and charm and not face the fact that sometimes, heavy emotional choices must be faced. He still couldn't take responsibility for the impact of his rejections or two-timing. Most of his final break-ups had been made on the phone from another continent. And now here he was calling Jonnie, the woman he had left for Kylie, in the hope that she could console him. Nothing could ever diminish my love for Michael but, honestly, sometimes I despaired of his emotional immaturity.

While Richard and I flew from San Francisco to Sacramento on the INXS Lear jet, Michael told me about Helena Christensen. He said Herb Ritts had introduced them on the phone and I should look out for her in a Chris Isaak video. He was obviously excited about this girl. I did not ask about Kylie. Michael and Richard got on well at that meeting. There seemed to be mutual respect and the fact that Richard and I were so obviously in tune with each other. We were transferred to a limo at the Sacramento airport. Fans lined the streets all the way to the venue. It was hours away from opening the doors. Richard and I sat alone in the Arco Arena, watching the sound check. When they were through we joined Andrew, Tim, Jon, Garry, Kirk and Michael for dinner and the members one by one headed off for a massage and a vitamin B shot, and finally the show was on. Richard held me in the wings on the same side of the stage where Kirk stood, a spot where I have always felt comfortable. We flew back to San Francisco directly after the show where I said my goodbyes to Michael, and told him I looked forward to meeting Helena.

CHAPTER EIGHT

Supermodels and the South of France

Arriving home from the office one day in September of 1991, Richard greeted me with a distressing message from Rhett. He had called from Amsterdam and was desperate to speak to me. He would call back in thirty minutes. Rhett was obviously in some kind of trouble. I had not heard from him in some time. He usually called Michael when he was in a crisis these days but lately he had been much more difficult to track down and a lot less willing to send Rhett a cheque.

As I waited for Rhett's call I thought about yet another upcoming family Christmas. We had settled on the South of France. Michael had been so excited about the prospect of showing off his villa. It would be my first visit there so I was excited too as I'd heard so much about it from Mother and Ross.

The phone rang. I grabbed it, accepted the charges and the moment I heard Rhett's voice, I knew he was in a bad way. He was broke, had not eaten for some time, had nowhere to stay and he needed a doctor. I wanted to fly to him but I got a number and told him to call back if he had not heard from me within the hour. I caught Michael just a day or two before he was about to leave the villa to wind up a tour of Europe and discussed the situation. He said he would arrange for a train ticket from Amsterdam all the way through to Nice. He refused to pay for an airfare, or to allow Rhett to bring his girlfriend. Although their bond was strong, and Michael loved Rhett very much, he was fed up with being used.

Rhett was ready to agree to anything. Once he arrived the two brothers talked things over and made an agreement. Rhett would stay at the villa and get well. He would be given a weekly allowance from Carole, the property manager. He would not really have any expenses as Carole had an account for food and incidentals. The idea was to keep him at the house, get his health back and to keep him off any illegal drugs before the family arrived for Christmas. It sounded good in theory. I called him weekly, finding him weepy and exhausted in the first month. Gradually he was more responsive and informed me that he was using the pool, gaining weight and getting a tan. I was delighted. I detected nothing in either the phone calls with Rhett or the private ones I had with Carole to suggest that he was up to his old tricks. How much trouble could he get into? After all, it was less than three months to Christmas and he had Carole, her husband Claude and their daughter Marie living on the property, taking care of his every wish. What a break: I was jealous!

Just before that Christmas in 1991, Michael bought a block of land sight unseen, in Southport on the Gold Coast of Australia. The asking price was AUS$1.3 million. He was in Europe at the time but Colin Diamond closed the deal after Michael OK'd the investment on the property. This is not unusual for people in Michael's position: not only is it time-consuming to look for properties but the price often goes up when a well-known person is known to be involved. This sort of thing was what he was paying Colin to do – to advise Michael on sound investments and do all of the legwork. Michael would see the land for the first time while visiting Mother and Ross on the Gold Coast in January 1992. The money was paid by cash transfer from Michael's bank account and the property was promptly placed in a trust company called Nextcircle.

Erin and I arrived in Paris ahead of Brent, Richard and his daughter Shawna, on 18 December 1991. Michael met us at the airport. He had only just arrived from London with Helena who had gone directly to a shoot. It was early evening, cold, and we took a cab to the little apartment they shared in St Germain des Prés. On the drive into the city he was as excited as we were on our first trip to France. He gave us a running commentary on the sights, just like a tour guide. I was not at all amazed at his knowledge of the history and stories he was telling us – it was so Michael. He always tried to learn as much as possible about any city, place or person he found interesting. Carole was teaching him French and I had never seen him so committed to acquiring a new skill.

He was preparing us for the tiny apartment he was so proud of. When we arrived at Rue des Canettes, we found that the street was no wider than an alley, typical in Paris. We climbed a winding staircase to the first floor, Michael struggling with our luggage. He opened the door, and with great flourish gave us a tour of the enchanting two bedroomed apartment which had a large living room with natural wood floors, a few good scattered rugs and original paintings and tapestries on the walls. Some of the artwork was Helena's own. He proudly told me how they had gone to the local market and bargained for the beautiful old furniture. He was clearly in love with not only the girl, but also the city, the language, and the whole lifestyle.

While we settled into the second bedroom, Michael made up a platter of fresh baguettes and cheeses. No sooner had we sampled the fine old wine he had opened in our honour and begun to catch up when the door swung open and in walked the most stunning young woman. At twenty-one Helena really was a heartbreaker, her green eyes mesmerizing. But beautiful though she was, as soon as she opened her lovely mouth, something must have provoked her that day for out of it poured a stream of complaints. She did not like the hairstyle they had given her for the shoot, she hated the make-up, the clothes, the waiting around, she was starving, she did not feel like bread and cheese – I was expecting her to say she did not like me either. It was impossible not to contrast this tall, blazing and apparently rather haughty, beauty who seemed utterly confident and cosmopolitan with the tiny Kylie whom Michael had felt he needed to educate. But comparisons are usually odious and I had long since ceased to detect a 'type' in Michael's choice of lover.

He made light of Helena's mood and suggested we all go to La Coupole for dinner. Erin was a wide-eyed thirteen-year-old and this was my first trip to Paris. We were happy to go anywhere. Off we went to La Coupole, Michael again pointing out the sights and sounds of the city. La Coupole is an enormous old restaurant, steeped in art history, and Michael had chosen it for just those reasons, since Erin was planning to take art as her college major. He was very animated and entertaining as always so the evening was filled with amusing stories, lots of laughter and excited expectations for the holidays. When he urged us to stay on in Paris it was tempting but impossible. I was disappointed that we were only spending one night there before going on to Nice, but we had made the plans months before. When you travel tourist class you must do things this way – Michael now had no understanding of what it was like to be cautious with money, but I would never have dreamt of talking about finances with him. I had not known during the initial planning that we would be staying with Michael and Helena and had been concerned about expenses for five at a Parisian hotel. Richard was a musician without a band so I was the chief breadwinner. Between us we had three students, Erin and Brent and Shawna, so we were on a tight budget. Richard was arriving later with Shawna and Brent, and they too would be staying overnight with Michael and Helena. It must be said that even though it was only to be for one night, this was quite a strain in a small apartment. If Helena seemed stressed, I can't really blame her.

By the time I realized that we could all have spent another night in Paris we could not change the train reservations. I was embarrassed about our financial situation but did not want to throw this on to Michael. He was already taking care of Rhett, and paying for Kell and Sue's vacation. Michael thought that Erin and I should fly down on Christmas Eve, but I told him that I wanted to get to the villa and decorate it for Christmas before the rest of the family arrived. I could not afford to take a flight, and I did not want him to pay for one. I mention this, because I want to stress that over the years I went out of my way to never take advantage of Michael's generosity, especially as others, friends and family, have done.

Next morning, Helena had a job and she left the apartment before we rose. Michael woke us up with breakfast and lugged our bags downstairs. This was not easy as we were carrying a mass of winter clothing, and bundles of Christmas gifts. We ran behind him, while he tried to hail a taxi and proudly directed the driver to Gare de Lyon in perfect French. I told Michael that we had chosen to travel by train because we had heard that the French countryside was so beautiful. Lately I had been used to seeing Michael with others around, people who carried the bags and had cars waiting so it was actually nice to see him in control and clearly he was enjoying the fact that he could walk around Paris and just be a normal person. I could tell he enjoyed being responsible for Erin and me. He took pains to explain which bank I should go to in Grasse to exchange my US currency, before running off to buy a stack of magazines and snacks for our trip, depositing us and our bags on the train, and waving us off.

The French landscape, as seen from the train, was indeed

breathtaking and I was glad circumstances had steered us towards rail travel rather than flights. I had faxed ahead to Carole but I guess both she and Rhett forgot or had the days mixed up, because we were not met at the station in Nice. Thirty minutes after I startled them with a call to the house Rhett arrived in Michael's Mercedes Jeep with a friend who had to be dropped off at nearby Antibes before we could go to the villa. As soon as I met this friend I felt uneasy. Even Erin was uncomfortable. Why was this person being 'disappeared' just as we arrived? I knew it was pointless to even ask the question. I was somehow sure that Rhett had been making friends as he does so easily and that the villa had probably been used for much partying. I was positive that the house was being cleaned up for our arrival. As I sat in the front seat of the car, which was approximately six months old, I noticed cigarette burns in the upholstery and wires hanging where the stereo should be. I asked Rhett about it and he just shrugged. I feared Michael would be furious.

After dropping off Rhett's friend I suggested we shopped for food as it was now close to 8 p.m. and Erin and I were famished. Rhett had said there was nothing to eat at the house. I had not exchanged my money into French currency but Rhett said that he had plenty of cash. So Erin sat in the car as Rhett and I ran around a supermarket stocking up on all kinds of delicacies. The bill came to about 400 francs (less than US$100). Rhett produced some large bills and handed them to me but when I proffered them the cashier gave me a suspicious look and called for the manager. The minute he arrived there was a commotion with everybody naturally speaking in French. Even to me it was obvious that the bills were counterfeit. I was so embarrassed and, without the language, could not rectify the problem. The manager insisted we leave. Rhett, never being one to back down, protested loudly. I ran out to the car with Rhett running behind and pleading with me to believe that he did not know the bills were no good. I yelled back that I believed him. Actually, it didn't matter to me if he knew the bills to be bad or if he had just been hanging around with people who had passed them on to him. Anyhow, the incident set the tone for my relationship with Rhett for the rest of that vacation.

By the time we arrived at the villa it was very late, so Carole sent Claude out to the local village for a pizza. I took a bath and went to bed. At about 2 a.m. I awoke to loud voices, music and laughing. The villa is two storeys high and built out of huge bricks with eighteen-inch walls. It is certainly solid but noises echo in the French countryside. I made my way downstairs to find Rhett entertaining. It had sounded like there were at least a dozen people there but there were only four highly intoxicated 'who are you to spoil our fun?' strangers staring at me. Without getting too heavy, and not wanting to embarrass Rhett, I asked them to lower the music. He told me that I could either join them or mind my own business and leave them alone. Deciding that, as usual, I was no match for Rhett's vicious tongue, I limply turned back to my bedroom and prayed for sleep.

In the morning I found extra bodies sleeping in the living room and by 9 a.m. decided that it was time they left. I went about the villa opening windows and doors to let out the stench of cigarettes, liquor and pot. I had just two days to get the home ready before the rest of the family arrived. Carole took us shopping before Rhett surfaced. Michael had given me a list of wines and liquors he wanted to stock up on and I had a long grocery list. We had agreed to take turns to cook but I was in charge of Christmas dinner proper. Michael had also given me specific instructions about sleeping arrangements. He was concerned that Mother and Ross and Kell and Sue should have the same size bedrooms, as he did not want anyone to feel slighted. The master bedroom was huge and the second almost as large, two others were about equally sized and another one was a little smaller. He told me to take the second bedroom and to let the others decide when they arrived. He was tremendously concerned that everything should be harmonious.

Rhett had bought a tree, which needed decorations, and he had also troubled to find and hang personalized stockings for each of us. It was touching: he could be so confusingly thoughtful and lovable at times. We threaded a garland I had brought from California up the staircase and tied huge red and green plaid bows at strategic points. Rhett found some mistletoe and strung lights over the tree. Mother and Ross arrived with dozens of tiny clip-on koalas, which they attached to everything. It was definitely an Australian Christmas. I stocked the pantry, the refrigerator, the liquor cabinet. By the following day this last had been considerably depleted so I went shopping again and this time I hid the liquor in Carole's house, hating being forced into the role of disciplinarian.

Then suddenly everybody was arriving. Even after just two days I was relieved that I would not be on my own maintaining law and order. Mother and Ross arrived first and there was the usual gabble of catching-up. That evening Richard arrived with a very happy Brent and Shawna. Michael and Helena had met them with a limo at the airport in Paris and taken them home to change and on to a Christmas party at Helena's modelling agency. This was all a great thrill for Brent: nineteen years old, his first night in Paris and his uncle takes him to a party with supermodels even though he was probably too shy to talk to anyone. Kell and Sue arrived, then Michael, who had massive toothache, which had necessitated a trip directly from the airport to the dentist. Helena's birthday falls on Christmas Day so she had flown to Denmark to be with her family and did not reach Nice until the evening of the 26th. Her parents came the following day.

On most nights before Helena's arrival, Michael, Rhett and Brent went out. Occasionally we would join them but I felt guilty about leaving Erin. The guys would arriving home in the early hours of the morning and sit in the kitchen, raiding the refrigerator, drinking more and laughing. Early one morning I went down to join them and was alarmed to see Brent with dried blood over his left eye. Michael, Rhett and he were laughing and saying 'Uh oh, we're in trouble now'. Naturally my reaction was anything but calm. It seemed that they had been leaving a club, which had a low doorway. Michael, being shorter than the other two, slipped through first and when Brent followed, he forgot to duck. They were like the Three Musketeers, laughing uncontrollably as they relayed the story and it was impossible to remain worried or angry for long as I watched these three guys who I loved so much bonding so well. They were all safe home, after all. Brent still has a little scar to remind him of that evening and one of his favourite vacations.

Even so, Michael was lonely and had trouble sleeping. During one of those early morning meetings in the kitchen, Brent suddenly went to bed and Rhett had already passed out. The house was full of sleeping people but Michael asked me to get dressed, as he wanted company as he walked around his garden. He grabbed three glasses and picked up a bottle of wine from the cellar. Richard and I just walked around with him as he described his plans for the west corner, the area beyond the pool and the unused basement. He was so enthused by this house. Then suddenly he suggested we take the Jeep and drive up to a little village on the hill to watch the sun come up. Halfway up the winding road, he pulled over and stopped at a favourite lookout. We got out of the car and sat on the side of the mountain. Richard pulled out his videocam and Michael quietly gave us an abbreviated version story of *Perfume*, a novel by Patrick Süskind, making the tale his own. We were spellbound and he enjoyed even the very small audience of two. I did not realize that it was not his story until Erin found the book in Michael's library and began reading it during that very vacation.

I was having trouble finding all the foodstuffs for Christmas dinner that I am used to in the United States and decided that I could not bake turkey without having yams to go with it. Two days before Christmas we went to a supermarket in Nice. Michael took one trolley and I took another, everyone else had a piece of the shopping list. When I asked for a turkey I was given something called a capon. Close enough, I thought, it looked like a turkey but it was just so small compared to the twenty-pounders we have in the States. I took two of them, but still no yams. I hoped to find some in one of the little villages near the villa: each one of them had a grocery store even if their stock was minimal. I had already found it a worry to find enough fresh vegetables and so on for up to sixteen people. The next day was a sightseeing day and I sent everybody in a different direction, telling them all to come back with yams. By that evening we had plenty for Christmas dinner.

Michael took me to Valbonne. It has cobbled streets and interesting little restaurants, which couldn't possibly seat more than fifteen in total. We were browsing in a shop when we heard some very scratchy music. 'Silent Night' in French, combined with the laughter of children, getting closer and closer. Michael stepped outside and within seconds he jumped back in and huddled me towards the doorway to take in the most wonderful sight. The music accompanied the youngest looking Père Noel I have ever seen, walking through the village with children hanging on to his coat, all singing. The wig and beard did not conceal this Santa's young appearance but this did not deter the little children from following him. Surrounded by the locals in the village, I felt that we had stepped into another century. The look of joy and pride on Michael's face to be sharing this with me was the best Christmas present ever. It was so obvious that he wanted his family to share in the deep peace and pleasure he experienced through the simple traditions of life in the French countryside. I was reassured and certain that only good lay ahead for him; what could possibly be lacking in his life when he had this perfect retreat?

Rhett noticed a poster in Cannes announcing a show by Lenny Kravitz. We all wanted to go and that night he piled us into the jeep, Rhett, Brent, Shawna, Erin, Richard and I. It was a crowded venue but the show was electric. Backstage I noted that Lenny ran a small, right operation, nothing like the large crew that INXS carried along. Michael found out that Lenny would be back late Christmas Day and invited him over to the villa.

On Christmas morning we all ran downstairs like children. Recently I came across a video that Richard made of that day, and I am so grateful to have this. It depicts an elated, jubilant Michael in his apple green suit walking around with a bottle of champagne in one hand and a jug of orange juice in another, pouring mimosas for us all. The fire was crackling away as we faced the mound of gifts tumbling out from the base of the little tree. The gifts that year were outrageously extravagant even if some of them had to be simply promised as we couldn't, practically, have them here in France. We had planned our surprises very carefully, calling and faxing for months. Mother was given a 1992 Honda from Ross, and Brent was blown away with a '65 Mustang from us all. I was astonished to find out that Ross had organized another joint gift for me – a laptop computer. We all went just a little overboard, but this was such a special Christmas. Later we dressed for dinner, Rhett in a red, white and black suit, which Michael had given him.

It was an incredible meal, not because I was the head chef but because we were together at one long table and this did not happen very often. Carole and Claude joined us with their little daughter Marie. We began the meal with very Australian Sydney rock oysters, which Michael had flown in, and ended with plum pudding and hot brandy sauce. The wine flowed, and there was much laughter, story-telling and forgiving. The phone rang many times during the meal, always with good wishes. Helena called several times throughout the day, and Michele also rang with her love. To Michele, Michael said 'Yep, getting out the cookbooks, doing all the cooking for the family.' He was revelling in the role of patriarch and host. I had already seen how much he enjoyed this role.

Later, when Lenny Kravitz arrived with his girlfriend, we were all delighted to see him again. He wore a huge cap over his massive dreadlocks. We were picking at delicious leftovers around the kitchen table and the conversation was lively. The first thing Lenny wanted to do was call his little daughter Zoe in the United States. After this he came back into the kitchen, removed his cap, and he and Michael headed for the music room. We all looked at the cap in silence, we had never seen such a huge brim. Ross tried it on and it fell around his shoulders, Mother took a photograph. I tried it on next. We were all in fits of laughter, Erin left the room, fearful that Lenny might walk back in and catch us. When he did return he did so laughing and said he wanted to show us the mass of tiny clip-on koalas he had attached to his dreadlocks. My children and I have seen Lenny perform many times since that Christmas and he has always been very gracious to us. His grandfather was backstage at one concert, a charming man. Lenny said he was staying on the road with him for a while. I don't think there would be many performers who'd take their grandfather on tour with them. I also met Lenny's mother, Roxy Roker, a beautiful and vibrant lady. She thanked me for making sure her son Lenny did not spend a lonely Christmas that year in France.

Helena arrived the day after Christmas and then her parents flew in. I noticed right away that her mother Ilsa often carried magazines bearing pictures of her famous daughter on the cover. She sat around the villa reading them and left them lying around on tables. This seemed curious to me; I always felt foolish purchasing a magazine featuring an INXS story. But I guess she really did have something to be proud about in her eldest daughter: Helena was hugely successful in her field and so beautiful – it was difficult to take your eyes off her. The villa has a huge satellite dish and we could get TV from all over Europe. One day between Christmas and New Year's Eve, a recorded interview with Helena came on MTV. I was fascinated to hear her refer to models over twenty-five as 'old cows'. She went on to say that she would not stay in the business that long. Considering she was already twenty-two and had yet to reach her peak, I thought this was a reckless statement. I decided that, ironically, she was showing her youth.

I found that I could not entirely agree with Michael's view that Helena was down-to-earth. For instance, even though she spoke fluent English, she invariably spoke in another language whenever

Clockwise, above: Michael and Michele Bennett in New York for her twenty-third birthday. **Right:** Michael and Michele. (Stevie Hughes). **Below:** Michele and Michael in Sydney, snapped by Patricia, 1984.

Left: Rhett in his casts, ready for an INXS concert. **Below:** The brothers in Japan. **Bottom:** Rhett, Michael, Tiger Lily and Zoe Angel, Gold Coast, 1996.

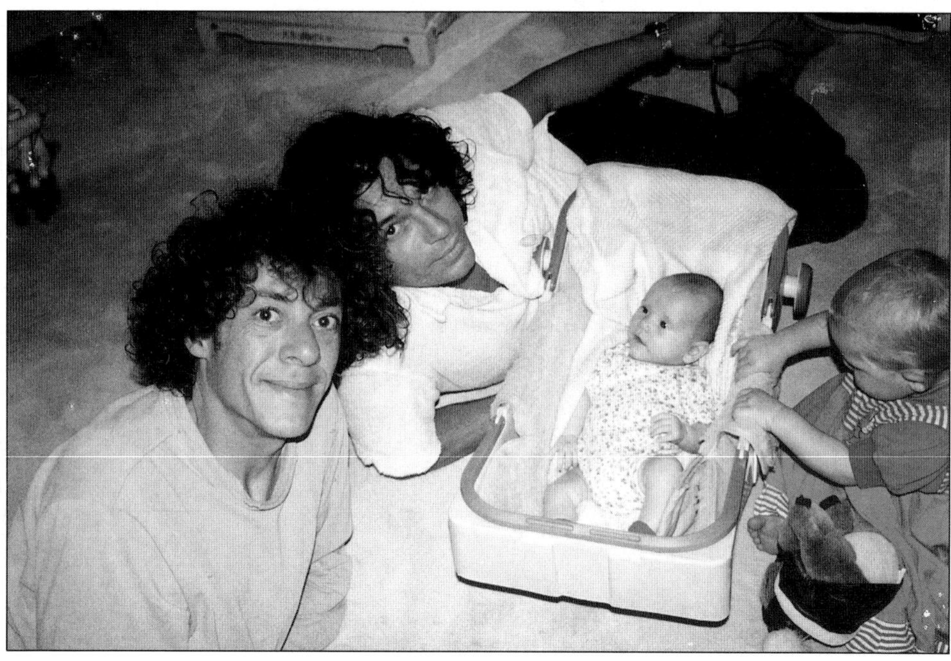

Right: We would often meet Michael on tour. Here he is with Rhett at the corner of Haight and Ashbury in San Francisco; note Michael's peace sign and retro tie-dyed jeans. **Below:** Michael and Rhett, Tambourine Mountain, Queensland, Australia, Christmas 1994.

Michael the Action Man. **Clockwise, top left:** With silver and gold medals at Kowloon Cricket Club, Hong Kong, 1971. **Top right:** Ready for the sights of the Gold Coast in a Tiger Moth, 1995. **Below left:** Diving and (**below right)** sailing in Tahiti.

Above: Michael always loved cars, even at seven. **Left:** Still fascinated by fast machines, Michael in Los Angeles, 1989.

Above: Michael in the driveway of his villa with his Aston Martin, 1996. **Left:** Michael skiing at Thredbo in Australia, 1982. Jeff is behind the skis, Wendy Murphy is between them in the background, and Debra is far right.

Clockwise, above: Michael and Tina in Los Angeles, 1983. **Top right:** Michael and three-year-old Brent in Los Angeles at Tina's rented house in Studio City, 1975. **Right:** Thanksgiving at Tina's home, 1996. It was a happy day. Although Tina knew Michael was stressed and unhappy, she never imagined that on Thanksgiving Day 1997, she would be speaking at his funeral. **Below:** Christmas at Patricia's Broadbeach home on the Gold Coast, 1993. Michael gave Erin an acoustic guitar and encouraged her to write lyrics.

Right: Tina with Michael and Rhett at Sydney International Airport, 1985. Tina was returning to California and Michael had arrived back from a tour just two hours before.

Left: Richard, Michael and Brent at a Christmas party at the home of Helena Christensen's agent in Paris, 1991. **Below:** The blessing of Tina's marriage in the beautiful garden of Michael's villa, 1996. Brent, Erin, Father Guerrero, Linda (the housekeeper), Ken, Tina, Michael, Patricia and Ross.

Left: Patricia at the entrance to the villa in happier times.

Right: Welcoming Lenny Kravitz to the villa, 1991.
Below: Christmas in the South of France, 1991. Richard, Susie, Kell, Rhett, Shawna, Brent, Tina, Erin, Patricia, Michael and Ross on one knee in front.

possible. Rhett had an Australian friend staying at the villa who also spoke French. If I were left alone with the two, Helena would break into French. Of course the girl would continue the conversation in French and I would feel excluded and foolish, even though it was they who were being rude and making me feel obliged to get up and walk away. She also had a way of directing all of her conversation to men. For instance, if Richard or Rhett was standing next to me and I engaged Helena in conversation, she would not look at me while answering but rather direct her answer to the man at my side. In this strange way we could have a whole conversation without making eye contact. It would make me crazy, leaping around trying to get her in sight. Richard noticed this and told me to ignore it. Easier said than done. My reaction only made me look bad of course. In my experience, women understand 'unsisterly' behaviour even as they may be enraged by it: some women, however successful or beautiful they are, may behave differently when they are possibly feeling threatened or inadequate. I could not imagine Helena feeling threatened by me or for that matter anyone else, but I believe that she was so used to being around so many other beautiful women that it was a reflex, she could not help herself. Eventually I decided that Helena couldn't have intentionally been trying to be nasty. Stunning as she was, I think she was lacking in confidence and this made her behave in a certain way around some people. I hoped that she would grow out of the habit in time.

We took many day excursions, sightseeing in a caravan of three cars, going to St Tropez, Monaco, San Raphael, Cannes and Nice. I have a video featuring the whole family in the kitchen while I am cooking. There is dancing, singing, and lots of ribbing and laughter. Rhett is doing his impersonation of a rap dancer, Kell flies by with a bowl on his head, Michael joins Rhett in the dancing and yells to me, 'Tina, baby, get with it, on the table baby, come on, you can do it' – referring to my ancient history as a 'go-go' dancer. It was a happy Christmas for all of us.

One evening we were invited to a neighbour's house where they had gone to a lot of trouble to make us feel welcome. It was a magnificent home belonging to a couple who owned, among other things, a local art gallery. They wheeled out a large cake, which was iced with the words 'Welcome to the Michael Hutchence Family'. Their teenage son had a music room filled with microphones, a drum set and guitars. He took Richard and Michael up there and it didn't take long for the music to start. Michael picked up a microphone and asked Richard to lead him into a soaring rendition of Hendrix's 'Hey Joe'. His voice was strong and it was evident that he was enjoying the departure from his INXS repertoire. The teenager could not believe his luck as he sat behind the drums. Downstairs the classical pianist was preparing himself at the grand piano but, deciding that the competition was too great, put off playing for a while longer.

Two days after Christmas, Carole and Claude told us they were getting a divorce – and they were both very relieved they had made the decision. Claude handed me a fresh glass of champagne and made a toast. He wanted to move to New York and drive a taxi. Carole said she would like to stay on with her job at the villa. It later emerged that she had been having an affair with Rhett. Michael was furious about this and angry with himself as well. He'd relied on Carole to look after Rhett and in doing so he had unintentionally thrown them together. He went about finding replacements and eventually hired a wonderful couple from the Philippines, Linda and Nestor Ventavilla, and helped them obtain their papers to stay in France. The change was all done through the villa trust company of course. It was for the best because although Carole had been a reliable manager she did not cook or clean, and Linda enjoyed doing both. Nestor came to love caring for the garden and Michael's cars.

New Year's Eve was ushered in with a barbie and fireworks. Michael, Helena and her parents spent most of the day in the kitchen preparing it. The barbecue is at the end of the pool – a good 100 yards from the main house – and the December temperature in the South of France stays around 40 degrees Fahrenheit at night. Michael wore a silk shirt, an overcoat, a straw hat and had hands turning blue from the elements as he cooked prawns and lobster and mahi mahi. Claude was down there doing his best, but Michael insisted on taking the chef duties. He would run all the way up to the house where the main party was drinking and then return to tend to his coals. Rhett and Brent had quietly bought the fireworks earlier that day and began to light them off the balcony at midnight. Below the balcony lies the firewood store. Although it was winter, it had not been raining and within minutes Claude was hosing down a small blaze at the side of the pool. This sounds potentially serious, especially when you consider the surrounding dry shrubbery and neighbouring villas, but there was actually very little harm done and Michael laughed louder than any of us.

Michael could sometimes seem thoughtless but this tendency was usually rooted in the absent-mindedness of a dreamer. He really enjoyed surprising and spoiling those closest to him. For instance, throughout this Christmas Brent had been craving a 'Big Mac' or anything that did not have that suspicious healthy gourmet look about it. When we arrived back in Paris – where Richard and I planned a week sightseeing with the children, Brent was keen to check out the nearest McDonald's at once, but Michael called our hotel and invited us to dine with him at a great steakhouse he had chosen just for Brent's benefit. Michael and Helena were only staying one night at their apartment so he gave me the keys and an open invitation to use his driver. This whole vacation had been such a success that we all agreed to get together as a family at least every other year.

During 1992, Michael and Helena travelled constantly. Her star was rising, and Michael was genuinely proud of her. After one evening at a nightclub in Copenhagen, Helena and Michael stopped for some takeaway food on their way to Helena's apartment. They were standing in the little street when a taxi attempted to drive round them. As Michael took his time getting out of the way, the driver leapt out of the cab and gave him a shove. He went down hard, hitting his head on the kerb, and sustained head injuries which he did not take care of immediately. Complaining of a persistent huge headache, he finally went to a specialist who found that the injury had hampered his sense of taste and smell. He did not speak of this much, unless he was drinking, but I noticed that he started to become short-tempered more often from then on. Eventually his senses returned to a certain degree, and I would notice him once again pass his wine under his nose, testing the bouquet, or sometimes he would comment on my perfume. However I do not believe his sense of smell and taste ever returned fully.

I saw less of Michael during the years he was with Helena. His career remained more or less stagnant whilst Helena's soared. He took on a whole new personality. When they visited, it was a quick dinner before 'we have to meet Kate (Moss) and Johnny (Depp)', or whoever. Michael was completely involved with Helena's work, friends and family. There were infrequent phone calls from resorts, occasional visits when Helena was in town on photo-shoots and postcards from exotic places and not much else. He had no contact whatsoever with Rhett. Mother and Ross were keeping up dialogue with Michael because they took trips to Europe every year but it was hurtful to read he was in Los Angeles but hadn't called me. To be fair I suppose he and Helena were very busy, they knew a lot of people in LA and rarely spent more than a week here. Thank goodness for faxes.

In October 1992 I had the usual entertaining fax from Rhett in which he wrote about how busy he had been having art directed four videos and worked on a pilot called 'Eye On Style'. He said he was no longer doing drugs (other than pot), but Kell was evidently treating him as though he was doing 'hard drugs', ending 'IT'S ENOUGH TO MAKE ME START!' He signed off, 'I love you, please remember that.' I did not see much evidence of progress in this communiqué from Rhett although I had to admit, he had the sharpest sense of humour which, thank God, never failed him.

In late January 1993, I had a fax from Michael and Helena. Michael thanked me for a birthday greeting, as, since he had been travelling around so much, he had not heard from many people. He'd evidently had an hilarious time in Denmark with Chris Bailey. He ended the note with a drawing of a big heart with an arrow and kisses through it.

Michael and Helena had each made enough money to switch careers and try something else if they wanted. I don't think they knew how lucky they were, most people have to go to a boring job day after day. But I was only a little envious. To the outside world they were living a glamorous jetset life, but Michael's self-esteem had taken a dive in the company of the Danish beauty. He was constantly reminded that he had not had a successful album in some time. He spent much of his time sitting in hotel rooms with friends, waiting for Helena to complete her work, or attending her shows – where he was invariably interviewed by CNN. I was feeling so left out of his life – the whole family felt this way. Apart from refusing to speak with Rhett, Kell often called asking if I knew of Michael's whereabouts.

I was so used to him travelling with Helena that it was easier to call MMA to get a number for him. One time when I faxed MMA London and Sydney simultaneously, I had a call from Michael within ten minutes. Without any greeting he said, 'Paris is my home, you know where to find me, call me here!' I don't think he had any concept of how different his lifestyle was. Of course his home base was Paris but if you added up the days he actually spent there, you would probably get three months of the year.

He went to Sydney without Helena and called Michele Bennett to invite her to a club. Michele had to decline. Early the following morning she had a call from Michael, not unlike other calls when he had been up all night, a little hungover and feeling miserable. Michele agreed to go to the hotel and help soothe him to sleep but she made it clear that he could not just call her at the times that he needed comforting and then disappear into the ether for who knows how long. Although she was his friend and would always be there in a crisis, she needed to know that they could have normal social interaction too.

In the spring of 1993, INXS came through Los Angeles on their Dirty Honeymoon tour, promoting their album *Full Moon, Dirty Hearts*. The album was not doing very well and they were no longer filling stadiums. In fact, this was downright disappointing compared to their previous tours. They fared a little better on the European leg, performing at the White Nights Festival in St Petersburg, along with Pearl Jam, Faith No More – and the Kirov Ballet. The venue for the southern California concert was Barker Air Hangar; a ghostly, unused aeroplane hangar in Santa Monica. The cool response to the new album was predictable. Michael had been frustrated with the musical direction of the band; he felt that while he was travelling the world and listening to new music, most of INXS were musically stagnant. Hoping for inspiration he invited the other band members to the villa to prepare before the recording. His plan was to fill the house with a lot of different, new music so they would be open-minded when they got into the studio. I called him one day while they were there and asked him how it was going. He said that it was not what he had hoped for and added that he was worried, sure none of them had progressed in their musical taste since *Kick*. In fact it was a disastrous collaboration. The dynamics of the band was such that each member was talented in his own way, and they all wanted to be the producer. Andrew had always been the leader in the studio, but Michael was so frustrated, trying to drag him and the rest of his band into challenging themselves to keep up with the new music scene. Grunge was in and INXS was not going to be able to compete with Nirvana at this rate.

There was something very unfriendly about that tour, and that time in Michael's life. Whereas previously, crew and band had been like a family, everybody on this tour seemed to be out of sorts. Michael did not even call when he reached LA, but I went ahead and made arrangements for 'will call' tickets, for myself, Richard, Erin and two of her friends. When I called Michael's hotel before the show, Helena answered, saying he was busy and suggested we come down to the hotel and ride to the show with them. I was working out the logistics in my head when she suddenly changed her mind, saying they would see us there. I had trouble backstage again. Eventually I saw Chris Murphy who physically stopped me from entering the 'inner sanctum'. I was furious and told him what a lousy job he was doing and that I thought they had all become self-important at a time when the popularity of the band was on the decline. He tried to placate me but I just wanted to leave. Only the potentially disappointed teenagers in my care prevented me from doing so.

After the show, we went backstage to a tent set up outside, where there were tables and chairs. This was unlike the usual backstage gathering, where the guests mill around with the band. Michael and Helena were holding court surrounded by approximately thirty people sitting in a circle. After a while I ventured over to the circle and attempted to get Michael's attention without being too obvious. He was flying and did not notice me. I finally stepped inside the circle and bent down to hug both of them. Michael was too far gone to notice, and continued to speak, incoherently to the group. Eventually he realized who I was and hugged me back without getting up. I don't think he could have done so without falling over. Helena simply ignored me. Michael waved at Erin and said he would be over to our table in a little while. Then Chris Murphy's assistant, Sam, came over and asked if I would speak to a fan of Michael's. It seems that he had refused to speak with her and suggested that I take care of it. I followed Sam, expecting to meet a teenager. Instead I came face to face with a fifty-year-old high school teacher and her seventy-year-old mother in a wheelchair. She gushed over the fact that I was Michael's sister, how lucky I was, and told me she had been a fan for years. Apparently she had organized her class into writing to the band in their very early days, and had become a huge fan herself.

I didn't quite know what to say to her, but recognizing she meant well, I was polite. I could not have known that this lady was obsessed.

Sam did not warn me that she had a habit of sitting in hotel lobbies for hours waiting for Michael, that she constantly sent him gifts and letters, that she drove the tour managers mad asking for 'will call' tickets, that she followed Michael around taking photographs of him. One week after this concert, I began receiving gifts and cards and even visits from her. She would call me, show up at my office and send me expensive gifts from Tiffany's. It was disconcerting to have someone I didn't know talking incessantly about my brother and bearing gifts I didn't deserve. And it is very hard to ask someone to leave your office when they are handing you a present.

When I talked to the other members of the band I noted that each had something negative to say about this tour and the business in general. Where had the magic and camaraderie gone? Of course I would have expected them all to mature, but the men I found myself speaking to that night were a far cry from the fresh, idealistic boys that I once knew. Michael came by to say Helena was starving, so he was leaving with his friends to find a hamburger. I never spoke of this incident with Michael and Helena, though I should have done. It was rude and shabby to treat his family this way. Looking back, I suppose that I avoided bringing these things up with him because I knew that I risked being treated in the same way as others who had forced confrontation: he would take flight.

Four months later, when he was visiting Los Angeles alone, I had a letter delivered to his hotel. It completely bewildered him. I had simply set out two pages on my feelings, about how perplexed I was by his busy yet unfulfilling lifestyle. I wondered why he was not doing something for his own career, or painting or writing or taking acting lessons, anything. He asked me to meet him at the hotel for the afternoon, and we would discuss it. He was acting very pretentious when I arrived. He said that he was shocked by my letter and dropped names of celebrities he had been hanging out with. I was not at all impressed with this: LA is full of celebs. This was a side of Michael that I did not like. We spent the whole afternoon thrashing out the dynamics of the family. At the beginning of the conversation I felt that Michael had taken on a very superior attitude, and his take was that I was all wrong about this. After all, as much as he loved his jetsetting lifestyle, he liked to be thought of as one of the guys. Here I was, essentially accusing him of being far too pleased with himself.

Now I realized that ours was a confusing relationship. Although

I was Michael's sister, I was twelve years his senior and throughout his life had performed some motherly duties as well. I was not impressed with the outside world's perception of him, I knew as I read or watched his interviews, when he was making up a story. He was a great storyteller and I always enjoyed his embellishments, but I wondered if some of his yarns would come back to haunt him some day. Sadly some of Michael's imaginative tales of his childhood and teenage years have been repeated, taken up and further distorted by journalists and by acquaintances who truly believed Michael was telling them his true history. Some of these accounts of his life are pure fabrication and for my family to read such inaccuracies is painful. It is one thing to announce to the world that your sister was a go-go dancer in a cage – thus conjuring up a seamy strip joint (though totally false, this tale did give the whole family something to laugh at) – but when a journalist reports that at twelve years old Michael was awoken one night by Mother and whisked off to the United States against his will, not only is a lie perpetrated but a mother's character is damaged. I think that Michael spiced up his stories simply because he loved to get a reaction, to entertain, to be the centre of attention. Asked the same questions over and over again he would become bored and 'tweak' the story.

On that day in August 1993 we sat soberly in a private room but were slinging attacks as if we'd been in a rowdy bar. It became clear that Michael now believed in his own publicity and resented my questions. Few of those who surrounded him ever did so. It made him feel very insecure. But he knew I would not lie to him and I loved him for no other reason but that he was my brother and a terrific guy. Fortunately he was in town for a week and we were able to spend some time together, and patch things up over the next few days. The fact was neither of us had ever been comfortable with conflict and residual bad feelings and now, he was really seeming mature about mulling things over, and coming around to see some sense in what I had told him. I think this is a 'man' trait.

By August 1993, Rhett had finally agreed to go through a rehab programme in New South Wales. He wrote a long letter as part of his therapy, telling me that he loved me and that he wished that we could heal our relationship. He told me not to feel responsible, for the drugs were his choice for dealing with his pain, and he blamed no-one but himself. I thought that it was very brave of him to admit this, and he wrote with such clarity. My heart went out to him. He wrote that he was happy Ross and I had found each other, and suggested that from now on we – the whole family – should all be more honest and open with each other, getting 'all the skeletons out of the proverbial closet'. I was relieved to read that he felt happy, safe, and healthy, surrounded by a community full of loving and caring people. The family had not been allowed contact with him for six weeks, and he was now asking that I let Michael and Tina know he was thinking of them and to write.

Christmas 1993 was spent on the Gold Coast. Mother and Ross were hosting and Helena's parents, Ilsa and Fleming, were their guests. Once again Ilsa arrived with a fresh new batch of European magazines. When she and Mother went to the local supermarket, she picked up some local magazines featuring Helena showing them to anyone who cared to look. Rhett had checked himself out of rehab for a short time to join us and was also staying with Mother and Ross. Helena and Michael and their guests, a model Gail Elliot, and her husband John were staying at the Mariott, and Richard, Erin and I had taken an apartment close to the beach. Kell and Sue had taken another one close by. Mother and Ross have great style when it comes to entertaining and they went to a great deal of trouble even to the extent of furnishing our temporary abodes with miniature decorated Christmas trees, fruit and flowers.

There was a definite deterioration in Michael's relationship with Helena who often appeared unhappy. She had frequently made fun of him before but in times past it had been playful and he was in on it – the sort of loving banter you observe between two people who are close. Now it seemed to us that the mood had changed. Michael often seemed unsettled by her remarks and it was obvious that it took him real effort to rise above the joshing with humour, which had always been his deliverance. It was painful to observe and I can only assume that he loved Helena very much to stay in the relationship. We were told that since it was Helena's birthday on Christmas Day we were to gather early for a Danish tradition. In Denmark it is the custom to wake your loved one on their birthday by breaking into the bedroom and jumping on their bed. If you fail to do this, it is bad luck.

Once again we had all tried very hard to seek out just the right gifts. Months before we arrived in Australia for this Christmas, Richard and I began combing antique and specialty stores up and down the California coast for the most appropriate, unusual gifts. I had Helena in mind when I came across a *Harpers' Bazaar* from the late 1800s. I knew that she collected antiques and treasured things, which had been cherished before. As much as I was excited to find this for Helena, I also collect pre-loved treasures and was tempted to keep it and replace it with something more conventional. The little newspaper – as this is the form in which magazines were printed back then – was bound and sealed so as not to yellow. I am not sure she knew what she was looking at when she ripped the gift wrapping off the package because, before I could stop her, she tore open the protective seal also and then tossed aside the gift. Oh well, I thought, at least it got to last a hundred years and made its way from Burbank to Sydney without becoming fish and chip packaging. We had also commissioned a friend of Richard's who specializes in large, chiaroscuro style portraits of celebrities, to paint Michael. He loved it. Gail's husband John said that I won the prize for the most original, loving gifts that year.

Mother received a lovely ring from Ross, Helena, a friendship ring from Michael and Richard surprised me with an engagement ring. The following day, the newspapers reported that Helena was seen with her mother, her sister and our mother in a bridal shop, choosing a gown for the upcoming wedding – as Michael had given her an engagement ring! Michael gave Erin a beautiful acoustic guitar. When we returned to California, she and her friend Linda formed a band called Bedlam Spiral and they began singing and writing their own material. Michael was thrilled, and encouraged Erin.

We spent New Year's Eve in Sydney, Richard, Erin and I dining outside at a restaurant in Knox Street, with Kell and Sue. Just before midnight, Michael's limousine pulled up right next to us and out jumped Helena, Ilsa, Fleming, Gail and John. Michael sat next to me, Helena was to his right. Adding to the commotion reverberating about the streets from New Year revellers was loud bickering between the two most recognizable guests. In fact, people were beginning to take notice of our table as much for the raised voices as for the famous faces. Again Helena and her parents wanted to act out a Danish tradition which involved everybody jumping up and down on their chairs. Michael was conscious of the attention we were creating and did not welcome the thought of any additional stares. I could tell that he was getting weary of these Danish customs. Eventually they departed for a local nightclub, taking Erin with them. Michael held Erin's hand protectively, after all she was his fifteen-year-old niece and she was not used to nightclubs. As they left the limousine at the club a photojournalist took a photograph of Michael and Erin. When it made the newspaper it looked as if Michael was with a new girlfriend. I imagine Helena was furious!

In that same week, Kell arranged for a long-time friend of his to take us all out on his boat for the day. It was a perfect day for cruising Sydney Harbour and it was a beautiful boat. As usual, we were driving caravan style, when halfway to the pick-up point Sue remembered that she had left lunch in her refrigerator. It was too late to turn back so we stopped to shop for a variety of oysters, crab, bread and side dishes. On our way out we ran into Ilsa who had been into the local newsagent to fetch all the latest magazines featuring Helena. When we arrived at the jetty, Kell introduced us to his friend who was obviously starstruck with Michael and Helena and Gail and John. I registered that Kell had missed me out in the round of introductions, but I was not aware that the friend had not even connected that I was part of the family. We had a fun day without pressure and not a photographer in sight, except for myself. Kell and his friend told funny stories and Michael and John got into the spirit and tried to top them. Ilsa spent most of the day flipping through the fashion magazines. Later, on the way back to the dock, Richard and I sat up with Kell's friend and chatted as he steered the boat through the marina. During the conversation I referred to Kell as 'Dad'. This long-time friend of Kell's looked at me, dumbfounded and embarrassed. He apologized: he had not heard any mention of me from Kell, during a forty-year friendship, and nor had he heard of Rhett. He was only aware of Kell having one child, Michael. He overcompensated with his apology and I felt sorry for him. He became very quiet for the rest of the way to the jetty.

I never did get used to these moments, although, certainly I had been through enough of them. It is easy to understand how this could happen: even then, you just had to walk into Kell and Sue's apartment to see a monument to Michael. I began sending framed photographs of my children to Kell and Sue after my first visit to their

Sydney home when I noticed they had absolutely no evidence of grandchildren in the photo gallery. I thought this was odd: most people are proud to show off their grandchildren. I don't know where they put those photographs, but they are nowhere to be seen in their home. Brent and Erin have been hurt by this slight over the years, but they are learning, as I have.

25 January 1994
Dear Tina,
Hope all is still OK, what a mess LA is in. [The 1994 earthquake hit two days after we arrived home from Australia.] Michael fell on stage Saturday night, had a bad sprain, a hairline fracture, and pulled tendon – he had to cancel a couple of concerts, and is unable to walk on the foot for two weeks – he is on crutches – still, in Melbourne Como Hotel – Room # 615. Rhett is coming up for a couple of days, should be here within the next hour.
Love,
Mother xx
PS: I forgot, Michael is under Mr Dick Shake!

Mr Dick Shake was one of Michael's more imaginative pseudonyms. Understandably it was one that Mother and I had a great deal of trouble using.

In late January 1994 Michael returned to the Gold Cost without Helena and was due at our house for lunch. Rhett was staying with us, having checked out of rehab, and Michael arrived two hours late. He apologized and explained that he had just bought a bowling alley in Labrador, fifteen minutes from our home, for $2.25 million cash and as it had a restaurant he'd had a sandwich there. He said he had decided to keep the same restaurant in place as it was bringing in considerable rent as was the bowling alley itself until it was decided to tear the building down and put up some townhouses or apartments. Michael was exhilarated at the prospect of investing for the future. The Paradise Lanes Bowling Alley gave him more of a thrill because it was commercial property and unlike the rest, was already working to make a return. He'd been told often enough to ensure that his investments worked for him – hence his glee at the thought of the rents already coming in. The bowling alley was on a large block of land with a view across the water to Bribie Island. The view could not be built out, so it was a wonderful investment.

Michael had arrived with a load of dirty clothes and asked to use our laundry. I guess life doesn't change too much just because you become a celebrity. Rhett already had a load in the washer and later he placed his jeans in with Michael's. When they retrieved the clean clothes from the dryer one pair of Michael's had a bulge in the back pocket which turned out to be a wad of sodden bills totalling a little over six thousand Australian dollars. Michael had totally forgotten about the money. I suppose it dried out all right but in those days it probably wouldn't have mattered to Michael if it hadn't. Rhett said he had heard of money laundering, but this was ridiculous! I thought about how things had changed, since that day Michael lost his little paycheck from the top of the houseboat.

Later in the same day, Michael asked to use our fax. I gave him some paper and a pen and left him alone. When I returned he was standing over the fax machine feeding it blank pages with his signature on the bottom and some with his signature in the middle. I assumed he was sending his autograph to someone, maybe to his fan club. He laughed and said that the faxes were needed for some business transactions.

INXS played the San Diego Sports Arena in April of 1994 and as I was unable to go Michael sent a stretch limousine for Erin and her two friends Linda and Tim from Bedlam Spiral. The kids had a blast, and he dedicated 'Mystify' to Erin. Michael took the same limo back with the teenagers as the rest of the band was staying in San Diego and he had to be back in LA for an interview early the following morning. Erin remembers many clamouring fans after the show. It was a claustrophobic, terrifying, experience being shuffled with Michael from backstage to the car. Halfway back to Los Angeles, they were pulled over by a highway patrol for speeding. Even though he had downed a full bottle of wine in the back of the limo, Michael leapt out of the back seat and went to the driver's aid. He had a word with the officer and told him that it was his fault as he had instructed the driver to speed up to lose some persistent fans. The officer shone a light directly into Michael's eyes and asked to see who the other passengers were. At this point it got a little touchy, after all he had two sixteen-year-old girls back there. Of course it was quite innocent, Erin and her friends were playing video games and no alcohol in sight as it had been put away by the time the officer put his head in the limo. His niece? Well, this took a lot more of Michael's smooth talk.

The following day I had a call from Michael who was in another limo on the way to the airport. He had just heard that Nirvana lead vocalist/lyricist Kurt Cobain had been found dead, the apparent victim of self-inflicted gunshot wounds. Michael was shocked as he expressed his sadness and disappointment that such a talented man would take his own life. He could not understand how he could leave his little child. He also said that we had lost the poet laureate of our generation. He continued to discuss it obsessively all the way to the airport.

He invited me to meet him on tour in Portland, Oregon, as I had recently broken my engagement with Richard and he wanted to cheer me up. Also he would have some free time between band obligations and Brent was now attending college there. Two days after his call from the limo, I checked into a room he had booked for me, next to his. I called him to let him know I had arrived and he came right over. The bellboy had flipped my television on to demonstrate the room features, and by the time Michael knocked on my door there was a reporter on the screen in front of the Cobain estate in Seattle interviewing grieving fans who were camping outside the gates. After hugging one another our attention was drawn to the television and Michael lamented about the pain Cobain must have been going through. Still, he could not understand or condone his actions, calling it stupid and senseless and selfish. He worried about copycat fans taking their lives.

Brent met us and we went with the band to the show where the reception this time was warm. There was a lot of joking around with the crew. The family atmosphere had resumed. When INXS went on stage, Brent headed out into the crowd and I sat in a little stairwell off to the side of the stage. I could see Brent push his way to the front and reach his hand out to Michael who was singing and laughing and slapping Brent's hand as he worked the audience. Just as soon as Brent could make his way to the front, the crowd would lift him up and move him back over their heads. He was crowd walking, having the time of his life, and meanwhile giving me heart failure. Seated at stage right, was a huge group of young people who had impaired hearing. I noticed that they had one person facing them who was signing the words to the songs as Michael sang. Michael spent a lot of time on this side of the stage, seeming to want to give this group more. In respect for Kurt Cobain, Michael sang a heart-wrenching rendition of 'By My Side'. He just said the song was for a very special friend who would be missed and asked that everybody take time to think of Kurt. In the light of the fact that we were close to Seattle and everybody was feeling sadness about the loss of the songwriter, it brought most of the audience to tears. Directly after this Michael switched to an up-tempo number and made his way over to my side of the stage, lingering there as he sang to me which forced the spotlight to shine into my little hiding place. I was embarrassed but it was a sweet gesture and it took everybody's thoughts back to the concert at hand. The whole exercise showed what a great performer Michael was.

Next day at breakfast Michael told me that he was exasperated with Kell as he had tried to persuade Kell to retire several times but he insisted on getting back into some new business venture. He just wanted him to retire and play golf. I had just heard that he was investigating the logistics of a car wash business. Michael rolled his eyes when I told him and said that this was *out*. He decided that he needed a movie to escape this conversation, so we went to an early show. A kind of brief sanity is evident in the exchange of the first of the notes below, both written soon after Portland.

24 May 1994
Hi Michael,

It was good to 'feel' the relaxation in your voice last night. The view outside of your bedroom window [at the villa] must be a slice of heaven. I remember seeing photographs of the sun deck when it was covered in vines . . . it must be getting that way now – I promised Brent and Erin that we would make a trip over there during spring or summer of next year. Erin and Linda have been getting serious about Bedlam Spiral; they have hooked up with a drummer named 'Fish'. They have been writing a lot lately also.

Take care and keep in touch.
Love,
Tina

On 16 June I received a naughty postcard from Michael, who was somewhere on the Ionic Sea. It featured a naughty picture of a Greek god with an enormous . . . He wrote, 'how's this statue for culture?' On the back he talked about sailing with some friends and reading Socrates. He sounded so relaxed and carefree, relieved that the tour was over, closing playfully: 'life has just begun. Love from the Ionic Sea + Me x Michael x'.

In a fax dated 8 July 1994, Michael commented on Erin's trip by road across the US with four friends to the twenty-fifth anniversary of Woodstock in upstate New York. He said he wished he could have dropped by. He and Helena had spent the previous weekend with friends at an outdoor festival called Roskilde in Denmark. They had stayed overnight in a tent to see Henry Rollins and the Specials, adding that they'd 'said hello to Björk and had a Real Viking Good Time!!' Evidently the garden at the villa was blooming, and he was excited by the pears, apples, plums, lemons, pink grapefruit, cherries and corn, all springing up.

In early October, Michael flew to Nashville, Tennessee, to perform without INXS in a special Elvis Presley tribute which had been organized by Priscilla Presley and included a mass of talent. Michael sang a wonderful rendition of 'Baby, Let's Play House', pouring his usual special blend of sensuality into it. He was never confident about appearing, never knew how good his voice was nor how special his phrasing. He just did not allow himself to believe that he touched people with his voice the way we all know he did.

By mid-1994, Rhett was spending time on the Gold Coast with Mother and Ross when he decided that he desperately needed to go back into rehab. He had been maintaining early nights, eating well and sunning himself but whenever possible he was also drinking a little (which in his case is a little too much) and still found it impossible not to party when the opportunity arose. When he did present himself back to the rehab clinic and they laid down the rules to him, he changed his mind and decided that he did not want to do it their way, so they invited him to leave.

6 September 1994
Dear Tina

Rhett phoned yesterday – he was still in Sydney. He said everything is definitely OK – and has met someone, her name is Kate and she was in Sirens. *I can't remember her surname.*

xxxxx Mother

Not long after this a photograph of Rhett and a very pretty girl appeared in Australia's *TV Week*, taken at an early showing of *Sirens*, a movie featuring two of Michael's friends, Ben Mendelsohn and Elle Macpherson. Also in the cast was the up-and-coming Kate Fischer. The caption read: 'Latest hot couple seen at celebrity gatherings is *Sirens* star and model Kate Fischer and Rhett Hutchence, brother of INXS's Michael.' *Inside Info*'s cameras caught them smooching at a Johnny Walker promotional party in Sydney. No serious romance was to develop, however.

My brothers may not have had everything in common but they did share a reluctance to commit in relationships. Rhett had been out of rehab for some months and after a short dalliance in the film industry in Sydney, he was living contentedly in Byron Bay, on the northern coast of New South Wales. By late 1994 he seemed to be coping very well. I had never before heard him sound so clear-headed and I was both relieved and happy for him and admired him for having the courage to face his life without a chemical crutch for the first time. He was living in a household with three women, one of whom was an exceptional person named Mandy Nolan. But there did not, for once, appear to be any sign of a big romance. She was a stand-up comic and an artist. Michael said that she was just what Rhett needed, someone with a wonderful sense of humour. In November Rhett delighted and astonished me with a fax addressed to Tina, Erin and Rio, our gigantic cat. Positive and playful, he talked of having designed and built a set for a local play in Byron Bay and started a monthly advice column – 'Just Add Vice' – in the local gig guide, and started to host a radio show on Friday mornings. He truly was getting his life together, and I appreciated the lovable rogue's sense of humour. He called in late December with the news that Mandy was pregnant and they were expecting in August. He asked me to relay the news to all. This was very exciting, so unexpected and we all hoped that this would be a turning point.

In the latter months of 1994 the Australian press had been reporting Helena and Michael's upcoming wedding plans. Speculation was that it would take place in Paris and that Helena had commissioned Gianni Versace to design the gown. Michael and Helena were of course friends with Versace – his villa was just minutes from Michael's in Roquefort les Pins. And goodness knows Helena (and her mother Ilsa) had hinted plenty to get a marriage proposal out of

Michael, but it had always seemed that he was just not ready to commit himself to marriage yet. The story about the Versace wedding dress – that was pure invention. Helena had shown no signs of what he called 'serious nesting', meaning, I suppose, that if he was going to settle down he would want his partner to feel that way too, but Helena was taking on more work than ever. Helena did buy a fabulous, full-length, satin gown. It was, however, an antique, yellowed with age. She hung this on her side of the closet in the master bedroom of Michael's villa. I assumed it was to remind him of her wishes. It would remain in the closet for a long time.

CHAPTER NINE

Mind Games

Christmas 1994 was unforgettable. Mother and Ross arrived into Los Angeles on 18 December, and within two days bought a 2,300-square-foot penthouse in my name. This was a huge surprise and outrageously generous even though Ross is a wealthy man. Michael and Helena arrived shortly after this, for a two-week visit. Helena was booked for some work and Michael was catching up on family. When Michael found out about my penthouse he asked Mother why she had not told him that I needed some financial help. She replied that just like her, I would never think of asking him.

Michael invited us to join them at the Ivy for dinner and joked that he had difficulty getting a table under his name so he used Helena's. He had a way of making a joke at his own expense, but I noticed an edge in his voice and I reckoned it bothered him more than he was letting on. Later we went back to the Sunset Marquis bar and settled around a corner table. Helena jumped on the phone and tracked down Kate Moss. It was as if she had decided that two hours was enough with the family. She and Michael had a confrontation over whether to stay at the Sunset Marquis bar or to move on to the Viper Room. Michael wanted to stay put. The atmosphere was thick. Helena finally suggested that she would go ahead in a taxi and he could join her later. I knew this was putting pressure on Michael and the mood had been brought down anyway so I excused myself and took Erin and Brent home. Mother and Ross also left.

The next day Michael invited Brent and Erin to join him, Helena, and Stephen Dorff to a showing of Stephen's new movie, *SFW*. Afterwards Erin, who was now sixteen, reported that Helena was flirting with Stephen Dorff. Erin couldn't understand why Michael would put up with this behaviour. Maybe he just didn't care any more, I said, and I had other things on my mind. The former owners of my new home had moved to the East Coast three months before we bought it so Ross had arranged for us to move in less than the usual thirty or sixty days. He had originally tried for Christmas Day but that was out of the question for me. Anyway, four nights after our dinner at the Ivy, I had a house-warming party. I wasn't really ready for it but since Michael and Helena were in town I went ahead. Although Michael appeared quite jovial, arriving with an exquisite bottle of wine, Helena kept to herself. Throughout the evening it was obvious from their body language that they were going through a rough patch. Michael bounced around conversing with many people, spending a great deal of time with Erin and her friends. One of my guests, an actor and a cigar connoisseur, had heard that Michael had recently started to appreciate cigars. He led Michael upstairs to sit by the jacuzzi overlooking the LA skyline where they sat and enjoyed one of his best Havanas. Relaxed now, Michael spoke of acting and settling in Los Angeles. He thought it was time to get serious about this aspect of his talents and expressed an interest in taking acting lessons.

Wandering around my new home, Helena stopped to look at a picture, which had been inscribed 'To Tina and Richard'. She thoughtfully reminded me that I was no longer with Richard and suggested that in future I should insist that the artist give me my own separate piece, as if the problem of division of spoils attendant to a break-up was on her mind. It didn't seem very optimistic or romantic to me, but with conviction she announced that she always did this. I knew that Michael was on the move.

Michael's birthday fell on the day of his departure and Mother, Ross, Erin, Brent and I were meeting him and Helena for lunch at the Four Seasons. I was pleased with the gift I had found him – a copy of the original script for *Citizen Kane*. Michael arrived an hour late and without Helena. Making a very poor excuse for her absence he admitted that he had not yet been to bed. This was obvious from his dishevelled appearance. He explained that he had been dancing naked on a friend's coffee table in honour of his thirty-fifth birthday, adding that you come into the world naked and therefore why not celebrate your birthday the same way? He looked around the room and saw his old friend Michael Hamlyn and went over to him. His film *Priscilla, Queen of the Desert* was winning awards all over the place. Michael had been offered the role eventually given to Guy Pearce, but after numerous negotiations with Chris Murphy, Murphy advised Michael not to take the offer. Michael regretted taking this advice as he knew that it could well have been a turning point in his career. Hamlyn was at the bar with Terence Stamp, his lead actor from the film, consoling him for not winning some Best Actor award for his role as a cross-dresser.

Michael seemed much too animated for someone who had not been to bed but that day I wasn't going to worry. We were just happy to be spending these last hours together, it was his birthday, and we were happy that he was happy. Helena was unconvincing when she called that afternoon to complain about her earache. I suggested that they delay their flight to Nice, as it can be dangerous to fly with ear trouble. Nothing doing, they were on their way to the villa and they departed that evening.

Three weeks later, in mid-February, Michael called me from the villa. He was in the mood for a talk and spoke a good deal of Paula, the by then estranged wife of Bob Geldof, and mother of three. She was well established as a British television personality and journalist with a high profile in the press. He did not say his relationship with Helena was over but mentioned that she was on her way to Denmark. He did not imply that he was intending to start seeing Paula, though he did harp on about how caring she was with her children. Apparently she had written several books on the pleasures of motherhood. He said that her girls were more than just bright, they were prodigies, all three with IQs running off the Mensa scale. I wondered how you would test a three-year-old. He referred to her as 'brilliant' so I guessed he was now hooked; I could always tell what was up when he called a woman brilliant. With Michael it was all or nothing. For instance, he would never just say that Paula's children were cute, funny and bright. They had to be beyond genius.

He was disappointed to learn that although I was familiar with Bob Geldof through his efforts with Live Aid and with the Boomtown Rats, I had never heard of Paula Yates until I was reminded of the interview she had done in New York for the London listings magazine *Time Out* (the one which had caused Virginia Hey to pack her bag and leave Michael briefly stranded) and I dimly recalled Jonnie's mentions of a Paula who made phone calls and showed up at hotels while they were on tour. Could this be the same woman? Very rarely does a British television personality make headlines in the United States as we don't get very much British television here, so for a while I remained truly baffled. This made Michael praise her more as if he wanted to be sure that I knew just how clever she was. I asked him if Paula Yates was a new friend and he said they had known each other for years ever since he appeared on her television show. Although he didn't say so I had the feeling that as usual he had already begun this liaison before cleanly terminating his relationship with Helena.

25 February 1995
Dear Tina,
Thought you would get a kick out of this story. What next!
Love, Mother

It was a story cut from an Australian magazine about Michael jilting Helena, Michael denying his involvement with Paula Yates, and Helena's new love interest – Stephen Dorff! I had heard rumours that Michael and Helena were having problems. At this stage Michael never mentioned Paula Yates to me and I assumed that it was not an important relationship, just something casual. Later on, the whole world found out as various photos and articles began to appear in the press. This sort of thing happened once before when Michael appeared on *The Tube* in England. I remember INXS teasing Michael about Paula's body-language when she interviewed him.

14 March 1995
Dear Tina,
Radio and newspapers are announcing Michael and Helena's secret wedding somewhere in Europe. Here we go again! Has the rain stopped yet? Love from us both,
Mother and Ross xx

Michael was seeing Paula discreetly as he was not sure where this was going and he had not finally split from Helena. They saw each other sporadically for about three months until she suggested that they go away for the weekend. Paula had evidently chosen a quiet country inn in Kent, a little place she had often visited with Bob.

Even though it was supposed to be a secret weekend getaway, the press had been tipped off by an 'anonymous' source that Paula was having an affair with an unnamed rock star.

The British tabloid press, always hungry for scandal, responded royally. Half of the inn was occupied by photojournalists. Later on Michael said that the dining room was full but he did not realize that most of the couples were members of the press. When a journalist friend of Paula's came over to the table she seemed astonished and hurried with Michael upstairs to their room. Before the weekend was over, Michael had scuffles with at least two of the photographers – one of whom brought assault charges. Michael was a lover and he loved women almost to a fault, in a protective way. What I think he saw in Paula then was a beleaguered, defenceless mother of three up against a Goliath by the name of Geldof. Soon after this incident Michael began telling friends and family that he thought Bob was out to destroy Paula because she had left him. He believed that Bob was so well connected that he had some influence when it came to controlling the press. Paula, too, had some powerful media friends.

It's important to remember that the British press has always had an ambivalent attitude towards Paula. The media can be fickle, changing their opinion without any fair reason, but in her case while some have always liked to knock her, in other quarters she is deified. And Paula does give good press.

Anyway, it figures that the combination of smart, sexy, female in distress would be an unbeatable combination for Michael. What a cad he would be, if *he* left *her* after such a public display. The photographs that made the newspapers showed Michael attacking a photographer, while Paula dashed to a waiting car. Of course what most people did not know was that while one photographer baited Michael, another stood aside waiting to snap the picture. These pictures were published along with stories about Paula leaving Bob for Michael, which was completely untrue. She had already moved out of their home. Bob had just procrastinated about giving the press a statement about their separation.

Michael may have been already smitten with Paula, but it had not been enough to actually end his affair with Helena thus far. Now, he had no choice but to commit to the relationship as he could not talk his way out of this with a humiliated Helena. But not only was his four-year relationship with her shattered, he was also eventually brought up on charges instigated by one of the photographers, and his former relative anonymity in Britain was forever lost. Up till that point, he had been rarely followed by the press and could usually put a hat and glasses on and go anywhere. But from now on the press was always waiting. Thus began his gradual but growing contempt for the media, the British tabloids in particular. He had experienced a taste of their manic desire to hunt down a celebrity for a fat cheque when he was with Kylie, but what he experienced at their hands in the three years he spent with Paula was pure malice. For Paula's enemies in the press corps, this new relationship of hers was an opportunity to paint her as a harlot. And when Paula sobbed about her mistreatment, Michael took it personally.

Several years had elapsed between Paula's first encounter with Michael and when they started to have this affair. In her own autobiography, however, she has written of her ongoing fascination with Michael, although of course she was still married to Bob Geldof. This time her rival had been one of the world's most beautiful international supermodels. British newspapers, always eager to attack the victor, taunted her with unflattering stories. One depicted a magnificent photograph of Helena next to a particularly frumpy photograph of Paula. The caption read: 'Would you trade this for this?' Michael could not understand why the press was so nasty to her. He blamed it on the saintly image of her estranged husband, Bob Geldof, making the fact that Paula was so brazen as to leave Geldof tantamount to a sin to many people, particularly readers of the British press. The person who wins in this sort of situation is usually the one with the most expensive public relations firm. If publicists were planting stories, it was a dangerous game they were playing, for there is no such thing as loyalty in the media. The press and those who follow it can turn at any time.

Poor Michael, I commiserated with him. It was a mixture of unimaginable pain and confusion, to find himself ostracized by the same press which had, up until now, treated him generously. He had spent his whole life basking in compliments which he really did not think he deserved and now, at the age of thirty-five, a pivotal age for a singer in a rock band, he was being publicly and painfully scorned. And for what? This, too, was undeserved. In his eyes, he was seeing a woman of whom a certain sector of the public did not approve, but what did his personal life have to do with anyone else?

I continued to fret about Michael's involvement with Paula's problems and concluded that it was insane for him to be so concerned about her collapsed marriage. I believe that one should finish one relationship before entering into another. It's true that Michael had a pattern of doing just the opposite, but he had never had the extra complication of being married and nor did he have children.

28 March 1995
Dear Tina,

Haven't had any further news from London as yet – but the 'Rag Mags' are having a field day. I've still not heard from Michael. And I'm very concerned, as he promised he would phone as soon as the case [assault charge] was over on Monday. The papers and magazines have been pushing this on TV as well. Poor Mike, he must be feeling so alone at times.

Love,
Mother

6 April 1995
Dear Tina,

We have finalized our itinerary for Europe, we will send you a copy. I have been getting calls from London re Michael . . . more like being harassed, so I phoned Sam at MMA and she has given me the number of the PR girl in Sydney, also in London. She said I should just refer any caller to those numbers, and if they continue they will hear from their solicitors.

Lots of love,
Mother

Michael was a strange combination of someone who ate well, took care of his body with workouts, usually drank moderately, but who also consumed a healthy or unhealthy amount of illegal drugs. Like many people involved in drugs, he reasoned that exercise and a healthy diet would counteract their effects. But mid-1995 Michael's illegal substance abuse had escalated. He particularly enjoyed hallucinogenics, and the 'balance' he sought was listing. Michael enjoyed drugs for the same reasons that most people do, of course – escapism. It was a relief from life's problems.

Paula, by her own admission, had jumped in the deep end of the drug culture at the age of twelve with a boyfriend while she was attending school in Malta. According to her autobiography, she was using heroin every afternoon and did 'lots of drugs as a teenager'. She maintains that she remained a teetotaller at that time. At all our family functions she was very fond of good champagne. So here we have Michael, fearless about experimentation with life itself but loath to create discord, and Paula – a self-proclaimed chameleon – who has the uncanny ability to say things that will stun print and television audiences and make headlines. I don't think it's surprising that the combination of these two people could be volatile and, at its worst, horribly destructive. Especially when you add drugs to the mix.

22 April 1995
Tina,

Will you still be coming in August to see Rhett and Mandy and his new baby, or wait until Xmas if we all go to South of France? Also ask Michael if he is coming out for the occasion in August, or will he also wait. Rhett said – 'As soon as he meets Mandy, he will know where I'm at now'!!! We leave for London next Sunday, Michael's driver will be picking us up at the airport.

Could you fax us Michael's new number? I can't tell you how good it was to see Rhett looking so healthy and happy – he is so over the moon and so gentle with Mandy and she is the same with him – they look great together and are looking forward to seeing you. He doesn't think Kell will get to Byron Bay (for the birth) as he can't afford to!

Can you believe this? Can't drive to Byron Bay but he can go to Europe. I'm also astounded that they already have plans for Xmas – obviously we aren't included. It makes me angry, especially with all the effort we all go to in order to stop Michael and Rhett from feeling pressured and feeling guilty and/or having to make decisions on who they should eat with on Xmas day – like you say, it's not as if we are all in the same country, so we have to work this through together.

Love, love,
Mother and Ross

24 April 1995
Dear Tina,

I'm pleased that Michael is happy about our plans for Xmas at the villa. I think it's best all around, at least we would get to see each other a lot more, and it's a great family get-together location – (kind of like the Kennedys! – at least I'm one! Was one. Ha Ha.)

In mid-1995 Ross and I were in London, staying with Michael in his apartment in Belgravia as his house on Smith Terrace in Chelsea was being renovated. Paula and Michael were not living together. She was living with her children and their nanny in another rented house. This was to be my first meeting with Paula Yates. I was curious to meet this woman and form my own unbiased opinion of her. In fact, I was determined to like her. When I did finally meet her I was totally captivated by the shy, sweet lady, who breezed into my son's apartment wearing a pink Chanel dress – nothing sexy, just a smart shift. She must have taken to heart his comments about Chanel, made seven years before during her *Time Out* interview with him. Her arms were filled with flowers for both me and for Michael. She had just taken her children to school and the plan was for us to spend the day together before meeting the children and their nanny Anita at the Connaught for afternoon tea.

We had such a lovely day. Michael's driver tipped us off that the paparazzi were following us everywhere but we honestly did not see them. Michael, Paula, Ross and I went shopping at Harrods, Chanel and Dolce & Gabbana, trying on clothes and shoes and lunching together. We returned to Dolce & Gabbana where Michael bought some black trousers, and I purchased a beautiful pale-blue suit.

Afternoon tea was interesting to say the least. The Geldof girls looked adorable and told me that both Paula and Anita had ordered them to be on their best behaviour. I found them really entertaining at that first meeting. Fifi, who was twelve at the time, was lovely, intelligent and friendly and looked unnervingly like her father. We talked about her school, friends and her love of horses. Pixie was about four years old and so cute. She insisted on Michael covering his eyes as she donned her new designer jacket and matching hat to surprise him. I could see that he enjoyed playing her game. I remarked on her hair colour, which was many shades of red and blonde and she said that she had coloured it herself, especially for me. She also said that her six-year-old sister Peaches had tried to put a stud in her nose, but it hurt too much, so she decided against it. Peaches was the livewire, very hyper, and she looked like Paula. I caught nanny Anita giving her the 'behave yourself' eye contact, as she stuck her little finger in every petit four on the silver tray.

On reflection it must have been a slightly stressful day for all of them. Paula, trying to maintain her demure young mum persona to make an impression on Ross and me. I must admit that Ross and I were enchanted. Later I had a touch of déjà vu about it, remembering going through the same scene with Tina, Michael and Rhett. Tina always trying to act so very sophisticated – she would be the one with the 'behave yourselves' glare in her eyes, inevitably aimed at Rhett. Michael told us once that whenever Kell paid the bill, Rhett would stay behind and 'nick' the tip left for the waiter. No wonder we were not too popular in some restaurants.

Throughout the week we saw lots of the girls and I came to like them more and more. And yes, I liked Paula very much as she made Michael laugh a lot and I told him so. His early days with Paula were undoubtedly happy – apart from the press persecution – and it would be foolish of me to deny this. She knew how to say and do just the right thing. One day we went to Portobello Road where some workman called out 'Hey Michael, that Paula's a babe'. Obviously journalists were following us, because this was reported in a magazine, only the workmen were quoted as saying something derogatory. On the way home she asked the driver to pull over and let her out, she said she wanted to go into a shop on the Kings' Road and would meet us at a nearby coffee shop. When she walked in she had a beautifully wrapped gift box which she placed in Ross's lap. He opened it and there lay a gorgeous spray of asparagus . . . made out of rich, dark chocolate. He had mentioned earlier that he loved chocolate. Another day when she noticed that I was reading Sarah Miles's autobiography, she said that Sarah Miles was a friend and that she had written another book which she showed up with the next day. I could understand why Michael was so charmed by her. I wanted to send good news and reassurances to my daughter.

4 June 1995
Dear Tina,

Michael has a brand new fax here. It was jammed, I finally fixed it and it spewed out about 12 faxes – some for Chris Murphy. Lots of news. We had dinner last night at a restaurant in Piccadilly called Bentleys with Paula and Fifi Trixibelle. It's obvious Paula and her children are crazy about Michael, and vice versa!! They will all be in Sth of France over July/Aug. He will be taking Fifi water rafting as she likes danger and excitement. They are looking forward to meeting you, Rhett, and Mandy – Michael was telling her a little of how Kell treats you, she thinks that is outrageous. You will like her very much.

Much love to you all,
Mother and Ross xx

One evening we went to San Lorenzo, a superb Italian restaurant and one of Michael's favourites. When Mara, the owner, came over to our table and Michael introduced us she hugged him and said to me, 'Mamma, don't you believe anything you read in those newspapers, I know your son Michael, he is like my son too. Very special, I love him.' Michael's friend, Michael Hamlyn, joined us with his wife Sara, then Paula arrived. Michael had wanted to pick her up beforehand, but she had insisted on meeting us there. She was again dressed in a very conservative fashion. She was still being very sweet and shy. What's not to like? I asked myself.

Dinner over, we walked outside and suddenly there was a flash of lights. About fifty flashes went off in our faces in quick succession. It was quite awesome and, as anyone who has had the experience of flash bulbs going off knows, it is temporarily blinding. We almost fell down the three front steps of the restaurant. We hurried on down the street and at one stage thought the photographers had left us but suddenly the flashes began again. These people wear sneakers, they creep up behind you and call out your name so that in your confusion you turn and oblige them with a startled stare.

The next day almost every newspaper used the shots, selling them to magazines in Australia and elsewhere. We were puzzled as to why there were so many members of the press and how they knew where we were. No matter how secretive we were, how often we changed cars, or went our separate ways to meet up at an unexpected location the press was always there – sometimes before we were.

During this visit, Michael took us to see his house in Smith Terrace, Chelsea, which he had bought in 1993. It was quite different from the other terraced buildings in the area. He had commissioned some major work which had been carried out by Australian architect Robert Grace to make it more open and airy, like a home you might see in a warmer climate, such as Sydney. He had concerns about the neighbours as they had already complained about the noise and disruption that all of the repairs were causing. As he described all the work that had gone into it, I thought it was sounding like a 'money pit'. But he was very proud of the investment. On a later trip to Australia, he left some papers in my home which included some of the accounts from Mr Grace. One account alone was close to A$300,000, and Michael still wasn't even living in the house.

Before we left London for the villa, Michael told us about another property, a house he had purchased on the Gold Coast, not far from our home. We were particularly excited as it meant that he would possibly spend more time near us. He said he would be back to see it later in the year. Once again he had purchased the property sight unseen.

Michael joined us in the South of France with his friend Chris Bailey who was helping him write his solo album. Chris has a wonderful Irish sense of humour and they spent many hours in Michael's music room. Music filled the house most of the time and the two men had such a rapport. It was one of the happiest times we ever spent at the villa. Paula called often, several times a day, and Michael laughed a lot while on the phone with her. After one call, he got off the phone and told us that she was discussing her new 'boobs'. She had very publicly, and thus to the consternation of many, decided upon breast enlargement. I couldn't see why she would want this but believed it was her business. I gather that quite a lot of people assumed that she'd chosen to have breast enlargement at Michael's request, or at least to please him, which is silly, as to my recollection most of his girlfriends were anything but buxom. At any rate, she said that before they took her into the operating room she wrote across her chest, 'make them perfect'.

I was glad to see Michael laugh so much, but I was concerned about the conflicting press that he was getting. One day I asked Chris about this new love of Michael's, and he told me not to worry, as far as Michael was concerned, this was nothing serious.

While Michael was staying with us on the Gold Coast in late 1995, Ross and I drove him over to view his house in La Spezia Court, on the Isle of Capri. This was another property he had planned to rent out. He was seeing it for the first time and wasn't expecting much as Colin Diamond had explained that although the land was valuable, he could not ask very much in rent because the house itself was very rundown. This surprised us as we had already driven by before Michael's arrival and we thought it looked rather well kept especially the grounds. He told us he had paid $1 million in cash for this house and a Bentley had been thrown in with the deal. He said that Colin told him it was a bargain.

As we sat outside the house with Michael two cars pulled into the driveway. One was a four-wheel drive, the other was a Bentley. Michael was very short-sighted so he did not recognize either driver, although he wondered aloud who was driving his Bentley. We drove off immediately, thinking that we were encroaching on the privacy of whoever was renting the house.

Soon after we arrived back home Colin rang and asked to speak to Michael who became audibly annoyed on the phone and told him that he was coming over to see his house. He refused a ride from Colin and asked Ross to drive him instead. They were met out front by Colin who took them inside for a tour. The house was impressive and stood on a large plot with a river frontage. Colin said he was staying there. He also said that his brother Stephen was temporarily living at the house. This surprised Michael who asked why he had not been told that it was being rented out to tenants. At this Colin asked to speak with Michael alone. Ross sensing that they wanted privacy suggested to Michael that he return for him in an hour. When he did so, Michael was in slightly better spirits.

About a month after this I was dining with my friend Susan. A friend of hers came by and Susan introduced me to Nicola Diamond, estranged wife of Stephen Diamond. Nicola suddenly began talking about Michael's properties on the Gold Coast. I asked her how she knew so much about my son's business and she replied that she worked at her husband's office. She said they kept a safe there containing all this paperwork with which she was so familiar. She mentioned the house on La Spezia, the block of land in Southport and the bowling alley at Labrador. I was quite astounded to hear this. I told her that I did not believe she should be speaking about Michael's business outside the office. She apologized and was obviously embarrassed.

As it happened Ross and I had sold our house soon after this and decided to use Stephen Diamond to close the sale as the buyer was leaving for Melbourne that day, and our regular solicitor was in Brisbane. Just before we left to meet Stephen, the mail arrived and with it a letter from Nicola Diamond. It was an apology for her behaviour. She said, 'I don't want Colin to find out . . .' When Ross and I were at our appointment, Stephen mentioned this incident and apologized to me for her indiscretion. I told him it was all right and that Nicola had sent me a letter of apology herself. He asked if he could read the letter. Reluctantly but feeling awkward, I showed it to him, but as I put my hand out to retrieve it, it got ripped. I was furious and in hindsight I am sorry I didn't recover it from the waste basket. When I mentioned that I thought Michael had made some excellent choices in his property investments, citing the La Spezia house as an example, Stephen agreed and in the course of the conversation took credit for finding all the Gold Coast properties for Michael. Later on when holidaying at the villa, I was reading a biography of Errol Flynn. A note fell out of the pages. It was from Stephen Diamond, writing apparently to congratulate Michael on the purchase of the house on the Isle of Capri. He had added a P.S. at the bottom saying, 'The Bentley has been thrown in'. This was one of the properties that Nicola had told me about. The letter aside, I was later to recall a coincidence. Errol Flynn had named his boat *Tigerlily*.

On 20 May 1995, Michael and Paula sent Mother and Ross a fax telling them that he had to appear in court on 22 August. Mother wrote to me shortly beforehand, but didn't allude to it.

15 August 1995
Dear Tina,
Spoke very briefly to Rhett last night, he was emotionally wrung out – hadn't decided on a name – Paula suggested 'Saucy Cupcake', however, he wasn't too impressed with that!
Love,
Mother and Ross xx

Rhett had become a father in August 1995 when Zoe Angel was born. He and Michael had not had much contact since Christmas 1993, their relationship strained due to many broken promises on Rhett's part. Although he had worked hard at turning his life around, there was so much bad history that Michael had found it easier to cut himself off from him. I called the hospital where he sat at Mandy's side, cradling the baby. You have never heard a more proud father. I flew out to Australia and surprised him a week later. I wanted to offer my support for the strength and courage he had shown and resolved to write to Michael about this.

9 September 1995
Dear Tina,
We saw Michael on the news last night flanked by reporters/photographers, etc, as he left court. I'm sure he was pleased with the outcome as he was only fined £825. I had imagined it would have been much more (even though he was set up by the photographer).
Yours,
Mother and Ross

8 October 1995
Dear Tina,
Yes, we have now decided to go to Sydney for Xmas, this of course depending on Michael definitely coming out. As of last night he is, but Bob's decision not to allow the children to come may change that. I doubt it though as he is really looking forward to it, and meeting Mandy and Zoe. Also catching up with Rhett after all this time. The last time was on the Gold Coast (1993). This trip will be good for Mike and Rhett to start again and become good friends. I am looking forward to seeing Michael and Paula, I do like her and we get along well. Wish you were coming.
Love,
Mother

A fax came through from Michael shortly after Zoe Angel's birth, expressing happiness for Rhett. They'd spoken and Rhett had 'said all the stupid Dad things'. Michael reckoned he'd be a natural in that role. He admired Mandy, as she seemed to have it all together. He'd recently commented on Mandy's profession – as a comedian and artist – saying anyone who could keep up an ongoing relationship with Rhett would need to have a sense of humour! It was Bob's turn to have the girls for Christmas, so they'd have an early celebration with them mid-December then head to Australia until 5 January.

Shortly before Christmas 1995 Paula and Michael came to stay with us. They had worked something out with Bob who agreed to send his children on a flight to Sydney on 26 December. Tina was unable to join us that year, a pity as there were a couple of family events as well as Christmas itself – the christening of Zoe Angel and – as it happened – Michael's announcement about the birth of his first child.

Ross organized a flight for Michael in a Tiger Moth. Michael, who had always wanted to be a pilot, was very proud of Ross's flying record and career. That day, Ross was having the pilot fly over our apartment block with Michael. Paula and I ran out to the balcony with the sound of every plane or helicopter. Michael wanted a photograph of himself flying and I got some great pure joy shots of him in the plane giving the thumbs up and waving. Later we had one of them printed on to a T-shirt for

Brent. The following Christmas, 1996, Michael had some cufflinks specially made in London for Ross, in the shape of the Tiger Moth.

During this same visit a radio station announced a competition to see who could tell them where Michael and Paula were staying. Over the three days they stayed in our home and they were not bothered, Michael's security people had taken great care to get them from the airport to us undetected. Michael rarely had the chance to drive his Bentley, which was often parked in the garage of our apartment block, but the day we went out for lunch at Mount Tamborine he drove it out. The owners of the restaurant are friends and they were careful not to let anyone know that we were there. There was a group of ladies sitting behind us, Paula heard their English accents and began getting agitated. Although these women were not taking any notice of her she complained quite unnecessarily, attracting ever more attention to our table. I had the impression that she wanted to be recognized.

Two days later, we all drove down to Byron Bay for Zoe Angel's christening as Rhett had asked Michael to be Zoe's godfather. We led, followed by Michael and Paula in the Bentley, who were followed by Tony the bodyguard. During our short stay in Byron Bay Michael confided in me that he and Paula were expecting a child but he was most surprised and a little disappointed when I told him I already knew. How? Someone had leaked the news just before they boarded their flight from London and it was in the British press. A friend had called to tell me. Michael asked me not to say anything to the rest of the family as he wanted to announce the news on Christmas Day. Also, he did not want to take anything away from Rhett on this special occasion for his little Zoe Angel. Evidence at last, perhaps, that Rhett could make us all feel happy and proud that he had done something right, and for once done something that Michael hadn't yet managed. To his credit, Michael could easily have trumped his ace with his own news about fatherhood, but chose to let Rhett have his day.

Our hotel was crawling with photojournalists but we managed not to let this spoil the special occasion. Ross and I were still finding it difficult to understand how the press always knew where Michael and Paula were.

In the morning Tony knocked on Michael's door and told him that he had just had a scuffle with some photographers who were staking out the cars downstairs. He proudly told a number of us an elaborate story involving a fist fight with one, smashing the camera of another and chasing after yet another. It struck me as odd that in the light of this Tony had not a scratch on him, nor was he even out of breath – it was the middle of summer but he was not overheated or dishevelled. Nor did he seem concerned about the possible consequences of destroying another's property. But Michael was grateful to Tony and thanked him profusely. One of the photographers that day who was really hassling us was Frank Thorne, who was later to write what we certainly considered to be a degrading article about Michael and me in the *News of the World*.

We continued on to Sydney where the four of us were booked into the Hyatt on the Rocks. Paula had yet to meet Kell and Sue. Michael arranged for Christmas dinner in the Hyatt Library. He was very specific with his directions for a perfect day. During the meal Michael announced Paula's pregnancy to the rest of the surprised family members. We called Tina in Los Angeles and he gave her the news, knowing that gossip from British newspapers would not have reached LA and the news would thus come as a surprise.

The only aspect that really surprised me about the news was the depth of Michael's surprise about it. Of course I congratulated him and wished him well. I thought he had survived a long, lucky streak considering no other girlfriend had announced this news before. I was also surprised that it would be with Paula, who already had three other children, was in her late thirties and had still not completely severed her relationship with her husband.

Just a few days after Christmas Mother called to say that Paula had to fly back to London urgently as her girls could not join her in Australia because one of them was ill. It was not critical, but when a child is sick it is always serious to a mother if she is a zillion miles away. Mother had confided that Paula was feeling very down about having to leave summer in Australia as Michael had rented a beautiful home in Palm Beach in preparation for the children's visit, and now she would be alone in the London winter for New Year's Eve. She suggested that I call Paula to give her my support and cheer her up.

I was a little hesitant, as so far we had only had phone contact. Up till now, if I called Paula's home looking for Michael, she would never offer much in the way of conversation. She gave me the impression that she was much too busy to speak to me; I always felt that I was intruding. Return calls from Michael seemed to dry up. I began to send my faxes care of Paul Craig in his London office or ask his office to have him call me. Michael and Paula were not actually living in the same place for very long at that stage as even when he eventually moved some of his clothes over to Paula's, he immediately went on tour.

Still, I had yet to meet Paula in person and thought my mother's suggestion a very positive and appropriate move towards someone who was carrying my brother's child. Checking my watch, I put in a call to the London home right away as it was early evening there. Nanny Anita answered and after some pleasantries, she said she would tell Paula I was on the line. After a few seconds and muffled voices in the background, Anita returned to the phone to say that Paula could not speak as she was reading a story to the girls. I thought that maybe she did not want to get caught up in a long phone call, so I asked Anita to pass on that I simply wanted to wish her a Happy New Year. More muffled voices and Anita returned to tell me that Paula was still unable to come to the phone. I wished them all a happy and fulfilling New Year, and said I hoped that she cheered up soon. I left my office number and hung up, but the call was never returned and I felt rather brushed off.

When I mentioned the call to Michael, he said, 'I think you're blowing this out of proportion, Tina. You don't know Paula, she's actually shy. She has a fear of telephones. She hates them, she can't even order room service for herself.' But her 'phone phobia' did not seem to have prevented her from making all those calls to Michael over the years when he was involved with other women.

I thought about the English and Australian magazines Mother had sent me, all featuring pictures of Lady Geldof in the most outrageous outfits and doing things like running through airports wearing tiny T-shirts and minuscule skirts topped off with a tiara in her hair. There were now breasts bulging out of near-see-through dresses as she walked around London. This was a thirty-six-year-old woman and I had difficulty marrying these images with that of a shy, retiring person. To be sure that messages got through, I continued to send them via Paul Craig.

CHAPTER TEN

Tiger Lily

Sweet sister T, she loved so long and hard
Kept to herself
Until that right man came along
Some men they lie
Some men they cheat
But now she's found
Someone who can be as strong

'I'm Just a Man' lyrics by Michael Hutchence

I had been divorced for twelve years and friends always told me that I would not meet anyone by working long hours and sitting at home. Michael said that nobody was going to knock on my door. Well, I showed him. Ken Schorr was a forty-eight-year-old divorced, successful businessman who moved into my building and literally knocked on my door in January 1996. After a three-month courtship with huge arrangements of exotic flowers arriving every day at my office, he asked me to marry him and we planned a wedding at Michael's villa for mid-July. It was Mother's idea to be married in the beautiful garden there and when I called Michael not only did he agree to the plan he was thrilled that the 'family' vacation home would be used for such a happy event. He always felt like we did not make enough use out of his favourite home, and encouraged me to involve Linda and Nestor in the organizing of it all. His only concern was that it was close to Paula's delivery date and said that he might have to bring her down from London by train. This plan changed several times; at some stage he decided to leave Paula in London and bring one of the Geldof girls. He finally arrived alone.

On 4 April I received a two-page fax from Michael regarding our visit and my marriage at the villa. He assured me that we should not let the fact that we had not had much contact lately get to us: 'although I'd obviously love to see more of everyone I know we all love each other and shouldn't let it get to us too much. You're a great sister I've always been proud of your many achievements and let's not forget my fantastic niece and nephew.' Mentioning Erin's plan to major in Art, he told me that his secret ambition was to be an artist and had decided to set up a space especially for that, and to get serious about it.

He went on to tell me about how he could feel his child's kicks and sang to her, and how excited he was over the pending birth. He added, 'Heavenly is one name we've been playing with – I'm also looking for a Polynesian name like Herani, Lani, etc.'

He discussed schedules, very diplomatically telling me that he had promised to give Kell and Sue a vacation in Europe and did not want to mess up anybody's plans. In other words, he wanted to make sure that we would *all* have our time and space at his 'family' villa.

He wrote of the turmoil surrounding Paula's divorce, custody fights and division of money and properties between her and Bob. He said that he and Paula had been through 'unimaginable hell with the press, the police (four burglaries), a fire, various litigations with 7 or 8 writs', and the fact that he had lost faith in society and the system. He offered me his Chelsea studio for my stay in London as in a bizarre court decision, as Michael was staying at Paula's house, his house in Chelsea was being used by Bob.

I felt so bad for him. How could anyone deal with all this turmoil? But I was impressed, not many men would stand by a mother of three, facing many legal problems. Of course I recognized that the impending birth of his daughter had a lot to do with his loyalty, but I was amazed that he was able to cope with all of this, even work on his solo album and write the new INXS album as well. There were many calls and faxes back and forth between Linda and Michael and Mother and me. Linda was excited for me and happy to have a wedding to organize, albeit a very small, private one. She was in a continual flap because the date we had decided on was Saturday, 13 July – the eve of Bastille Day. In France, this is like Independence Day in the United States, or Australia Day on Sydney Harbour – party time and everything is booked up or shut down.

The United States would not recognize a marriage in France between two US citizens not resident in France and the French government would not give us a marriage certificate at such short notice. It would have to be a symbolic wedding, so Ken and I were formally married in Los Angeles two weeks before I left. The final plans included Erin and me spending a week in Paris to do the things we do best – shop, visit all of the museums and art galleries and the French cinemas. We had a marvellous time, Erin was only days away from her eighteenth birthday, and we treasured this time as a kind of symbol of her move into adulthood.

While we were in Paris Michael called to check on our plans. He told me that Paula had redecorated the inside of the main house. He said that as a surprise she had Nestor repaint almost every room and he wanted my opinion. Erin and I flew to Nice, ten days before everyone else. Nestor was waiting at the airport and we greeted each other warmly. He had his own opinion on the new decor, with a running report for the thirty minutes it took to reach the villa. He was very distressed, and almost in tears at describing how Paula had insisted he paint the beautiful aged wood beams in brilliant colours! In his eyes, this was sacrilege, and when I saw it, I had to agree.

Before Paula's work the whole interior had been white, with lovely thick natural dark wood beams. Helena had been instrumental in the choice of furniture and decorative objects. Old candelabra were placed throughout the rooms, there were fine paintings and antique pieces, all very tasteful, and in keeping with the traditions and spirit of the beautiful old home. I find it difficult to describe the 'feel' of the place as it later stood. All I can say is that the interior resembled a bordello, old and falling apart. Paula had had old smelly chairs, some with stuffing coming out, driven down from her house in London. They now had ridiculous old pieces of fabric thrown over them. I have never before seen so many fabrics and patterns and ugly colours in one room. The living room alone was painted in a yellowy-green, baby waste colour. Everything, even the stairways and lamps, had odd pieces of fabric flung over it. There was such disharmony that it was actually uncomfortable to sit in many of the rooms. I changed bedrooms three times (there was an unwritten rule at the villa – 'first come, best bedroom') and finally settled on the tiniest one in the house, because Paula had not got to the walls yet. I tore down the fabrics which festooned the rest of the room.

Before this makeover the house had been available for hire as a location for fashion shoots, commercials and movies. I saw one aerial shot of it in a magazine where they claimed it was Helena's property! Now, it was deemed unsuitable and the house was eventually taken off the books.

The weather was brilliant and the gardens looked magnificent. Nestor always worked very hard, and loved Michael's garden as his own but he had outdone himself in readying it for my wedding. The rose garden was flourishing and I basked in the scent of fresh blooms each day. Sometimes I could see baby rabbits hopping away as I approached the flowers. One evening Linda and I were going over the table setting for the reception when I noticed that we were missing a crystal wine glass from a set of twelve. I commented to Linda about this and she told me that she had to discard one. Why would you 'discard' an expensive crystal wine glass? She was embarrassed as she told me that during a visit to the villa in mid-1995, Paula had used one of the glasses to take a home pregnancy test, afterwards leaving it in the bathroom. Linda felt that it was not enough to clean the glass, she simply could not use it to set a table knowing this. I made a mental note to look for another one.

Michael called before arriving in Nice, and asked for his Aston Martin to be at the house. As with most of Michael's cars, it had actually spent more time in his mechanic's garage in Nice than in his garage at the villa. Nestor and I drove off to collect it. It is awesome to navigate those bends in the South of France in an automobile like this. Michael's romantic attachment to this magnificent piece of machinery was understandable. When he flew into Nice the day before the nuptials I was shocked when he walked towards us. He was hunched, his face was bloated, and his hair was dyed a harsh, unbecoming black. His shiny curls were all but gone, replaced by dull, unnatural black tufts. When I enquired about the new hair colour he replied that Paula messes with her hair colour all the time and she fancied this on him. I thought, what was he going to allow her to change next? He announced that he was on a health kick and refused any alcohol, apart from champagne. I do not know how long he had been abstaining but he did not look healthy to me. Looking back, I remember not only his shocking physical appearance, but also his quiet manner. He seemed to be preoccupied but I attributed this to imminent fatherhood. Calls from London, with updates on Paula's condition, were coming thick and fast. When I asked about his feelings on the birth of his daughter, he spoke enthusiastically about the future. But his eyes remained dull. It was almost as if his spirit was broken.

On the morning of the marriage blessing, which was set for 3 p.m., we stocked the house with fresh oysters, shrimp, lobster and other delicacies and of course champagne. I was getting ready in my room, which was next to Michael's master suite and we were sharing a bathroom. He walked out as I entered and I noticed some prescription drugs on the counter. He was looking so unhealthy, his face was pale and still slightly puffy. On the label I read 'Michael Hutchence' and 'Prozac'. When he came back into the bathroom he zipped me up and gave out a wolf whistle. I asked him then what the Prozac was all about. He replied that it had been a troublesome year, he loathed having to spend so much time in London and sometimes he got so low he needed it. I had not heard much about Prozac and it was a hurried conversation as we were both running late, and Father Guerrero was waiting in the garden to bless my marriage. I made a mental note that I needed to speak at length with Michael. But when? He was only in the South of France for one more night during that visit as Paula was due to give birth at any moment, and I was off to a honeymoon in Venice.

During the reception on the terrace Michael played his solo tapes. These were songs, which he had recorded separately from INXS at his own expense, and he was hoping to put them together as a solo album. The music was quite different, and varied. Some songs were edgy and there was a little blues thrown in. His voice sounded better than ever. We were all impressed and asked to hear some of the tracks over again. On the two evenings Michael spent at the villa he took Erin, Brent and his friend Dan to a number of all-night clubs, returning for breakfast. The kids had a wonderful time. As Erin tells it, wherever they went, they were taken directly to a reserved table and drinks were automatically brought over. On the first evening, the four sat at a café and discussed many things, including drugs. Michael expressed his concern for Rhett, and wondered aloud if he was staying clean. He admitted to having tried heroin himself but assured them that he had quickly stopped, when he learned how destructive it was, and how habit forming. He said that it had made him feel ill. He made it clear to them that he indulged in illegal substances only lightly, preferring to occasionally heighten his senses with pot, or ecstasy.

At some point he disappeared from the club for a short time and when he returned, Erin said, it was obvious that he had taken something that spurred him on to dance and move around the room, bringing girls over to the table, introducing them to Brent and Dan. He later admitted that he had found some ecstasy. On the second evening Ken and I had left the villa to be alone and Michael and the kids were taking a late-night swim when he jumped up and told them to get dressed, it was time to check out the clubs. He thought that Brent and Dan couldn't possibly be having fun, after all, they hadn't met any girls.

On the roads back to the villa, Michael, at the wheel of his Mercedes jeep, drove directly over several roundabouts. When they reached the house he continued ahead to property behind his, and did some more four-wheel driving, squeals and laughter pealing over the quiet countryside from the three passengers in the jeep. This pattern of behaviour continued over the long weekend until Michael returned to London for the birth of his first and only child.

I returned to the villa the following day before continuing to Venice, but Michael, in his usual way, avoided the subject of depression and Prozac, making it clear he wanted to enjoy his time at the only private retreat he had. By now he could not walk out of his front door in London without being mobbed. With its large electric gate and driveway this was the only home which could not be invaded by the press. However, in speaking with friends after his death, I discovered that Michael had not been entirely truthful about his involvement with drugs when talking to Erin and Brent. I can understand why of course, and appreciate that he did not want to divulge the full extent of his substance abuse to his niece and nephew. I now know that Michael was hiding his dependency from the whole family. By mid-1996, he was very fond of opium and ecstasy and a physician in London was prescribing him Prozac. I should have remembered from my concerns about Rhett that people addicted to substances are often accomplished liars about their level of dependency.

Heavenly Hiraani Tiger Lily Hutchence was born on 22 July, nine days after our wedding was blessed, whilst Ken and I were continuing our honeymoon in Paris. Linda broke the news when I called the villa. Upon reaching Michael in London, I could barely get the words of congratulations out before he embarked on an excited description of the birth. He was naturally ecstatic over watching the birth of his little daughter. Paula's original idea had been to have friends at the house while the birthing process was going on (although not necessarily in the same room!) and he had invited us over to London for the event. I declined this invitation because I wanted to savour the rest of my honeymoon. I knew I would see the baby soon anyway. In subsequent phone conversations we discussed his new daughter, his upcoming tour and new video clips. We did not get a chance for serious conversation on the merits or demerits of Prozac until we spoke at my home in California in November of that same year, when he came for Thanksgiving dinner.

Ross and I were on our way to the villa for Tina's wedding to Ken, intending to continue on to Santa Margherita and Portofino before returning to the villa to see our new grandchild, who was due in late July. We stopped off in London to visit Michael and a very pregnant Paula. Paula was moving house as she and Bob were doing a swap. After one more court date, in a very unusual compromise, Bob was moving into Michael's house in Chelsea for six months. I felt sorry for Paula as her house was full of packing crates and wondered if she was quite ready for the birth of her baby. Michael assured me that there was plenty of help for her and somehow it would all come together.

Michael wanted us to return to London for the birth but watching a home delivery was not my idea of fun. Anyway, I was worried about Paula having the child at home. Though she had her other three children at home, she was now thirty-seven years old. I worried about her diet, for she certainly didn't look healthy. I didn't voice my concerns but I didn't support the idea either. After a couple of days getting re-acquainted with the children, we flew to Nice. Nestor met us at the airport, happy to see us again. As we drove he talked of the changes that had been made to the villa – the drama it had caused, what the colours were like and the number of times he had to redo things. Most of all, he expressed his horror at Paula insisting he painted the lovely old dark beams in outrageous colours. Linda gave us another lovely welcome. Tina and Erin were already there: it was my birthday and they had organized a cake. The garden was as peaceful and colourfully fragrant as usual but the interior of the house startled me. Tina had warned me about changes but I thought she might have been exaggerating and so was unprepared for what I saw. The peaceful old farmhouse had been made over with the bright bordello look Paula seems to favour. She had proudly said, 'I did it myself.' What a shame she had done so before Tina's wedding.

After the wedding party we took the train to Genoa, where Ross had a car waiting to drive us to Santa Margherita about an hour away. When we checked into our hotel room there were three messages for us, but before I had time to look at them Ross began fiddling with the television as men do. As I was opening the first message, I looked up to the television screen and to my surprise there was the news with a photograph of Michael, Paula and Tiger Lily. It said on the screen, 'Welcome Heavenly Hiraani Tiger Lily – Congratulations Paula Yates and Michael Hutchence.'

My three messages read: Michael phoned, please call him; Linda phoned, please call Michael; and Michael phoned, please call, it's a girl! I phoned Michael and the line was always busy. Linda rang to say that as we were driving out the gates of the villa, her phone as well as the house phone were ringing. It was Michael wanting to speak with me as Paula was in labour. She could not reach us until we arrived at the hotel, almost eight hours away. Meanwhile Tiger Lily had arrived. I put the phone down and Michael called through. He was so happy, said Paula was well, and gave me the vital statistics. He said they were drinking champagne with a few friends, and he was a dad. He couldn't believe it. I sent our love and kisses and hugs and he said he would call back later that day.

Ross and I walked down to the little village to find a florist, and after choosing some flowers to be sent to Paula, Tiger Lily and Michael, went back to our hotel to unpack and toast our new granddaughter. On the way we passed a news-stand and saw the story was front page in an Italian newspaper.

Later, I phoned Michael and Paula back, and Michael's manager Paul Craig answered the phone. We spoke of Tiger Lily; was she beautiful, who did she look like, the usual things. He knew I was against the home birth, but he said that there were two trained midwives in attendance. He said that Tiger Lily was healthy and so beautiful, I was not to worry. We spoke several times over the next ten days. I had asked Paula what she needed so that I could have everything ready, but she kept saying she needed nothing for Tiger Lily. When we arrived at the villa we went shopping immediately and chose a gorgeous stroller with an umbrella for the garden and a car seat, as we knew they did not have one.

They eventually arrived by charter flight, and as there were so many of them, Ross took another of Michael's cars to help transport them to the house. Nestor attached the baby car seat in one of the cars, and he and Ross set off for the airport. Linda and I were jumping out of our skin at the villa, awaiting the arrival of the baby. Ross told me that Nestor had had a job persuading Paula that she couldn't hold Tiger in the car, such was French law. But attached to her as she was, she of course finally agreed that the car seat had to be used.

When they arrived at the house, it was a fight between Linda and me as to who was getting first cuddle! Paula was pretty cool towards me that day, a very different Paula to the friendly, breezy one we had met a year before. To be fair, we mustn't forget she had just given birth, and the travelling may have tired her. I gave her the little stroller. The children took it outside to play, but I never saw Tiger Lily in it. Michael later thanked me.

Tiger Lily was such a sweet, pretty little baby, sleeping all day long, as did Paula between feeds. In any case, I did not get to see Tiger Lily until around 6 p.m. each evening when Nanny Anita would bring her downstairs. We were in the bedroom next to the master bedroom and I never heard a peep out of the baby.

We sat around the pool, Michael joining us on and off, Ross swimming with the Geldof girls who are brilliant swimmers. If Michael was out on business, or working in the garden, he would return and ask me how his lovely daughter was today. I would say that I had not seen her, or Paula. He would bring her down to me, until it was time for the next feed or to see her sisters. The girls had been through this pregnancy too and had waited so long for Tiger to arrive that they naturally wanted to see their sister.

One day, Ross and I had gone to a neighbouring village, Michael was shopping with Linda and Nestor, and Anita was down the end of the garden. We returned to find something of a scene involving the children, who'd been pretty mischievous. Michael arrived home not long after us and exchanged words with Paula about it. Linda and Nestor were also very upset. There was a lot of mess to clear up, and not all the damage was reparable. Had it not been for the baby making Michael's set-up more of a family unit, I think they would have resigned.

We were leaving the next day. I had ordered a vase for the villa from the glass blower at the art gallery in Valbonne and Michael was readying to drive with us to collect it. Suddenly, Paula came racing out the front door, running ahead of us, barefoot and with her hair uncombed. This was the first time I had seen her out without Tiger Lily in the whole time we had been there. It seemed they were not speaking. She jumped into Michael's jeep, but Michael started the motor of his Peugeot, and motioned to Ross and me to jump in. Paula jumped out of the jeep and into our car as Michael was backing out of the garage.

There had been an exhibition of beautiful work at the gallery and there was a photographer from *Paris Match* covering it. He came over to me, pointing to Paula sitting outside in the car, and asked, 'Is that who I think it may be?' I replied, 'You got that right.' He said, 'That's Paula Yates?' and walked away shaking his head. I was really surprised that he didn't attempt to take a picture of Paula, as she wasn't exactly looking her best, barely recognizable, and I thought this was what photojournalists lived for. Instead he turned back to Michael and asked if he could take a photo of Ross handing him the vase and it ran in *Paris Match* two months later.

CHAPTER ELEVEN

Confrontations and Tangled Relationships

Michael arrived in Sydney ahead of Paula, in September 1996, to promote the album *Elegantly Wasted*. One evening he dined with Michele and some other friends along with Colin Diamond and Australian barrister Andrew Young. Bob Geldof's name was raised a number of times. Michele says that Michael got very worked up about him, talking of 'Satan Bob' as a play on the 'Saint Bob' handle the press had given him.

Michael was convinced that Bob had special power and was above the law because he was so revered in the United Kingdom – after all, he was knighted. I also think that due to travelling, house moves and the fact that he was not responding to messages, Michael was not enjoying much contact with his old and faithful friends. I began to picture him living in a bubble, pervaded by only a select few.

INXS were promoting their album and due to perform at the ARIA (Australian Record Industry Awards) ceremony in September 1996. Paula arrived in Sydney with Tiger Lily and joined Michael at the Sir Stamford Hotel. Ross and I were staying at the nearby Ritz Carlton so that we could spend some time with them. At first Paula was busy having fittings and deciding on hairstyles, and we were all invited to the home of INXS's publicist, Shawn Deacon, for a party with some industry people. Paula was sitting between Kell's wife Sue and me on a sofa, breastfeeding Tiger Lily. She suddenly motioned us to listen to a secret she wanted us to share. In hushed tones she announced that Michael had finally asked her to marry him and they would be making the announcement shortly. We were both quite surprised, but congratulated her. Sue rushed off to give Kell the news and I stood up and walked over to Michael who was in another room. I kissed him on the cheek and congratulated him. He said, 'What for?' When I told him what Paula had said he threw his head back and laughed, saying, 'That's silly, she's just having you on, we're not getting married.' I was still standing there in shock when Kell, who had by now heard the news from Sue, came up to give him his best wishes also. Michael just shook his head, continued to laugh and said, 'She's just having you on, I'm telling you.' Kell and I just looked at each other. I continued to pay attention to Tiger Lily that evening, but tried to steer clear of conversation with Paula. This was made even more difficult because Michael wanted to party on with his friends and he sent Paula back in the car with us.

The following day, two days before the ARIA show and while Michael was at rehearsals, Paula called to invite me to go out shopping with her. I thought this was strange because she was always grumbling about the aggressiveness of the press when she went out and things had been so awkward when we'd last seen each other, two months earlier in the South of France. After some consideration I decided to go so we made plans for me to meet her at the Sir Stamford. I still wanted to get to know her properly for Michael's sake, and I wanted to see Tiger Lily.

When I arrived she was very chatty and pleasant, and I was even allowed to play with Tiger Lily. Time passed and I mentioned our shopping spree. She said, 'I can't go. Tony [the bodyguard] said it's better I stay in. We'll have some tea and talk.' As with most Australian hotels, there were tea facilities in the room and I made the tea, thinking this was very strange as she was acting like a close friend – in fact, my new best friend. She began to ask me about Kell. How we met, about our marriage, about the divorce, how he reacted when I divorced him. She told me about her problems with Bob and with her mother. It was a strange conversation to be having with her, all very 'girlie' and confidential. Then she told me that she might not be attending the ARIAs. I was astounded and asked her why. She told me it was all no use, that Michael had told her he was not going to marry her. She said she had tried everything. What do you say? I suggested that she try harder. She said that there was nothing more she could think of doing. Paula admitted that she had been asking Michael to marry her for some time now but he always refused. Privately I felt that if he were going to marry her he would have done so much earlier in their relationship when he was so wildly enamoured with her. At one point the phone rang, and I stepped outside on to the balcony to give her some privacy. When I came back inside, Paula jumped up and said she now had to make a call. I went to the other end of the room.

The following day Ross and I went to a movie and on our way back as we passed their hotel, I noticed about thirty photographers outside. My heart jumped. I had no idea what was wrong but I was sure it had something to do with Michael and Paula. We decided to go back to our hotel and call from the room. Michael answered and when I asked if he was all right he said yes, all was well. I mentioned the press outside crowding the little street. He said, 'Don't worry, I have no idea why they are there. Come on over if you like.' I was thinking that maybe the press had picked up on the idea of a possible wedding. Michael assured me again that all was okay, so I decided not to go over until the next day as I did not want to talk through that herd of paparazzi.

In the morning the newspapers and television were flashing the headlines, 'Drugs Found in Paula's House – Under the Bed'. My first thought was that this could not be true. I have been in that house and she slept on a seven-foot futon, there was no 'under' to that bed. I called Michael who said Paula was leaving to go home to sort this out. She said it was a set-up. Michael asked me to go over before Paula left for the airport. When Ross and I arrived at the Sir Stamford Michael was deeply concerned and really did not know what was going on. Anybody in England who read a newspaper knew they were out of the country. Michael was worried that Bob was going to take Tiger away from them. I thought this was unlikely. Certainly he had legal leverage as far as his own children were concerned, but what would Bob Geldof have to do with Michael's child?

But Michael was convinced that the authorities would think him an unfit parent with this latest development and that Tiger would be taken away from them. He was petrified of losing his daughter, so to prevent a possible ugly scene at Heathrow they decided that Paula should leave for London to face things alone the following day, the day of the ARIA ceremony. Michael would return with Tiger at a later date. Mandy would take care of Tiger Lily, as it would be impossible to retain a trustworthy nanny or nurse at such short notice, considering all of the intimate information being discussed.

That night, Michael sang 'Searching'. 'If you could face the pain, and I could do the same, it would be clear tomorrow, but would it start, but will it start, again'. He did so with such feeling, and I wondered how he could be in such control with all that was going on around him. Mandy had stayed at the hotel with Tiger Lily and Zoe Angel.

The following day Michael chartered a flight to take him, Mandy, the two babies, Colin and Tony to his house on the Isle of Capri, an inlet at Surfers Paradise on the Gold Coast. Colin advised that Rhett should not stay at the house, nor should Mandy or Michael leave it. Rhett came back to stay at our apartment, which is near Michael's. In retrospect I see that this must have been hard for him and it did cause a lot of resentment. Michael and his minders were worried sick that the press would find them. Ross would play pool with Michael to pass the time and we would take food in for them. Mandy and I repeatedly heard Michael complain to Colin about having Tony there, saying that the house had an excellent security system and he did not need someone looking over his shoulder all the time, but Colin was concerned about intrusion. Michael did bring Tiger Lily to our house for dinner one night and he arrived with Tony in tow. I asked him to leave us for a couple of hours so that we could have some family privacy. Michael did not object to this: I think he felt relieved.

The following day Michael called and invited us to the beach. He knew of one down the coast which was very private. He asked us to be downstairs in thirty minutes, and would we bring an umbrella for Tiger? We packed for a day at the beach and waited downstairs for almost an hour before calling Michael's house. No answer. Then Tony rang to say he had taken Michael to the beach and they would not collect us as he had checked out the area and had seen several photographers. He did not want to subject Michael and Tiger to that circus. We could see no visible signs of paparazzi and from our balcony we can view both front and back entrances to our secured building and would have noticed them while looking out for Michael's arrival. We were disappointed at not spending the day with them, but we thought little of this and waited until the following day to see Michael and Tiger. Michael and I did not discuss this incident at all. However, Mandy recently said that what Tony had confided to her and Michael was that he had heard that *I* had called the press to tip them off that Michael would be by the house shortly! To this day I regret that Michael allowed so many people to make decisions for him, and it hurts so much to know that he could actually have imagined that I had betrayed him. Now it is too late to set the record straight.

While Michael was hiding out with Tiger Lily, Colin visited us. He told

Ross and me about a piece of property he and Michael had purchased near Lombok, in Indonesia. Colin said that Ross and I would be able to stay there. He and Michael explained that they were building several homes on the plot – enough room for the whole family. Mandy actually saw a video of the property while she was staying at the house and told us it looked like paradise.

We have since found out that it was during this visit, in fact the day after arriving on the Gold Coast, that Michael revised his will. He had not signed a new one since 1992 when the only beneficiaries were the immediate family, Rhett, Tina, Kell, and myself. It was therefore imperative that he now include Tiger Lily, by then nine weeks old. Michael told Mandy that he was going to Colin's office to take care of some business and on 3 October 1996, he made and signed a new will. Again, it was straightforward. Apart from generous gifts to both Amnesty International and Greenpeace, he bequeathed 50 per cent of his assets to Tiger Lily, which she will not see until she is twenty-five years old, and the remaining 50 per cent is divided evenly between Rhett, Tina, Kell, Paula and myself. Colin was named as guardian to Tiger Lily. The executors were Andrew Paul (Michael's Hong Kong based accountant) and Colin Diamond. Colin's brother Stephen witnessed it.

It must have been signed in a hurry, unless Michael had his mind on other things, because his own daughter's name is incorrectly spelled as 'Hirani' and Tina's was typed as 'Christina Ellen', when it should have been Christina Elaine. My name is given as Anne Patricia, when it should have been Agnes Patricia. I have never been known as Anne. You might overlook one mistake, but out of this will's six beneficiaries, three of the family names were incorrect. This was a straightforward will, without any special conditions; our names had all been correct in his previous one.

Over time Mandy noted that the extreme stress and paranoia that Michael exhibited in Sydney upon the initial news of the drug charges gradually lifted. He spent time with his daughter and spoke of the many plans he had for the house on the Isle of Capri. Eventually, Colin arranged for an Australian passport for Tiger and Michael left the secure confines of his house and once again tested his nerves by returning to London. He took with him a nurse for Tiger. She was hired by Colin's father, from a local hospital and Michael referred to her as 'Bentley'. I felt so sad for Michael having to live this way, and all the time I was reading in the press that I had little Tiger Lily in my home.

The real story behind the 'drugs bust' is still a little hazy. Newspaper and magazine reports feature both Anita and Gerry Agar, Paula's publicist. Boosting Paula's image must have been a daunting task given the amount of negative press attention she seemed to attract. As I've read it, the story goes that Gerry's daughter was spending the night with the Geldof girls in Anita's care at Paula's house. Paula and Michael were away, and Sophie was friends with Paula's children. When Gerry returned to pick up Sophie, Anita confided in her that in the course of trying to find the manual to Michael's jeep to turn off the alarm, which had gone off in the middle of the night, she came across an envelope containing a couple of Smarties tubes, themselves containing a brown substance.

Later, it was alleged that the brown substance was opium. Gerry and Paula were famously to part ways, but no convictions were ever brought. However, this did not prevent the press in both Britain and Australia devoting yards of column inches to speculation and analysis of the situation. Paula and Michael were once again in the eye of the storm.

In November of the same year, INXS was in Los Angeles to shoot the CD cover for *Elegantly Wasted* and I invited Michael over for Thanksgiving as the other band members were going to Jon Farriss's home. He arrived with photographs of Tiger Lily and was surprised to discover that Paula had neglected to send one to me. He left his with me instead. My other guests were Venetia and Gary Berwin, and their son Sacha. Erin and Sasha had begun pre-school, together with President Ronald Reagan's grandson – who used to arrive at school every day accompanied by his own two secret servicemen. Michael loved hearing about this.

Michael was always excited to run into fellow Aussies and he had not seen Gary and Venetia for some time. I had first introduced them in 1983. He spoke of his house on the Isle of Capri, and he and Gary traded stories about deep-sea diving and boat racing. A dinner party was never dull when Michael was a guest. That night he told us a story about four-wheel driving through the outback of Australia with Helena Christensen. It was one of his typical vehicle-in-distress tales. Apparently they had attempted to cross a running stream, and had become stuck in the mud by the edge of the water, which housed who knows what kind of snakes and critters. He took on a wonderful, heavy Aussie accent when describing the locals who had helped them out of the mud.

Gary later said:

I was particularly glad to see Michael that day and we went about catching up on our lives. When we first met his manager was trying to put a record deal together in the United States and I owned the Hollywood Athletic Club, also known as the Berwin Entertainment Center. The BEC was known as a happening place because of its famous rock and roll tenants. It housed Van Halen, the Beach Boys, Blondie, Jose Feliciano and Baby O Recording Studios. Michael sent me a video to present to my tenant and friend Lionel who headed up Island Records. Lionel was preoccupied with Bob Marley and his new hit, so nothing came off with Island and INXS. Sometime in 1985 my wife Venetia and I were dining with Lionel. The subject of INXS came up, and I reminded him of the tape I had given him. Lionel's eyes grew wide and he made as if to bang his head against the table, saying 'No, no, that was INXS?' Needless to say he was very upset with himself about this missed opportunity.

Michael and I laughed about this that Thanksgiving and we talked about many other things, too. He impressed me as he spoke of his concerns about nature and the environment as I am also an advocate of conservation. I was so impressed that this rock and roller was so sensitive to mankind and nature. Michael was involved with some marine environment projects and was putting money into studies, his positive participation meaning he was using his fame to some good.

After dinner Michael and I talked about his plans for 1997. I asked him about his solo album and he replied that he doubted that he could get the record company to release it until his obligations with INXS were completed for *Elegantly Wasted.* Anyway, he was still perfecting it. He spoke of a US tour for the *Elegantly Wasted* album and although he knew he couldn't take a little baby on tour he expressed his sadness at missing out on daily life with Tiger Lily. Other band members had taken children on tours, but Michael did not believe in doing this, and it distracted him. This is why he had always wanted to wait until he had a more stable home life before having children. He told me he despised his life in London, something confirmed by his manager Paul Craig, who once said that upon landing in London, Michael would literally pale before his eyes. Michael blamed most of the turmoil in his life on the complexities of Paula's situation, although he could still not understand why the press persecuted her.

As he spoke he picked at his purple nail polish which had been applied by the make-up artist for the shoot the day before.

Throughout the evening he had few kind things to say about Bob Geldof but I had trouble believing all the calumnies. He said that Bob was trying to gain custody of Tiger Lily but the more I told him that this was ridiculous the more adamant he became. I really don't think he was looking at things rationally. I asked him about the 'drug bust' and he just insisted that the opium that was alleged to have been found at Paula's had been planted by Bob, and that private investigators could prove that it was Bob's doing. He said that he had a lawyer, Andrew Young, who was a 'pitbull', an unbeatable force in a negotiating situation. Michael said that although he was an international lawyer based in Australia, he had a lot of powerful friends.

I thought about all of the published photographs I had seen of Michael playing with the Geldof girls. This would be hard on a caring father if he knew of Michael's views about him. When I pointed out that a high-profile figure such as Bob Geldof couldn't be that bad and get away with it and suggested that he was exaggerating, he reacted like a teenager defending something his parents disapproved of. It wasn't my business to comment. It felt like I was walking on eggshells. This continued to be a problem over the next year as I became increasingly aware of Michael's volatile state of mind and did not want to risk igniting it. It was truly Catch 22, because I was loath to bring anything up that would upset him further.

My brother spoke of moving to Los Angeles to pursue an acting career. Being realistic, he recognized that he would fail to give it his all if he lived outside of the United States. Never before had he expressed an interest in a Los Angeles home to me. He said that he could not take the depressing London weather and looked forward to the endless sunshine of Southern California. He said, 'I give it six months and Paula and I will be back here with the kids.' I was thrilled. Finally we would once again be living on the same continent, even in the same city. It gave me hope, for I knew that distance would possibly soothe tempers and heal wounds between Paula and Bob. This would make Michael's life more tranquil, although I doubted that he could bring the Geldof girls with him without fierce opposition from Bob.

After his death I found out that in the thirty-two months that Michael spent with Paula, most of them on the road or in his own homes, he only actually had a half-dozen conversations with Bob Geldof. So his strong impressions of him are all the more bizarre. Only when I look at the photographs from Thanksgiving 1996, do I see how, physically and mentally, Michael was far from well. In the pictures his face is slightly bloated, his body hunched over, and it reminds me of how, when he spoke of Geldof, his eyes shifted and darted in a manic way. Many people who have seen those pictures and heard me describe his manner have since suggested that it was obvious that he was using heroin, if only occasionally.

At Christmas 1996 Michael and Paula brought the Geldof girls and Tiger Lily to his house on the Gold Coast. I was on crutches that year, due to a back injury. He wanted to drive over to see us in the Bentley and we made arrangements for it to be parked in the lot beneath our building but they arrived in the four-wheel drive. Michael was not very happy, as he did not get to drive his beloved Bentley often. Ten minutes after they arrived, Colin Diamond was buzzing our security door with another man. As Colin and this man stood outside on our balcony talking, Michael walked out to join them and he and Colin had a heated argument. I heard Michael threaten as he walked back in 'and it's my house too you know!' I would not understand the significance of this remark until after his death.

On this same day after Colin and the other visitor had left, Michael was in Ross's study, looking at his old flight logbook. He was always fascinated with Ross's medals and memorabilia. As I recall, Paula came over to me and quietly said she was aware of something that would involve details of our family life being made public. I grew terribly anxious. To change the subject I admired Peaches' dress even though it was much too large for her. Paula said it was hers. Pixie chimed in that they had packed some really special dresses for this trip and made reference to a wedding. I enquired about who was getting married and they just giggled, saying that their mother had a really special blue dress, but that they could not say more.

Michael and I had a running joke. I once wore a red dress to an awards show, and when Michael complimented me on it I said 'I will wear it to your wedding'. It became 'the' wedding dress and from then on whenever Paula mentioned a wedding, I would ask Michael if it was 'time to bring out the red dress?'

We had champagne, as usual, during that Christmas dinner. It was the first time I had seen Paula drink. Michael gave Ross the pair of cufflinks in the shape of the Tiger Moth and Ross still treasures them. Ross had given Michael the bomber jacket which he had worn in Korea. Michael loved it and called a few weeks later to tell us to watch him wearing it in an interview.

In January 1997 Michael returned with Paul Craig to Hong Kong to present a special for MTV. He gave a tour of Hong Kong through his eyes. He was happy and relaxed, but when it was time to return to London his mood changed. A little later he flew to Los Angeles with the rest of INXS to promote *Elegantly Wasted*. While he was in town, it was Jonnie's birthday and he celebrated it with her. During that evening he had several volatile calls from Paula and after the last one he got off the phone and poured out his concerns about his many problems in London.

INXS worked the press and played some warm-up shows in anticipation of the March release of *Elegantly Wasted*. They played two private acoustic shows at ABC Studios in Sydney for the Australian media; six days later, a special show in Aspen, Colorado, which was recorded by VH1 called *INXS Rocks the Rockies*; ten days later they were in London to play on the television show *TFI Friday*; most of the following four weeks was spent promoting in London and Paris. The tour began on 4 April, and on 16 April while in New York they appeared on the *Rosie O'Donnell Show* where Rosie called Michael a 'cutie-petootie'. On 20 April they played a show in Dallas with Matchbox 20 and Beck; David Letterman had them on his *Late Show* from New York where they performed 'Elegantly Wasted'. They spent the next two months doing shows and promoting in the United States, United Kingdom, South Africa, Scotland and Wales – where they played a festival with several other groups – and headed on to Germany to play the Rockpalast Festival with Simple Minds, Sheryl Crow, and Nenah Cherry among others.

In April they played the Mayan in downtown LA. It was an excellent show. While they were in town, Michael took Ken, Erin, her boyfriend Joshua and me out to a wonderful brunch. When I hugged Michael he winced in pain and explained that he had fallen and bruised his ribs while working on a video. I observed him laugh out loud and hold his side while in conversation with Joshua, who has a wonderful dry sense of humour, which Michael appreciated immensely, but his ribs hurt him every time he laughed. Part of the conversation centred around royalties, as there had been stories in the news about the Beatles and the Rolling Stones selling off much of their publishing rights. Michael's comment was that he and Andrew owned theirs outright and would never part with this income, as it was ongoing.

He left us with some copies of *Elegantly Wasted* and I played it over and over, liking it very much. I have always tried to listen to new INXS music as an objective fan for the first day or so. Then I listened to the lyrics more carefully, trying to figure out what he is saying, or who he might be referring to. But it was Erin who saw that the song, 'I'm Just a Man', referred directly to our family. I played it again and listened carefully. There he was, singing of Rhett's pain and struggle with substance abuse.

I immediately called him in London, and told him I thought it brave to bare his soul like that. I wanted to support him, as I was certain that it had been difficult to release those words for the world to scrutinize. At the same time I wondered how the rest of the family would read them. He thanked me profusely but by the end of the conversation he was sobbing and he made me cry also. I was glad I had called and assumed that his tears were a reaction to the fact that I had acknowledged his bravery. Rhett told Mother that he played that one track over and over. Mother wrote Michael a poem in response, and faxed a copy to me.

I got your message, heard it loud and clear,
A very private message, for all the world to hear.
I knew our lives had changed for ever
The day we took that plane,
The two of us so quiet, my reasons then seemed sane.
I had to take you with me, my love for you so strong,
Couldn't leave without you, yet couldn't carry on.
Didn't mean to hurt your brother. My reasons seemed so clear –
He was born with so much anger, and I lived a life of fear.
I didn't want to marry, was feeling too much pain,
But we marry for wrong reasons, hoping we can love again.
'He' knew that there were two of us, he said 'Don't worry Hon',
She will have my name. But soon we had two sons.
'She' became invisible, unacceptable – a daughter.

He's lived too long the Eastern Way –
Girl babies sent to slaughter!
If that sounds hard, it's meant to be. He really didn't try
To be a husband and a Dad, it means listening to our cry.
He didn't seem to notice, didn't seem to care,
He had his sons, his trophy wife, but he was never there.
He never kept his promises, he left us all alone.
I couldn't really cope with this, and ran far away from home.
You're so sensitive in nature, very much like me,
Though some may call it arrogant,
The truth's hidden deep inside of you and me.
Yes! I got your message, heard it loud and clear,
A very special message, for all the world to hear.

Michael phoned me during the European leg of the last tour, in late June 1997. They had reached Vienna, and for the first time I could 'feel' his depression. I asked him what was wrong. He said, 'I can't take it any more, I don't want to finish this tour. I'm so unhappy.' He was worried about money. The fighting between Paula and Bob had been escalating and making him crazy. I asked him to try to hold on, finish the tour and think about the baby. She was his first priority, he assured me. He loved Tiger so much it hurt.

But over the course of our conversation I had a growing sense that he was feeling trapped on tour, and the perpetually escalating tension surrounding the whole 'Paula/Bob' situation can't have made things any easier. I knew Michael to be non-confrontational by nature. I was concerned by this conversation with him from Vienna. I wished I could be there to give him a hug and reassurance. I knew he was fragile, but the idea of his suicide did not cross my mind. At worst I thought he might walk off the tour. Yet I did feel helpless and so far away. When I called back Michael asked us to come over to Los Angeles where he would be taking a month off. He would be arriving there in the first week of July. I was pleased: we would have the chance to talk, and I could see Tina as well as reassure myself that he was basically all right. Since Ross and I were both retired, we were fortunate enough to be able to make arrangements to head off right away. We checked into the same hotel as Michael. When I saw him he looked so happy, and I was instantly relieved. He said he had anonymity in Los Angeles, he felt free to walk around without the media following his every move. He was temporarily released from the Paula/Bob pressures and his spirits had lifted. It was nice to have two of my children in the same city at the same time. Maybe too nice to spoil things by too much heavy talking . . .

Between his other commitments, including discussions about his future film work, we spent a lot of time with his friends, old and new, and he seemed so proud and loving when he was with us. I had not seen him this happy in a long time. We would sit around the pool at the hotel and talk about old times. It was also great to see the rest of the band.

On our first evening, Michael told us to be down in the lobby in fifteen minutes as there would be some limos to take the whole band to a private screening of *Face Off*, a movie starring John Travolta and Nicholas Cage which featured a track off the *Elegantly Wasted* album. When we reached the lobby Michael introduced us to a very tall, attractive girl, whom he described as a journalist doing a special behind-the-scenes story for *Rolling Stone*. My sixth sense kicked in at once but I said nothing. We all enjoyed the movie, went back to the hotel and sat around the Sky bar, which is owned by Cindy Crawford's husband, as the restaurant was closed. I spoke with the 'journalist', whom I will call Blair, who questioned me about Michael's upbringing and his siblings, and also told me about her parents, while Michael went off to find someone who would get us some food. I asked her why she did not take notes and she said that she had a retentive memory. She reminded me of the younger Helena I had met seven years ago in New York.

The following night Ross and I went to the final INXS concert at the Greek Theatre in Los Angeles. Tina and Ken came along with Erin, Joshua, Brent, Milan and some other friends. The Greek is a beautiful outdoor venue, like a theatre in the round. I could tell from the audience that a lot of the crowd were long-time fans. Michael was performing better than ever. Afterwards he appeared to be looking for someone. All of a sudden, he raced downstairs and arrived back with Blair and her two friends. I introduced her to Tina who noticed that she had a throwaway camera and thought this strange for a journalist as they usually have the best equipment or even a top-notch photographer with them. The rooms backstage were crowded. I glanced up to see someone wearing a woolly cap pulled down almost to his eyes. He was peeping around the door but didn't come in. I brought this to Michael's attention and he walked over and brought back his friend Johnny Depp.

Over the next ten days Michael and Martha Troup were busy with meetings at studios. Tina, Ross and I had run into an old friend, Peter

MacGregor Scott, with whom Tina and I had worked in Hong Kong and who produced the Batman movies. He was working on pre-production for *A Perfect Murder* with Michael Douglas and Gwyneth Paltrow. He was interested in meeting Michael and Martha and I passed their contact numbers over. Peter had long been interested in Michael's career, but had not seen him since we left Los Angeles to return to Australia. I actually sat next to Martha one morning as she waited for Michael and people were coming up to her, offering deals. She said, 'Wow, this is great. I don't even have to walk out of the hotel.'

I saw a lot of Blair too. Blair getting into a limousine and heading off to the San Diego show, Blair stepping into a limousine on the way to a Santa Barbara show, Blair constantly getting out of the hotel elevator, even though she lived in Los Angeles. I liked her very much and rather hoped she was more officially 'with' Michael. She was so obviously making him happy and she had shown a sincere interest in our family background whenever she had spoken to me. Michael said that she was not only beautiful, but smart too.

Blair in truth was no *Rolling Stone* reporter but was studying communications at a local college while she was working on an acting career. She met Michael while waiting in the lobby of his hotel. She was standing near the reception desk, when Michael walked up and asked a clerk about how to get in touch with Liz Hurley and Hugh Grant who were also staying there. They had given him their pseudonym and room number but he had forgotten both. Quite correctly the clerk behind the desk could not give it out. Blair and Michael had a short conversation and soon he had asked her to join him for a drink with some friends. She remembers something that I find very significant. Within minutes of their first conversation Michael surprised her by very pointedly explaining who he was when there was no need. Of course she had recognized him, but I think she would have been interested in him anyway. Great sadness washed over me when she told me this. I had never before thought of Michael as being in need of recognition. His self-esteem then must have been at maximum low. Initially Blair was hesitant to take Michael up on his offer. But she did find him attractive and extremely witty and this evening turned into a four-month liaison. During this time, Blair brought out the old romantic and charming, playful side of Michael.

One evening she emerged from the bathroom to find he had strewn the bed with rose petals. Another time they had a whole evening free and he asked what he could do for her. When she told him she wished he would not have to take a phone call for once, he responded by leaping about the hotel suite, wrenching the phones out of the wall jacks, announcing, 'Done'. He could just as easily have called down to the front desk and requested them to hold all calls. When she arrived at his suite on their first dinner date, Blair discovered that in order to please her he had ordered a dozen different selections on the menu, as he wasn't sure what she would like.

Whatever his own tormented agenda might have been, Michael told Blair that his child was the most important person in his life. Both Blair and Jonnie witnessed his anger and desperation over his relationships. Blair and Michael were sitting in a bubble bath with a drink when he became melancholy. He spoke of his love for Tiger Lily and the hopelessness of the upheavals he had been through over the previous few years. He could not understand why the world he lived in attracted so much drama. He began to sob, and suddenly smashed his glass against the wall in frustration. Even after Paula arrived in Los Angeles for a short visit, Michael continued to see Blair. She was determined not to chase him and continued with a social life, which had been buoyant prior to Michael. But often, while she was with her friends, Michael paged her to meet him at Johnny Depp's house. If she agreed, it was with the knowledge that he would not be returning to his hotel and Paula that night. She told me how often Michael spoke of his love for his daughter, and his fear of losing her. On one appropriate day the undemanding Blair simply brought a small stuffed tiger for him to take on the road for comfort.

I had spoken with Martha who was in Los Angeles earlier on some INXS business for Paul Craig. That day she was very dismayed about the ticket sales and said that she was not going to let this happen to the band. She would insist that the record company purchase tickets and she was determined that the venue be filled. She was also worried about the other dates but Los Angeles was the most important. She must have pulled the right strings because the amphitheatre was filled. Actually INXS, along with their support band the Cunninghams, received some wonderful reviews. One writer said, 'Both bands delivered. The Cunninghams gave every indication of being an extremely rockin' club band. As for INXS, they put on one very slick, professional, and entertaining show. Michael Hutchence is so natural it's scary. Of course, I was too busy motivating in the aisle to give them less than a stellar review. I couldn't help it, there's just something about them that makes me sweat.' The Cunninghams were signed as the support band on the West Coast tour, and lead singer Seven Pearson, who has gone on to lead another band, Jimmy Girl, later recalled for me his first encounter with Michael.

> *It was the third show that I finally had the balls to go up to Michael. There were about ten or fifteen fans surrounding him as I watched from afar. He was gracious and very happy to be a part of these fans' precious moments. I have to admit I was a huge fan as well, and when I finally had the nerve to introduce myself to him he made me feel like a long lost friend. That's when I realized the special thing about Michael; he made everyone feel that they were a part of his world. I told him he smelled great, to which he replied, 'I do, don't I?' We laughed, and I felt I was in good hands. What inspired me the most was the camaraderie INXS had between themselves and those around them. To this day I try to create the same kind of friendship with my bandmates that they held. Their roadies, managers, family and friends are what matters and I realize that their twenty years together is a tribute to that.*

The day the band was travelling on to San Diego I was meeting Mother for lunch and as I walked into the lobby of the hotel, Martha stepped out of the elevator and approached us. She talked about a deal that had been made involving a commercial for the theme park Sea World and whether this had been a wise move. She suggested that I talk to him about it – not that I felt any expert. We were huddled together discussing the matter when Michael approached. As he hugged me, I therefore asked him if we could talk briefly before he got into the limo. When I doubtfully mentioned the issue he looked very sad and shrugged. He said he was concerned about Paul Craig's well-being as he was considering letting him go; Paul had a family, and he had been there when others had not. I agreed that Paul was a nice person and that it was difficult to let someone go. But I encouraged him to think of his career and the rest of his life. Michael said he would give it some thought. He looked miserable and I wished that I had not said anything, although I still hoped that I had done the right thing. How lucky Michael was with so many people to look after him, I thought. He had an accountant so that he never had to worry about making the cheques out to the utility companies, or the telephone people. He did not have a mortgage, and he did not have to balance his chequebook. He had a financial adviser who looked out for his investments and a manager who believed in him and was willing to work hard for him.

Just then we were interrupted by some fans who had gifts for Michael and were asking if they could get a photograph with him. I recognized one of them as the schoolteacher with the Tiffany boxes. I really detested that we so often had to have conversations out in the open like this, with people standing by watching and waiting for the moment to approach. He came back with another hug and told me not to worry, he would think it over and do the right thing, and he followed Blair and Martha into the limo. Blair later told me that the discussion of 'legitimate music versus fish' – some of the band were concerned that supplying music for the Sea World commercial undermined their credibility – continued all the way to San Diego. I believe 'New Sensation' ended up in continual use on a Sea World commercial for at least twelve months after Michael's death. Three days later Michael called Paul Craig with the bad news. Martha was now his sole manager. I remember thinking, everything will be smooth from now on, Martha will take good care of him.

Eventually, it was time for Paula to arrive. We were downstairs with Michael, waiting for her car. It was getting dangerously close to the time that he had to go and tape a television panel show called *Politically Incorrect*. A car was waiting to take Michael and Martha to the studio just as Paula came running in. She was holding Tiger and the driver was carrying an overnight bag. Michael was excited as Paula had told him that Tiger was now walking. She had called him from London a week earlier to say that she had got down the front steps to her house and went 'running' down the street. Michael hugged and kissed Tiger, then placed her on the marble floor of the hotel lobby and encouraged her to walk, but she just plopped down on her bottom. Again I felt sad for Michael. He was needlessly embarrassed and disappointed.

There was drama from the minute Paula arrived. She announced that she was going to the studio with him, even though she also said that

Tiger appeared to have a fever and that she had lost her bags after travelling for approximately twelve hours. Things sounded terribly complicated, and I didn't envy her.

On an afternoon when Michael and Martha had some meetings I called the room to see if we could take Paula to lunch. She said she was having a hairstylist come to the room for a colour job. I asked if I could take care of Tiger while she was doing this and she said she would prefer to have her in the room to feed her. When Michael arrived back at the hotel he spotted us at the pool and asked had I seen Tiger? No, but I would love to, I replied. We went back to our room and he called and asked us to come up. While we were still on the phone talking about Tiger's fever and I suggested Pedialyte, a product that Tina had mentioned, I could hear Paula yelling in the background as she overheard his side of the conversation. She demanded to know who he was speaking to. He answered, 'I'm talking to my mother.' I recall that she issued a tirade of swear words, adding that she had four f—ing children, had written fourteen f—ing books on child care etc, etc. Michael was angry with her: I think this was a Paula whom he did not like. Once again he was embarrassed that I had heard her.

Ken and I were joining Mother, Ross, Michael and Paula at the hotel for dinner. I called that morning to re-confirm and when Paula answered I thought she was in a mood not to be reckoned with. She seemed very angry, and told me that Michael had not arrived home until breakfast time. I chose not to ask her to elaborate, having a very good idea where my brother had been, but felt this was a private matter. I just wished Michael could learn to be more honest. My assessment was that Blair was giving him the support he longed for at the time, so why couldn't he confront Paula instead of making it hard on himself? I had realized by then that he still had a strong and passionate attachment to her. This did not, however, prevent him from seeking simpler pleasures elsewhere. I wished that he could be confident enough to convince Paula and establish that he wasn't yet ready to commit to just one woman, let alone marry her. He had made it clear to those closest to him that he saw his role as a father as paramount. But like most performers, he wanted approval all of the time, and dodged uncomfortable situations. He may not have known how such evasions can eat away at the subconscious. Other women had accepted that sooner or later Michael would move on and even though the break-up might be difficult and painful at the time, they bowed out gracefully and remained friends. I think Paula found it hard to walk that route.

When we arrived we found Mother and Ross by the pool waiting for Paula to bring Tiger down. Eventually a shoeless Paula appeared, wearing a fantastic dress, Tiger on her hip. I remarked on Paula's exquisite dress and she told me that Michael had taken her shopping on Rodeo Drive, where they had spent far too much. Although I'd heard so much about her from Michael, this was actually my first face-to-face meeting with Paula. Most of the photographs I had seen were unflattering, but Mother had often assured me that she had beautiful skin and could be very attractive in real life. I thought she looked much older in person. It was difficult to believe that she was the same age as Michael. Perhaps I recall things in a different light, since now there is so much history and grief. But even then I resented Paula for what I saw as not taking responsibility for herself. After all, she had come across in her autobiography as a woman with strength as well as warmth. But in my view, given what I had heard, she had encumbered Michael with her problems. She seemed to me emotionally dependent on Michael and I just could not marry this up with her public persona. I begrudged her that, and I suppose it coloured even my first impression of her. But as I watched I could see that she could be wonderful with him.

We sat around the pool until Michael and Martha arrived, he carrying the small toy tiger, which Blair had given him, and he presented it to Tiger Lily. Molly Meldrum, along with several other friends, came by for a chat. Michael appeared to be happy in the company of friends. He kept introducing Mother, 'This is my mother. Isn't she great? No surgery!' When we were ready to go in for dinner the maître d' came over to Paula and gently requested that she retrieve her shoes. She told him that she did not have any shoes. There was no cute smile and apology about her shoes being upstairs in her room. Surely she'd worn some from the airport? What had she gone shopping in? I wondered. She was reminded that California health law prohibits anyone without shoes going into an eating establishment. It rarely has to be enforced. Michael jumped up and took the surprised maître d' aside to put him in his place. When he returned to the table he confessed that he had embarrassed himself as he had mistaken this mild mannered employee for someone to whom he had given concert tickets. He had demanded to know why the tickets had failed to buy him some grace. This maître d' had no idea what he was talking about, he was just doing his job. Michael said he would have to think of some way of making it up to him.

Paula meanwhile seemed oblivious to the attention our table was attracting, although the rest of us were embarrassed. She was not asked about her bare feet again. Things calmed down until shortly after the main course was served, when there was a burst of flashbulbs at a table outside on the patio. Even though the cameras were not professional and the person taking one of the pictures had his back to our table, Paula became agitated and insisted that the photojournalists were stalking her, making Michael jumpy. Sitting to my left, with Tiger's high chair on his other side, he leaned closer to me in case the culprits were trying to catch a photograph of him with Tiger. It took the four of us to convince them that this was just a table of friends taking social photos of each other. Michael and Paula both launched into a tirade of how difficult their lives had been with the press persecuting them. I did not see why they thought they had a problem in Los Angeles, because LA is the celebrity capital of the world, where people did not know Paula's name let alone her face. Even when Michael's star was shining brightest he had never been hassled in blasé LA where there are always dozens of more famous faces around.

Paula picked at her food and before we completed the main course said she was tired and wanted to go to the suite with Tiger. Michael quickly announced that he was going to the Viper Room to see Johnny Depp. So much for a getting-to-know-you family meal. I guessed he needed to do this in front of us to avoid a scene. Paula threw him a 'not tonight you don't' look, but had already committed to leaving the table. Michael ignored it and escorted both her and Tiger Lily back upstairs. It was a very abrupt and uncomfortable finale to dinner as Michael did not return to the table until well after dessert and coffee.

That same week, Tiger Lily celebrated her first birthday and Erin's nineteenth birthday fell four days later, so I organized a small lunch at home. Michael was so attentive with his little girl. I have many photographs from that day and although his eyes are bleary he is beaming with pride in all of them and seemingly oblivious to whoever else was in the room, although I remember him laughing with Joshua.

Paula said she loved the pictures of my wedding dress and asked to see it. In my dressing room she told me that she was planning a wedding on one of the South Sea Islands. I asked her if she had a date and she replied not as yet, but that she would soon. I thought she was kidding herself. It was clear to me that Michael was not going to marry her, besides, she never seemed to announce an impending wedding when Michael was in earshot.

On our last day a worried Michael came to our hotel room at the Mondrian for a talk before taking off with Martha for meetings with producers. We knew that we would not be seeing each other until December when the family would be spending Christmas together. I remember Michael saying that Paula had changed a lot, that turmoil seemed to appear around her. I imagine this would have been hurtful and shocking to Paula had she heard it. But as I've said before, Michael had a non-confrontational nature. The constant stories in the press of an upcoming marriage were not funny any more. He said that he was worried about the stresses of her lifestyle and her legal bills were soaring. After his death some of his friends said that he had aired the same concerns to them. I asked about his plans for the future and he said he had signed with an agency for his acting, and had been offered some work in the States. He seemed excited by these possibilities. He had been taking some private acting classes and his life had changed for the better. Los Angeles was where he wanted to be and his only concern was his daughter. He would like to be able to anchor himself in Sydney and commute to LA. He still seemed to fear that Bob had the power to take his daughter away.

He hoped to get Paula out of London with Tiger Lily and the Geldof girls. I thought that it was one thing to want Tiger to be in a safe environment away from the glare of the tabloids and close to relatives but I was doubtful about the rest. It was such a dilemma for him. How could he have his daughter close by when her mother had three other daughters whose father resided in a country he no longer wanted to live in? I later wrote him a carefully worded letter about all this. My letter was in his hotel room when he died.

When leaving my room that day he took my face in his hands and said, 'Ignore the things you read about weddings, until you hear it from my lips, don't you believe it.'

We had invited Paula and Tiger Lily to have lunch with us around the pool; this would give me a last opportunity to see Tiger before we left. Michael advised me to ring Paula and remind her of the plan as he would be out until the early evening. I called soon afterwards and Paula was not in her suite so I decided to start packing as she had accepted our invitation the previous evening. I called her room a few more times, always leaving a voice mail message. Anyway, I was concerned that Tiger might still be running a temperature, though Michael had not mentioned it. Nor had he mentioned that he had stayed out all evening with Blair and the huge fight which unsurprisingly ensued. Ross and I decided to have our lunch and then went back to finish packing. I called their suite around 5 p.m. to see if Michael had returned and still hopeful of seeing Tiger before we left. Paula answered the phone, sounding sleepy and I hung up, embarrassed that I had woken her. Fifteen minutes later, Ross answered the door to a very agitated Paula, carrying Tiger. I asked her what happened. Why she could not come to lunch or answer our calls?

She said that the last thing she needed was me laying into her. She said she'd been up all night on the phone with Bob – evidently there was a court hearing that day. She said words to the effect that she wouldn't have lunch with me that day or ever, and Michael should have told me that. I cannot replicate her vocal style, especially as it was littered with the 'f' word. I felt myself shaking with shock and my heart was pounding so much I could hear it. Ross was also shocked, his face was white, but like me did not respond to this outburst. When I finally got my voice I told her that Michael had asked me to call her but it would have been nicer if she had called us out of courtesy. I recall her screaming words to the effect of, 'That's his problem not mine, I don't want to talk to you now or ever.'

I said, 'I know that, Paula.' Even when I had called to wish her a happy birthday, she had said 'can't talk' and hung up. She did the same to Tina and Kell, and has never once acknowledged our Christmas or birthday gifts to Tiger or her other children. I had wanted so much to like her, Michael's happiness was so important to me, but I felt she intimidated me, and I didn't want to say anything to Michael about how I felt she treated us when he was not around. I'd heard from him that she said she needed to be part of a family as she had been abandoned by almost everyone she thought loved her. I'd now come to the stage where I thought, if this is the way she behaves I'm not surprised. I think things changed when Tiger Lily was born. After that, it seemed to me none of us mattered. In my experience Paula can turn from timid to intimidating in seconds. That day, I felt crushed. In retrospect this was one of the worst days of my life.

I never wanted to lose Michael's love or trust but sadly for me Paula was part of his life, and clearly we weren't going to get on. An enduring regret is that I invited her to lunch that day, a devastating end to a happy reunion with Michael and the last time I was to see him.

She had left Tiger on the couch in our suite and gone back to hers. I sat there feeling ill, not knowing what to do or say. Paula had never before even allowed me to have Tiger for five minutes alone. Tiger is such a sweet, placid child and I wanted so much to cherish this short time, as it was only an hour before we had to leave. However, not knowing what was going on, and being only certain of one thing – that at that moment Paula was capable of saying anything that came into her head – I decided to take Tiger Lily back to her mother. There was no answer. I went back to our suite and then Tina arrived.

When Ken and Erin and I arrived at the Mondrian Hotel to say our goodbyes to Mother and Ross it was evident to us all that something traumatic had just taken place. Little Tiger was there without Paula for one thing. Mother was sitting on the couch with her while Ross worriedly looked out of the window. I walked over and hugged Mother and could feel her heart pounding. Tiger was smiling and playing with Mother's handbag. Erin picked her up. I hugged Ross and his heart was all but jumping out of his chest. Mother motioned me to speak with her in the bathroom where she could hardly get the words out in an attempt to explain what had just taken place. I then left her to compose herself and went out to Ross. He told me exactly the same story. We were all trying to keep calm so that Tiger would not feel bad vibes. Their concern was that their car to the airport was due in less than an hour and they would have no time to rectify this horrible incident.

Ross called for their luggage to be taken down to the lobby. We rang Paula but she did not answer her phone. It was decided that I would stay with Tiger if their car came before Michael arrived back. As we waited downstairs, Tiger was laughing, making cute baby sounds to our songs and games, oblivious to the commotion surrounding her. We continued to call Paula's room, to no avail. Finally, just before Michael's arrival, she appeared with a smile and giving no hint of recent anger. Mother and Erin and I continued to hold Tiger who simply giggled. For once Paula did not insist on taking her, and Tiger did not make any motion to go to her mother. When Michael ran into the lobby it was minutes before Mother and Ross's departure. I was holding Tiger and said 'There's Daddy'. She stretched her arms out to him. There was great, silent, tension. Paula seemed to me to display an upset expression the minute Michael ran in, which seemed in turn to puzzle him. Mother and Ross, depressed and bewildered, said their goodbyes with the saddest of faces. As Mother leaned in to say goodbye to Paula she whispered, 'Let's forget about today'. If I had not been with Ken and Erin I would have followed them out to the airport to help comfort them. Yet I also wanted to stay and explain to Michael what had taken place. Instead, the valet handed me my keys and motioned to my car which was blocking the driveway, so I had to say a hurried goodbye too.

How many times have I castigated myself over this. Why didn't I just ignore the valet or have Ken take the car? I should have stayed and spoken to Michael then and there. I wish I could have told him things from our point of view. How were we to know, although we would be speaking with him over the next fifteen weeks, that this awful day would be the last time Mother and I would see Michael alive. The last bone-crushing hug, the last infectious smile, the last wink, the last wave – the last picture I have in my head of Michael alive.

Michael had stayed out all night with Blair and Paula was angry – and I was the one in her line of fire, I suppose. Michael then came back to find Tiger with Tina and me. I don't know what he would have made of the situation. He seemed confused when we talked about it later.

I wrote to Tina shortly after I returned home, saying how devastated I was by the incident. Something had blown up out of all proportion, had become terribly exaggerated. And I doubted we'd really get to the bottom of it with Michael. I so never wanted to lose his love or trust. He had so much on his mind right then; his career, Tiger, all the litigation problems that circulated around him and Paula.

But it was a sad ending to a special holiday, which started out so absolutely happy, just perfect. All of Michael's friends were so nice to us, it was lovely seeing Tina, Brent, everyone, although I hadn't got to see much of Tiger. She is so precious, and Michael was so sweet with her.

I really didn't want to worry him – he had enough to think about, and he would no doubt have to be loyal to Paula, which I understood. I just hoped against hope the incident didn't mean I would never get to see Tiger at all. If Michael didn't marry Paula, she might be unlikely to go to Australia with him. If they split up, who knew what the custody arrangements would be.

Shortly after Mother and Ross left Los Angeles, Paula's children arrived. I left several messages with Paula, and even at the front desk, but I never received a call from Michael. When I finally did catch him he said that he and Paula were taking the children to Sea World and Disneyland and they would be staying down the coast at a beach resort. It may have been my imagination but I felt an aloofness. Paula and the girls returned to London immediately after this trip. Michael was already on his way to see Blair before Paula's flight took off.

When Michael called about two weeks after we left LA it was as if nothing had happened. I asked him if he wanted to talk about that last day, at the hotel, and he declined. 'Well, I do,' I said, and I proceeded to tell him my thoughts. He was very quiet and listened, then Ross took the phone and said, 'Everything your mother has said is true, Michael.' He handed the phone back to me. Michael said, 'I'm so sorry you had to go through that. I love you Mum, and I know that Ross would never lie to me either.'

He was about to continue his US tour and since he was on the road, we only spoke sporadically. During one conversation Michael told us that he had taken an unscheduled flight back to London between shows after receiving a phone call from home, where there had been something of a domestic crisis which sounded rather disturbing. He said, 'I think that Paula and the girls would be better off in Sydney, closer to the rest of the family.' I could only agree.

A month before arriving in Australia Michael had Martha issue a press release denying any upcoming marriage. The story had been that Michael and Paula were planning a wedding, on Bora Bora this time.

Martha's dismissive statement said that it was totally untrue and it was something which was dragged up every year when he came out to see his family in the hope that a story could be conjured out of their assumed surprise about it.

Michele Bennett had several calls from Michael while he was in Los Angeles. She said he sounded strange, a little out of it, scared and angry. On one call he began laughing for no reason and rambled. Just as she was enquiring about his mood, there was a knock at his door and several noisy people came in. He hung up without saying goodbye. A few days later in Sydney, at a fortieth birthday party for Tim Farriss, Michele saw Colin Diamond and spoke of her concerns. He blew her fears aside and assured her that Michael was fine. He was great, he was happy and he had no problems on the home front.

CHAPTER TWELVE

The Unravelling

When INXS went back on the road Michael gave Blair the tour book, and made her promise to call him at any time. He rang her from each city and made airline tickets available to her. He had planned to meet Blair and some of her family in Miami after a show in New York. At the last minute he cancelled: there was an emergency in the London home, with which he was in daily contact. There always seemed to be a new crisis being reported from the London home. His mind was in constant chaos overload – all to do with the London home front.

The 'Elegantly Wasted' promotional tour continued on 22 August with a show in Chicago featuring The Violent Femmes, Matchbox 20 and Meredith Brooks. The following day they did a show with Echo & The Bunnymen and Sarah McLachlan, and six days later a festival with BB King and Bob Dylan in Kansas City, Missouri.

In St Louis, where he heard of the death of Princess Diana, Michael loudly condemned the outrageous predator tactics of the press. He was obviously thinking of some of his own experiences. With a heavy heart he stepped onstage that night and amidst forgotten lines and missed cues gave one of the worst performances of his career. Blair knew how heartbroken he was over Diana's death and later, when he asked her what she thought of the show she felt constrained to lie that it was great as usual. They returned to the hotel to take in the news reports in silent grief.

However, others were more forthright. One fan sent a letter to *People* magazine in December 1997, after it had run a tribute story on Michael.

Those attending the INXS show in Wallingford, Conn., on Sept. 22 might disagree that 'Michael was performing better than ever.' The once controlled, graceful performer was anything but 'elegantly wasted'. It's hard to understand how those closest to Michael Hutchence did not see he was in trouble. It was apparent that if he did not get help, the comparisons to Jim Morrison would inevitably prove all too true.
Kathy Charbonneau
Bethany, Conn.

Indeed Michael did not display his usual professional brio at all during this tour. He told several people that he was concerned about his finances and he was plagued by constant updates from London on the perils of Paula and the press. His tensions were reflected onstage. Whereas in the past he had shed some clothing between songs for effects and segue, now he was using the device as what appeared to be a desperate, showy, plea for approval. One or two of the other INXS members approached him individually to confront him on his excessive drug use and depression. They talked between themselves but never actually had a stand down with Michael to force him to do something positive about getting help. Kirk said that the dynamics of the band were such that the other members did not feel as if Michael was very approachable as he had distanced himself from the other members long before this on the *Kick* tour and they never felt like they could tell him anything.

However on the edge Michael may have been, the band continued to tour. Blair continued to meet him in various cities. Sometimes they just read books or watched television and other days they worked on acting techniques.

Michael had accepted a cameo role in a small independent film called *Limp* which was being shot in Canada. His character was that of a jaded record producer who applauds the brilliance of Kurt Cobain's suicide, saying how great it was because it increased record sales. Michael was very excited about the project and asked Blair to help him with lines. He desperately wanted to do well and worked very hard for what would amount to about seven minutes screen time. Michael invited Blair to accompany him to Vancouver, where he was shooting, but not only was she concerned that her presence would distract him, she was a private person who did not want others on the shoot to know of her involvement with Michael.

*

INXS completed their North American tour on 27 September 1997 in Pittsburgh, where they appeared in a show with Savage Garden and 10,000 Maniacs. Then Michael took a short break in London before heading to Los Angeles to continue work on his solo album. While in London he consulted Dr Jonathan Boreham, the general practitioner who had been treating Paula for some time, and asked for a referral to a psychiatrist. Dr Boreham referred him to Dr Mark Collins, a consultant psychiatrist from the Priory Hospital, Roehampton, London, who later, in the course of the investigation following Michael's death, confirmed that he had seen Michael twice during this time, and that Michael had already been taking Prozac for many months. He said that Michael's partner had accompanied him on his first visit. He noted in his statement as areas of stress for Michael concerns over an ongoing dispute between his partner and her ex-husband regarding finances and child care. '[Michael] had concerns about the effect of this on his partner and also concerns over the future direction of his career and how his band INXS would be received on its forthcoming tour . . . From what he said it was apparent to me that he was committed to and happy with his relationship with his partner and he loved her and their daughter.' He also noted that Michael showed no signs of physical or psychological dependence on drugs, and said that in his opinion he did not show any indications of suicidal thinking.

During this visit to London he and Paula discussed Christmas plans. Michael wanted Tiger Lily to join him in Australia where he could show her off to his family and friends. For the first time in four years we were all planning to be together, and in Australia. I understood that Paula wanted to arrive early and bring Pixie and Peaches on the Australian leg of the tour, send them back to their father for the holidays then have them return for twelve weeks while she took some work on a new Australian show.

The two of them met with Bob – a rarity – to talk things through. There was a fair amount of negotiation, and Michael told me of a number of formalities that had to be gone through as a result of the Geldof-Yates custody arrangements.

On 6 November, shortly after the initial meeting with Bob in London, Michael had flown to New York and after five days there he arrived in Los Angeles to continue working on his solo album before joining INXS for the Australian leg of their tour. He checked into the

Bel-Age Hotel, which is in walking distance of the Viper Room – where he spent much of his time that last week before heading to Sydney. He neglected to call several of his usual friends, choosing instead to see acquaintances who were known to be heavy substance abusers. His old friend Nick Conroy visited him in his suite, which was full of people, and noted to Michael that these were not his friends. He sensed that Michael was in a place which was hard to reach and left after a short time telling him that when he was ready to get back to basics, when he needed him, that he would be there for him. Even suggesting that he come stay at his apartment for a while. Michael declined but asked Nick to reconsider and stay, when he said he had to leave, Michael hugged him, and assured him he would call.

Michael only saw Blair once, at his hotel, where she returned some clothes that he had left at her apartment and told him to take care of himself. She sensed that he was in a state that no matter what she said, she could not get through to him. She left his hotel room in a hurry and he ran after her, following her to the car. He had company in his room and she did not want to discuss anything in front of others. He said it would be all right, that he would call from Australia. She replied that she had a feeling that they would not see each other again.

The talks about the Christmas arrangements went on. During a conversation with Michael on his last weekend in Los Angeles, he told me he had devised a plan which involved Paula doing a radio show and maybe taping a weekly television show in Australia. Several shows could be taped over a relatively short period directly after the Christmas break. He might not be married to Paula, but he felt responsible for her as she was the mother of his child. So much had been made of the Geldof, Yates and Hutchence triangle in the press that he felt responsible, appalled that people might think of him as the bad guy.

He said that relocating Paula to Australia for a while would keep Tiger closer to family and allow him to divide his time between Sydney and Los Angeles. This was a turnaround from the strategy he had discussed a year earlier when he had planned to bring Paula and Tiger to California. I asked him if it was definite. He replied 'Pretty much. Well, um, we're working on it.' He was loath to return to London, that much was certain. I did not ask him about the Geldof girls as this was a decision for Paula and Bob to make.

Michael arrived in Sydney from Los Angeles on the evening of Tuesday, 18 November and checked into the Ritz Carlton, room 524, using the name of a popular Australian landmark, Murray River, as his pseudonym. He made his first call to Blair from his room the following morning. He called again on Thursday morning for a longer talk and again that evening for an even longer one. Rhett was in Sydney, staying overnight before catching a bus for the Gold Coast. He and Michael made plans to see each other that evening but after a six-hour rehearsal Michael had gone back to the hotel and fell asleep, succumbing to jet lag and exhaustion. By the time Rhett called him from the hotel lounge to ask Michael to join him and Mandy with some friends it was after 11 p.m. and Michael was too tired. He and Rhett had a minor argument and when Rhett left for the Gold Coast early on Friday morning he was irritated as well as disappointed as he had not seen or spoken with Michael in ten months.

According to the hotel's records, Michael did not call Paula until Friday morning. The first call lasted seven minutes. Soon afterwards he called the London home again, this call lasting twenty minutes. Then he rang Mother on the Gold Coast and had a long conversation.

Michael phoned me when he arrived in Sydney and we made plans to see each other the following week, as he would be performing in Queensland. He phoned once more on Friday morning and we spoke of Christmas plans. I suggested that as we would all be together it would be a good opportunity to have Tiger Lily christened. Firstly he seemed hesitant but then decided it was a good idea. He sounded frail. I think he could see that things were a mess. I called Kell and warned him that Michael was depressed and suggested that he not push him for any definite plans.

On Friday morning Michael called Michele Bennett at her office. They spoke for approximately ten minutes and made plans for breakfast Saturday morning. The conversation was centred around the tour and his disenchantment with it. He also expressed concern about Paula's custody problems and spoke of his desire to get back to a simpler way of life. He was tired of dealing with problems. He was looking for the silver lining.

He also called actress Kym Wilson, whom he had dated briefly in the early nineties, who had left him a message. 'Mr River, if the current is flowing right it should lead you to the basement from about 8 p.m. till late. Love very much to see you. Hugs and kisses, love, Kym.' This alluded to a benefit play she was involved with which was being staged at a venue called the Basement. Kym did not answer her phone and Michael left a message apologizing for being a no show the previous evening and suggesting that they meet up on Friday evening after his dinner with his father. He spent the afternoon rehearsing with the band, seeming to be in great form. None of them could have foreseen that this would be their last time together.

That evening, Michael met Kell and Sue at 7.30 p.m. and drove to one of his favourite Indian restaurants for dinner. Kell remembers him as pensive and quieter than usual at first but brightening up enough to fall into some of his usual mimicry. Nonetheless he confessed that he was burdened by his troubles in London and elaborated upon Paula's custody difficulties, their expenditures, and the overall gloom of life in the United Kingdom. Kell sensed that Michael was very worried, and tried to pursue this line of conversation. Michael, in his usual way, changed the subject. In the weeks following this dinner, Kell went to great lengths to ensure the accuracy of his statement to the police. In his final version he said that Michael was concerned about the court hearing in London, he did not trust Bob and hoped that the court would rule in their favour. He said that he missed Tiger very much and needed to see her. Despite this, Kell maintained that Michael was in good spirits, telling jokes and relating stories. He even said that when they dropped him off at the Ritz-Carlton, Michael had danced through the main entrance.

Returning to his hotel at 10.30 p.m., Michael changed and went downstairs to the bar to wait for Kym Wilson and her boyfriend, barrister Andrew Rayment. When Kym and Andrew arrived at 11 p.m., they found Michael sitting in a booth with a girl each side. Kym remembers introducing Michael to Andrew and suggested that they order drinks. The girls left to return to their dates and Michael said he would prefer to go up to his room as he was waiting on a phone call from London. As they were leaving Michael made a joke about getting out without paying the bill. He was quite theatrical about it and appeared in good spirits. The barman came after him and asked him to sign the tab before he could make a getaway. With drink in hand, he laughed and signed the bill.

Up in his room Michael told Kym and Andrew to help themselves from the mini-bar. Michael sat on the bed as they relaxed and talked. He finished his drink and opened a beer as he explained that the call from London was about the outcome of a court ruling on the departure of the Geldof girls for their Christmas vacation in Australia. He said that he was quite nervous but hopeful as he wanted to see Tiger Lily, who would, of course, be grounded with her mother if the other girls could not fly out. There was a script on a chair and he also talked about the film he had just worked on. Martha called from New York and told him that Quentin Tarantino did not want him for the original small role he had tried out for in his new movie *From Dusk Till Dawn* but had something much better in mind. She also said that Harvey Weinstein from Miramax had made favourable comments about him. It was a long conversation and he was excited about all of the positive aspects relaying the gist to his guests. Martha concluded by telling him that she would see him Sunday night. Actually she knew that she would not be arriving into Sydney until Monday, but she wanted Michael to feel a little more secure, as she was later to tell Sydney detectives.

Kym, Andrew and Michael settled down to their drinks and to talk about Michael's plans for a career as an actor. But after a time he began to speak to them also of the problems in London. He said how much he loved Paula's children and that he thought it unfair of Bob to prevent the children from going to Australia early. He said he considered himself to be their father, besides, he wanted to see his daughter. He said of the 1996 alleged opium bust that he was convinced that Bob had set Paula up. He spoke quite openly with Andrew about Paula's legal battles, obviously feeling comfortable in the knowledge that he was an attorney. He also railed against the way the press had behaved in all of this. He told them that this was his last tour with INXS and that he even considered cancelling the Australian leg if the outcome of the court appearance in London did not go their way. He could not stand to be without Tiger Lily. He must have seemed like a man obsessed and possessed.

Throughout the evening Kym and Andrew occasionally stepped out on to the balcony as Michael received or made phone calls. Kym does not recall Michael exhibiting anger or despair during this time, nor does she remember any outbursts on the phone before she and Andrew had to leave. She does not recall him being wasted, just frustrated and anxious. At some stage Michael said that he wanted to go out and Kym demurred, reminding him that the London call was the reason they were waiting in his room. Michael replied, 'I know, but sometimes I just want to run away.' Kym and Andrew were tired and at some stage she was falling asleep. Michael roused her with, 'I need you Kymmie. Please stay awake.' According to Kym's statement to the police, he handed her two small empty plastic bags containing a white, powdery residue and said, 'Here you are, suck on this.' Kym says she then asked what it was and Michael said, 'Leftovers.' It was literally the remaining traces of cocaine from a previous indulgence. Andrew did not take any of it.

Andrew remembers that by about 4.30 a.m. he was falling asleep. Kym was exhausted too and he said that they needed to go home to bed. It was 5.30 p.m. Friday evening in London. Michael decided to call London one more time to find out about the court matter before they left but the number was busy. The phone log from his room shows that Michael called Nick Cave at 4.45 a.m. and stayed on the line for almost eleven minutes. Andrew Rayment remembers this call prior to departing. He says that around 4.50 a.m. Michael had not heard anything else from London and insisted that they take themselves home to bed. They had helped him get through most of the night, and he could await alone the all important call, as it would surely be in the next hour or so. Before leaving, Kym and Andrew noted their mobile numbers in his address book which was lying on the bed and told him to call if he needed to as they would be just a short distance away from the hotel. He suggested they have breakfast later then changed his mind, remembering that he was meeting Michele and then said, 'Let's go out tomorrow night.' As they left he lay on the bed and said, 'I'd love a Valium.' Kym replied that they had none and they drove to Andrew's parents' home, just ten minutes from the hotel.

As to what happened next, since Michael's death my mother and I have spoken with (amongst many others) Michele, Kym, Bob, Martha and Kell about their recollections and understandings. Naturally we have pored over the coroner's report, dissecting each individual's police statement and all the time frames. Bob Geldof's

Clockwise, above: Michael and Kirk in the spotlight, performing the beautiful 'Shine Like It Does'. **Right:** Michael with Jonnie. **Below:** Michael and Richard Lowenstein in Cannes, 1992, the year of *Dogs in Space*. (Chris Plytas)

Michael and Kylie Minogue in Cannes for Christmas 1990. (Pearl Bailey)

Left: Michael and Helena at the villa, Christmas 1991.
Below: Paula, Mandy, Rhett and Michael, Christmas 1995, at the Hyatt Hotel in Sydney. Paula had just announced her pregnancy to the family.

Above: Michael with manager Chris Murphy (right) and Ian 'Molly' Meldrum (left) backstage at the Entertainment Centre, Brisbane. **Left:** Our first Christmas at the villa, 1990. Pearl and Chris Bailey, Michael and Kylie.

Right: The beautiful and intelligent Virginia Hey (left) with manager Martha Troup – Chris Murphy in the background, 1988. **Below:** Bridget Fonda, Michael and John Hurt in *Frankenstein Unbound*, 1980.

Above: Combined birthday celebration for Tiger and Erin in Burbank, July 1997. Tina, Paula, Patricia and Michael, the proud daddy, holding his precious little Tiger Lily. **Left:** Paula, Hiraani and Heavenly Hiraani Tiger Lily, September 1996, in Clontarf, Sydney.

Right: Tiger and Tina on Patricia's last day in Los Angeles – after that confrontation with Paula, 29 July 1997. **Below:** Paula, Michael and Patricia with Tiger Lily at the villa in the South of France, 1996.

Left: Michael and Tiger at the Mondrian, Los Angeles, August 1997.

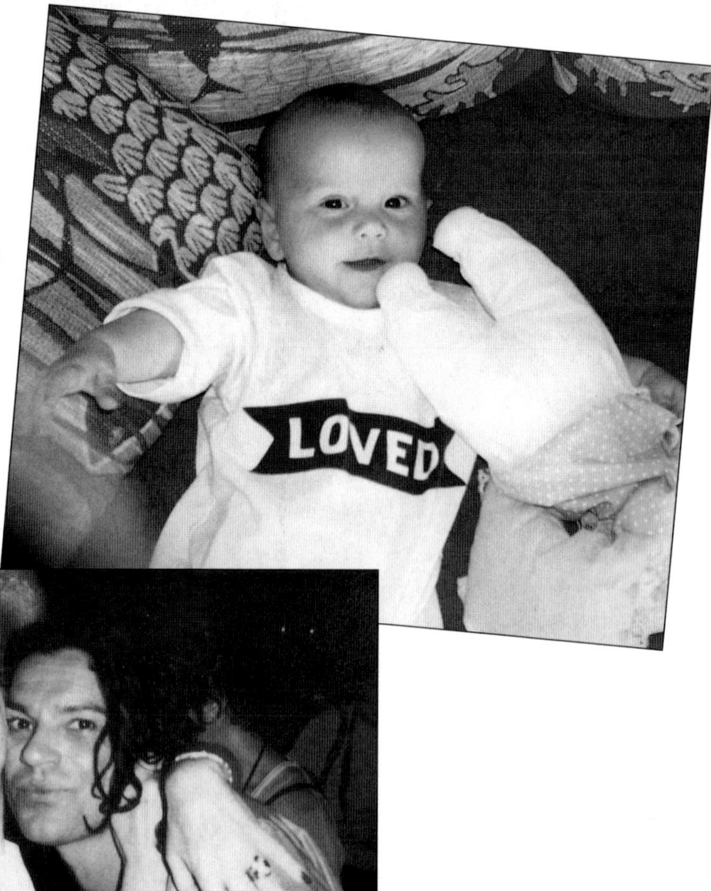

Right: Tiger Lily, Main Beach, Gold Coast, 1996. (Ross Glassop)
Below: Patricia and Michael at the Mondrian Hotel in Los Angeles, 1997. This is the last picture of Michael and Patricia together.

statement was mostly word for word conversation and he was very generous towards us with his time and sympathy. We are familiar with Paula's statement, but have not had the opportunity to have a straightforward discussion about events.

The guest in the room next door to 524 awoke to noise coming from Michael's room and glanced at her clock. It was just after 5 a.m. She heard a loud male voice obviously having a heated phone conversation, as she could not detect another voice coming from the room. According to the Ritz Carlton phone records, this was not an outgoing call. Out of all the police statements the only incoming call around this time was from Paula. I can only assume that she made a call to Michael after arriving home from the court hearing. The detectives handling the case did not request Paula's phone records and her statement to the police does not give detail. However, both she and her friend Belinda Brewin state that they called Michael when they arrived home from the hearing. Michele made her phone records available to the detectives without them requesting it.

Of course, no one can be sure what transpired in this conversation. Paula contends that she said that she would not be bringing the children out to Australia and that Michael was distraught when she told him of the hearing postponement. She said that she could not leave without Pixie and Peaches (Fifi was not scheduled to join them). Paula stated that Michael was terribly upset and said, 'I don't know how I will live without seeing Tiger. What will happen?' She said that he sounded desperate and couldn't stand a minute more without his baby. He told her that he would call Bob and beg him on his knees to allow the children to depart for Australia early. She said that he did not sound as if he had consumed much more than a drink. According to the police report this is the extent of Paula's statement about her last call to Michael. The remainder of her statement is concerned with background on her discordant relationship and financial woes with her former husband. Belinda Brewin says that she took the phone and spoke to Michael after he had talked to Paula. She told him not to worry and he replied, 'Yeah, thanks Belinda. How's Tiger?' She said that he sounded fine.

Looking at this logically I wonder why – knowing that he was under great stress, even under the care of a psychiatrist, and after hearing the desperation in Michael's voice – Paula didn't attempt to alleviate his anguish by travelling to Australia with Tiger, and telling him then that she was going to do this. There was nothing preventing her from doing so, thus making it possible for Michael to at least spend time with his daughter. Bob Geldof is an extremely devoted father who has never had trouble sharing responsibility for his daughters' day-to-day care and I would have thought could willingly have stepped in if their mother had gone ahead of them to Australia. The Geldof girls could have joined Paula in Australia for Christmas later. It would have been very difficult to tour with three children anyway, so why not have them join the family on the Gold Coast for the Christmas celebrations once the pressures of the tour were behind Michael?

But my crucial question is, did he sound fine, or was he desperate? It is hard to reconcile Paula and Belinda's recollection of Michael's disposition on that first phone call after the court hearing with the tone of the conversation between Michael and Bob afterwards, not to mention the impression he gave Kell, Sue, Andrew and Kym. Bob took a call from Michael as he waited for Fifi's school bus. It was made at 5.18 a.m. Sydney time and lasted just over a minute. In his statement to the police, Bob remembers Michael's phone manner as being the same as it had always been during the very few times he had called in the past. Low voice and a little sleepy – a voice I'd heard many times myself, but his manner was sarcastic as he obviously believed Bob had been causing problems.

'Bob?'

'Who's that?'

'It's Michael man. Are you happy?'

'I'm okay. Listen, can you call back in ten minutes? I'm on the other line.'

'Ah man, can you call me?'

'I can't, I don't have your number.'

'Hold on, I'll give it to you.'

'I'm in the car and I don't have a pen.'

(Sighs of exasperation) 'OK, I'll call back.'

No yelling or argument, so this could not have been the 5 a.m. conversation the hotel guest next to Michael's room overheard. After a brief call to Paula at 5.31 a.m., Michael called Bob back at 5.38 a.m. and his tone was as before. As his theme was familiar to Bob (who had once reported a call from Michael as harassment) he did not have any hunch that this exchange was going to be any different. Michael's calls to Bob in the past had been hectoring and threatening. Most of them, and I reiterate there had not been many more than a half-dozen in a thirty-month period, were marked by offensive fantasies such as his fears over Tiger Lily's custody. Michael would say that he knew of wrong doings by Bob and had proof. Bob knew that he was innocent of all this and he would not rise to Michael's accusations. Such lofty calm would further enrage Michael.

Bob simply told Michael that he could not allow his children to miss their last three weeks of school. Michael called Bob 'little man', as he had done in previous conversations. 'I'm their father little man, when are you going to realize that?' But it seems doubtful Michael would have known the full scope of whatever Paula and Bob's negotiations had been – after all, it was their business. Bob says he did not appear to be depressed and was sleepy rather than loudly aggressive, but he did not seem to hear Bob when he tried to explain his point of view. Michael continued as if not hearing, speaking directly over Bob, saying 'I hate you,' repeating that he was Pixie and Peaches' father now. Bob replied that he was glad he felt that way, and he preferred that his children spent time with someone who cared so much.

Michael only became more agitated and rambled on without making sense. Between expletives he accused Bob of trying to take Tiger away from him. Bob, with what seems like extraordinary patience, offered to sit down with him and his lawyer to go over it and assure him that he had no interest in taking his daughter. This call ended at 5.54 a.m. when Michael slammed the phone down. I shudder and shiver when I consider how misjudged Michael's tactics were.

After going over Michael's conversation with Bob, I realize that it is doubtful that Michael was fully aware of all the events that took place in court that Friday, when the departure date of the Geldof girls had been discussed. The court records clarify the various to's and fro's between solicitors, and why there was going to be a further delay before the Geldof girls' Christmas plans could be finalized.

The hotel room's records show that he did not make any more calls to Paula, and he did not have a mobile. But for the coroner's report to state that Michael did not speak to her again is a strange assumption – after all, she said herself that Michael had told her that he would call Bob and beg him to allow her to take the girls to Australia the following day. I would have thought they would have wanted to discuss the outcome of his call to Bob, as she was holding tickets for a flight to Sydney departing 22 November. But the hotel had no log of incoming calls. In her statement Belinda Brewin says that she asked Paula when she had last spoken to Michael, and Paula told her it was around 6 or 7 a.m. Sydney time. The coroner cites Belinda as witness to the call between Michael and Bob. This is puzzling as she was at Paula's house when Bob was talking to Michael on a mobile phone. What she had said was, Bob *told* her about the call the following morning.

The records show that Michael did ring Michele, whom he was due to meet for breakfast in a few hours. She was asleep and did not hear her phone so he left a brief message on her machine at 6.09 a.m. He sounded drunk and just said that he wanted to speak to her. The only thing that is clear from here on is that he undressed and took a short nap. Something woke him. The fact that some of his belongings seemed to have been hurled around the room as if in anger, suggests that something made him lose his temper. When Michele rose she played back a message from what she describes as an inebriated Michael and called him back at around 8 a.m. There was no answer and she assumed that he had fallen back to sleep, so she left a message.

There were only three more outgoing calls from Michael's room, two of them to Martha. The first one was to her New York office, which she had left for the day. He left a message at 9.42 a.m. Sydney time, his voice agitated and angry. He said, 'Martha, Michael here, I fuckin' had enough.' The next message was left at her home nine minutes later. His voice was slow and deep and mumbled. He just said, 'Martha, it's Michael.' He returned Michele's call at 9.54 a.m., sounding wasted as he did when he had been drinking all night, but this was no different from dozens of other calls she had received from Michael over the years. He said that he was just over-tired and upset but speaking, in Michele's words, 'normally' and not angrily. Michael said that he had to see her. Nothing alerted her that this call was any different from the many calls she had had over their eighteen-year friendship. As they spoke he became distressed and told her that he had been to sleep for a short time, but was still tired and did not know how he was going to get through the band rehearsal which was scheduled for noon that day. He began to cry as he said that he could not sleep and that he just needed her to come over to the hotel.

Michele promised she would be there and advised him that he should skip rehearsals, suggesting he call someone in the band and explain. He agreed to do so. As she stepped into her shower with her phone, she told him to expect her in twenty or thirty minutes and said he should lie down and try to rest until she arrived. Michele dressed and flew out of the house, taking with her the book by her bed. She had soothed him to sleep many times in the past by reading to him and she thought it wouldn't hurt to try again today.

Then Michael rang down to the front desk and left a message for tour manager John Martin, also staying at the hotel. The note said, 'Mr River is not going to rehearsals today.' When Michele arrived there she made her way up to Michael's room, knocked on the door and listened for him to open it. No answer so she knocked again and even tried the door. Still no answer. Michele thought it had been no more than twenty-five minutes since she had been speaking to Michael but according to phone records and the time she scribbled on the note she subsequently left for him, it was more like forty. She decided that he must have gone back to sleep and went to the house phone next to the elevators to call his room. Four rings and no answer so she decided that he must be in a much-needed deep sleep and did not want to wake him. She wrote her note at the lobby, saying that she was worried about him and that she would stay in the area in case he awoke. He could call her mobile number. She asked for the note to be slipped under his door and left the hotel to walk around the neighbouring shopping area. Then she sat in a café with a newspaper, and waited for Michael's call.

Martha had already spoken with John Martin at approximately 7 a.m. Sydney time, explaining the London court developments which meant that Paula and Tiger would not be joining Michael for the tour. Then John had breakfasted and done some work in his room before receiving a call from Kell asking if he had seen Michael. This call was received at about 11 a.m. Kell said he thought they had had a great time the night before, and it had been a late night, so maybe Michael was sleeping in. Kell and Sue had dropped Michael off at the hotel at 10.30 p.m., but of course this wasn't exactly a late night for Michael! John returned Martha's call after speaking with Kell, and finding the message from Mr River under his door. It was around 11.15 a.m. when John spoke to Martha and she told him to let Michael sleep for an hour or two longer.

At 11.50 a.m. a hotel maid was doing her rounds and knocked on the door of room 524. There was no answer so she used her master key. When she attempted to push the door open it was obvious that there was something obstructing it. With great force she pushed it open to find Michael's naked body on the floor. He was in a kneeling position facing the door. Much has been made of the fact that he was nude but Michael had usually slept naked since his teens and it was obvious from the crumpled bedding that he had at least been trying to sleep.

He had used his black leather belt to tie a knot on the automatic closure at the top of the door, and the fall of his head forward into the loop had been so hard that the buckle had broken. The room was chaotic: clothes on the floor and over chairs, and two suitcases were open on the floor. Scattered around were a number of medications including a Becloforte ventolin inhaler for his asthma, Nurofen tablets for pain, Zoviorax 200 tablets, and two other containers filled with unidentified pills. In the bathroom lay an open packet of Prozac capsules and some nicotine patches. The management was alerted, then the relevant authorities. He was pronounced dead.

An hour after Michele arrived home, just before noon, things happened in quick succession. The authorities had not taken steps to keep Michael's name from the press, and it had already been reported over radio and television. She heard the terrible news when her old friend Jenny Morris called her. She assured Jenny that the person at the Ritz Carlton could not be Michael as she had spoken to him less than three hours before. All the same, Jenny dispatched her husband Paul to Michele's apartment to help if need be. After this Michele desperately tried to call Michael and was told that there was no Murray River registered. She then tried to call the police but no one would speak to her. Rhett phoned and told her what had happened but she could not believe them: she had spoken to Michael and although he was exhausted and upset he was definitely not suicidal. Rhett told her to call Kell, who asked her to get over to his apartment.

When she arrived the police were there and asked her to come to the station where they interrogated her with questions, which seemed to assume that she had actually been in the hotel room with Michael. They conducted the interview as if she were a suspect. She was in grief and disbelief and she insisted that they take her to see him. It was only then that she was convinced that Michael was really gone.

In subsequent interviews Paula contended that she had proof that Michael's death was accidental. She is positive that he was involved in a sex act, auto asphyxiation eroticism, which went wrong. She has never set forth firm evidence but she continues to keep the idea alive, quite simply maintaining that it was impossible that Michael would choose to abandon her. She participated in a TV documentary in August 1999, which centred on her theory that Michael had accidentally taken his life. The producers relied heavily on Paula's comments and innuendoes, some of which were upsettingly brazen to us. In reading Paula's statement to Detective Inspector Duclos there is no mention of this being a possibility. Her statement, taken four days after Michael's death, cites Michael's despair at not seeing Tiger Lily before Christmas and the battles with her ex-husband as a possible cause. The detectives treated Michael's room as a crime scene: this, I am told, is always the first procedure in a suicide case. The local Rose Bay detectives went through not only room 524 but also the balcony, the room above Michael's which is the gymnasium, and the roof. They checked to see if there was any evidence of forced entry and any trauma to Michael's body, which would suggest a struggle. They took statements from people who were not even in the country at the time and each statement is consistent with Michael being in a deeply depressed state. They also looked into the possibility of AAE. The coroner, Derek Hand, and Detective Inspector Duclos found no reason to endorse this theory and nothing to substantiate it later. We also categorically refute it.

In the aftermath I have studied some powerful literature on depression and its effects on individuals. I spoke at length with one particular specialist who assured me that it would not make sense for a person in deep depression to feel the sexual urge this act requires. The one thing we knew for sure was that Michael was depressed, so we may be sure that his libido was low. Add to this, Michele's conversation with him. As no one else has come forward and there were no more outgoing calls, as far as we know Michele was the last person to speak with Michael and she states emphatically that sex of any kind was definitely not on Michael's mind. The AAE theory is ridiculous. The aspect of such speculation which makes my blood boil is that to my mind it is a despicable legacy to lay out there for Tiger to read about in the future. You have to wonder what the merits are of pushing this idea. I think Paula may support it as she cannot accept that Michael would deliberately choose to leave her. Some have suggested it might have something to do with the terms of Michael's life insurance policy, but its beneficiaries were the other members of INXS. (This is not unusual when someone is in an integral part of a company, or in Michael's case a band, when such an incident would presumably bring hardship on the remaining partners who could not continue their business obligations.) And in any case the insurance policy was honoured, its benefits duly paid out to the band.

We will never know what went through Michael's mind in those last few minutes nor why he could not hold on when he knew deliverance was on the way. But deep depression can cause someone to feel hopeless and helpless and quite beyond the rational and logical thought processes that should have kept Michael going until Michele reached him. Maybe, confused and befuddled by fatigue, too much alcohol and another cocktail of drugs, he simply lost his mind. We will never know exactly what phone calls he received and what was said. But it is obvious that Michael was pushed beyond his limit – he was already a man on the edge. Many people were aware of this and the police statements confirm it. He had been mixing both prescription and illegal drugs for at least two years and legal or not, drugs are known to distort the mind. His perception of his life that day would have been contorted beyond his capacity to handle it.

Michael had many people watching out for his needs. On the business side, a personal manager, an accountant, several lawyers, an investment adviser, a tour manager, a bodyguard, a publicist, a record company, a management company for his acting career, not to mention roadies and assistants. He had friends and family who loved him but were unable to get beyond the frenzy in his mind. My mother and I both happen to think that it takes real courage to take your own life. We also think that the deep depression that Michael was experiencing and the drugs and alcohol he had taken made it impossible for him to see a solution. It was a split-second resolve made in anger and despair. The fact that there was no suicide note says to us that Michael made a snap decision. In his own words uttered repeatedly over the last five months of his life, he just 'couldn't take it any more'.

CHAPTER THIRTEEN

The Funeral Service

We had been booked into the Sir Stamford, one street away from the Ritz Carlton. We turned down a side street and into an alley behind the hotel. Even there, I spotted some huge camera lenses resting on shoulders. One of the men explained that the building, in particular the front entrance, was surrounded by photojournalists. Entering the hotel from the parking area, we were instructed to remain in the vehicle as they checked for more photographers. I doubt the press would recognize, or be interested in Martha or me, but they were just doing their job. We were also checked in under the 'Edwards' name. A security man was stationed nearby.

I gave particulars of my children's flight, and hurried off to my room, exhausted. I noted that it was five doors away from Rhett's but resisted knocking on his door, I just wanted to get in to call Mother. She said she would let Rhett know I had arrived. She sounded so anxious to see me, I just dropped my bag and ran directly to her room.

I had never seen her so distraught. If I had thought my heart would break when I heard the terrible news about Michael, when I saw my mother standing there, in such agony, my whole body crumbled. I simply held her for a long time, and then Ross held us both. We were united in a grief we never imagined we would ever have to bear. Then Rhett and Mandy arrived with Zoe, who looked totally bewildered. They had been to the Ritz Carlton, as Rhett wanted to look at Michael's room and the makeshift memorial outside the hotel lobby, and they had been followed by journalists back to the Sir Stamford. After a brief conversation, Mandy and Rhett left with Zoe to return to their room, inviting me to stop by. Ross, Mother and I sat in their suite trying to make sense of this nightmare.

While I was there she took a call from Kell, who reiterated that he wanted Mother to call the PR wizard Harry Miller. She told me that Kell had come up with the idea earlier that day after noting the growing swarm of journalists surrounding his apartment and our hotel. With Paula arriving the following morning, he thought we needed some help controlling what was shaping up to be a frenzy. Again he asked Mother to make the call. Kell and I also spoke briefly, and he gave me the number of the morgue. He suggested I call early and have them delay the autopsy so that Martha and I could go to see Michael together.

Mother already felt as if people were manipulating her. Where to stay, what name she would be under. I told her that they probably thought it was for the best. Photographers were already clustering and all they had to do was follow Rhett who, at a little over six feet tall, with dreadlocks and wearing a Hawaiian print shirt, was quite conspicuous. For reasons of his own he had made several trips to the Ritz Carlton – in particular to room 524. It was almost as though he was inviting photographers and journalists to take his picture or talk to him and I'm sure he sensed our unease about this, but that's Rhett. He cares little for convention and has always been prone to do the opposite if he feels he is being pressured in any way. Returning to my suite, I resisted knocking on his door, as I could hear many voices coming from within, and the last thing I wanted was to be with strangers.

Early next morning I called the number Kell had given me for the Glebe Morgue, but was only able to leave a brief message for someone to call me. By 9 a.m. I had still not received a return call. I checked the number with Kell: he'd given me a wrong number and by the time I got through I was informed that the autopsy was to begin in less than an hour. Too late. I could go afterwards, the counsellor told me, but I wanted to see Michael whole. She assured me that I would not see any incisions. I was truly upset about this, I felt that somehow it would not be the same if I had to see him after medical examiners had been all over his body. But there was nothing I could do – there were so many things already out of my control. Slowly I placed the phone in its cradle, my attention was drawn to the television news. It showed footage of Paula arriving, the anchor person describing how she had arrived on a 6 a.m. flight from London and had gone directly to the morgue . . .

I called Martha and said that Mother and I would be right over. We wanted to tell her about the meeting which, at Kell's insistence, Mother had set up with Harry Miller. It was important that Martha be kept up on our decisions, and liaison with the band was necessary.

As usual, Martha was on the phone when we arrived. I wondered when she ever had a chance to take care of her own needs. We sat on the couch and half watched a television special on my brother's extraordinary career, while we filled her in on the plans to involve Harry in an attempt to control the media circus.

Back in my room, the hotel manager called. Apparently the Ritz Carlton had sent over all the cards, flowers, stuffed animals, photographs, candles and loving messages being left by fans outside their lobby. He asked if they could all be sent up to my room. I suggested that they also send some to Mother's suite. I was not ready for the buckets of flowers that would arrive each day. Throughout the week, we received more and more bouquets from friends around the world, to the extent that the Sir Stamford ran out of vases. We filled our baths with flowers, sharing them with Mandy and with Erin too when she arrived. One day they were delivering as I was running out my door. I looked around the room, which was completely overwhelmed by floral arrangements, and having no more room in my tub, I simply placed some in the toilet bowl until I returned. But the flowers were very comforting. I liked to breathe in their scents, which represented love and respect from fans and other special people. That love had given Michael pleasure every time he stepped on stage. I'm sure those who left or sent the flowers and mementoes thought it such a small sign of respect that we would barely notice them, but it meant a lot to the family. During that horrendous week, they reminded us all just how much Michael was loved.

We began our meeting with Harry in Mother's suite. Kell was late, the band's minders were picking him up. I did not understand why they always had to collect him. Didn't he have a car? Last I remembered, he was driving Michael's Jaguar. When he came in, he greeted me warmly and wished me happy birthday. I had forgotten that the day before had been my birthday. Who could remember anything so insignificant when we were facing the crisis of our lives? Kell then went on to explain why he had not brought a gift with him! I couldn't believe it, our world had caved in and he is discussing my birthday. Considering this stepfather of mine had rarely ever remembered it in the past, it rocked me. I decided he must be in shock. There were many interruptions during our meeting. Kell's phone, Harry's phone and of course the phone in Mother's suite. Lots of questions, too many opinions.

Harry Miller is a dynamic personality who commands attention. His mobile on constantly, you just know that he is working on two dozen deals at once. I was actually intrigued that he was helping us. He was accustomed to representing celebrities, and we were just civilians. But he seemed to understand and size the problem up immediately. His plan was to shut down the press outside the hotel by sending out a statement to the effect that there would be no press releases unless they came from his office. He proposed that we allow just one television channel in the cathedral, where the funeral was to be held, thus avoiding the danger of what he called 'a bum fight' in the church. Channel Seven was interested, and they agreed to feed small segments to other international networks for the evening news.

During this meeting, Kell kept asking if anybody had heard from Michael's financial adviser, Colin Diamond. Someone said that he was on his way in from Indonesia. From what I understood, Michael and Colin had purchased some land on a small island off Lombok there. Michael had told me that they were building separate houses for us all. However, I could not understand why Kell considered it so important that Colin be in Sydney, except of course, to attend the funeral. Kell became extremely agitated and claimed that he needed peace and quiet to make a phone call. He went to the door of the suite and I assumed he was standing in the hallway, but when I opened the door to call him back in, he was nowhere to be found.

I eventually found him twenty minutes later, making a call from the hotel breakfast room. He did not see me at first, and was saying something about someone being in mid-flight. I wish I had been more observant at the time. He looked surprised when he saw me and cut his call short. He began rambling on to me about some abalone cargo, which he had to get out that very day to Hong Kong. It was obvious that he had not been speaking about abalone, which he traded in, but who cared? I asked myself, we had just lost Michael. How could he even pretend to focus on a shipment of fish? I left him to make another call.

When he arrived back in Mother's suite, it was obvious that he had spoken with someone who objected to Harry because if he had been positive about his involvement when he left the room, he had done a 180-degree turn by the time he walked back in. He announced that perhaps we had been too hasty in contacting Harry – even though it was he who had insisted on Mother calling Mr Miller; it was she who had been hesitant. Now he wanted to think about it. Think about what? The wagons were already circling, and this man was offering to take away the circus. Harry, to his credit, said he would leave it with us and to call him if we needed help. His office was only ten minutes away.

Once Harry had left, Kell said that we should look through the phone book. Maybe there was someone else who could do a superior job. Who is better than Harry Miller? Mother and I asked. Why this change of heart? The important thing was to get the press shut down. Kell said he would give it some thought and hurriedly left the hotel. Mother, Ross and I were confused. An hour later, in a phone conversation to Mother, Kell told her what he now had in mind. He wanted someone who could represent us in the media. In other words, he saw this as an opportunity to make money. His exact words were, 'You know I'm thinking that – why should a roadie or someone make money out of this? It could be a house for Rhett.'

Shock does not even come close to describing the feeling I had when I heard him say this. Who had said anything about receiving money? Certainly not Mother or Ross or me – or even Harry. Who could give a thought to profiting from this horrible tragedy? I think Kell must have been crazed with grief and shock. When I thought back on how Michael had sought his privacy and loathed media attention, I could well imagine how sad this would have made him.

How do I know he said that about a house for Rhett? Because, I was on the other line. It's important to realize that not one single call was taken in that room without someone else on an extension. We were all paranoid, due to what Michael had relayed to us over the years about the press. The journalists were really beginning to mount in number and we were all on our guard. I had counted thirty-two photojournalists across the street alone, with huge lenses trained at our windows and several more on the other side, downstairs in the underground car park and directly outside the front door of the hotel. Although it was blazingly sunny weather in Sydney, we had to keep our curtains drawn at all times.

When Mother replied that all she wanted was for the circus to stop, and the trusted Harry to do this for us, Kell finally agreed to return to the hotel and sign an agreement allowing him to handle the press and the arrangements for just one camera to be in the cathedral. It was agreed that it would be unobtrusive and at a distance behind the congregation. This was done with absolutely no money exchanging hands: Harry was doing us a favour. If Channel Seven made money by selling to other networks, that was their business. For our part, it put a stop to potential pandemonium in the church. Another suggestion Harry made was to put a gag on the coroner's office in regard to the official autopsy report. Harry explained that there was already speculation in the press, and the coroner's report might spark even more tabloid fodder when it was released in two to three months' time. He made a quick call to an attorney, a friend of his, who took care of this immediately.

Over the ensuring months Kell was to tell this story two different ways. To one journalist he said that in relation to Harry Miller's involvement, Ross and Harry had shown up at his apartment where they barged in and demanded that he sign a release for Harry to handle the press. In Vince Lovegrove's book, *Michael Hutchence*, he is reported to have said that he rose from a nap around 11 p.m. on Sunday evening to find a note under his door. He said it was from Ross who had delivered it there with Harry, and it said that he should call Mr Miller regarding dealings with the press. Both stories are ridiculous. To begin with, Mother had not even contacted Harry Miller at this stage. Not only was she putting it off, but it was Sunday evening and she did not have Mr Miller's private number. She knew it could wait until Monday morning when we were all thinking more clearly.

How Kell was planning to capitalize on this catastrophe, we did not care or dare to ask at the time. However, we found out about ten days later when he announced that he had retained an entertainment attorney and had made a deal with Channel Seven in Sydney, for an interview with him and Rhett. They reportedly received AUS$175,000 for the thirty-minute interview, and neither had denied this figure to me. Anybody who watched it must have realized that Rhett was in no condition to be exposed on national television. He was drowning in grief and anger, and I feel it was inappropriate for Kell to allow his younger son to appear on national television this way.

Martha called from her mobile. She was on her way back from a long interview with the police. We were arranging a rendezvous, as we were going to the morgue and did not want to be followed by these relentless and thoughtless people with their cameras. We had to be careful, as so far, the journalists had managed to snap pictures of each of the other family members leaving the morgue, even with police escort. The side fire-escape seemed the logical answer. Answering a knock at my door at one thirty sharp revealed a minder standing with a hotel employee holding a massive key ring. She took us out a locked door and down some stairs to an exit where there was a van waiting. The minder was pretty serious about it; I thought it was silly. Who knew me? But he was just doing his job.

Martha was waiting in the van and told me some of the highlights of her interview with Detective Inspector Duclos, the chief investigator on the case. She had given a statement to the police, but felt that apart from the fact that she knew Michael was depressed and that he had left two desperate phone messages for her, she had little to offer. During our drive she was going over the phone log from Michael's hotel bill and had figured out who most of the numbers belonged to, but asked me if I recognized the ones she did not. I wasn't much help.

She had also been to see Paula, who had arrived with Tiger Lily and an entourage which included her friend Belinda Brewin and Belinda's fiancé, the barrister, Andrew Young. I remembered Michael telling me about Mr Young. Michael had said that he had not only been helpful in negotiations between Paula and Bob Geldof, but had also helped out with damage limitation during at least one of their crises. The papers reported that it had not been a smooth flight from London.

She was in her hotel room under sedation, and had, according to Martha, asked to see me alone. I was surprised, as I would have thought that the first person she would want to see would be Mother, if only as one mother to another. After all, we had only had brief telephone conversations and I had actually only met Paula four months previously in Los Angeles. Perhaps she thought I occupied neutral territory, as so far I was the only one in the family she had not had a mild clash with. I declined a meeting for the time being and Martha said she understood. As it turned out, the only time my mother or I saw Paula in Sydney that terrible week was at the funeral, where it was impossible to speak.

We reached the morgue and hurried inside. It was summer but I was shivering. There is no way to create a warm ambience in a morgue. It must take a special type of person to work in a place like that. I thought of all the times I, in my job as a make-up artist, had actually demonstrated the colours and special stippling motion with a sponge to create a cadaver for film. In fact it was to this very morgue, in the late eighties, that we would bring our students to view bodies so that in time they could create a more realistic corpse. Not once on any of those visits did I imagine that I would ever be visiting a loved one in this place, especially not Michael. The memories of the smells and bodies had made me nauseous then, and even more so now.

A counsellor was waiting for us. As we sat with her, Martha asked some tough questions. I was glad she was doing it in front of me and not my parents. She asked about drugs and their attendant paraphernalia, alluding to illegal substances, and was told that there had been no evidence thus far. Definitely no suspicious circumstances. Martha and I went in to see Michael together at first, then I left her alone with him. I could hear her weep loudly.

It was my turn, and the counsellor had left a small envelope and scissors next to Michael. I wanted some of his beautiful hair. My mother was right, he did look as though he was in a peaceful sleep. I tried to hold his hand, but it was cold and stiff. I stroked the hair on his arm and rearranged the hair on his head. I gently clipped three small locks of that curly hair of which I had always been envious. One each for my children and one for myself. I ran my fingers over his eyelashes and expected him to pop open his piercing, chocolate eyes and say, 'Just fooling, Sis.' His cheeks were so cold, I wanted to warm him up. I felt that if I could just throw myself on top of him and make him warm, he would come back to me. I noticed a small cut over his left eyebrow and a little dried blood. At the time I wondered how and where this had happened, and feared foul play. Later, at least this extra, horrible, dread was lifted when I learned that the cut had probably occurred when his body fell forward and his face hit the door of his hotel room. I stroked his cheeks and kissed him over and over. I whispered loving thoughts to Michael, hoping he could hear me. After a long time, I pulled myself away with difficulty and walked outside.

I turned back, compelled to see him again. The counsellor told me to take all the time I needed. 'All the time I needed.' I wanted another thirty-seven years.

Michael was more than a brother. Long before Erin and Brent, there was Michael. He was the first child I held in my arms, the first baby I bathed and soothed to sleep. I had learned most of my mothering skills with Michael. My brother's life was extraordinary and full, and I'm sure he gave me more love and laughter than many get from their siblings, but I wanted much more. I felt cheated, I wanted to stay there, be with him in case a miracle happened. But I finally pulled myself away for the last time, and felt incredible numbness as I was driven back to the hotel.

A meeting was about to begin in my mother's suite. Mother, Ross, Rhett, Martha, Andrew Farriss, INXS publicist Shawn Deacon, the funeral director Rodney Claxton, his assistant Marcella, Harry Miller and myself had assembled to make arrangements for Michael's funeral and final resting place. Arriving late, Kell announced that he had just come from a meeting with Colin Diamond who had informed him that Michael had stipulated in his will that he wished to be cremated.

Everybody in the room was visibly shocked. There followed a short discussion on this astonishing news. In our family a request to be cremated had been unknown. Andrew Farriss sat shaking his head and looking at the floor. Martha, who was seated on my left, looked at me incredulously, asking if Michael had ever said anything about this to me. He had not. But then, he was a young man so why would we speak of such things? We all questioned Kell who had been so keen on an elaborate funeral service, and a monument of some kind. I'd always thought a large headstone was only for those with a grave. He said if Colin said it was in his will we should respect Michael's wishes.

I was getting increasingly anxious to meet Mr Colin Diamond as I was curious as to why Kell was not making any kind of move without his OK. I assumed that I would have the pleasure shortly as he was in town for the funeral and Mother had left a message at the Sheraton for him to call her. This aside, we all agreed that if Michael was to be cremated we, just his immediate family and his brothers in the band, would take a boat and scatter his ashes over Sydney Harbour. He had loved that place. Rodney Claxton said that the Premier of New South Wales had offered all the security we needed for the day of the funeral. We still had to decide on the day however. There were only two houses of worship in Sydney which could accommodate a large crowd, St Mary's and St Andrew's Cathedrals. Rodney Claxton suggested that St Andrew's was the better for security reasons. He made a call to check on either availability and reported that Thursday afternoon would be the best time for St Andrew's.

Rhett objected: he thought that it should be on Saturday because it would give extra time for people who were arriving from overseas to pay their respects. He was adamant and insisted on a vote. He was voted down. Do disputes about our dead brother have to start so soon, I wondered. Rhett also wanted an open casket but Mother and Kell did not. How are you going to file 1,000 mourners past a casket and maintain security? You can't frisk people coming into a church as you can at a rock concert. Once more he was voted down. The last thing we needed was to make this even more of a security nightmare. We had to think about who should be in the cathedral and how we would control the guest list. Someone suggested passes and someone else suggested a password – 'Tiger Lily'. This was getting ridiculous. We were all stunned and bereaved, yet here was this parish council meeting with a whole set of different agendas and some egos needing attention too. Rodney Claxton suggested that along with the irises we agreed upon for the casket we should have one large, beautiful Tiger Lily and we all liked this idea. Later a newspaper reported inaccurately that the flower was placed there by Paula with a note from her and Tiger. Paula did not join us to help make any of these decisions. She could have taken part in the planning but we were told when we gathered that she was highly sedated, resting in her apartment at the Quay West.

On my right Andrew Farriss, Michael's devoted friend and writing partner, was meticulously taking notes. He agreed to speak for the other band members at the service. Rhett said he would like to speak, and Mother asked me to say something. Mother and I had seen the television presenter Richard Wilkins on Channel Nine the previous morning, speaking eloquently about Michael, and Harry said he would approach him about leading the eulogies. Two years later we read that Michael was not an admirer of Wilkins, though this statement had been made in Lovegrove's book by a friend of Michael's who wanted to remain anonymous. If this was so, nothing was said by Andrew or Martha that day. Rhett wanted to be a pallbearer along with the INXS members. Andrew was hesitant to be a pallbearer as he was already unsure if he was up to speaking and afterwards 'carrying my best mate on my shoulders'. This was perfectly understandable and my heart went out to him. Andrew and Michael had shared a long and very special, enduring friendship. He has always been a thoughtful, circumspect man and takes his time before making a comment on anything. Rhett suggested that Brent stand by in the event that Andrew found that he was not up to it.

We also had to decide on the music. Martha suggested we ask Nick Cave to sing 'Into My Arms'. Although Mother and I had not met him we knew that Nick was one of Michael's close friends. Martha said she would ask him. Next day we received a call from Harry saying that Nick Cave's manager specified that he did not want to appear on the televised service but that he would sing for his friend's funeral if his face did not appear on camera. Of course Mother agreed, and Harry suggested that Channel Seven show footage of Michael over the song.

It was soon getting very noisy in the hotel suite. Rodney Claxton asked Mother, Ross, Kell and myself to join him and Marcella, his assistant, outside to go over the service announcement for the newspapers. I don't think he meant to leave Rhett out but I do think that what he had witnessed in the suite made him apprehensive about asking for his opinion. It was a while before we came up with the correct wording and the order in which to place Michael's loved ones and when completed it was faxed to several international publications. He then asked us to make up a list of INXS music we would like played although it would have to come down to just two songs. Incredibly, Kell suggested 'Stay Young'. Mother and Ross requested 'Never Tear Us Apart' and 'By My Side', and these were settled on. We adjourned, with Rodney Claxton making an appointment for Mother and Kell to meet with the Dean of St Andrew's to discuss the service.

We all felt like prisoners. Mother remarked that if this was the way Michael had to live most of the time she could understand his depression. There was always somebody stationed on the third floor entrance, but Mother said he was one of Michael's bodyguards, although when Michael was in Los Angeles he hadn't needed them. The sun was brilliant outside, but we all had to keep our curtains closed, and were told to give notice if we wanted to go anywhere. I thought this was crazy: nobody knew me. I supposed that Rhett, having lived in Australia most of his life, might have been more recognizable – but so what? He's an outgoing guy who didn't mind the attention at all, although he did not refrain from threatening the press if they got too close. That afternoon, Ross and Mother wanted some bottled water. I slipped out a side entrance and into a shop across the road where I saw a newspaper on the counter with some headline about Michael and Bob Geldof. The place was quiet with only one other customer. As I waited for the man to fetch the water I tuned into the conversation between the sales person and the other customer beside me. 'Of course he bloody killed himself, what do you expect with Prozac and booze?' the salesperson said. I felt immediate anger rise up inside and found myself screaming at the stunned woman, 'Shut up, shut up, you didn't know him!' Both women looked at me in disbelief as if I were insane. At the time I was. I was insane with grief.

I finally asked Rhett what really happened to Michael. At that point I knew none of the physical details and had been afraid to ask. I had not read any newspapers but I knew Rhett had been over to the hotel room several times and had also spoken to the police. As I looked around my own room, I could not work out how it could physically be done; I could not see anything to thread a belt through which would take the weight. Rhett led me to the door of my room. He looked up at the closing mechanism, the long metal hinge which prevents the door from slamming and pointed while he told me. From then on, I could not go out of my room without looking up at the mechanism and thinking about how desperate Michael must have felt to deliberately do such a thing.

Brent and Erin arrived from Los Angeles. I was so relieved to see them. They were bewildered about having been ushered in via the hotel's parking area instead of through the main entrance. Eventually, Brent and Erin came and went as they pleased, but I would never trust myself to leave the hotel without either Brent or Ross at my side after that first incident. I also worried that I had nothing to wear to the funeral, as Erin seemed to have packed my bag with more shoes than dresses. Knox Street, where we were staying, is known for its dress shops, so I took the children with me across to the boutiques while I searched for something black and conservative. I tried something on in the first shop and burst into tears. Erin asked the salesperson for tissues and a glass of water. I couldn't go through with this and decided just to buy the first decent dress in the first shop we tried. Erin hugged me and said, 'It looks really good on you Mom, Michael would be proud.' As we hurried past the photographers, Brent put his arm around me. Trying to lighten things up, he mocked a tough-guy attitude and whispered, 'You want me to smash a camera for Michael, Mom?' I thought, how courageous my children were to see some irony in this. They were handling this situation better than I thought they could have. Michael would indeed be proud.

Mr Claxton had arranged an appointment with the Dean of St Andrew's Cathedral to discuss the service and funeral arrangements. When Ross and I arrived we found that Kell and Sue had brought along Kell's sister Croy. The Dean began by suggesting to Kell and I that we tell him about Michael – where he went to school, his career, what he was like as a child, that sort of thing. Before I could form any words, Kell went into a dissertation of his private and complex problems with Paula and Bob Geldof. He pushed on to the divorce, child custody fights, stipulating that Geldof was the demonic cause of it all. He was turning this into a counselling session! I kept asking Kell to get on with the real reason for us being there and was ignored, so after about fifteen minutes of this, I rose and said, 'Call me in when you are ready to discuss our son.' I walked outside. Ross settled me in a chair and returned to the room to see if he could get them back on to the reason for our being there. Kell continued on. After about ten minutes, Ross said, 'That's enough. I am going back outside to bring Patricia in and you had better be prepared to talk about Michael.'

I returned to the room and we got through the meeting. The discussion over, decisions made, we went out into the cathedral to meet Mr Claxton. He showed us our seating arrangements in the church. We returned to the Sir Stamford for further meetings on the final funeral arrangements – cars, flowers, security. Halfway through, I noticed that drivers and bodyguards were coming in and out having discussions at the other end of the room. In fact, there were many uninvited people, and the room was getting so noisy with various cellphones going off. I was so distressed by this that Mr Claxton suggested that we adjourn to the hotel breakfast room. We had literally been forced out of our own hotel suite. Kell, who continued to whisper into his cellphone, came scrambling behind.

Mother wanted a collage of family photographs to be placed near the casket. She had brought some with her. Rhett collected some from the lock-up he shared with Michael and Erin had brought some from Los Angeles. Since she and Mandy are the artists in the family it was decided to let them take care of this task. I visited Erin's room that night while she and Mandy were working on the large board of scattered family memories. I had not realized that the work would leave Erin drained and depressed. I tried to keep little Zoe occupied because she wanted to help and she kept rearranging the photographs. Poor child, it must have been such a confusing week for her. She kept saying, 'Daddy sad. Daddy cry. Zoe cry too.'

While we were cut off from the world, engulfed in such sad undertakings, Colin Diamond and Andrew Young were visiting their other client Jon Farriss at his home. There were several people in the house, drinking their grief away downstairs as Jon sat upstairs in the master bedroom. Diamond and Young were overheard by several of Michael's friends discussing Rhett in a contemptuous way. Rhett is not one to let things rest and over the course of that day he had been playing detective as usual, asking a few leading questions of Colin Diamond. This was mainly concerning Michael's state of mind, how no one in his management or the band could have been so blind as not to notice the decline in his mental well-being. He wanted to know how these people could have ignored this situation. He was also asking questions about Michael's financial position. Anybody who knew Michael was aware that no matter what transpired between the brothers, whatever temporary estrangements, Michael loved Rhett very much and the feeling was reciprocal. Rhett was following his instincts, asking the questions we all wanted to ask.

Many things happened the day before the service. We began hearing reports that remaining members of INXS were unhappy with our decision to restrict the press, including televised coverage of the funeral, although none of them actually called us to say so. Not even Martha had said anything about that. Now Rhett decided that he did not like the idea either. I agreed with my parents and felt restraint was the best way. Anyway, it was their decision. Except for the die-hards, most of the photojournalists had by now dispersed from across the street. They had been told that everything had to go through Harry, so we knew that there would be no shuffling and fighting for places in the cathedral because only one network and one photographer had permission to be there.

The day before the funeral I heard from Michael's hitherto elusive financial adviser, Colin Diamond. Martha had told me that I needed to speak to him but he had cancelled every meeting. I thought now he was calling to change yet another plan, but the man on the other end of the phone explained that he did not have long to talk as he had been up most of the night at a hospital with Tiger Lily. He said he had taken her there after she had suffered a seizure. Colin Diamond has since discussed this publicly, in a short-lived magazine called *AXS*, the masthead of which cited Andrew Young as 'Legal Adviser'. Kell confirmed that he too had heard about this, from Martha, who had accompanied them to the hospital. This news of Tiger of course gripped me with alarm, and I called Martha and Tina to talk about my anxiety and concern.

Despite the chaos that Mother had endured in those five days and given that she had been expected to make decisions on her elder son's funeral service and was forced to say goodbye to him in a very public way, we tried to think about positive things. We were all concerned about Tiger and how we could help Paula out at a time like this. Mother even asked me if I would be willing to return to Australia and help raise Tiger if this proved to be a sensible option. I did not think it through but agreed without hesitation. In fact I was rather charmed by the prospect of raising another child, especially Michael's Tiger Lily. Of course I had a life and two children of my own in California, and I can't imagine this would have been an option Paula would have been keen on, but for the moment, in the midst of such a crisis, I wasn't thinking straight about anything.

After this call, Ross, Tina and I went back to working on the list of friends and family for the cars when the phone rang again. It was Kell, furious as he reported a meeting with Paula the previous evening. They had had a disagreement over the plans for the next day's service. After our confrontation at the hotel in LA just four months before – since when we had neither seen nor spoken to each other – I assumed I was *persona non grata*. News of the seizure meant that I was seriously concerned for Tiger's welfare. But having now heard of Kell's account of his encounter with Paula, I doubted that she and I would have a very positive meeting when we came into contact.

The next slice of news to hit us in the morning newspapers came the day before the funeral. In an interview the Dean of St Andrew's announced that his 'house of worship' was open to anybody who wished to come and pay their respects to Michael. This presented us with a huge problem. We had tried to ensure that the service would be as private as possible, considering the number of friends and the celebrity status of some of those who were coming to the church. Now this man was throwing the doors open to the public. It was also not generally known, even to the press and certainly not to us, that the Dean usually has his own video crew which offer videos and audio tapes of special services performed at St Andrew's. No doubt the proceeds go to a good cause, but I can't even begin to express the anger we continue to feel at discovering for ourselves so late in the day that the cathedral expected to film and tape Michael's service for financial gain. It seemed to us so wrong when the Church's principal obligation in such circumstances is surely to offer comfort in grief, rather than to see the occasion as a business opportunity. Maybe in less sensitive circumstances it might be fitting to make use of this facility, but given that we had taken steps to restrict the press it just didn't seem appropriate. The only solution was to ensure that the programme for Michael's service did not contain the usual promotion details on the back, and that the church cameras were not operating. We informed Harry Miller and Rodney Claxton of our wishes.

I was in my mother's suite when Martha called to say that Michele was in the hotel. Would we see her? Of course we would. She walked in looking as beautiful as ever, but frail and shaken. I had so many mixed emotions, knowing that Michael had loved her so truly and so long. We hugged and I brought Erin in to see her. She had been just a little girl when they last met, and they greeted each other warmly. Talking with Michele brought back floods of memories. She said that she had felt in talking with Michael that past week that he had come full circle, that he seemed strong and ready to begin again. She added that with the encouragement he had received from the motion picture industry in Hollywood he was optimistic about his acting career and also wanted to establish a simpler way of life. He could accept that it would take some effort to cross over to an acting career and he was prepared for that, but he wanted his personal life to be less complicated.

Eventually Michele asked about Rhett. I took her to his suite and was surprised again to find a room full of people. Since Rhett had been to his and Michael's Sydney lock-up, he was now sitting on the floor going through a box of Michael's personal papers. He was sharing some of Michael's most precious thoughts with a room full of people! He even pulled out an old letter from Michele and began reading it aloud as she sat there horrified. I begged him to put the box away, but he didn't. Fortunately, knowing Rhett for many years, and through Michael, Michele understands and accepts Rhett's unconventional behaviour – you just can't stay mad at Rhett, and in a funny way you love him for what he does.

That afternoon a memo was placed under every door in the Sir Stamford and presumably sent to each business on Knox Street. It stated that at 1 p.m., Thursday, 27 November the street would be blocked off for a short time. The police had advised that this was for the best in order to get the cars lined up for the procession to the cathedral. I realized that although I had many wonderful memories of my beloved brother bouncing around in my mind I still had to come up with something to say to express my feelings in the cathedral. The fact that it held 1,000 people and the service was to be telecast live did not bother me. I would simply be there for Michael, his brothers in the band and most of all for my family and I wanted to do my best for them. I realized that it would be Thanksgiving for Erin and Brent and me. Our last Thanksgiving holiday had been spent with Michael and I felt compelled to mention this. Erin had arrived with a book of poetry by e. e. cummings. She suggested a verse which spoke of one's passing but it was not quite right. As we flipped through the book we came across another which gave some hope and was fitting to the occasion and the man. Just as my mother was relying on me for support, I was also relying on my children for strength.

Mother made arrangements for us to go to a beauty salon. She thought it would make us feel a little better if we looked better. Lloyd Lomas, the owner of the salon, kindly offered to come to us on the morning of the funeral but I was in need of a little more help. I slipped out the side entrance and ran down the alley to Lloyd's salon. It was very low key and none of his staff knew who I was. It was greatly appreciated because in the eternity of those past four days I had noticed that people in and around the hotel were staring at us, almost waiting for someone to break down. When he had finished weaving his magic he guided me down an alley, through some doors, and then I was back in my hotel room. Cars were arriving to take us to the funeral parlour at 6 p.m. for the final viewing. At the appointed time, we made a short, sombre ride to see my brother for the last time. We waited while Kell and Sue had their time alone with Michael. When Kell emerged he seemed aloof and distanced. I could not quite define my unease and since nothing untoward had transpired between us I put it down to his expression of grief.

Andrew arrived with Martha, just before we entered the chapel. I greeted her but immediately felt a strange detachment from her as well. I was well aware that a funeral parlour is not a place for warm ambience but I do imagine that in most instances, friends and relatives try to comfort each other. I felt no empathy from Martha who, up until then, had always been so friendly. Again I put it down to overwhelming distracted grief. Mother, Ross, Brent, Erin and I went into the small chapel together. Michael lay there so peacefully, dressed in one of his beautiful suits sent over from his stage wardrobe. We stood around the casket and each of us placed something special with him – photographs and letters. Mother and I had each brought with us a flower from those sent by well-wishers. I laid a lily by him and Mother placed an iris in his hand. Then she began to weep. Brent and Erin were standing back a little and gradually came closer as we spoke to him. Mother stroked his hair and I noticed that they had attempted to cover the cut on his eyebrow by rearranging his curls. Strange as it sounds we were all comforted by how peaceful he looked. There had been such a change in his face over the last year, he had rarely looked at peace.

Just as it was getting too painful to bear, Andrew came in and put his arms around us. He talked to Michael and then said something that gave us real solace. He reminded us that Michael would not be alone on the other side. He was referring to his mother Jill, who died in 1993, who had always loved Michael and knew him to be Andrew's brother in a way. She had died much too young. Andrew said, 'He's not alone, he has my mum to look after him and they'll have each other now.' My mother managed a painful smile. He went on, 'She'll take care of him for you.' I can't explain why this gave us relief from some of the pain. It just did: the idea that a loving and familiar face was waiting to care for him there, I suppose. Mother's face lifted when she realized what his words meant. We will always be grateful to Andrew for that loving, unselfish thought. Over more than twenty years of backstage meetings and various social gatherings, as well as award ceremonies and so on, we had come to know all the boys in the band pretty well. INXS staying together for so long was partly due to this unspoken importance of this extended family. But I guess Andrew will always be the most special INXS brother of all because his friendship with Michael began with him defending Michael from bullies at school all those years ago.

I walked outside to give Mother and Ross some time alone. Rhett called me over and began objecting to the proposed live telecast, trying to enlist my help in cancelling it. Now, for someone who took so many trips over to view the flowers, cards and stuffed animals outside the Ritz Carlton, never once disguising himself but wearing, au contraire, brightly coloured shirts which were likely to draw reporters' and photographers' attention, I would not assume that having one camera at the back of the church would be a problem. I struggled to keep quiet. For some reason, it was OK for him to be organizing a wake but he objected to Mother and Kell controlling their son's funeral. Our discussion was getting heated because he could not bring me round to his way of thinking. He tried to drag poor Andrew into it. I said that there is no way for us to really know the pain that Mother and Kell must be going through. We have nowhere to learn to become parents far less to know how to deal with this most unnatural thing – the death of a child. I mumbled that we just try to deal with sorrow as it arises and as a parent this was a tragedy that I hoped neither he nor I ever had to face.

I tried to hug him as we left for the hotel. He was stiff at first but softened. I also hugged Andrew, who had joined us outside and heard most of this difficult conversation and he agreed with me. Then I joined Mother who was waiting to leave. As we walked away she noticed some programmes, which had been printed by the funeral parlour. The front read 'Thanksgiving for the life of Michael Hutchence – January 22, 1960 – November 22, 1997'. But, sure enough, the back cover still invited people to purchase video copies of the service for $25. The audio tape was priced at a bargain $5. My blood boiled again. Mother was almost beyond fury and insisted that the programme was reprinted before the ceremony. I wonder how those who criticized my parents for the carefully restricted telecast which was beamed to international destinations and for which they took no money, would feel about those videos and cassettes being on sale for the next few months, if my mother hadn't stopped it right there and then.

Mother and I were confused by the unfriendly 'messages' we were getting. There seemed to be some sub-text or hidden agenda that we were excluded from. For one thing, apart from some beautiful flowers from Andrew and Shelly Farriss, and a phone message from Tim Farriss, we had not heard from the rest of the band. We found this very strange, as in the past we had all been part of an extended family. I realized that they were grieving the loss of a good friend, and creative and business partner, but having been in each other's lives for twenty-four years, I thought a call to my mother could be expected.

On the morning of the funeral I woke with a pounding heart, shaking and sweaty. Memories came flooding back. As I lay there trying to calm myself I put my hand out to feel for Ross who was sleeping quietly and peacefully beside me. I was trying to take long breaths, concentrating on exhaling slowly while pushing all of the air out, hoping this would slow my heart rate. I did this for some time but still felt I was hyperventilating. I looked at the clock beside the bed: 4.25 a.m. I could hear voices from the street below. Cars, voices, shutters being opened. I got up and went to the bathroom. My face looked swollen and puffy – I had cried myself to sleep again. How could I get through this day?

I pulled back the heavy velvet curtains and opened my windows wide to get some fresh air. As I looked down to the street below I saw an outside broadcast van pull up, then a couple of photographers arriving to stake their claim outside the hotel entrance. I could see their cigarettes glowing in the dark – the sun still not up – and I watched them moving around and chatting to each other, getting ready for another day in the quest for that front page shot.

It started to grow lighter. I looked up at the sky and suddenly from out of nowhere I saw two birds – two doves. They were chasing each other across the sky, criss-crossing back and forth in front of our bedroom window. I could not believe my eyes. I will never forget that moment. I felt they were sending me a message to tell me Michael was at peace. I wanted to wake Ross, but could not tear myself away. I could not help but recall a beautiful photograph of Michael standing and holding a dove in his hand which was used in an advertisement for Amnesty International. It was one of my favourite photographs.

By this time my panic attack had subsided but I was still feeling strange. I went back to bed and thought about those doves. When Ross woke up and made tea for us I told him my story, and he listened with tears in his eyes. Ross is a very special and gentle man, and he loved Michael dearly.

I showered and tried to prepare myself for the day ahead but was feeling so shaky, bewildered and teary I did not think I could cope with the day ahead of me. Ross insisted on sending for a doctor, who arrived about an hour later and said I was under such extreme trauma and stress and needed to take something to calm me down. She offered me a tablet; I asked her what it was, and she said it was a Valium. I panicked, as I hardly ever take an aspirin. She sat talking to me for some time, and I eventually decided to take it to get me through the day.

Lloyd came to my suite to do my hair and Erin's. He was astounded at the likeness between Erin and Michael. When my dear friend Jan and her daughter Cassie arrived they gave me a stone to hold and rub – it was meant to calm me more. They also made me some 'calming' tea. By this time I was so calm, I was almost comatose! Cassie, a former student of mine, had won the BAFTA award for her make-up on *Priscilla, Queen of the Desert*. She offered to make up my swollen eyes for me. I remember reminding Cassie to keep my eyes very soft. I never usually let anyone do my make-up for me. Then there was a knock on the door and Harry Miller came in to discuss certain final arrangements to control the filming. He knew Jan and they chattered on about old times. I remember listening to the chatter and even interjecting occasionally myself, while at the same time wondering why I was feeling so animated. When they all left to allow me to dress, I went over to the window. The stillness was eerie. The outside broadcast van had left, and all the photographers too. Knox

Street was deserted, but for a few pedestrians standing outside the hotel – not a car in sight, or even a taxi on the rank outside. But there was no sign of the doves now.

As I took off my dressing gown a wave of sadness overcame me, my Valium-induced calm giving way to a flood of tears. The outfit I had decided to wear that day was the suit I had bought that happy day with Michael in London.

Thursday 27 November 1997 fell on Thanksgiving Day itself. It was also the day that we would be giving thanks for Michael's life. Mother called and said that she was on her way with a statement for me to check through before I read it on a radio show. Actually her thoughts were very concise and I had to change very little. She left and the phone rang while I was still furiously correcting details. It was Harry. I took the call, thinking that he was going to discuss this whole radio interview business, but before I had time to draw breath, he transferred me direct to the Alan Jones Show. I later found out this has the largest listening audience in Australia, and that Mr Jones can be quite caustic. I thought I had nothing to worry about in that respect as he was also a client of Harry's and I was given to understand that he was doing us a favour by allowing us to put our case across to his audience. He began by asking questions about Michael as a child and extended his sympathies to the family. He then said that many people were curious and suspicious of our motives and feared that we were trying to make money out of tragedy. I then read out Mother's statement, improvising here and there. I flatly denied that we were getting a cent for the live telecast and added that we were indebted to Harry for his help. It was important for me and Mother to establish this as Harry had been horribly impugned and we wanted to do what we could to correct the record.

Later, when I went to check in with Rhett, I was alarmed to find his room still resembled Grand Central station, with a constant flow of people. He was still publicly going through Michael's boxes. He suggested I came along with him to see Paula before the funeral. Rhett had only met Paula three times, at Zoe's christening and then again at Christmas 1995 and 1996. These were very happy occasions and he and Paula had got on well. He had not seen Michael's deterioration in 1997, had not even spoken with him other than briefly the morning before his death. Though he had heard stories from friends, he was oblivious to the turmoil Michael's life had taken on with their domestic problems. He did not know of Michael's depression. Out of respect for my mother, I declined to go with him. Paula had yet to call her, and I did not think that right.

I went to see Martha. She was taking phone calls in between trying on dresses which friends had sent over. She had been too busy to go shopping, she explained, and would have to make do with a borrowed outfit for the funeral. She was waiting for news on her husband Bill who was due in from New York an hour or so before the service. Bill had known Michael since the early days of INXS when he was first employed to check their contracts with the record companies. We wanted him to say something at the crematorium. As I waited for her to become free to speak to me she took a call clearly pertaining to the seating in the cathedral. I don't know who was on the other end but she would stop every now and then and say into the phone, 'Just a minute, I'm not sure about that one, Tina's here I'll ask her.' Then she turned to me and asked something like, 'What do you think, should the [tour] crew be seated in front of the girlfriends?' We both agreed on that one. Michael respected the people he worked with for so many years, and they should be seated directly behind the band.

When I returned to my room, slightly disquieted, I found several messages. Chris Murphy, Wendy Murphy, Hiraani, Jonnie and many others had rung. There was also a fax from Gibson and Tina Kemp, my good friends in London, sent via a mutual friend in Sydney. It had been difficult for friends to find us as we were all booked in under assumed names. Gibson had sent me a beautiful, uplifting verse on the passing of a loved one. I decided to read it out at the cathedral. I also thought the INXS brothers would find some comfort in it as it was from such a dear old friend and the words were so fitting:

And from those lips which did sing,
a rose beget the spring,
do not stand at my grave and cry,
I am not there, I did not die.

These lines were written by an unknown soldier from World War Two.

As I dressed that terrible morning and tried to keep myself

together, a friend of Michael's came to my room and gave me a beautiful crystal to hold at the church, along with some calming tea. Actually I had taken a Valium and was approaching *Valley of the Dolls*-style calm. All I had to remember was to stay in the first limo, sit on the right side of the church, and walk up to the podium with Rhett.

I went to my mother's suite, stopping briefly in the lobby where a few relatives and friends had gathered. Mother was also sedated. She does not believe in drugs of any kind and she rarely ever even takes aspirin, but it was obvious that today she would break her rule. She was wearing the pale blue suit she had bought when she had first met Paula. Little had she thought then that she would be wearing it for an occasion such as this. Rodney Claxton had already delivered a satin-lined box which contained the small, silk, purple and yellow Versace kerchief from Michael's coat pocket and the six beautiful Vivienne Westwood buttons he had carefully removed from his jacket before closing the casket. Mother had asked for these items the night before but was surprised when he brought them to the hotel. She chose to carry the kerchief for comfort. After the funeral Mother divided the buttons between Rhett, Brent, Erin, Martha and myself as keepsakes. The sixth and best she kept and has had set into a ring. Shortly before we had to reach the lobby the phone rang. Nick Cave was on the line. There were no words of condolence and he was quite businesslike as he explained that he was willing to sing 'Into My Arms' for Michael's family but reiterated that he objected to being seen on television. We were confused as we had already gone over this with Channel Seven and assumed that the message had reached him. Mother assured him that the only image on the screen during his song would be Michael's.

After greeting our friends and relatives in the lobby we had to depart – quite early, as we were to pick up the INXS brothers and Paula plus her entourage from another hotel. As we walked from the quiet of our hotel to the limousines I looked up and saw people hanging out of windows and lined up and down the street. I realized they weren't gawking, they were paying respects. The first car carried Mother and Ross, Kell and Sue, Croy and me. Rhett, Mandy and Zoe, Erin and Brent, our aunt, Maureen and our cousin Melissa were in the second car. INXS members and partners rode next. The other cars carried close friends and family to the church. We were terribly moved by the outpouring of grief from crowds along the route. Mother and Ross and I were taking it in of course, lost as we were in our private thoughts. Kell and Sue found it necessary to comment upon the turnout for Michael, saying things like 'Look at that person with the banner', 'Look at all the flowers', 'What a gorgeous day it is for Michael'. I was on edge by the time we reached the Sheraton and definitely felt like taking another little yellow pill, just about remembering my 'Right side, right side, right side' mantra.

The careful plan was to break the two front cars just ahead of the Sheraton entrance so that the three other cars, including Paula and her companions, Belinda Brewin, Andrew Young, Tony the bodyguard, Nick Cave and presumably Colin and Stephen Diamond, could pull in behind and follow to the cathedral. This would mean that Paula was in the fifth car, a potential insult to dignity and status that had not occurred to me. We had no wish to slight her. Besides, we had rather gratefully accepted the advice of our funeral director who was used to orchestrating these miserable occasions.

The door of our limo opened all too soon. I was out first and was greeted by the Dean and a blaze of flashbulbs. I cannot remember what the Dean said, but as he spoke, I was aware that people were running behind me into the cathedral as if on their way to a gig venue. I still felt light-headed. Right side, right side . . . As I walked, blinking, across the threshold of the packed and dimly lit cathedral, flashbulbs, blazing sunlight outside and Valium all playing their part, INXS's publicist Shawn Deacon caught my arm and congratulated me for coming across so well on the Alan Jones Show. I just hesitated for a few seconds, then I was shoved several times by people running through the door behind me as my parents were still trying to enter the church. Then the way was finally clear for me to walk down the centre aisle to take my place in the front pew; the front *right* pew.

I was aware that many eyes watched to see who might be walking to the front and felt suddenly weakened without certainty of my family behind me. Almost there, not much further, right side, right right side. Oh no, it can't be. The right front pew was occupied. There sat Tony the bodyguard, Nick Cave, Paula's friend Belinda and sitting with her feet up on the railing was Paula, bouncing baby Tiger on her bare, extended legs. I realized that the people running into the cathedral ahead of me while the Dean and Shawn were detaining me must have been Paula and the others from her car. How else could they have been in their seats before me? Behind them were the band, the crew and some of the girlfriends. I quickly glanced back to see my family still detained at the door. Feeling the weight of many eyes upon my back, I just slipped into the front left pew. My parents were visibly confused and upset when they finally made their way to the front and saw me seated on the left. Not realizing that I had failed to reach the front first they thought that I had made the mistake and Kell was furious with me. Of course it was the fault of the funeral director because he had not properly directed traffic. Who knew that it had become a first come, first seated affair? I was expecting an usher or a cordoned-off area. I still do not know why it had been allowed that everyone could choose their own seating after all that planning. There must have been some sort of plan that the band's crew and girlfriends had been told about. Why else had Martha taken the call while I was in her room that morning? I do not know if our original, respectfully traditional and formal, seating plan had been tampered with by others but it was unsettling and upsetting. Then again, who could have known that the occupants of the two front cars would enter the church behind the occupants of the fourth and fifth limousines? By the time Rodney Claxton realized the mistake the cathedral was just about full.

Perhaps to some this just seems like an unfortunate muddle. I'm acutely aware that silly, snippy pride and concerns about breaches of conventional protocol were insignificant on the day. We were all there to wish Michael our love and that was the only thing that mattered, finally. However, the fact that, despite my Valium haze, I recall this confusion so keenly and with such pain suggests that the memory of some other agenda lingers.

We had two choices. Either we could ask everyone in the first six rows on the right, which included the band, to move to the other side in an orderly fashion while about 1,000 pairs of eyes looked on. The other was to sit on the left, which is what we did. Seated directly behind the enormous collage of family photographs, I couldn't even see my brother's casket. Rodney Claxton moved the collage but replaced it with the enormous arrangement from Bono and Ali. I could now just about strain to see the corner of the iris corsage lying on top of the casket. The piano from which Nick Cave was to deliver his song and the pulpit where the Dean was giving his address were both on the other side. Everything had been arranged to ensure that right side could have a better view of proceedings. This is why the family is traditionally seated on the right.

I did not see Rhett until we arrived at the cathedral, and when I saw him I wondered to myself why he had chosen to wear such a loud outfit for this sad occasion. It was a red and grey striped suit Michael had bought for him in Paris, which stood out vibrantly among everyone else's more sombre colours. Then I realized he had chosen it for the same reason as I had mine – to remember Michael.

We walked up the aisle to take our places only to find them already occupied by Paula, Belinda Brewin, Andrew Young, Martha Troup and a few others. We were confused, but saw other seats on the left were vacant and so sat in those. Mr Claxton came to us to apologize, and asked me if I wanted to ask them to change seats. I looked across to see Paula with her legs up on the front pew, jiggling them around in front of the Dean. I decided it would be more embarrassing to move, and we stayed put. I did not think moving would embarrass Paula, as she was doing a good enough job of that herself.

More unhappy surprises were to come. Just before the service began Paula slipped out of her seat and came across the aisle with Tiger Lily, as if for a social chat. It was the first time I had noticed what she was wearing. There, leaning over the pew, and facing the television cameras, was Paula in a short, tight, red and black dress with a plunging neckline. She had Tiger Lily dressed in matching Chinese pyjamas.

As she approached Kell and Sue they smiled broadly. I guessed they were so stunned that they had forgotten what had happened the day before. They kissed Paula and Tiger on the cheek. Then Paula moved on to me. I did not feel I could be a hypocrite and embrace her, and I turned my cheek away as Paula attempted to kiss it. After kissing Tiger, I told Paula to go back to her seat as the service was about to begin. Ross did the same. Nobody else could have possibly heard this exchange but many saw the interaction and there was an even deeper hush in the church. Tina was next in line but by that time Paula had decided not to press her luck. Returning to her seat, Paula put her ankles back up on the railing and jiggled her legs again. Belinda hit the leg closest to her, obviously trying to get her to behave herself. They went through this routine several times throughout the service. In normal circumstances we would be together with Michael's child and her mother. This had been my first interaction with Paula since her outburst at the Mondrian four months before.

Tina and Rhett had each written a eulogy for Michael and went up to the lectern together to deliver them. It must have taken so much strength to overcome their grief enough to do that. I looked at their pained faces, and have never felt so much love and pride in all my life.

The sound of Michael singing 'By My Side' filled the church. As the service began, Kell alerted Rhett to a photographer standing over on my side, about thirty feet away and not bothering anyone. This was the one photographer Kell had agreed to allow into the church beside the Channel Seven camera crew. Without warning, Kell had Rhett leap out of his seat and very pointedly demand the poor man move. Something had definitely happened in the last twenty-four hours but my head was too fuzzy to address it. I only wanted to focus on Michael. It was as if there was a secret society to which Kell had been admitted and Rhett had been ordained but I guessed that they hadn't had time to tell Mother and me about it.

The service began smoothly. Then, just as Nick Cave was singing, a man in the balcony yelled, 'This is how he did it Paula, this is how he died', and attempted to jump. Someone caught him before he fell but as he crashed against the side of the railing he smashed a light bulb. Glass splinters shattered all over two of my friends, one of whom was very pregnant. Security rushed to bundle the intruder off to a police van. I blame this disturbance on the Dean, who had invited one and all to come into the service. I later found out that this person had been allowed in simply because he was carrying a guitar.

Andrew was moving when he spoke of his friendship with Michael. Then Rhett and I walked up together and as I began to speak I felt my throat constrict. I pushed on trying not to look in my parents' direction, for I knew I would never be able to finish. I tried not to focus on any faces, especially the ones I knew, but faltered when I looked out at one point and locked eyes with Chris Murphy. Rhett put his arm around me and I continued. He was very nervous, reading his prepared eulogy fast, but it came from the heart. He told of his close relationship with Michael and how wonderful and how difficult it had been at times, to be his brother.

The service ended, the music for 'Never Tear Us Apart' swelled, and again Michael's voice rang through with his beautiful lyrics. 'We could live, for a thousand years and if I hurt you, I'd make wine from your tears, I told you that we could fly, 'cos we all have wings, but some of us don't know why.' I could feel it through my body and the pain was excruciating. We followed Michael's casket down the aisle and as we got to the door, where we could see Andrew, Jon, Tim, Kirk, Garry and Rhett placing the casket into the hearse, a friend of Michael's, whom I did not recognize at first, pushed through next to Mother's ear, and yelled, 'Three cheers for Michael.' The crowd outside responded. My poor mother had taken all she could stand, I watched her sink back against Ross.

We passed groups of mourners on the side of the road on the way to the crematorium and were so touched. I don't know if they could see into the limousine, but we mouthed thanks to them for coming out in tribute to Michael. We reached the crematorium with only the immediate family and friends, although as we exited the cars and I looked up on the hill I was surprised to see that we were surrounded by what looked like the whole of the New South Wales police department. When we were asked to enter the small chapel behind the coffin, Paula turned on her heels and walked away when the Dean stopped her from walking ahead of the immediate family members. Bill gave a fitting and beautiful speech. It was hard to watch Michael's casket being engulfed by the flames, so final.

It was only when we all met outside the crematorium that I really noticed who else was there, as the cathedral had been a blur for me. We wandered around and spoke with INXS members and some very special people who had been influential in the success of my brother's career, including Chris Murphy, who was taking his death especially hard. Kym Wilson came over and introduced herself to me. She offered me her phone number should I want to ask any questions about that last night. I doubt she has the answers to the questions that I would have for her. I think that only Michael or God would be able to answer those.

Kell was in a limousine with Sue and Croy. It was hot and humid by now, and he wanted to leave. Ross requested another car because we were not ready to leave. This was impossible, I looked over at the car we had arrived in and saw that it had steam pouring out of the engine. Also I could see that guests who had not originally gone to St Andrew's with us in the limousines were now getting into them whilst some of our relatives had apparently been left stranded at the cathedral. No doubt the same rules had applied as when we were on our way into the church: it was first come first seated – in a limo! Film footage of the exterior of St Andrew's later confirmed this, I saw no humour in the situation then – and little now. It reminded me of the backstage hangers-on, determined to claim close connection with the band.

On the way back to the Sir Stamford I was seated next to Croy and next to her was Sue. Across from us was Mother, between Ross and Kell. There was incessant chatting from the other three about which relatives were buried where. Mother and I looked at each other, and I could see that she was about to lose it. Kell was speaking very loudly, as he had forgotten his hearing aid. Then he started on about Rhett. Why didn't Mother speak to him? He needs to be pulled into line, he said. She defended Rhett, praised him on a beautiful eulogy and told Kell to speak to him himself if he had something to say. She told him that she did not want to speak of it now, we needed some quiet time to ourselves. Kell exploded and then Mother did lose it. Without looking, she flicked her hand back; her heavy gold bracelet caught Kell on his open mouth. He immediately began pummelling her head with his fists. I couldn't believe what I was seeing. Ross interposed and put a stop to it. In my head I was saying, Michael, please don't watch this ugliness. Climb inside my mind, and I will tell you how much we all love you.

By now, Kell was covering his bleeding mouth with a handkerchief and moaning about all the work he just had done on his two front teeth. We later found out that Mother loosened five of his new caps and caused several months' worth of dentist's appointments. But despite this scene, Sue and Kell's sister were clucking away like old hens. Mother begged them to be quiet, buried her face in Ross's chest, and took out something to dab at her tears. It was the Versace. Recognizing the precious silk from Michael's jacket, Sue's eyes grew large and then squinted into furious 'pins'. I was trying to find something interesting to watch out of the window, while I literally sat on my hands to stop the impulse I had to hit someone. I could not look at Mother for fear that I would burst out laughing as people sometimes do in a tense situation. It had certainly changed the mood.

Mother's wrist and cheek were bruised and swollen by the time we got back to the Sir Stamford. She must have whacked Kell harder than I thought, but he had connected with her also. As she left the car, holding her wrist – which had a tooth indentation – she said, with great aplomb, 'I hope I don't get rabies.' But we had further concerns about the incident: the tabloids. After all, Rodney Claxton's assistant Marcella who was riding up front with the driver had overheard everything. With the price of a good story these days, all this could be all over the newspapers by tomorrow morning, we thought. The three of us, Ross, Mother and I, took her aside and begged her not to discuss this with anyone. She gave her word and as far as I know she has kept it.

There had been no sign of Colin Diamond at the funeral. I would not have known this, as the cathedral was so crowded, but heard later that he did not attend. We called Martha who was at the wake by now. She said that her husband Bill was to have a conference call with Colin later that evening and she assured us she would make certain that Colin called Mother. She told her, 'It's important that he talk to you.' We wondered what could have been so pressing that it kept him away from his friend's funeral; it didn't make sense that he would fly in from overseas for two days and not attend the ceremony he had come for. In his later *AXS* interview he is quoted as saying that he had gone to Queensland to get a second opinion on Tiger's condition. Although he made the trip without Tiger! Mother and Ross did not attend the wake but I went for a short time. I did notice that Rhett was particularly cold towards me. Mandy later told me that it was just down to whatever substance he was on. I did not see Kell and Sue as they were in a very noisy area that I was avoiding. I guessed that Mother had not done that much damage, as it certainly did not keep Kell away from the wake. Paula, Belinda and Andrew Young were not there. I spent my time with people who had been close to the band in the early days, old friends with comforting, familiar stories. Little Stevey Murphy, Michael's godchild, was now a beautiful teenager. Hiraani and her husband sat close by and talked softly about what a beautiful man Michael was. Molly Meldrum came up to me and complimented me on my choice of words for the service. I was pleased to see my children were enjoying themselves with their Australian relatives: they needed to let off some steam after the week they had been through. The following day Erin told me that when they were standing downstairs afterwards, waiting for the cars, Kell, his sister, and Sue came down and completely ignored them, driving off in the only remaining limousines. How mean to take his anger out on the grandchildren.

We were all featured in the newspapers the following day, amidst photographs of Paula's cleavage. Excerpts from the service played over and over on newscasts. I would walk past a television and suddenly hear my own voice, the painful start of reliving that day over and over. We read that Paula was returning to London with Michael's ashes. In panic I called Paula at the Quay West. We just wanted to know if she had already left Sydney. Paula's voice came down the phone in a very matter-of-fact voice, 'Hello Tina'. I found myself placing the phone on the cradle, realizing that I had nothing pleasant to say to her. So we knew she had not left, but what about the ashes? Surely that part of the story must be another mistake? Rodney Claxton assured Mother that Paula was not leaving with Michael's ashes; he could not release them to anyone due to a document signed by Colin Diamond as executor.

I am at a loss for words to explain our confusion upon hearing this. This was my mother's son. My brother. What could Colin Diamond possibly have to do with his ashes? We understood that he was a financial adviser, but just how far did his powers extend? We would soon find out. Apparently he had signed the statutory declaration required under New South Wales Public Health Regulations before the remains of a dead person can be cremated. But why, and did Kell know about this? After all, it was he who had broken the news of Michael's wish for cremation, he who had been in constant touch with Colin Diamond. Could this connect with the strange sense of distance we felt? Kell did not return our calls that day.

CHAPTER FOURTEEN

The Ashes

It seemed impossible that I had left my comfortable, busy, orderly life in Los Angeles less than one week ago, where the only issues coming up might have been finding suitable gifts for each family member, and who was going to feed the cat while I was out of town. Hard to believe that just six days ago, each of us, Mother, Kell, Rhett and I, were contentedly going about our lives and looking forward to spending Christmas together in Australia. What had transpired in those six days had made them feel like an eternity. Our contentment had been shattered, and the pain and loss would be with us for ever. So much was out of our control, even worse, some outside forces were dividing us just when we needed each other the most. Michael, the one person who had always brought us together, was no longer here to play that passive, reconciliatory role. I wondered how we would pull ourselves out of the depths.

We were all leaving the following day and wanted to do something appropriate with Michael's ashes and bring some peaceful resolution. Our last discussion about it had been three days before when Kell suggested that we scatter them out in Sydney Harbour. Rhett and Mandy were flying back to Byron Bay, Mother and Ross were returning to the Gold Coast, my children and I joining them there before departing for California on 4 December. When would we all be together again? I could not believe that Colin Diamond had the power to put a hold on the ashes and thus prevent us from symbolically putting Michael to rest.

Early on Friday morning, with Mother and Ross standing by, I called Colin's brother Stephen at the Sheraton. He kept repeating that since I was a beneficiary he could not speak to me. I'm afraid I screamed into the phone that I was not speaking as a beneficiary, I did not know the rules as I had not been a beneficiary of any will before this, and did not particularly care to discuss that aspect. I just wanted to know about the ashes. It was obvious that someone else was in the room as I could hear a man's voice in the background commenting on the conversation. After one of my questions, Stephen began to answer and this other man yelled, 'You don't have to tell her that!' My mother was on the other line and heard it all. My frustration mounting, I asked him to explain why his brother had put a stop to releasing my brother's remains, and what right he had to make such a personal decision. He said that his brother was executor of the will, trustee and guardian of Tiger. When I repeated the question, he still gave me no specific answer. And nor would Stephen tell me where Colin was. He refused to help us in any way.

That night I was so exhausted: it felt as if all of my emotions had been drained and laid on the sidewalk for strangers to trample. I was to leave with Mother and Ross the following morning. I fell asleep fully dressed, but was roused by a knock at my door just before midnight. To my relief it was Rhett. 'Anything you want to tell me, Tina?' he hissed. An alarm went off in my weary head. I motioned him in and asked him to explain himself. He just kept asking the same thing over and over. 'I'm asking, anything you want to tell me?' He sat across from me, his rage barely controlled. Then he began pounding my head with cushions and yelling. I told him that he should tell me what was bothering him, but he only continued, shouting louder and louder. What was he talking about? Was it the incident in the limousine? Rhett was reeling out of control and it was obvious that he was either on something or coming down from something. I was aware that Rhett was hurting and angered at the world. I shared his grief but it was useless to take it out on each other at this time we so desperately needed to be united as a family. I attempted to soothe him, but his rage was too far gone.

I can't remember everything that passed that night in my room. Many things were said in anger. At one stage, when he jumped up from the couch and bore down on me to say something particularly hurtful, I attempted to slap his face. He grabbed my arm and it turned into a full scale tussle. We ended up in the hallway and by the time he marched out slamming the door, I looked down to see my clothes ripped, and my room littered with flowers. Flowers? The same flowers which had been left outside the Ritz Carlton, out of respect and love for Michael. How ironic. How tragic.

I was seriously shaken and nursing an ache in my side. Bewildered and emotionally shattered, I was not sure what he had been told or by whom, but I had a pretty good idea it had to do with the incident in the limousine, and it was a different scene to the one I had witnessed. I couldn't imagine how, but from the line Rhett was taking, it seemed to me that he believed I was party to some wrongdoing against Kell. Even though it was past midnight, I called Kell at home. When he answered he said, 'Never call me again as long as you live.' I put the receiver down and looked back at the horrible mess in my room. Fearing I would not be able to clear it all myself, I called Mother. While I waited for her, I tried to put some understanding to the ill feelings that were surrounding us. Why were Kell and Rhett so angry with Mother and me? What had been said? Mother arrived and we went about soaking up the water and setting the flowers back into their buckets. Apart from anything else I feared that housekeeping would report that my room showed signs of a confrontation and leak the news to the tabloids as 'Hutchence Sister Trashes Hotel Room'.

Lying in a bath the following morning I could practically see the changing colours of the bruises on my stomach where Rhett's foot had connected. I felt that I had lost two brothers in the same week. I felt angry with Rhett at the time; later on, I felt sorry for him. It was a terrible time for us all. We have reconciled since, and I will always love Rhett very much. He was in a rage over losing his brother with whom he had not had a chance to truly reconcile. Though Rhett and I have reconciled he has never been able to discuss this incident with me. I do forgive him and I will always love him. I also know it was the drugs that pushed him over the edge. Rhett's true nature is a loving one.

We left for the Gold Coast two days after the funeral. I was feeling numb at this time, so drained of emotion and so confused as to what went wrong. I felt that everything had been taken away from me, my son, my involvement in his funeral arrangements, his body, and later, his ashes and most of all, our dignity. I found it hard to live with this, and resolved that from now on I was going to fight for justice and the truth.

From the minute we arrived at Mother's the phone was never quiet. We finally switched it over to the answering machine. If we did happen to pick up, the answer to all journalists was a definite 'No comment'. They were depositing letters in the mailbox, offering us a lot of money for an exclusive interview and an 'inside scoop'. As angry as we were and as much as we had to get off our chests, we were not interested. Mother would not touch the phone unless she was dialling out. One of those she did call was Rodney Claxton. She requested a copy of the statutory declaration signed by Colin Diamond and relating to Michael's ashes. He promised to fax it through as soon as he could obtain a copy from the crematorium. Four days after the funeral he faxed through a copy of the document. We read it over and over. It had been filled out in Colin's handwriting – Mother recognized it from other papers at her house. We were alarmed to read the following questions and answers:

Q. Have all near relatives of the deceased been informed of the proposed cremation?
A. YES. [At this stage Mother, Rhett and I had not]
Q. Has any near relative of the deceased expressed any objections to the cremation?
A. NO. [Mother, Rhett and I had never been consulted]
Q. Did the deceased leave any written directions as to mode of disposal of the remains of the deceased?
A. YES.
Q. If so, what direction?
A. CREMATION.

Michael's address had been given as 13-17 La Spezia Court, Isle of Capri, QLD 4217. Mother was bothered by the signature on the very bottom of the page, under that of the Justice of the Peace or notary. She said it looked familiar and realized it was Stephen Diamond's. She and Ross had used Stephen two years before when they had sold their former home and their own solicitor had been unavailable. Stephen had also drawn up new wills for them. They had had no reason not to trust him, but they hadn't happened to use him since. Mother called Rodney Claxton again and asked him what he had seen in writing to ascertain that Michael had wanted to be cremated.

He answered that he was told by Colin Diamond that the request was in the will. We later received a document that had been sent to him which stated that he was to collect Michael's ashes and make sure that they were released to no-one but Colin.

We were outraged. How was it possible for someone other than Michael's next of kin to take 'possession' of his body? I began calling the Diamonds' office on the Gold Coast as we were very suspicious and we wanted to see that will. A woman representing them informed me that Colin was in Hong Kong and his brother Stephen was on his way back to the Gold Coast. She said that Stephen had told her to give me the phone contact of the co-executor whose office was in Hong Kong, Michael's accountant, Andrew Paul. She informed me that this was where the original will was kept and that everything would be handled through Mr Paul's office. Stephen would be the Australian liaison. Having no confidence in Stephen, I began juggling time zones and tried Mr Paul's office for two days before he rang back. The conversation only alarmed me more, as he told me that he did not have a copy of Michael's latest will and assumed it was at Stephen Diamond's office. Also, he was amazed to hear that he was the co-executor, and even more surprised to hear that Colin Diamond was in Hong Kong. He suggested that Colin could be in New Zealand, but insisted that he did not have a phone contact for him.

We were more concerned than ever before. A trusted friend advised us to consult an estate lawyer. At the time we did not understand why we needed such advice. Frankly, the only thing that concerned us was the issue of his ashes. We simply wanted them released so that we could end this ordeal. But we were becoming increasingly suspicious that the request for cremation was not in Michael's will. It had not been in the first one. We were angry with ourselves for taking Kell's word for it.

Spite and jealousy are evil emotions to harbour especially when they last a lifetime. Strangely enough, Kell and I had been able to maintain a reasonable relationship over the past few years. He and Sue had driven up to the Gold Coast to spend Christmas at my house with the rest of the family; we had met up in the South of France and attended many functions together with Michael in Sydney. Our relationship had been a series of harmonious phone calls and meetings in the last ten years. How else could we have shared family vacations and celebrations? But this very workable relationship seemed now to have disintegrated.

Perhaps it was odd that I needed to get this sorted out but somehow, even in my numbed state, my feeling was of forces that had somehow gathered me, and which were working away behind my back. Despite having no reason to believe there would be problems with Michael's estate, I decided to take the advice of my friend and ring the lawyer. During the initial talk we spoke of the ashes and how agonizing it was, not to be allowed to lay him to rest. I still hoped we might be able to ceremonially scatter Michael's ashes on Sydney Harbour when Tina returned in three weeks' time for Christmas, even though all the children would not be present. There was no other discussion of what the will contained as at this stage none of us had seen it. Next day we received a faxed will from Andrew Paul's Hong Kong office, and within the hour, another from the Diamonds' Gold Coast office. This was allegedly the will Michael had made while hiding out on the Gold Coast in 1996, leaving half a million US dollars to Greenpeace and Amnesty International and 50 per cent of the remainder to Tiger Lily, the rest to be divided between Kell, Rhett, Tina, Paula and myself. The most important thing to us was that justice was done and the right provision made for Tiger. As we searched the two pages for the request for cremation our fears were confirmed. It was not there, positively no mention of it.

When we realized that the will did not contain directions for cremation, we wondered about what it did provide for. Our anxiety mounted. Tiger's future financial security was at stake – we wanted reassurance that the executors would take care of her and preserve her inheritance.

In the ensuing months Tina and I were savaged in the press and also by people we had believed to be friends, all because we had retained a lawyer. It never occurred to us that people would view this as an attempt to get money out of the estate. Our concern was, and always has been, that justice was done. Michael had been a public figure but surely his family had a responsibility to ensure that his wishes were respected.

Certainly the people who worked for Michael when he was alive, the lawyers, financial advisers, and managers, had their duties as far as his business affairs were concerned, but as far as his remains went, we felt that they were treating him like a piece of property. We felt a decision had been made that robbed us of lovingly laying Michael to rest in dignified peace.

Kell denied knowing anything. He stuck by his original story that it was Colin Diamond who assured him that the request was in Michael's will. I knew that Kell had told some tall tales in the past about his travels and such but for some reason I was unwilling to believe he would deceive us on something so serious as this. It was a shock to read some eighteen months later in Vince Lovegrove's account of Michael's life that Kell said he decided to split the ashes three ways, after a call from Diamond who reported that Paula and Mother were arguing over them. Mind you, when Diamond and Kell would have had this discussion, Paula had only been in Sydney for twenty-four hours, and Diamond even less. When did all these harassing phone calls take place? Mother has her bill from the Sir Stamford for her room as well as mine, and there is only one call to the Quay West and this was the call I made from my mother's room the day after Michael's funeral. I asked Kell about this recently and he told me that he did have such a conversation with Diamond. It was only much later that he wondered if he had been misinformed. He said that Diamond was running the show for those couple of days he was in Sydney and yes, he indeed gave the directions for three urns at Diamond's suggestion. One for Paula, one for Mother and one for himself.

We had all been stunned by Kell's announcement that day about Michael wanting to be cremated. I was certain that Kell knew perfectly well that Mother had no contact with Paula that week: we didn't even known her hotel pseudonym until the day after the funeral. Why was Kell so ready to believe Paula and Diamond without even asking Mother? It would not occur to any of us that a girlfriend would even want to take Michael's ashes back to a city he had at first loved then later came to loathe. But further, why did Kell not assume that his ex-wife, the mother of his child, the child they had *both* just lost, might have had something to say about her son's resting place? It was a decision Mother and Kell should have made together. I don't believe that Colin Diamond should have had a say in it, and nor should Paula.

I called Rodney Claxton and I asked him how come Colin Diamond had the right to decide what would happen to Michael's ashes, and he told me that it was a very unusual situation. He had also never heard of a girlfriend requesting the ashes. He said when a person is not married, and does not have a child who can make these decisions, the ashes would automatically go to the parents, in most cases the mother. When I asked him if he had any proof that the request was in the will he said Colin Diamond assured him it was. And he said he believed him because Kell had also said that was true. Why wouldn't he believe the father? Besides, the document was signed by Stephen Diamond as a Justice of the Peace.

A letter from Stephen Diamond arrived at Joanne Kelly's office on 3 December for Mother and me, after she had requested a meeting between all interested parties. It informed us that his brother Colin had disbursed over $60,000 of his own money to cover the funeral costs. He suggested that Mother (being the only relative with the means to do so) could reimburse him. We later found out that the bill hadn't been paid, and in fact was not settled until some time in 1999.

This letter certainly seemed to me to be in extremely poor taste. My mother was still in shock over losing her son just eleven days before. It was an outrageous letter to send. When asked for an accounting of the bills, she was not offered any. The account for the funeral parlour, normally the responsibility of the estate and which the executors normally pay, had still not been taken care of eighteen months after Michael's death. The letter further assured us that Colin had every right to sign the statutory declaration – in order 'to put a stop to Paula Yates returning to the United Kingdom with the ashes'.

This did not even address the fact that Michael had not asked to be cremated or that the decision was up to both parents, not some financial adviser who had not even attended his client's funeral. We were also informed that Colin was far too busy to speak with us, due to the complexity and size of Michael's estate. This last remark regarding the estate would change several times over the next six months, depending on what the executors were being asked. We would be intermittently told that Michael had nothing left or hear more about the 'enormity of the estate'. At that time the executors were too busy to meet us and barely had the time to correspond with us.

Soon after arriving back home on the Gold Coast I called Linda at the villa. They had seen the report of Michael's death on the television and had then been contacted by Paul Craig, Michael's former manager, to say that someone would be in touch to take care of things at the villa. Over the years we had viewed Linda and Nestor as more than employees and I knew that they would be upset by Michael's death. Linda sobbed and told me that Norman Leighton, whose offices in Nice and Monaco were where Michael's company Leagueworks was lodged, had driven up with a colleague and had taken an inventory at the main house. There was a search for papers and certain possessions removed, others locked or stored away, others disposed of.

At the time all I thought about was, doesn't his family have a say in any of this? Surely there were personal letters and notebooks containing his writings – far more precious to us than documents pertaining to his business affairs.

Linda also told me that she had already received a fax from Kell, which in essence said that she was to send a crate of Rhett's belongings on to Sydney and then she was to await future instructions from either himself or Colin Diamond only. She assured me that she had safely stored articles belonging to Ross and me in her home.

Given that we felt we had grounds for concern, I asked Linda to come up with a hiding place for what we assumed was important paperwork, preferably off the grounds of the villa. Linda suggested the home of Father Guerrero, the priest who had blessed Tina's marriage. That night Nestor drove with Linda into Nice where she deposited the papers in Father Guerrero's safe. Linda mailed the originals of these papers to me some months later. Along with some other documents Michael had left at my house, these became the most important papers we had when trying to unravel Michael's affairs.

Amidst many reservations as to what was now going on I left for Los Angeles. I was due to return in less than three weeks for what would surely be the saddest of Christmases. Jonnie had left a message inviting me to a celebration of Michael's life. His friend Nick Conroy from his very early days with the band was hosting a luncheon at the Café d'Artiste, a little restaurant in Hollywood. Some of those present were Pamela des Barres, Nick Egan, Stewart Copeland, and old friends from Australia like Lian Lunson, Sherine Abeyratne and Karen Ansel. Even the Los Angeles businessman who had brokered the deal for Michael's Aston Martin came to show his respects and remember Michael.

While talking with some of Michael's closest friends that day I learned that he had spoken to many people beside myself of his discontent on the home front. It was clear that he had been extremely worried about his finances and yet I could not imagine why. Then things lightened a little: I was sitting with Nick and Jonnie when Blair arrived with her roommate who had also been to INXS's last Los Angeles concert at the Greek Theatre in July 1997. I went over to her and without a word we hugged. We talked for a while and then I brought her over to meet Jonnie, who introduced us to a photographer whom she used to date, but who was now dating Kylie Minogue. What a complicated world we live in.

Shortly before Christmas, Blair wrote a beautiful letter to my mother which included the following:

> *I don't know what words I could say to let you know how sorry, sad, and devastated I was for you, the family, the band, Tiger, and selfishly – for myself. This feeling inside me continues to grow and I am at a point now that I wish I could enable myself to just plain forget everything – but that is far from possible and won't make it go away. I spent time with Tina before I left LA, as I'm sure she told you. It felt good to be close to her – I suppose it's the extension of souls coming together. I miss Michael. Forgive me for sounding selfish – but I do. They say human beings are made up of energy and that energy never dies. However, a big part of my heart has died. I only wish I could have sent him some love before God called him home.*
>
> *We go through life not understanding why we are here, how we got here, what we're supposed to do and why we leave. Michael had a very full life. He filled so many with joy through his talent – yet another extension of his soul, giving to others. I remember at the show in St Louis, three disabled people were in the front seats next to me, Michael spent so much of his show on that side (of the stage) that they figured I knew him. They asked if there was a way they could get to meet him – I made no promises – however, when we met backstage I asked him and without hesitation, he told me to grab them. The smiles on their faces showed me the proof that even the smallest act of caring can make a difference to a person's smile. Michael's heart was full of gold and the only thing he knew was to give it away.*
>
> *I am sorry I never took the time to say goodbye to you, I am sorry that Michael and I were not honest and I'm sorry for being a 'secret'. I am not that type of person – but he needed to be cared*

about and he wanted someone to listen to him, so I did. When I felt things were . . . growing – I tried to walk away – but he wouldn't let me. Your son was nothing less than amazing and I hope you accept my prayers, my sorrow, and all my love.

On 8 December I faxed Andrew Paul in Hong Kong noting that, despite leaving many messages, I had been so far unable to reach Colin or Stephen Diamond. I requested use of the villa for February, March and April of 1998. I felt that this notice would give them plenty of time to reopen the house, I reminded him that I had been married at the house the previous year and it was special to my whole family. I faxed this through twice and finally received a reply three days later. I did not consider it satisfactory. He suggested that he found it hard to believe that I could not reach the Diamonds. He further told me that as a beneficiary I could not contact him directly, I needed to go through legal counsel. I later received a professional opinion to the contrary. Executors' duties include those of taking care of the estate and serving the beneficiaries. He went on to say that although he understood my sentimental attachment to the villa it would have to be sold, due to the cost of upkeep. I shot a fax back saying that the family would like first right of refusal.

I had sent a similar fax to Colin Diamond. My later reply from his brother Stephen was most distressing. It stated that Michael had never in his lifetime owned a villa in the South of France. On the same day that I received the fax refusing my stay at the villa, Linda sent Mother a copy of a fax which she had received from Norman Leighton on 5 December 1997 which had informed her that Paula and Belinda and their children would be using the villa over Christmas and asked her to stock the pantry for their arrival. He said that the trustees for the villa had OK'd it. Also he asked Linda if she could list which items in the villa belonged to Paula.

Over the following three months we would be told that Michael's London home was not his, nor did he own a Peugeot, an Aston Martin, a Mercedes Jeep, a Cherokee Jeep, a Bentley, a Ducatti motorcycle or various other vehicles I knew to be his. The home on the Isle of Capri – even though Colin Diamond had given this as his domicile at the time of his death – the bowling alley and the block of land in downtown Southport were also evidently figments of our imagination. We were informed that not even Michael's ongoing income from publishing and performing rights to his music, not even his solo album which Martha Troup and Paul Craig had told me he had personally bankrolled, belonged to him. I kept going back to that day over lunch when he assured us that no matter what transpired, neither he nor Andrew would ever sign away their publishing income. But above all in this situation, how could there be any sort of provision for Michael's daughter?

While dining in LA with Jonnie and Michael's friend Nick Seymour, formerly of Crowded House, Nick told me that he had recently run into Nick Cave who complained that it had cost him a huge amount of money for his attorney to ensure that he was not on the Hutchence funeral footage. I couldn't imagine why, since we thought we had taken care of this with one phone call. I do not know who he made the cheque out to, but as far as we know it was an unnecessary expense. At home after dinner there was an urgent message from Mother asking me to call about a fax she was sending. When I read it I felt physically ill, it was so humiliating. The *News of the World*, in London, had reprinted a photograph of Mother and Michael, taken in December 1993 when Helena and her parents were visiting the Gold Coast. The headline read 'Hutch Told Mum of Bondage Ordeal'. It was a detailed and completely fabricated story which claimed an unnamed 'friend of the family' had revealed that Michael had told Mother of a bondage session that he had endured several months before his death. Mother remembered Michael saying 'Look Mum, you just don't know what they will do, they sometimes alter the picture to create a story, or make up a story to go with the picture.' This story was repeated in other magazines.

Mother was so traumatized by this despicable story that she had a major health setback. To add insult to injury, Kell accused her of selling the story. Ironically, it was Kell who had retained an entertainment lawyer to handle and oversee lucrative offers for interviews with him! Mother called me again, sounding frailer and sadder than ever before. Stephen Diamond had responded to our lawyer about Michael's ashes. My mother had requested to know when they would be released and she was now informed that she could 'collect her third' as soon as she wanted. Her third! What happened to her son? But on contacting the funeral parlour, our lawyer was told that no authority to release the ashes had yet been received.

Ken and I had separated. It had become clear that I had entered the marriage without taking enough time to really get to know him, and now that there was so much stress and sadness I found that I was looking for comfort and reassurance that I felt he wasn't able to offer. The sadness of the break-up was compounded by the memory of the blessing of our marriage in Michael's French garden only the summer before. However, we had booked our flights for the Gold Coast for Christmas so we decided to go together. You know how people say that when things are so miserable in these situations you may as well be together? Don't you believe it. The trip together was a mistake. We thought we could at least remain amicable but he began to get on my nerves. For instance, during our stopover in Sydney I visited the restroom. When I returned he had struck up a conversation with an Australian couple about my family. As I approached them I noticed looks of commiseration from his two new friends. I was furious and told him so. From then on every time I looked up, these people were staring at me. Let's just say that there were other incidents which I don't care to report here, and Ken flew back to LA much sooner than planned.

On Christmas Eve our attorney received a fax from Stephen Diamond. It advised us that the executors (at this stage his brother Colin and Andrew Paul) had not decided when and where they would probate the will. He noted our correspondence concerning an address to send Christmas gifts for Tiger but suggested that we contact Paula directly. Since we had asked him for an address for this very reason, it was obvious that we could not do that.

The communiqué also informed Mother that the funeral directors now had the proper authority and she could collect her urn containing Michael's ashes. I thought this a callous fax considering the timing. Merry Christmas to you too!

His final point was that 'to the best of [the executor's] knowledge and belief' Michael had not purchased nor owned at the time of his death a villa in the South of France, but if we should have any information to the contrary, we were invited to let him know.

As if facing our first Christmas without Michael wasn't difficult enough. It was as if he had never existed, either. Once again our lawyer contacted Rodney Claxton who told her that he had still not received any instruction from Colin Diamond. Mother was on the verge of collapse. Over in Bali Kell, Sue, Rhett and Mandy were celebrating Christmas. Kell and Rhett had been handsomely paid for various interviews. Rhett called on Christmas Day, and after talking to Mother he asked to speak with me. I finally took the phone; he spoke, I listened. I couldn't bring myself to speak to him or to return his seasonal wishes. Without a word, I handed the phone back to Mother.

Upon my return to Los Angeles, I took a chance and called London to speak with Michael's former personal manager, Paul Craig. I asked him if I could post late Christmas gifts for Tiger and the Geldof girls via him. He did not have an address but said that he would probably be able to get it to them through friends. I was truly frustrated at the thought that business associates of Michael's, the very people who in the past had tracked down phone numbers all over the globe, people who had so much access to both him and Paula before 22 November, suddenly did not know where to find Paula and Tiger Lily. What did they think I was going to do, show up on her doorstep?

Paul congratulated my family on the decision we had made to have the funeral televised. He said he had spoken to many people who had not been able to get to Sydney to show their respects and that they had felt closer watching it in their homes and added that although it was late he hoped that we would accept his condolences. I told him that I was surprised that he had not come to Sydney for the service. He replied that he was two hours away from departing London when he received a call from someone in Sydney who advised him not to go. He vacillated and since this person had been insistent that it was the band's idea, he cancelled his flight. I do not know who it was that made the call and Paul would not divulge the identity. At a moment like that I could see why Michael despised the Chinese whispers and peripheral garbage of the music business.

Due to the international dateline, 21 January in the United States would have been Michael's thirty-eighth birthday in Australia. Colin Diamond had finally sent a letter allowing release of his ashes two days before this and two months after his funeral. Mother flew to Sydney to collect them. I knew she would be very sad. I was due to catch a flight home from Washington where I had been lecturing. As hospitable as everyone had been it was a very difficult time emotionally. I found it increasingly hard to be around people. I called my office in Los Angeles and asked them to arrange for Mother to receive an arrangement of lisianthus from her favourite florist. I called her the moment I arrived home. She thanked me for the flowers and told me that Michele and Ross had also sent beautiful blue flowers. I wasn't at all surprised that Michele had thought of Mother on Michael's birthday. I chose that day to give my 'Michael' button to a friend, a jewellery designer, to be made up into a ring.

Next day I began to see a doctor about my obvious depression. Over the phone she asked me some questions before we began to decide just how urgent it was, and how much therapy I might require. She asked me if there had been anything out of the ordinary happening lately. I said my brother had committed suicide. She said that this would be a major reason for stress and depression. Then she asked some simple questions about my lifestyle. The last question was 'Single, married . . .?' I replied that it had almost slipped my mind that I was going through a divorce. There was a silence and then, in a very controlled voice she said, 'How fast can you be here?' My job was becoming more demanding and I wasn't sure how long I could go on. After speaking with the psychiatrist I decided to go on 'leave of absence'. I really thought that I just needed a rest away from people and I resisted medication for the first three weeks. I relented when my analyst finally convinced me that it was the only way I was going to get through these tear-filled days. She prescribed an anti-depressant. It made me nauseous so I only persisted with it for two months. It did help, but I could not stop wondering how Michael could have been on these drugs for two years. They do alter your perception of the world.

Early in February, while Mother and Ross were visiting Los Angeles, I received a call from a member of the Australian press, saying that Kell had just sold another interview, a five-page one at that, which was due to hit the news-stands any day. He had been in the papers every week since Michael's death and had sold innumerable interviews to magazines. I asked her to read it out to me. It was mostly a rehash of anything else that had been written along with some of Kell's own thoughts. Now he was quoted as saying that he and Mother had divorced when Michael was twelve years old and that he had obtained custody of the boys. The piece does have him stating that Michael had denied that he would be marrying Paula; however, he is also quoted going on about Michael's devotion to her. This and various other statements made in the interview would only perpetuate more untruths. For instance the article has him completely dismissing the fact that Michael was battling depression when he died and chooses instead to report that he died from a combination of 'drugs and booze' – his quoted words, not mine. Perhaps Kell was trying to say that it's somehow more manly to die that way than through depression . . . Anyway, the coroner's report had not even surfaced yet.

The journalist reading this to me was the one who had broken the news of Michael's death to Mother. She asked me if I wished to make a statement. I had to think about this, as so far both Mother and I had remained quiet. But this latest was ridiculous and I agreed to say something in redress. I sat around the dinner table with Mother and Ross and a friend who wrote as I dictated a statement which read:

> *Truthfully, it saddens me to hear these fabricated stories regarding my brother's personal life. Especially coming from family members. It is painful and embarrassing. In this last assault, I will agree on one thing, and that is Michael had no intention of marrying Ms Yates. The only woman I have ever heard him say he would wed is Michele Bennett. It was not common knowledge; however, people in Michael's inner circle knew that he had been trying to get out of his relationship with Paula Yates, with whom he was very unhappy. – Tina Hutchence.*

Honestly, this is all I had intended, a statement which I assumed would be placed out there like a press release. Within four hours it had become a full-blown story, photographs and all. I was faxed some questions which seemed reasonable at the time and I answered them. I was sent some other questions which I declined to answer. I thought that the statement might show up on page twenty of an Australian magazine. Not being privy to the ways of the press, I had no idea the commotion this little story would raise. What's more an abbreviation of the coroner's report was released the following day and my phone began to ring ceaselessly so I took it off the hook. I was informed that Australia's Channel Seven had a crew on standby in Los Angeles should I choose to make a statement. I chose not.

Mother, Ross and I dined with Erin and Joshua and his parents, Nancy and Michael. We came home feeling relaxed for the first time in weeks. It had been a laughter-filled evening. Both Nancy and Michael are professors of psychology and they had some really amusing stories. They even encouraged Mother and me to join in with some funny stories from our days together on set. I delighted in watching her laugh and not only did she join in the conversation, at times she was the centre of attention delivering riveting tales of our years in Hong Kong. As I watched her she became younger as some of the pain she wore on her face was erased for a few hours. I thought back to some of the happy times our family had shared around a dinner table when it was a fight to get a word in as each of us would be so animated.

When we returned home a little before midnight, I found a fax from Kell. It had been less than a day since I had done the fax interview, four days before it was due to reach the news-stands. But Kell had obviously been tipped off with a very sketchy outline of what I had said. I say 'sketchy' because he was obviously guessing at what I had really said and had jumped to conclusions. In this – his reply to my statement – he reprimanded me for exposing who he termed 'that poor little girl in Los Angeles', referring, I assumed, to Blair. From what I understood he had no knowledge of her, but concluded that others had told him of Blair's existence. I had certainly not mentioned anyone in Los Angeles. Although he had said some terrible things to both Mother and me in the past, this was the most hurtful. These were two pages of vile, unprintable accusations. He said that I was the destructive element of the Hutchence family and a disgrace to the name. I could not understand where this was coming from, as I had not even mentioned him in the interview. I had just wanted to make it clear that Michael had loved his child but had been nowhere near to marriage to Paula. I suppose Kell felt he was being blindsided and wanted to lash out on the defensive in case I had said anything hostile about him, but I felt he was attacking the wrong person. I realized that he was in a bitter state, one from which he would probably never recover. Still, it is hard to read something like this from the person you have called 'Dad' for thirty-nine years.

Sleep was fitful that night. I was jarred awake by a call at 2.40 a.m. from a cheery-voiced Belinda Brewin. She spoke to me as if we had actually met. She said we had a problem. I thought she meant something was wrong with Tiger. No. The problem was that we needed to do some 'damage control' because Paula was very upset about reports in the press that I had said Michael was marrying someone else. Here we go again I thought, my words taken out of context. I told her that

I had not said that and that that was all I could say to her in the middle of the night. She said, 'Oh God, I'm sorry, I will call you back in the morning.' Although I was very drowsy I wondered why Paula wasn't calling herself.

Belinda did not call in the morning. I dropped into my office and left my answering machine on. When I arrived home there was a message from a very agitated Paula. So here we were at last, ten weeks after Michael's death. Paula had still never once spoken to my Mother to relay news of her grandchild. We had called everybody we could think of to obtain a contact number for her but to no avail. It took a pending magazine story to propel Paula into finally calling me. She said that it would be on my head after tonight if I did not do exactly as she wished. Her exact words were, 'Tina, I have fifty journos outside of my house [at that point it was obvious that she held the phone up to an open window as I could hear voices calling her name in the background]. You have not attempted to get a hold of me and Tiger, I suggest you ring Belinda. It's literally a circus out here because of what you said out there. We have to do damage control. It's your responsibility from tonight on.' Click. Again, she neglected to leave a phone number. I was glad we had a paper trail of the many times we had attempted in vain to locate them. The faxes stretched from attorneys and accountants to Martha and even Paula's own attorney.

I had no intention of killing the story. I thought somebody needed to stand up for Michael's integrity. Our lawyer faxed over a cover story from the Sydney *Sun Herald* dated Saturday, 14 February 1998. It was written by a journalist whom we had been advised to ignore, and was all about the rift in the family. In actuality, the rift was something the press had invented for there had been no public display, each of us grieving on our own terms and turf. However, the press was getting a lot out of Kell, who at that point was willing to speak to anyone with press credentials. Because of his bitterness, rage and grief, he was spilling out anything that had ever made him angry over the thirty-nine years he had known Mother. However, Mother and I had not had much contact with Rhett or Kell and certainly not with Paula.

Rhett had been quoted with a paraphrase of my words – that is he told the journalist to publish a statement from him which mirrored my statement in the magazine article one week before! 'It saddens and embarrasses me, etc.' It stated that the men in the family had sided with Paula for the sake of the child. To a large extent it discredited Mother and me. I felt that this article and the previous one had been deliberately planted to discredit Mother and myself. We resolved that we were in for the long haul, and we were fighting for Michael.

The other beneficiaries, Kell, Rhett, and Paula, had as far as we knew been as quiet as mice about the will. But if there were to be no assets, Paula especially had much to lose; after all, she had Tiger Lily's future to think of. The actions we were contemplating undertaking would help all the beneficiaries, but without the help of others who presumably also had evidence of Michael's holdings, it would be a long battle. We were not heartened to learn from Kell and Rhett that they were in contact with the executors.

I was walking past my fax machine when a newspaper article began rolling in. In an interview with Colin Diamond's ex-wife Robyn, headed 'Will Protects Tiger Lily', the Sydney *Sun Herald* published what we considered at the time to be the most defamatory piece so far, although the courts later disagreed with us. It portrayed Mother and me as money-hungry relatives who had caused Michael to set up special trusts to protect his daughter from us. In fact it had quotation marks around clutching and greedy. It said Mr Diamond's ex-wife, Robyn, told the *Sun Herald*: 'Michael set the whole thing up to protect Tiger so that she would inherit it one day. She's a little baby and he made Colin sole executor because Colin knows the family story.' Mrs Diamond is quoted as saying that the problems over Michael Hutchence's will stemmed from members of his family wanting more than they were given. It went on to say that past problems between Colin and Paula had been resolved. 'They had a bit of a kerfuffle shortly after the death but now they are fine.' The Melbourne newspaper, the *Age*, ran the same article under the headline: 'Star Feared Greedy Relatives', with a curious byline.

The article stated that Michael had a baffling, worldwide network of trusts and holding companies in which to bury a fortune estimated at $40 million. Mr Diamond, it said, had legal control over them, and of assets previously thought to have been the rock star's property, including music publishing rights, a flood of royalties from record sales, a global property empire and a fleet of luxury cars. Mrs Diamond is quoted stating that Michael had put everything into trusts and placed them in the care of her ex-husband because he wanted to protect his money from relatives. The most damaging and outrageous misinformation in the piece referred to Mother and me in the last paragraph, which said, 'The star's mother, Patricia Glassop, and sister Tina appear to have been shut out of any major inheritance.' It says that Kell is thought to be the beneficiary of at least one trust fund, however.

Coming from the woman who lived next door to Michael's financial adviser, his ex-wife with whom he has two children, this was more damaging than any 'close source'. How could she be associated with an attack on two people who had so tragically and publicly lost a son and brother? There was so much misrepresentation in this article. The fact is that we had never questioned the will. Why would we? It expressed Michael's wishes, and he had been very generous and fair. This article gave the impression that we were trying to take food out of Tiger Lily's mouth, when the fact was we just wanted Michael's wishes adhered to and to ensure there was indeed something for her – which there wouldn't be if there was nothing of any value considered to be in the estate. In his will, Michael had not made reference to separating his assets, he just asked for all of his assets to be divided between Tiger Lily, Greenpeace, Amnesty International, Mother, Kell, Rhett, Paula and myself. It was very convenient for those who thought otherwise to accuse us of trying to steal from Tiger, claiming to be protecting her interests themselves. We were concerned to ensure that there would be something left for her when she came of age.

It was simple. Michael had set up trusts to house all of his properties, cars, bank accounts, and even his ongoing income. This way his tax burden was lowered. When a person with this arrangement passes on, there should be an executor in place to disburse the assets accordingly, in the interests of the estate. We knew at least enough of Michael's financial dealings to have an idea where the assets might lie, and therefore felt it appropriate to ask some difficult, delving questions. We wondered if this had sparked the press interest.

All we were guilty of was loving Michael, being devastated by his death and of wanting to be sure that he was not made a victim one more time. But the angry responses we were meeting with made me begin to question his love for me. But although our time together over the years had been sporadic, due to our separate continents, he had always been so loving and supportive. I could not let fear of the consequences impede my resolve, and affect what I knew to be true in my heart.

The article implied that Michael did not love us. Mother said that if we were to question Michael's love now we would go out of our minds. I agreed but it did not help my physical and mental pain. We were becoming increasingly isolated. Those few close friends who knew how to reach us said that we displayed dignity in our silence and commended us for not speaking to the press. They did not know how difficult it was to keep quiet at times when so much misinformation was being flung around. We felt we had been portrayed as the grasping mother and sister from hell that Michael had not cared to be around. Before this we had thought we were doing the right thing for Michael but now we just wanted to hide. But going to ground did not mean giving up.

CHAPTER FIFTEEN

The Christening

Four months after Michael's death, I had a surprise call from Paula. She had arrived in Sydney with Colin Diamond, Belinda Brewin and Andrew Young. She began by announcing how furious she was with Tina for telling the world that Michael was not intending to marry her. Suddenly she became soft and sweet as she said that she wanted to stop all of this and that she wanted Tiger to know her Grandmother, that Michael would want it. I could certainly agree with that. We discussed the prospect of getting together, she gave me her departure date and phone and fax number and told me to call. But then things disintegrated when she returned to what Tina had said in the press. We exchanged further words, then the conversation neared its end. Suddenly she said, 'Oh please, Patricia, let's not talk about anything else when Michael's ended up hanging on a doorknob.' Then she hung up. I was stunned and appalled.

But I did desperately want to see Tiger and attempted to fax Paula on her suite's private line to set up a time for me to go to Sydney. I had the wrong fax number, so I called the Quay West where she was staying and got put through to her. She said that she would find the correct number. Then Martha came on the line. We talked a little, mainly about Tiger, and she said that she had been in town for about five days on INXS business. Paula never did come back to the phone. I obtained a fax number from reception and sent a message that I would like to come down the following weekend. I then called Mandy, as I had read Paula was denying to the press that a christening would be taking place. I asked Mandy if she was going to a christening for Tiger Lily, and she said she would be there and mentioned it was Monday or Tuesday but she wasn't sure as it was being kept quiet, adding that Belinda would be calling everybody. I thanked her very much, mentioned that I had not been invited and hung up.

The next evening Belinda called to ask if I could come down sooner as they were leaving that weekend, enquiring if I was attending the christening. I said that I had not been invited. She indicated that Paula was supposed to have sorted this but must have forgotten. I agreed that she was quite agitated when we spoke. Belinda said that it would be a small affair, only about forty people. They were sending cars and she offered to send one to the airport. I accepted her invitation with apparent joy. Actually, I couldn't imagine how I would manage to keep my composure given all that had happened. But I couldn't bear to miss my granddaughter's christening.

Ross refused to go. He is a very tolerant man but could not forgive Paula for apparently not inviting us herself. But he was nonetheless unhappy about me going alone.

There was an extremely unflattering article about Colin Diamond in the Sydney *Morning Herald* the following day. Before I could finish reading it I had a call from Paula, who seemed to be of the belief that Tina and I had given information and how dare we! The piece was an exposé of Michael's business affairs and nothing to do with us. There was nothing derogatory in the story about her or Michael. She reiterated that Michael would never leave her. I had taken enough, I repeated that he had left her and he had done it a long time ago in Los Angeles where he had been seeing someone else. Paula was not fazed.

Ten minutes later Belinda called me to check where I would be staying for the christening. I replied that I was intending to make my own way to the church. I said I would check back with her in the morning to confirm the location. Afterwards, I was called by a trusted journalist friend who informed me that Paula had sold the christening story to a UK publication. The journalist said an Australian magazine was offering $20,000 for a photograph inside the church. They were prepared to pay for my accommodation and flight expenses, provide a picture-ready camera, and give me a cellphone to contact the person I was to pass the film on to, if I could get one picture to scoop Paula. I did not care for the money nor did I have the courage to carry this off.

Rhett had been invited to the christening, and we had been keeping up a relationship with him if only through Zoe. I mentioned the offer and to my surprise he decided to go for it. He had already been angered by being told that there were to be no photographs taken, even by family, at what was meant to be a special occasion for Michael. I told him to think about this before making any decision and if he did decide to go through with it, he must be extremely careful.

The day before the christening Paula called me again and we had a regrettable exchange. My point was that with great pain we had accepted that Michael had committed suicide in order to move on.

She made several more calls so I left my answering machine to pick them up. Things had got into a terrible state, and I was worried.

Paula made several similar calls throughout the day to me in California as well. Agitated that she could not reach me, Paula made a call to my office manager, who took a message with words to the following effect: 'I have a famous human rights attorney in my room along with five attorneys, and they have decided that she and her mother are in an issue of human rights against Tiger Lily. She had best call me immediately if she ever wants to see Tiger again.' My niece was crying in the background. Formally, we requested that we not be harassed, suggesting we discussed setting up a time for some visitation with Tiger Lily if that's what was being proposed.

Even after this Mother received another call from Paula. She sounded extremely upset and Mother was very concerned. She phoned the police and begged them to please look into it and to keep it confidential – they promised to take all precautions, but a story did appear in the press. Two days later the police were notified that the problem was that Michael's mother was calling Paula and harassing her over the will. A story ran confirming this.

The night before the christening Paula called Michele Bennett and asked her over for a meeting at the Quays. She told her that Michael would want her to see his daughter. It all began very friendly, with Paula finally asking Michele about the events of 22 November. Paula wanted to know if Michael had said that he loved her. Michele assured her that there had been nothing romantic between herself and Michael in the past ten years and told Paula what she thought she wanted to hear: that as far as she was aware Michael had loved only Paula. The visit only lasted about half an hour, and the next day in church Paula walked past Michele without so much as a nod of the head.

One week later Paula told a journalist that Michele had been loving and supportive as they had spent the whole day together before the christening and that it had been so comforting to see her in the church.

Rhett decided to take the magazine's offer of $20,000 for one shot inside the church. Mother had made it clear that as long as he was bound to do it, we were desperate to get a picture of Colin Diamond while he was about it. We didn't have one, and we wanted to be able to identify him for future reference. The news organization sent the camera and extra film to his hotel room, for him to take on to the ceremony. It was a tense day as I waited for word. Rhett had been calling Mother and lately always asked about me saying, 'Give Tina my love.' I think it was hard for him to pick the phone up and call me himself. I could never stop loving Rhett and as Michael's lyrics go, 'there is nothing said that cannot be undone', I knew it was just a matter of time before we would speak again.

When we finally heard from him, he was scared. He had gone through with it and handed over the film, signed the contract and even talked them into allowing him to keep the equipment. He said that security had removed some film from his camera, but this was after he had given the crucial film to his contact at the magazine. He was worried about the fact that he did not notice other people with cameras in the church, so he could easily have been identified. He did not want the photographs to be on the front page and requested that one picture, a group shot, not be used – as he was obviously not in it, having been the lone photographer.

He was so scared he broke down. I was very surprised to hear this as Rhett has been known to take some huge chances with his health, his freedom, and even his life. This was not a gangster movie, but it felt like one to him. Sometimes I have to remind myself that although my younger brother is a tall man, with tremendous physical presence, he is inherently fragile and not too practical. It says something about him and his character that for whatever reason, Rhett has barely worked in the conventional sense and hasn't had to learn how to deal with life's realities as most people have.

He did not tell us immediately about the remarks Colin Diamond had made about our mother. Later he said that he had a meeting with Kell and Diamond at DB's Coffee Shop on Knox Street during the week of the christening. During this meeting Diamond expressed his anger toward any legal action that Mother might bring against the two executors. According to Rhett, Diamond's comment was, 'I would like to slit her effing throat and she's not getting a cent.' Rhett said that he found his remarks threatening not only to Mother but to himself as well, which is saying something for Rhett. Kell later verified this.

Mother assured Rhett that there were other cameras in the church. She called the editor of the magazine to explain Rhett's position. The editor advised her that she understood his alarm, there was a photographer lying in St Vincent's hospital with reported bruises, cuts and injured back muscles due to an incident at the same occasion. This photographer claimed he had been shoved backwards, smashing his head on rocky ground. The editor called Rhett and advised him to have a large gin and tonic. Mother told him to switch hotels. He was also feeling pangs of guilt over making money from Tiger's christening, but Mother reminded him that others were making much more, and others still had made plenty of money off Michael's back over the years. He would have been a lot happier knowing that Rhett received the cash as opposed to a photojournalist stranger.

Rhett told Mother that during lunch at Mezzaluna Restaurant he placed his camera on the table in front of him and Colin Diamond himself walked by and snatched it up, pulling out the film. But he had already dropped off the precious film. Fortunately, he did get some clear photographs, which were printed in the following edition of the magazine.

Rumours did fly about Rhett taking money away from Paula and Tiger. This was so unfair – I had seen photographs of Paula leaving designer shops holding packages and on vacations and thus assumed she was keeping her head above water. Besides, if Diamond was complying with Michael's wishes there was no need for panic over Tiger's immediate future. Anyway, she was reported to have sold the nineteen posed photographs they used after the christening to *OK!* magazine for a tidy sum. Reportedly, the family was supposed to receive some of these official photographs. None of us ever has.

Mother heard from our friend Hiraani who had been at the christening. She said that the ceremony took all of ten minutes without a word from a family member or even an INXS member. Michael's name had not even been mentioned. She reported sadly that when the guests moved to the Mezzaluna for the luncheon they were told to wait before sitting down as Paula was downstairs having photographs taken with Tiger for the magazine. Two hours later Paula appeared in a different outfit, with a tired and cranky Tiger. Just as they were about to eat she said she was tired and left them to finish their lunch. 'It had overtones of a rent-a-crowd,' she said. The evening newspapers in Sydney reported that not only was the christening ceremony over in record time but that the baptism certificate had been left on a pew in the church. They published a photograph of the certificate in the paper. Among the godparents listed were Belinda Brewin, Martha Troup, Josephine Fairley, Andrew Young and Colin Diamond. Knowing my brother as I did, I am certain he would have chosen at least one close friend or family member to be godparent to his child.

Another nasty story appeared in a Sydney newspaper and was repeated in London. The 'feuding Hutchence women' were again taking food out of Tiger Lily's mouth. I was so very tired of it all.

On 31 December 1998, Erin's twenty-one-year-old friend Linda from the defunct Bedlam Spiral was found dead, apparently from an overdose. She had been travelling by road from the West Coast to New York to seek fame in the music industry. Ten days later her mother flew back to Los Angeles with her body and she, along with Linda's brother, arranged a funeral. About two hundred people attended, mostly under twenty-five. It was an emotional service. Afterwards I walked over to a small group of Linda's friends including my daughter, and without exception they all told me that the service was all wrong. They were all upset that they had not been consulted on the music and eulogies; they were angry. I surmised that their anger was misdirected and they were confusing it with the pain of losing a good friend. What was Linda's grieving mother and brother to do, cut off in their pain from those friends closest to their daughter and sister? Did any of the kids approach her mother? I asked. Erin knew exactly what I was referring to. It was a lesson in life and death.

By late April 1998, the newspapers were reporting that Paula had made an attempt at suicide. We were concerned for Tiger's welfare but had no idea who her nanny was since Paula had let Anita go in the wake of the 'drugs bust' incident in 1996, and the nanny who had gone to London with Michael at that time had returned to Australia.

Through friends I found out that at that point it was a joint effort between Belinda and a succession of temporary or part-time nannies. I sent a fax to Bob Geldof's attorney, requesting that he call me in relation to Tiger's whereabouts and well-being if he could.

Attn Sir Bob Geldof

Re: Heavenly Hiraani Tiger Lily Hutchence

Recent events surrounding my niece's mother have led me to contact you in an effort to gain some insight into the well-being of Tiger. Surely as a caring parent – and I can tell you are – you can understand my angst. Naturally I am concerned; should I be? Contrary to the understanding Ms Brewin has of the action being taken against my brother's executors, this action was brought about especially for Tiger Lily and her mother. We have never, ever disputed the terms of Michael's will. I may be contacted on the above numbers at my home in California.

Sincerely,

Tina Hutchence

Two days later Geldof's attorney called to enquire on the exact nature of my request. I explained as best as I could. Next day when I picked up my phone I heard, 'Tina? Bob here.' It was a very satisfying, if bittersweet, ninety-minute call. I wished that I had felt confident and comfortable enough to have made that call twelve months before. He gave me his private number and encouraged me to call any time. Sometimes he would be walking down a busy street, or in a meeting, at a restaurant or on the way to the airport but he always took my call. It meant so much to Mother and me to have this link with Tiger's world.

On 16 April 1998 I received an eight-page fax containing copies of letters sent to the attorneys acting for Colin Diamond, Andrew Paul and the trust companies in Hong Kong and Queensland, Australia, representing Michael's holdings in Britain, France, and Australia. A press release read:

HUTCHENCE RELATIVES LAUNCH ACTION AGAINST EXECUTORS OF ESTATE

Patricia Glassop and Tina Hutchence, the mother and sister of the late Michael Hutchence, have commenced proceedings in the Supreme Court of Queensland in relation to his Estate.

In the proceedings, in which the Executors, Colin Diamond and Andrew Paul, have been joined as Defendants, Mrs Glassop and

Ms Hutchence seek orders for the administration of the Estate including the furnishing of accounts by the Executors.

They also seek declarations that certain assets held by the other corporate Defendants were in fact beneficially owned by Michael Hutchence at the time he died and that these assets form part of his Estate available for distribution to all Beneficiaries in accordance with the terms of his will.

The Defendant companies are registered in Queensland, the United Kingdom, France and the British Virgin Islands and the assets include properties on the Gold Coast, London, France and various bank accounts and other assets held by companies in the British Virgin Islands and Hong Kong.

Notice of the Writ has been personally served on the Executor, Andrew Paul, in Hong Kong on Thursday evening. The other Defendants are in the process of being served. Letters have been forwarded to solicitors acting for Colin Diamond in both Hong Kong and on the Gold Coast requesting that they accept service on behalf of Mr Diamond or that they advise of his whereabouts in order that he can be personally served with the Writ.

Well, this was what we had been waiting for. I sat next to my fax machine and read the pages over and over. We still had a long road ahead of us but it was a start. There were copies of letters to the other beneficiaries Greenpeace and Amnesty International inviting them to join us as Plaintiffs. Amnesty International did join us. The best part of the fax contained copies of letters addressed to both Rhett and Kell, inviting them also to join us in the proceedings. A unique approach at setting about mending a family divided. Michael would have savoured that.

CHAPTER SIXTEEN

A Visit to London and Nice

By July 1998 reports from London about Paula's health were shocking. She had apparently checked into a private clinic for grief counselling. I could not sleep after seeing some sad photographs of Tiger Lily with what I thought looked like a black eye. It was very hard to know how things were from such a distance, and with no information, formal or informal. I had also read a disturbing article in the London *Sunday Times* written by Tim Rayment chronicling the events leading up to and beyond the alleged drug bust at Paula's house. The one thing that jumped out of the pages was a statement from Andrew Young, who had been described as Paula's 'Sydney-based barrister', about Tiger's health. Ross decided that I must go to London to see if there was a way to see Tiger. We do feel Tiger has a right to know us and we would like her to grow up knowing we tried, we cared and that her family loves her.

I hated leaving Ross behind and was full of apprehension on the flight but it was good to know that Tina would be meeting me there in a day or so. We would give each other strength. When she arrived, we phoned Paula's lawyer, hoping to organize a visit with Tiger. Belinda Brewin phoned me saying that she was looking after Tiger and that Paula would allow me a visit, but not Tina. We arranged a time for her to bring Tiger to my hotel the next day. I did not know what to expect, as we had not met Belinda Brewin personally, although we'd spoken when she was in Australia for the christening.

We'd arranged a private meeting room with the manager. We had no idea what to expect. I was apprehensive but hoped it wouldn't show. All I wanted was for my granddaughter to feel normal as she'd had enough traumas in her young life already. We went back to the suite to await their arrival. About a half-hour later a message was pushed under the door: 'Belinda won't be able to come today, but probably tomorrow.' A day or two later, Belinda called to say she would be at the hotel at 10.30 a.m. Tina was not to be present. She arrived at 12.15 and when I walked into the private room she immediately asked where Tina was. I answered, 'Up in her room.' Belinda paused and said I could send for Tina. I called Tina who had been very despondent over Paula's edict. I wish I could write about my visit with my granddaughter, but it was a private time.

Belinda said Paula was at home and she was doing fine. She said that she was planning a holiday for a month in Spain with her children and she would hire a new nanny and housekeeper for Paula and Tiger in her absence. I could see that Tiger was tiring so I decided to end the visit but said I would like another one soon. She agreed, suggesting a meeting in a park close to her house the following day. Belinda and Tiger drove away in Michael's Jeep Cherokee. Via Belinda and Paula's lawyer, we later made another plan to see Tiger the following day.

The following day Belinda made an appointment for 12.30, changed it to 2.30, and then showed up at 3.30 p.m. Tina had been out shopping for Tiger Lily's birthday – she was turning two in five days. Again, Belinda announced ahead of time that Tina was not to see her niece, but I decided to ignore this. When she arrived at the hotel I asked her to bring Tiger to my room and Tina was simply there. Tiger had been to a hairdresser for a shampoo and trim, Belinda told us. Tiger Lily was happy and friendly, but didn't seem to know us, which could have been upsetting, but we knew we had simply not had a chance to develop a rapport as we had not been allowed to have a continuous relationship with her.

Belinda's mobile phone rang constantly and she would take the calls outside the room. When she began asking questions about our litigation, I explained that we really could not discuss it. We also talked about Michael's solo album. But the visit was to come to an abrupt end. Belinda left without taking Tiger's gifts and although we left a message with Paula's attorney for them to be picked up at the reception desk they never were. Rather optimistically perhaps we tried to set up another meeting but this was to prove impossible. We even went around to Paula's townhouse. After many unanswered phone calls and faxes Belinda abruptly left London for Australia with Tiger Lily without informing us, the day before her second birthday. Paula's attorney sent a message to our hotel, which said, 'I have instructions from my client that I am not at liberty to give you any information on Tiger Lily.'

Belinda has visited Australia a number of times since, and even visited Mandy when staying in Byron Bay with her boyfriend Andrew Young. As you might suppose, seeing her pictured in magazines walking along with Tiger or posing for the newspaper with her causes me great pain when I am not allowed any contact with my granddaughter whatsoever. On each of these visits she has made to Australia with Tiger Lily, even if she has been paraded in front of the press, I have not been able to arrange to see her.

With little to do but look at Michael's home, which we wanted to see in case it ever came on the market, we took our cameras and walked to 24 Smith Terrace. I recalled the day Michael had brought me there. I described to Tina where he had been standing and how he had told us about the style of the house when he had first purchased it. We took some photographs, and I noticed a metal plaque on the gate. It was the Australian flag, stuck on. I tried to peel it off as a keepsake but it would not budge. Two days after visiting Smith Terrace we found ourselves in Chelsea again and decided to walk by the house one more time. When we did, to our surprise, the little Australian plaque had been removed.

Later that week we had a very long lunch with Bob. I found him to be very caring and warm: he must be a fantastic father. He walked us back to our hotel and hugged us both and parted with encouraging words.

We decided to visit Michael's villa in the South of France before returning to our respective homes. I rang Linda and Nestor to prepare them for our arrival. During the conversation she told me that Bono had been to the property and had scattered white rose petals on the lawn after saying a prayer for Michael with Father Guerrero. In his friend's memory, he then planted a tree on the grounds of the villa. We were so touched by this beautiful and loving gesture, from one friend to another. Bono told Linda that he missed Michael terribly.

Half an hour after this conversation Linda called back and advised that it would be best if we did not go to the villa, as there were still helicopters circling overhead and the press might follow us from the airport. I thought this over-dramatic and could not imagine that the press could still be so aggressive eight months after Michael's death, especially in rural France. I said we intended travelling to Nice no matter what. Nestor took the phone from Linda and I asked him why we were not allowed to go to the villa, as this was the message he was conveying. We all knew that besides a visit from Bono, Helena Christensen had also been to the house to collect clothing and spend time in the garden. Who knows who else had been there. This was Michael's home that he had, in his own words, 'purchased for the family'. We still had personal belongings there. However, it was certainly made clear that we weren't very welcome.

All this made me so depressed. I needed to go to the house, needed to touch, to smell, to feel Michael's aura. Not in a morbid way but as any mother who has lost a child so suddenly could understand. I needed to be in his surroundings, as did Tina. I was beginning to feel betrayed even by these two people who had been so close to our family in the past. We did not know who to trust. Linda phoned later and suggested that if we still wanted to visit her she and Father Guerrero would meet us and take us to stay at his home in Nice. Her plan was that we could stay there during the day and be driven to the villa undetected at night.

The idea of this almost shabby secrecy was unacceptable. The following day we flew into Nice, where our plan was to rent a car and drive directly to the villa. In our haste we had neglected to obtain the necessary visas and were detained at the airport. We were beside ourselves, sitting in a room seemingly full of immigration agents who were interrogating us. Finally they pronounced that we would be escorted to the next available flight back to London. I was in tears of frustration, the language barrier making it even more difficult to make them understand our position. Tina opened her passport and pointed to the Hutchence name in the hope that one of the younger men would understand what she was saying. She kept pointing to me and saying 'the mother'. Finally one of them became interested and began to speak in broken English to us. Finally he said, 'Ah, this is the mother of the chanteur Michael of INXS.' That way we negotiated a twenty-four-hour reprieve, with stiff penalties if we missed checking in by 5 p.m. the following day.

By the time we made our way to the rental counters all available vehicles had been taken for the Bastille Day holiday weekend and there was no answer when we rang the villa. We booked ourselves into a hotel in Nice and got some sleep. At 7 a.m. I telephoned Linda. Nestor said that she was not there but he would have her return my call. An hour later I called again and this time he said that the executors had told him not to allow us on to the grounds. As I was admonishing him for this Linda took the phone. Through her tears she said that it was much too dangerous for us to come to the villa. All of this cloak and dagger stuff was getting us down, but knowing we only had a few more hours in the country, we decided to try anyway.

What had happened to the devoted employees of Michael, the couple who previously would do anything to ensure his comfort and that of his family? These were the two most grateful people on earth when Michael guaranteed their working visas in France and extended money for their children to attend better schools in their native Philippines. Linda worriedly agreed to meet us in our lobby and drive us to the villa. Alas, when she arrived in Michael's Peugeot with Nestor they had changed their minds and would only agree to take us to the airport. As we stood outside by the car he unloaded a small box which contained family photographs, the vase I had bought at the gallery in Valbonne and left at the villa and some of my son's clothing. Two shirts, a pair of trousers, and two jackets. One of these was a favourite, a worn, three-quarter-length, ripped leather one. Tina and I touched and smelled the garments, hoping to get closer to Michael, but there remained no trace of him on the fabrics at all. When Tina took a photograph of the car which clearly showed the number plate we knew connected it to Michael, Nestor attempted to stop her. He was very edgy, as if he was worried that someone would see us together.

On the way to the airport I noticed Michael's asthma inhaler, his tapes and a half packet of cigarettes in the doorside pocket, just as it had been when he was still with us. At the airport Nestor and Linda showed us a new contract they had been issued with, dated eight days after Michael's suicide. They referred to this as a 'secret contract'. Linda again cried and said she prayed every day for Michael's soul. I was angry with them as I thought they were being disloyal to Michael. He had adored them and had given them every assistance he could, including financially, and had helped them obtain the necessary papers so they could stay and work in that country.

In calmer, or as Michael might have said, karma, moments later, as our legal efforts progressed, I was often to bless Nestor and Linda for storing for us, and then sending on documents which have proved to be vital. I realize that they did so at some risk so I feel no more bitterness now.

Three months later, visiting Mother and Ross, we noticed that Michael's block of land in downtown Southport was up for sale. I stopped the car and walked into the realtor's, making up a story as I went. Posing as Meg Wells, assistant to a wealthy Canadian, I enquired about the property and heard that the sellers wanted a quick sale, and yes, cash would be preferable. Our lawyer made an application to the Supreme Court and had the sale stopped. And my little ruse was reported in the Australian newspapers in a more positive way than we might have anticipated earlier. Much too soon to say that the tabloid tide was actually turning, but Australian rags, like their British counterparts, do love to support an underdog and can be shamelessly fickle about changing sides. Maybe this time they liked the idea of giving fair dues to the battling and beleaguered women in Michael's family and it now suited them to take that position, if not exactly championing ours.

Of course I was speaking with Mandy, but it wasn't until I returned to Australia one month before the first anniversary of Michael's death that I spoke with Rhett. I met him in Byron Bay where I played with little Zoe before taking off by ourselves. We sat down in a local pub for lunch and he asked about Erin and Brent and as is Rhett's style, before I could finish answering him, he leaned into the table and said, 'Why Tina? Why? Do you know why?' I just said, 'Our brother was a very unhappy man, Rhett.'

Over the next ten months we stepped up our quest for Michael. The second defendant and executor, Andrew Paul, filed application for probate in Hong Kong. However, he could not proceed to obtain the grant in Hong Kong as our lawyer had lodged a caveat in the Probate Registry. In August 1998 Andrew Paul brought an application in the Supreme Court of Queensland. It was agreed that we would withdraw the caveat in Hong Kong and enable him to proceed to obtain a grant of probate there, provided that he filed an unconditional appearance in the proceedings in Queensland which at that date he had not, and that he would obtain a reseal of the grant of probate in Queensland, which he did in January 1999. On 20 May 1998 Colin Diamond had purported to renounce his executorship.

With the help of Martha and Bill Leibowitz, Colin Diamond set up a deal with V2 records for Michael's unreleased solo album. They had not invited the family to listen to any of this music, had not informed us of their plans. Our response to this went over and beyond matters strictly legal; they may have been within their legal rights to proceed in that way, but we felt that our moral rights had been savaged. Whether they should have been an issue or not, considerations of courtesy and good manners obviously left the frame some time ago.

Our intention was not to hold up the release of Michael's solo album. We knew it had been important to him, but we wanted to be sure of what would happen to the royalties.

CHAPTER SEVENTEEN

Putting the Pieces Back Together

Just before the first anniversary of Michael's death, Mother, Erin, Brent and I received an apology from Kell. He had given some very unflattering interviews about us to various publications and collaborated with Vince Lovegrove in a book which included some scathing statements about Mother. Now he explained in a letter that he wanted us to come together for a dedication ceremony for a memorial for Michael.

We were torn as we had already invited Kell and Rhett to a private ceremony at the Sydney church where Michael had been baptized. We had gone to great lengths to keep it a secret, arranging with the pastor of the church to have a simple remembrance and dedication ceremony after which we were to plant a beautiful native Australian tree in Michael's memory. It would be a place we could always go to sit in tranquillity and think of Michael. There would be no plaque to mark the spot, we really needed it to be private, to keep something special for the family and only the closest of friends. The problem was that Kell had already told the press about his memorial site and announced it on the internet. We were not ready to do anything so private in public. He also announced that he had invited Paula, which would mean that it would be impossible to keep the media away. He later mentioned that Paula did not reply to this invitation.

As both services were planned for the same day, even the same time, Rhett called to persuade us to cancel our plans and come to Kell's chosen memorial site at the Northern Suburbs Crematorium. He and Kell had already scattered the ashes from the second urn over Sydney Harbour but the first urn was still in California. Mother and I had so far not done anything symbolic for Michael and we needed to do something that felt right to us both. Mother, Ross and I eventually went through with our ceremony surrounded only by the elders of the church, and Kell and Rhett had theirs – with the media. Later, some of the guests, notably Michele and Hiraani, who had been to Kell's service, came by the Sheraton for a small, private afternoon gathering which Mother and Ross had organized. Hiraani came up to me and told me that she had visited the 'Michael tree' on her way to the hotel. Michele arrived with flowers and encouragement. Referring to the front page of the morning newspaper, where a journalist had exposed my 'Meg Wells' undercover effort, she said, 'Well, with your picture on the front page, your career as a detective is over.' Nonetheless I think I have learned enough about estate litigation over the last twenty-six months to pass the Bar exam.

Michael had kept a residence in Hong Kong until 1995, when he began to spend more time in London. The monthly rental on the place where he then stored his personal possessions was ridiculous. Why hadn't the family been asked if we'd like to have something personal of his? Andrew Young had been authorized by Colin Diamond to collect everything which had been taken from his hotel room by the police, and Paula had kept everything from the London home. We assumed that the contents of the villa were still there, but where was the need to continue paying storage fees in Hong Kong when the family had been offering to go through the effects? We had asked that his storage container in Hong Kong be shipped to Sydney, but the request was denied. After much arguing back and forth, it was agreed that Tina and I could go to the lock-up in Hong Kong to sort out those personal belongings. Permission was given by Andrew Paul who promised our solicitor that we would be given all the help we needed. This was something that had to be done. It was already eighteen months since Michael's death.

Ross made my flight and hotel reservations and on 24 May I left for six days in Hong Kong. I was not looking forward to this task but it had to be done. Tina would be meeting me there, neither of us knowing what to expect, but we would be a comfort to each other as we always have been in any crisis. This was to be a sad and sentimental trip for both of us, but one we would have reconsidered if we could have predicted the nightmare it became.

I had last been in Hong Kong in 1993, when Ross and I stayed at the house Michael shared with Jon Farriss. Music industry awards hung on all four walls of the living room and the shelves were sinking with the weight of others. I had been used to flying in and out of Kai Tak and now we were landing at the huge new airport, connecting to trains and buses going to any area on the mainland and Victoria Island. Moving walkways, shops and restaurants galore evidenced the growing prosperity of Hong Kong. It resembled Disneyland. Driving to the hotel I was astounded at the changes. The new bridge is like a longer version of the Golden Gate Bridge in San Francisco. It was around 9 p.m. and every shop was still open. As my car neared Kowloon it seemed more daytime than night, people were everywhere. It was not the Hong Kong I knew of the past, but the memories were still there . . . bittersweet memories.

As they came flooding back I could hardly swallow for the lump in my throat. I thought back to the earlier years when I first had come here. These now seemed mostly good, as can be the honeyed and distorted way of memory, thank heavens. Michael was just a little boy then. I thought about how he loved his music, how his life had turned out, how he followed his dream. But he would never get to see his beautiful daughter growing up and Tiger Lily would never know her daddy. At least with his work he had left his mark in this world and there will always be a permanent reminder, a legacy for her to cling to. He had been ready to 'start all over again' as he had said to Michele in that last week, when he decided that he 'couldn't take any more', his words to me in June 1997 in his call from Vienna and again to me three days before his death. This was a journey I would have preferred not to be taking, an unnatural one, and one I had never envisaged. Parents expect to leave their children behind, it's not supposed to be the other way around. The driver interrupted my reverie to tell me we had arrived at the hotel. We had decided to stay on the Kowloon side to be closer to the storage company at Shatin, in the New Territories.

I went to my room, unpacked, showered and waited for Tina to arrive. She was coming from Los Angeles via Tokyo, and I expected her at the hotel around 11 p.m. It had been Brent's birthday two days before and also his graduation, so she had driven six hours to visit him in Monterey. He was one of only three students graduating in Global Studies so she was a very proud mother and her weekend had been a full one. She left Monterey and drove another six hours back to Los Angeles to catch her flight to Hong Kong. It was delayed two hours and then again in Tokyo another two hours. I had fallen asleep and woke up with a start when the phone rang with a call from her driver who said that her flight had still not arrived. An exhausted Tina finally reached the hotel around 4 a.m. We talked for a while and then tried to get some sleep as our appointment with Andrew Paul was at 9.30 a.m. Four hours later we prepared ourselves for the ordeal although we were both jet-lagged, Tina more so than I. It was also humid, and the job ahead of us was going to be stressful.

We were going to an area where English is rarely spoken. The first two taxi drivers did not know the address, but a third finally agreed to take us and we arrived on time. Andrew Paul was flanked by two associates and handed me Michael's passport as promised. I signed for it gratefully, the only reminder of my son I had received so far. We then walked around the corner to the storage area. I felt numb, not knowing how I would cope with the job ahead. Tina and I had barely spoken on the way there, both of us so full of sadness, but comforted by just being there for each other. Andrew Paul asked the attendants working there to open the enormous crate belonging to Michael. It looked roughly the size of a one-car garage. They started pulling out cartons and cases and opened them one at a time, methodically going through each one before allowing us to see what was inside.

Andrew Paul told his two minders and the packers to watch that we did not take anything without his permission. Thus we had to ask him if we wanted a book, a T-shirt or even letters we had written to Michael over the years. There were some family photographs, including one of a tiny Erin. On the back was her little girl handwriting: 'To Michele and Uncle Michael love from Erin xxx'. Tina had to get clearance to take it. We waited while Andrew Paul consulted his right-hand man, a big, seemingly unfriendly individual who spoke to Andrew Paul in Cantonese most of the time.

I was allowed to pack a box of clothes for Rhett, but as the storage area was not air-conditioned it was difficult to find anything worth saving. Almost everything in the boxes appeared to have been laundered and pressed but was mouldy due to the humidity, or battery operated equipment had been thrown in with the clothing and the acid had leaked. It appeared we were taking far too long just looking at this clothing, and I overheard Andrew Paul say to his assistant, 'Let them have this shit.' He then tossed a case at us and told us to take the clothes back to the hotel to sort.

So it went on for a couple of hours in the incredible heat. We were feeling so tired, so humiliated and so sad and angry for Michael to be treated this way. We had an inventory of the items in the crate and I was anxious to see if the paintings and Michael's music awards were there.

They unpacked and photographed some awards, porcelain and bronze artefacts and artwork including a painting by Michael. They said that all of this had to be valued for sale. I objected strongly as I felt that Michael had earned his awards and I am sure that he would not want them to be sold to strangers. He would have wanted his family and his daughter to have them. Of the scores that he had received, only about twenty-four were there and I wondered where the others were. We asked if we could divide these few awards six ways, with eight of them for Tiger and her mother but Andrew Paul would not allow this. He said we could not have 'anything of value'. But about four weeks after our visit to Hong Kong he decided that the awards were worthless after all! To him they may have been worthless, but not to Michael's family.

Just before they broke for lunch I noticed a large envelope addressed to Michael from his previous financial adviser, Gordon Fisher. Andrew Paul immediately began going through its contents. Tina walked over and watched him put the papers aside but we weren't allowed to look at them, but she glimpsed enough to see that these were private papers of Michael's and believed we should be privy to them. As we were in an industrial area and had no idea where to eat, Mr Paul kindly called us a cab, giving orders to the driver to take us to a small hotel about two miles away. We had no idea where we were going.

Arriving back at the storage building, after about an hour, Tina asked to see the papers but Andrew Paul refused. When she complained, the large man got heavy. We eventually managed to obtain some copies.

At about 3.30 p.m. Andrew Paul decided he did not want to open any more cartons. He allowed us to take some old clothes and books, packed in the two battered suitcases. When we walked through the ornate lobby at the Sheraton people stared at us; we must have looked like refugees from a war zone. We were physically and emotionally drained when we got up to our suite and too tired to eat. We just ordered hot chocolate and sat on our beds leafing our way through Michael's books, finding a few cards and letters we had sent him over the years and a lot of fan mail. There was one letter which I had to keep as it was so sweet. It was from a girl in Japan who had sent him a teabag and invited him to sit down and drink tea with her. She gave directions on making this tea, included a drawing of him drinking and the words 'Let's drink together, yum, isn't that delicious?' Much of the fan mail had not been opened. It was a really sad time for us, but at least we had some private time to look at a few remaining pieces of his life. If only we had been given that time earlier that day.

Arrangements had been made to meet back at the storage building at 9.30 a.m. the next morning. We arrived on time but Paul and his men did not bother to get there until 11 a.m. We were not to touch anything until they showed up and when they did so it was another fraught day, and a short day at that. Paul arrived, checking his watch and telling us that he did not have a lot of time. Our nerves were shattered, it was hard enough anyway to 'feel' Michael in this atmosphere and this approach was heartbreaking.

When Paul called a halt there were about twenty cartons in the crate as yet unpacked. According to the packing papers there was an almost endless list of items which we had not seen as yet, including a set of Christofle silver, which Paul claimed was definitely not in the crate. I enquired about Michael's guitars and other musical equipment. He said there were none, conversely adding that it probably belonged to Jon Farriss now as the list had been made up by the insurance company and they had combined both storage units to save money. He said that Jon had taken his things back to Australia recently. Then Paul told the crew to nail up the crate and said he was leaving and that was the end of the inspection. We were astounded and asked about the following day; he said that was impossible as he was leaving on a business trip to London in five days and had no time. We suggested that he leave his deputy in charge but he would have none of that. He had promised us his full cooperation but had treated us with disdain. He checked the few things we had to take back to the hotel, walked us outside to a cab, took my hand and said, 'I'm doing my best'. I believe it: this was as good as it got with him.

Paul did not come to the scheduled meeting the following month in Sydney, but sent his lawyer who brought the awards and paintings. They decided that the awards could now be shared among the family. We were to choose which ones we would like to have. Paula had been quoted in magazine articles as having already been given many of Michael's awards from members of INXS. If they did, I did not understand how they had them to give to her or how they even had the authority to do so. INXS have denied that they did so. Still, it was hard to believe that with all the awards Michael had won in different countries over the years, there were only twenty-four left.

Ross and I were ushered into a small meeting room and asked to wait. A woman walked in, handed me three awards and asked me to sign for them. I asked where the rest were as there were supposed to be four each and I was collecting Tina's for her. She said we were only getting three between us now as Kell had been in for a private meeting with Andrew Paul's lawyer and they decided between them that this was the way it should be. The lawyer had returned to Hong Kong that morning and the awards had been dispersed, so there was nothing I could do. I called Kell about it and he said the lawyer had requested the meeting and had insisted on sending the rest to London. I don't know who is looking after Tiger's awards, but I hope they will be there for her when she grows up. Why were we being treated like the enemy? Rhett came to our hotel later and wept as he showed us his award. He had chosen a beautiful *Kick* award which, when Tina and I saw it in Hong Kong, was in perfect condition behind glass. It had photographs and the album cover displayed in a huge frame. By the time it had reached Rhett it had been taken out of its protective frame, the backing removed and folded many times to fit into a suitcase.

Kell did not elaborate on his meeting, but everything in that crate was shipped to him, the estate paying for the shipping and Kell paying for it to be deposited in his garage. He chose what he wanted and sent the rest up to Rhett. Tina and I were given two books, which we had given Michael, two pieces of pottery and a couple more shirts. Later Kell told us that there was a wardrobe of Michael's stage clothes in perfect condition, but said that he intends selling them. As Tina says, 'We must put it out of our minds as we do not need the hurt and anger,' and that is about all we can do.

Perhaps the most callous and almost silencing aspect of the treatment of Michael's things emerged when Kell enquired at Paddington Police Station about the ring Michael always wore. He was informed that it had already been collected but was handed a bag. Astonishingly, it contained the leather belt, which our son had used when he took his life.

When Kell told me about the encounter at Paddington Police Station and the way Michael's belt was presented to him I cried for hours. I cried for Kell, for myself, Tina, Rhett, Tiger Lily and all of his friends who miss him, and I cried for Michael. I was drowning in my tears.

Our family will never be the Waltons or the Brady Bunch but we have mended some major rifts, which makes it possible to communicate at a certain level. Rhett looks healthier than I have ever seen him. He stands strong in his private war against illegal drugs. He has two beautiful little girls now since Sophia Rose was born in February 1999. He has made some visits to Bali and his latest trek to Tibet was for Michael – he's even thinking of taking up Buddhism. He says he has found some inner peace.

Kell's health has not been great but he continues to keep Michael's spirit alive on a website devoted to his son's memory. He can be seen on television and in newspapers and magazines disputing things that Paula puts out on the airwaves. He has been quoted in an interview talking about an unsuccessful bid to gain custody of Tiger Lily, indicating his intention as being to make sure she was taken care of while Paula regained her health. In the midst of his negotiations to take physical custody of Tiger, he contacted Colin Diamond and asked if he would support his endeavour by funding a live-in nanny for her. The answer was no. After this, both Paula and Belinda cut ties with Kell also.

Michele and I recently met in Melbourne, where she was producing her first feature film. She never changes, always soft spoken, gentle, and caring of others. We spent our time together taking turns telling gloriously funny, poignant stories about Michael. I am sure he was looking down and enjoying every minute of it.

It hurts to know that journalists, specifically those attached to glossy magazines who pay for a story, are allowed access to Tiger when requests for visitation from her own flesh and blood are turned down. I've seen many English magazines featuring Paula and Tiger on the cover, with pages of photographs of mother and daughter in Paula's home. One I read, written by a friend of Paula's, Josephine Fairley, depicted Paula as the ever-loving, perfect homemaker. She described how Paula made breakfast for the crew of photographer, assistants and stylists. This was particularly amusing to me as I know that Paula used to pride herself on the fact that she did not go near a kitchen. For the time being Paula and Belinda seem determined not to allow us to see Tiger. But Mother and I do believe that she is entitled to a relationship with her grandparents, uncle, aunt, and cousins. Let's say that finally we remain optimistic about the future and a relationship with the little girl who Michael loved.

Writing this book has been a release at times. It also brings out the anger I feel so often when reminded of certain periods in Michael's life, when many people around him pushed him over the limit. He had his faults, but essentially he was a gentle, caring soul, a wonderful son and a man who brought a lot of joy to many people. He will live in his writing and his music. Our prayers were answered when our litigation reached mediation, and I am glad we did not let go until there was some justice. But I wonder if we will ever have clarity for the reason he had to leave us and his child as he did.

Michael had announced many times that he did not want to be a forty-year-old, starving rock and roll frontman, forced to play small venues to pay the bills. He was proud of his investments and had spoken of how he thought he had set his affairs up in an ironclad manner.

Two and a half long years passed after I started litigation to ensure that all beneficiaries of Michael's will were treated as he intended, especially my granddaughter, Tiger Lily. I asked Tina, Rhett and Kell to join me – even though at that time I had not realized it would be such a long, heartbreaking, sad, stormy and expensive legal journey. Tina responded in a heartbeat, and thank God she did. I know I could not have gone this far without her support or the support of my husband Ross. Rhett and Kell declined at first, and when they changed their minds things had proceeded too far. We also asked Paula to join us, but received no reply other than a telephone call to our lawyers in London to enquire what the letter from our Australian lawyer was about. Regardless of statements made by various people, we never fought with Paula over the litigation.

The legal system in Australia is based on that of the United Kingdom, and it can prove to be very expensive. You don't just have a lawyer; you must also have a barrister who goes to court with you. All their fees can come to seem astronomical to the layperson. In our case we had to have two barristers, as our lawyer was based in one state and our case was being heard in another. This meant that each time we appeared in court we were paying for three legal representatives. And the time in court was only part of it: the barristers with us in court on a particular day would have to be briefed for up to several hours on our case. Considering we had fourteen defendants, the details were more complicated by the day.

The claims we made against the defendants were numerous, their main thrust being that by not including Michael's assets in his estate they were not administering it as he had wished. After his death, key people around Michael also voiced their concerns about this apparently assetless estate, and to those we are grateful. If he had no assets, why would he have made a will? The will was perfectly clear and straightforward, and made provision for his child.

We had to foot the legal bill ourselves. Such a suit as we were filing could not be heard on a contingency basis in Queensland. Amnesty International, another beneficiary, had believed in us and came on board early on. By mid-2000 when we approached a court-appointed mediation, our costs were close to AUS$500,000. But we knew if we could not come to an agreement at the mediation, we would to go court even if this would break us.

Thankfully, we were able to settle. We were able to tell the world that 'after mediated negotiation, the parties have resolved the differences between them and the litigation will not continue. [We] all agree that that is all that it is appropriate to say publicly having regard to the memory of the late Michael Hutchence and the interests of his daughter, Heavenly Hiraani Tiger Lily Hutchence.'

Tina caused a bit of a furore when she answered a journalist's question on how she felt. Her response was, 'I'm ecstatic.' But she was expressing a feeling we all shared, which was one of relief at getting our lives back.

There has been a lot of speculation in the press as to the value of Michael's estate and who will get what, but this is not based on anything that can be firmly stated. At time of writing, the will still has yet to be executed.

Epilogue

When the first pages of this book were written, it was just a thought, a way of trying to understand the reason for this loss, a way to work through my grief and the pain of losing Michael and the way it happened.

I had kept thinking if he had had a serious illness then maybe I could have come to terms with this tragedy, but this wasn't the case – or so I told myself. However, the truth is that depression is an illness more debilitating than one easily detected by a physical injury or a painful illness. And I understand this so much more now because since 22 November 1997, I too have experienced its grip. My depression was so debilitating that I could not get out of bed – I could not walk or even move without enduring excruciating physical pain. I spent a week in hospital going through every known test there was – x-rays, blood tests galore – but nothing at all showed up.

My wonderful husband Ross carried me, bathed me, fed me, and put up with my tears and anger throughout until I was able to bring myself out of that horrendous period. I had to realize that no matter how much I screamed or cried nothing in this world could bring Michael back, and I had to focus on picking up the pieces and get on with my life, even though a child's loss can never be replaced.

Michael was a gentle loving boy, who loved life and certainly tried to do all he wanted to do in the time he lived. Most importantly he lived his dream, and his songs and beautiful voice live on. He had a love of travel and listened and learned, he loved to read and was mindful and caring with his family. We had a very special bond. That is the Michael I really knew, and I loved him unconditionally. I remember one night I was standing backstage watching one of his concerts and he used a word I didn't approve of. He suddenly realized I was there and said to the audience, 'Oops, my mother is here, I'm not allowed to say that word – she will tell me to go to my room.' He then turned to me and said, 'Sorry Mum'. It was a family joke – I'd say that to him whenever he came up with something I didn't approve of, and it always used to make him laugh.

Well, he has now gone to his room, and I know he is looking down on me and helping me through life until I see him again.

Two years ago when Michael's loss was raw there were thoughts I wanted to express about him, but I was in shock and unable to share the most private feelings. This past year has held much pain and anger but rising above it all, memories. At first I wanted those memories to fade because they involved immense heartache. As time passed, I wished for more memories and found myself asking my children for more details of special times with their uncle. I am one of the fortunate ones, as I can remember Michael as a child. He was very happy and sweet-natured and a wonderful mimic with a great sense of humour. All of these qualities assembled to produce a man with a charismatic personality, who happened to be a poet and a man of music. Those closest to Michael knew that his powerful presence was not a figment of publicists' imaginations.

Some say that fame should not change the dynamics of a family but unfortunately it does, if only because of the influences of the outside world. We have all discussed this at length over the twenty years that Michael was involved in the music industry and we tried to convince each other that his fame was a separate issue. But it wasn't. Many times Michael said that what he did was just a job – but even he knew this not to be true. Michael was perceived as someone special and magical and we know his talent was unique, his lyrics haunting. His work has taken on a life of its own, and we are fortunate that this endures. I could not listen to Michael's music for months after his death and felt guilty about this. Having said that, it was hard to avoid as every radio station seemed to play it in high rotation. Obviously plenty of others did want to hear it. Now, I rejoice and thank the Lord that, unlike most families who lose a loved one, we can turn on the radio and hear his voice.

I'm part of you; you're part of me; there's nothing said that cannot be undone; flesh and blood . . .

These were lyrics to one of the last songs Michael wrote and after I listened to it, I called him and he told me that this song represented hope. It was telling us all that even though relationships can be fragile, we are all a part of one another, and we should be always willing to forgive and start anew.

In the end he was, in his own words, just a man. A brilliant, very gentle and caring man, I think, and one who gave us a lot of love and left us many beautiful memories, which live on. We who knew the private Michael must remember to be happy and grateful that he was fortunate to achieve most of his dreams. So many times and in so many ways he took us on the journey with him. He clearly thought of himself as an ordinary man leading an extraordinary life. We should give thanks for that extraordinary life.

Rest in peace at God's side sweet brother: I hope that somehow you know that you will always be in our hearts.

Index